READY-TO-USE
GEOGRAPHY ACTIVITIES
—— FOR THE ——
AMERICAN CONTINENTS

*Lessons and Skill Sheets
Featuring North
and South America*

**THE CENTER FOR APPLIED
RESEARCH IN EDUCATION**
West Nyack, New York 10994

JAMES F. SILVER

Library of Congress Cataloging in Publication Data

Silver, James F.
    Ready-to-use geography activities for the American continents :
    lessons and skillsheets featuring North and South America /
    James F. Silver.
        p.   cm.
        ISBN 0-87628-355-5 (spiral).--ISBN 0-87628-356-3 (pbk.)
        1. America--Geography--Study and teaching--Activity programs.
    I. Title
    E21.6.S55   1996
    910'.7--dc20   96-22856
                                                       CIP

Printed in the United States of America

10 9 8 7 6 5 4 3 2 1

ISBN 0-87628-355-5 (S)   ISBN 0-87628-356-3 (P)

Dedication

American Continents is dedicated to those members of the Department of Elementary and Early Childhood Education at Trenton State College—professors and administrative staff—who give generously of their time, efforts, knowledge, and expertise to the education of teachers.

Special thanks and appreciation are given to Dr. Anthony Conte, Dr. Timothy Hornberger, Dr. Frank Spera, and Dr. Edward Watson—all of whom have taught me much.

In addition, in this dedication I want to remember Professor Joseph Burcher and Dr. Charles Carman, both now retired, who over the course of many years gave freely of their experience and knowledge to encourage my writing endeavors.

James F. Silver

ACKNOWLEDGMENTS

Several individuals and publishing houses have been of immeasurable help in the creation of *American Continents*.

Mary Salerno, a graduate of Trenton State College's School of Business, who is now a freelance computer and word processing expert, processed and made camera-ready the complete narrative, including most of the charts, graphs, tables, and diagrams. She applied both technical skill and resourcefulness to all that she did.

Steve Busti, a Trenton State College graduate who majored in the graphic arts and art, drew most of the 170 maps and many of the 120 illustrations in *American Continents*. He did more than simply follow instructions; his maps, diagrams, and illustrations are models of accuracy, clarity, and distinctive style.

Lorna Jean Elliot, who received her B.A. from Susquehanna University, PA, and her M.A. from the Bread Loaf School of English, Middlebury College, Middlebury, VT, copyedited the entire manuscript and answer key. Her ability to find and address matters needing correction or clarification was remarkable.

Special thanks to David Evanetz, freelance artist, who drew the illustrations on pages 64, 84, 94, 120, 126, 150, 152, and 158. Special thanks also to artist Carlos Garzon for his illustrations on pages 65, 76, 190, and 222.

Very special thanks are also given to Silver Burdett Ginn Company for permission to use instructional materials from books published by them and authored by James F. Silver—including skillbooks for *Changing New World*, *Learning About Latin America*, and *American Continents*. The last page of this book lists the page numbers in *American Continents* where Silver Burdett Ginn's copyrighted materials appear.

ABOUT THE AUTHOR

James F. Silver received his B.A. in Social Studies from Montclair University, his M.A. in History from Boston University, his M.A. in Educational Administration from Montclair University, and his Ed.D. in Curriculum and Instruction from Pacific Western University in Los Angeles. Professor Silver also studied the psychology of reading at Temple University in Philadelphia, which led to his New Jersey state certification as a reading specialist.

Professor Silver's experience includes nine years as an elementary school teacher and principal in Morris County, New Jersey, and more than 35 years in the School of Education at Trenton State College, New Jersey, where he is now Professor Emeritus in Residence.

During his educational career, Professor Silver has written numerous teachers' manuals, geography and history skill development books, and achievement tests for Silver Burdett Company. He also wrote the two-volume *United States Yesterday and Today* for Ginn and Company. He is author of *Geography Skills Activity Kit*, *World Geography Activities*, *American History Activities*, all published by The Center for Applied Research in Education. Previous to *American History Activities*, he authored *Environmental Awareness*, published by Kendall/Hunt Company. The last four books cited above were written on the professional level for in-service teachers.

ABOUT THIS RESOURCE

"The world is becoming smaller and smaller" is not a reference to its physical dimensions; rather, it refers to the fact that in the past 200 years transportation and communication have advanced at accelerated rates, the effect of which is to bring people and nations much closer. Transportation over land by foot, horse, and horse and wagon, or over water with human- and/ or wind-powered boats remained basically unchanged from the beginning of time through the eighteenth century. Lack of fast and efficient transportation and communication brought about immeasurable numbers of deaths and amounts of property loss. For example, the last battle of the War of 1812, the Battle of New Orleans, was fought after peace had been declared. The battle was over and many soldiers had been killed before the leaders on both sides heard the news of peace. Another example of the effects of poor communication can be put in the form of a question: How many people have been killed and properties destroyed because people were not warned of an oncoming hurricane?

Today, via air travel, any place on earth can be reached in a matter of hours. Ocean trips that once took months can now be completed in a matter of days. Land journeys via trains and automobiles can carry people and goods from New York to San Francisco in less than a week. In the days of covered wagons drawn by oxen or horses accomplishing the same trip in five months was remarkable. The coming "Age of Space" will probably bring even greater efficiencies in communication and transportation.

That the world is smaller, in a figurative sense, makes the teaching of geography more imperative than ever. Where are those places we are trying to help, as in the Peace Corps, with instruction, food, money, medicine, and other materials? Is Bosnia, where American troops have been sent, a real place? Many of our young men and women have been killed or injured in places such as Somalia, Grenada, Iraq, and Saudi Arabia—and yet, many Americans would have great difficulty pointing these places out on a blank map. What would have been the effect, geographically and politically speaking, if Quebec, in 1995, had succeeded in seceding from Canada to form a new nation? Is it possible to understand, really understand, history if knowledge of where the events took place and the geographic conditions that shaped those events is lacking?

American Continents attempts to develop understandings of the people and places in the western hemisphere so that young people, as future citizens, will have stronger foundations of knowledge with which to make wise decisions—decisions that will affect not only their own lives, but also the lives of people in other parts of our hemisphere. Perhaps Americans living in 1800 may not have been significantly affected by conditions and events in other parts of the hemisphere, but in today's "smaller" world, ignorance could be very costly in both material (trade, products, etc.) and nonmaterial human ways.

Building A Place Name Repertory

Knowledge of how people live in a particular country or region, how they interact with their environment, how they live, and how they handle internal geographic problems are all part of a thorough geography education. Along with these important considerations we would want students to learn techniques and approaches for solving problems, either alone or in groups, that have geography as a basic consideration. What course should the United States take in establishing trade relations with our neighbor Mexico? How can we become less dependent upon oil from nations that are thousands of miles from our shores, a situation that influences our economic, political, and military relations with them? What humanistic responsibilities does the United States have to countries that are underdeveloped, devastated by war or internal strife, or suffering from natural disasters such as hurricanes, droughts, and famine? Within the United States, how can we conserve our forests and mineral resources, protect animals in danger of extinction, and eliminate air and water pollution?

The first requirement in developing solutions to such problems is to have command of some basic information and the research skills necessary to uncover or verify further information. Satisfactory solutions to geography problems will not be found unless the following question can be answered: Where are the places under consideration, and what basic details of distance, direction, climate, terrain, proximity to water, neighboring countries, natural resources, and past history are known? As Sir Joshua Reynolds wrote many years ago,

Thinking Point
Invention, strictly speaking,
is little more
than a new combination
of those images
which have been previously gathered
and deposited in the memory.
Nothing can be made of nothing;
they who have laid up no materials
can produce no combinations.

American Continents is concerned, then, with providing instructors and students with facts about the western hemisphere that will help students make "new combinations" to solve problems. Along with providing basic information about every major constituency in the hemisphere, it suggests teaching methods useful in conveying that information.

The ability to "see" in one's mind the major continents, countries, cities, waters, mountains, deserts, and rivers of the world is one of geography's essentials. Educated individuals in conversation with other individuals usually don't carry a globe or atlas to be consulted every time there is reference to a place. Neither do they, when reading a newspaper, magazine, or book, have a file of maps by their side. Just as one learns the basic arithmetic facts and formulas, rules of punctuation and grammar, rules for playing tennis or chess, one should learn the organization and conformations of the world. Of course, if there is a need for "looking up" an obscure rule of a game or the location of a remote mountain village in the Himalayas, one might have to use a reference book. The point is: there is a basic core of geographic knowledge that every educated person should possess.

So, one of the objectives of *American Continents* is to help students develop a place name repertory and associate meaning to the places recalled. In order to accomplish this objective the following procedure is recommended:

1. The places to be memorized should be met first in contextual situations.
2. The places should be put on a list.
3. Practice on the places should be conducted on a daily basis. Practice should be carried out using blank maps, that is, there should be no labels on the maps, just as there are no letters on the keyboard when one is learning touch typing. However, boundaries, cities, and other physical and political features should be shown and identifiable. Outline maps, such as those in the appendix of *American Continents* can be made into transparencies for projection, and/or the maps can be projected on to cardboard or window shades and then traced.
4. As students encounter new locations they should be added to the list.
5. During the practice sessions the instructor should refer frequently to locations previously learned.

6. Occasionally during practice sessions students should be asked to make "associations" and provide information about a place. For example, the instructor points to the Humboldt (Peru) Current and asks, "Current?" After a student has identified the current, the instructor might ask, "What can you tell us about it?" The response could vary: "a cold current flowing northward along the coast of Peru," or "attracts many fish which provide food for Peruvians and others," or "large flocks of birds feed on the plentiful fish, and the birds, in turn, produce fertilizer for crops," and so on. Then the instructor moves on to the next map identification problem.

The practice need not be long, but it should be intense and fast-moving; ten minutes would suffice provided the practice is consistent on a daily basis. Practice need not take place during social studies/geography periods; it can occur before lunch, at the beginning or end of a school day, or any time the students need a change of pace.

Instructors who have followed this routine have reported phenomenal success. It is not unusual for typical fifth or sixth graders to master 300 or more place names in a year. Success begets success. Students begin to drill each other and invent games; for example, they may use a stop watch or clock as they compete to see who can locate a certain number of places, say fifty, in the shortest time.

Instructor's Pages

All of the "Instructor's Pages" in *American Continents* have been designed to help instructors enrich their teaching. For example, in *American Continents* each of the fifty states has been allotted two facing pages, one page for the instructor and the second page for student activity. The Instructor's Page offers background information not ordinarily found in textbooks. For example, about one-quarter of the instructor's page for the state of New York has a section titled, "New York City: Some Superlatives." The remainder of the page contains information about Niagara Falls, and the Welland Canal that bypasses the falls. A large scale map shows the locational relationship of Niagara Falls, the Welland Canal, Lake Erie, and Lake Ontario. The map could be made into a transparency that, when shown, would enhance the instructor's presentation of the geographical situation and increase student understanding.

All of the states' instructor pages have been written on a readability level that would be within the capacity of most students who will be studying the geography of the western hemisphere. This was done purposely for it offers instructors at least 50 more student application pages. Instructors may photocopy these pages, distribute them, and assign a student or group of students to read them and, perhaps, prepare a lesson or presentation themselves.

Those instructor pages that are not concerned with the fifty states are designed differently. They offer specific information and suggestions that have to do with methodology. Although portions of such pages are suitable for student use, the entire page is on the instructor's level. For example, the book's section on South America contains suggestions and an illustration about early Spanish missions; another page contains information, diagrams, and suggestions for teaching about seasons of the year south of the Equator. In one part of the section about Canada, specific instructions are given for having students engage in a hands-on activity that involves the making of a "TV filmstrip."

Student Application/Activity Pages

The student application pages, approximately 200 in number (including 50 of the instructor's pages specifically written for possible student use) are designed to develop both subject matter understandings and the facts that support them. Also, every application page concentrates on developing one or more skills in the following ability categories: work-study, classifications, maps, graphs, charts, diagrams, pictures, tables, and reading comprehension. The abilities are made up of a number of skills, each of which is treated at various places in *American Continents*. As an example of the extensiveness of coverage, the following is a breakdown of the skills that contribute to the ability to read maps and that are practiced on student application pages.

- Using cardinal and intermediate directions
- Using latitude and longitude to determine location
- Using latitude and longitude to determine direction
- Using latitude and longitude to determine distance
- Using latitude as a climate indicator
- Using various kinds of map projections
- Using highway maps for locating places, following routes of travel
- Using keys/legends of maps as a means of identifying symbols
- Using map scales to compute distances
- Interpreting elevations from the flow of rivers
- Transferring and organizing data gained from maps to another graphic device such as a table
- Transferring table and chart data to maps
- Interpreting and making physical maps
- Locating places on maps through the use of an index
- Taking information from maps and organizing it into a map index
- Identifying map locations from written descriptions
- Comparing air distance, overland distance, and sea distance through the use of data found on maps and in tables
- Reading historical maps
- Recognizing countries by their conformations
- Understanding earth-sun relationships as shown on maps
- Using color, shading, and hatching to identify regions
- Following a route of travel
- Reading road maps

Examples of student application pages on which specific skills are developed:

Page 189, *The West Indies: Puerto Rico*: the map skill is identifying the quadrant in which a place is located and transferring the information to a map index.

Pages 176 and 177, *Mexico: A Map of Its Highways*: The map reading skills developed are following routes of travel, identifying places met, and calculating distances traveled.

Page 59, *Southeastern States: A Table of Facts*: The work-study skill developed is taking population information from a table of statistics and reorganizing the information in a picture graph.

Page 166, *Eskimos and Their Environment*: The picture reading skill is reading a picture for the facts it shows, making a listing of them, and then *combining* the facts to write a story about the situation depicted in the picture.

Activities, Puzzles, and Games

The "Activities, Puzzles, and Games" section of *American Continents* offers students numerous opportunities to engage in learning experiences that are interesting and productive and that will reinforce subject matter learnings and further develop skills. Some activities require students to work independently, some place students in small groups that require cooperative learning, and some engage the class as a whole while the instructor directs. Most of the activities lend themselves well to learning center activities.

Some activities have tangible outcomes—that is, at the completion of the activity there is something that can be seen, heard, or manipulated. "Making an Information Disc" is a learning experience that produces an end product that students will be proud to take home and explain to their families. "Geo Bingo!" offers an exciting and informative class activity where everyone competes on an equal basis and, yet, "luck" is an important factor. The "United States Travel Game" offers opportunities to review information in an enjoyable way; after playing three or four rounds of the game there is little doubt that many students will know the answers to the 56 subject matter questions.

The supplements described above and others listed in the Table of Contents will offer changes of pace in normal classroom routines. Students may not recognize them as a means of conducting practice; even if they do, they undoubtedly will look forward to the next "game" day.

Outline Maps

A variety of blank outline maps of North America and South America are included at the end of *American Continents*. These maps should prove useful to instructors who want to devise their own activities.

Answer Key

At the end of *American Continents* is a complete answer key to the questions and problems presented on student application pages. In most cases, exact answers are expected; however, in evaluating answers to inference-type questions or questions requiring distance measurement, some latitude should be given.

Table of Contents

Map Reading Skills

LINES OF LATITUDE HELP IN LOCATING PLACES NORTH AND SOUTH

1. The following suggestions for understanding and reading latitude will help your students in their study of the geography of the American continents. Later in this book longitude will be treated in a similar manner. *Note*: Practice has shown that it is not effective to introduce latitude and longitude simultaneously; this leads to confusion. The approach is to learn latitude thoroughly, then learn longitude, then put the two grid elements together.

2. After the suggested latitude lesson has been taught, the following page can be photocopied and distributed.

Suggestions

1. Distances north and south of the equator are measured in degrees of latitude. Places on Earth are either north or south of the equator or directly on the equator.

2. Knowing where a place is in reference to the equator serves two main purposes: (1) it helps to locate a place on Earth, (2) it provides clues about the climate of a place, especially with regard to temperature and seasons.

3. Latitude is measured in degrees as in a circle. From the equator to the North Pole is 90°; likewise, from the equator to the South Pole is 90°.

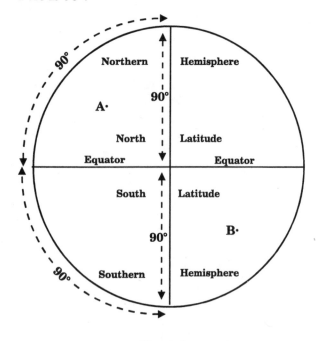

Figure 1

4. It is necessary to designate whether a place is *north* or *south* of the equator. Place **A** in Figure 1 is in the north (N) latitudes; place **B** is in the south (S) latitudes.

5. Since it is important to locate places accurately, parallel east-west lines are drawn across the globe at intervals of 10° or 20°. The figure that follows shows intervals of 10°. Thus, place C is 60°N, place D is 30°N, place E is 20°S, and place F is 50°S.

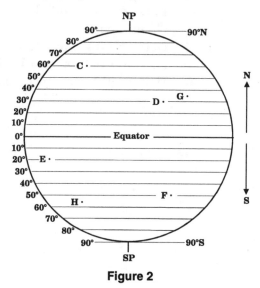

Figure 2

6. Places are not always located on a line of latitude; often, they are located between lines. In such situations it is necessary to interpolate the position between two numbered lines with as much accuracy as possible. For example, G is approximately halfway between 30°N and 40°N. So, it would be reasonably accurate to read G as 35°N; likewise, H as 55°S.

7. At this point in the lesson draw on the chalkboard (or use a transparency) a large circle with some numbered lines of latitude. At random print various letters north and south of the equator. Have your students identify the latitude of each letter.

8. Point out to your students that, in general, as one proceeds north or south of the equator the temperature decreases. However, it should also be realized that other natural elements may influence temperature: elevation can decrease temperature; proximity to water can lower or raise temperature; and winds may bring warm or cold air masses to a region.

USING LATITUDE TO LOCATE PLACES IN THE WESTERN HEMISPHERE

1. Study the map to determine the latitude locations of the following places in the American continents. Circle the better choice.

Place	Approximate Latitude	
Point Barrow	69°N	71°N
Churchill	55°N	59°N
Ottawa	55°N	45°N
Portland	54°N	46°N
Washington, D.C.	39°N	41°N
San Francisco	38°N	33°N
New Orleans	30°S	30°N
Mexico City	19°N	19°S
Bogota	6°S	4°N
Quito	0°	10°S
Brasilia	24°S	16°S
Buenos Aires	25°S	36°S
Punta Arenas	53°S	60°S

2. How many degrees of latitude are there between:

New Orleans and Quito?
 __ 30   __ 25

Portland and Buenos Aires?
 __ 82   __ 78

Point Barrow and Punta Arenas?
 __ 112   __ 124

3. Using only latitude as an indicator, which city in each pair of cities listed below would have the colder climate?

a. __ New Orleans   __ Brasilia

b. __ Bogota   __ Buenos Aires

c. __ Point Barrow   __ Punta Arenas

LINES OF LONGITUDE HELP IN LOCATING PLACES EAST AND WEST

1. Lines of longitude differ in several regards from lines of latitude. Lines of longitude:

❑ are north-south lines. They are not parallel to each other. The lines converge at the poles.

❑ extend from pole to pole. Each line covers 180° of the globe.

❑ are either east or west of the Prime Meridian (0°). Of course, some places are located on the Prime Meridian.

❑ are generally measured in increments of 15°; thus, the sequence is 0°, 15°E, 30°E, 45°E and so on to 180°E. The same method of enumeration applies to west longitude: 0°, 15°W, 30°W, and so on to 180°W. The reason 15° is used as an interval is that the earth rotates west-to-east towards the sun 15° every hour; thus, 24 hours (one rotation of the earth) × 15° = 360°. **Note**: It is not uncommon for map makers to enumerate lines of longitude at 10° or 20° intervals: e.g., 10°E, 20°E, and so on.

❑ are often shown on flat maps, especially Mercator projections, as lines that do not converge at the poles; the lines are vertical and parallel to each other. This approach is useful when locating places; however, sizes, shapes, and distances close to the Arctic and Antarctic regions become grossly distorted—to such an extent that Greenland appears larger than South America, and the Antarctic continent stretches across the bottom of the map from edge to edge.

2. The Prime Meridian and its counterpart on the opposite side of the globe (180°) divide the world into two parts: the Western Hemisphere and the Eastern Hemisphere. **Note**: See Figures 1 and 2.

3. To some extent all flat maps are distorted. This is so because the world is spherical. When one tries to flatten such a figure, distortion will occur. The only device that shows "true" world distance, shapes, and sizes is the globe.

   The truism stated above can be demonstrated as follows:

a. Obtain a hollow rubber ball. Cut the ball in half horizontally.

b. Identify the top of one half-ball as the *North Pole* (NP). Identify the bottom edge as the *Equator*. Sketch a map of North America on the half-ball.

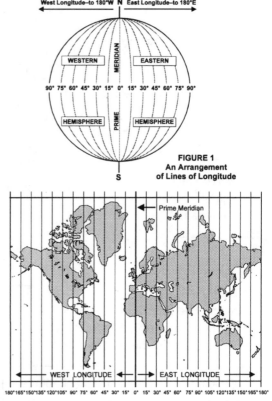

**FIGURE 1
An Arrangement
of Lines of Longitude**

FIGURE 2 Lines of Longitude on a Mercator Projection

c. Demonstrate to your students that you cannot flatten the half-ball.

d. Make three or four cuts from the North Pole to a short distance from the Equator. Make one cut all the way through the Equator.

e. Flatten the cut half-ball. Point out to your students that when the half-ball flattens the north polar regions spread far apart, while the equator remains basically intact.

f. Explain that mapmakers connect the gaps in the northern parts, but with the result that there is a great enlargement of the northern areas.

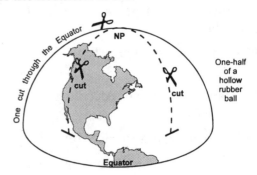

Name: _____ Date: _____

USING LONGITUDE TO LOCATE PLACES IN THE WESTERN HEMISPHERE

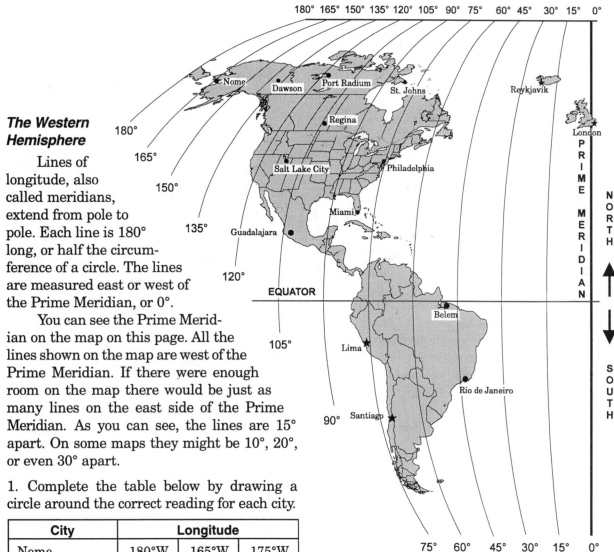

The Western Hemisphere

Lines of longitude, also called meridians, extend from pole to pole. Each line is 180° long, or half the circumference of a circle. The lines are measured east or west of the Prime Meridian, or 0°.

You can see the Prime Meridian on the map on this page. All the lines shown on the map are west of the Prime Meridian. If there were enough room on the map there would be just as many lines on the east side of the Prime Meridian. As you can see, the lines are 15° apart. On some maps they might be 10°, 20°, or even 30° apart.

1. Complete the table below by drawing a circle around the correct reading for each city.

City	Longitude		
Nome	180°W	165°W	175°W
Dawson	136°W	149°W	125°W
Reykjavik	30°W	15°W	21°W
Regina	115°W	104°W	94°W
Salt Lake City	112°W	102°W	119°W
Philadelphia	81°W	75°W	70°W
Miami	98°W	90°W	80°W
Guadalajara	115°W	103°W	95°W
Belem	48°W	41°W	58°W
Lima	83°W	77°W	67°W
Rio de Janeiro	50°W	43°W	37°W
Santiago	77°W	64°W	71°W

2. Only lines of longitude can accurately tell you whether one city is farther west or east of another city. For example, Salt Lake City appears farther west than Port Radium, but Port Radium is closer to the 120° line. So, it is farther west than Salt Lake City.

✎ What city is farther west, Port Radium or Guadalajara? _____

✎ What city is farther west, Rio de Janeiro or St. Johns? _____

3. How many degrees apart are Belem (48°W) and Lima (77°W)? _____

✎ Miami (80°W) and Nome (165°W)? _____

DETERMINING DIRECTION WITH LATITUDE AND LONGITUDE

On maps without lines of latitude and lines of longitude, direction appearances may be deceiving. In Figure 1, it appears that A is farther north than B, and that A and C are the same distance west.

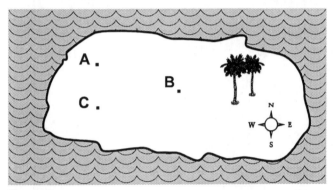

Figure 1

However, if we take the same map and on it draw lines of latitude and longitude (Figure 2) we see that our impressions were incorrect. Point B is north of the 20°N line of latitude, and Point A is south of the same line; thus, point B is farther north. Likewise, A is significantly farther west than C (A: 62°W; C: 59°W).

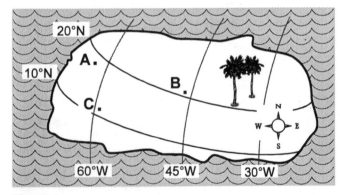

Figure 2

Suggested Procedure

The grid figure in the next column and the accompanying questions will provide an opportunity for your students to practice finding directions via the grids of maps and globes. *Note*: A transparency may be used, and/or the column may be photocopied and distributed.

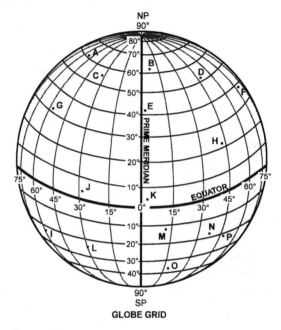

GLOBE GRID

Figure 3

1. Which point is farther west?

a. A or G? _____   c. L or C? _____

b. C or J? _____   d. I or G? _____

2. Which point is farther east?

a. B or O? _____   c. D or H? _____

b. H or N? _____   d. B or M? _____

3. Which point is farther north?

a. I or N? _____   b. E or F? _____

4. What point is almost directly south of D? _____

5. Name all of the points that are west of the Prime Meridian.

_____

6. Name all of the points that are north of the Equator.

_____

LOCATING PLACES WITH LATITUDE AND LONGITUDE

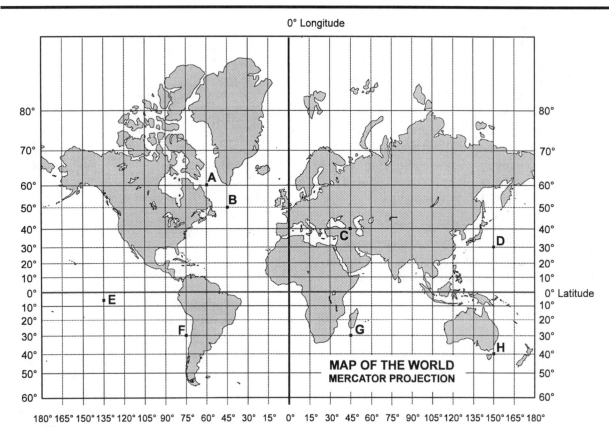

Latitude and longitude are used together to tell the exact location of a place. To tell where a place is located, you should state its latitude first, then its longitude. When you state latitude, you should indicate whether it is north (N) or south (S); likewise, you should indicate whether longitude is east (E) or west (W). For example, place A on the map is at the intersection of two lines: 60°N and 60°W. Notice that E is between two numbered lines of latitude and on a line of longitude.

1. Write the latitude and longitude of the places shown on the map and listed in the table below.

Place	Latitude & Longitude	Place	Latitude & Longitude
A	60°N–60°W	E	
B		F	
C		G	
D		H	

2. On the map print a dot and a letter at each of the locations listed below.

I at 30°N–45°W L at 70°N–155°E
J at 50°S–30°W M at 15°S–150°W
K at 40°S–45°E N at 55°N–165°W

3. Answer the following questions by writing a √ before *Yes* or *No*.

a. Does the 30°W line of longitude touch any part of South America?
___ Yes ___ No

b. Does the 75°W line of longitude pass through South America?
___ Yes ___ No

Challenge

a. Start at point **A** on the map.
b. Go south 40°. Write a **w** at that point.
c. Go west 90°. Write an **x** at that point.
d. Go north 20°. Write a **y** at that point.
e. Go east 10°. Write a **z** at that point.

What is your latitude and longitude at **z**?

_____

USING LATITUDE AND LONGITUDE TO COMPUTE DISTANCES

The scale of miles found on most globes and maps is useful in computing distances between places. However, the grid system used on maps and globes may also be used to determine distance. Following are procedures, sequences, and examples that will help your students learn how to measure distances along lines of latitude and longitude. The accompanying application page will provide your students with opportunities to apply what they have learned.

1. The distance around the world on the Equator is approximately 25,000 miles. If 25,000 miles is divided by 360° (the number of degrees in a circle) we find that one degree of longitude at the Equator is equal to approximately 70 miles.

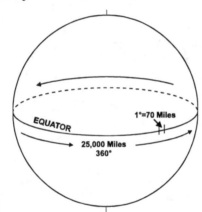

Figure 1

2. The lines of latitude become shorter in circumference as they approach the poles; although, of course, they continue to be made up of 360°. If the circumference in miles of a particular line of latitude is divided by 360°, the result is the number of miles per degree. Figure 2 tells the approximate number of miles in circumference of every tenth line of latitude between 0° and 90°.

3. Because all lines of longitude are the same length, approximately 25,000 miles, each degree of latitude crossing a line of longitude is also 70 miles approximately. *Note*: The distance around the earth from pole to pole is shorter than the distance around the Equator because the earth is slightly flattened at the poles. (Equator: 24,902 miles; longitudinal: 24,859 miles.)

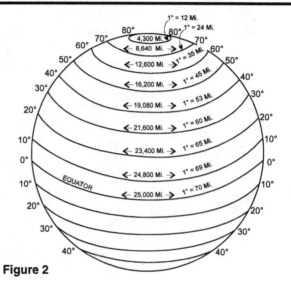

Figure 2

4. The following figure and explanation may be used as an example of how to compute distances on a map grid.

Figure 3 shows that from point **A** (10°E) to point **B** (40°E) there are 30° of longitude. The numbers in Figure 2 tell us that 1° on the 10° line, north or south, equals approximately 69 miles. Thus, 30° × 69 miles yields a distance of approximately 2,070 miles between A and B.

Likewise, an airplane that flies from point **A** to point **E** on the 10°E line of longitude flies 20°. A degree on a line of longitude equals approximately 70 miles. Therefore, the plane will fly approximately 1,400 miles (20° × 70 miles).

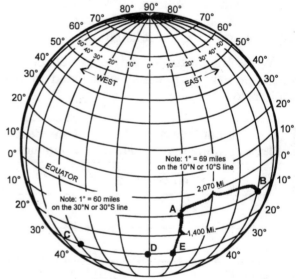

Figure 3

Name: _____ Date: _____

USING LATITUDE AND LONGITUDE TO COMPUTE DISTANCES

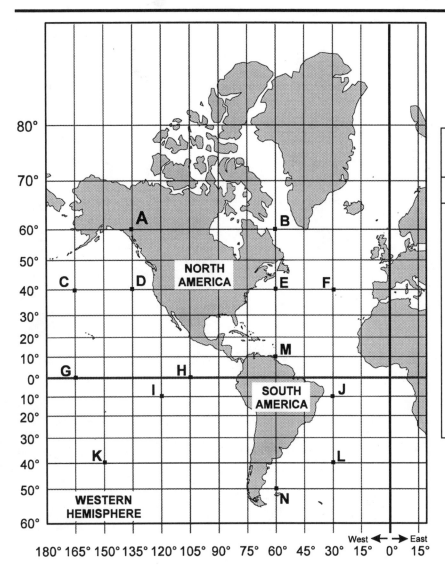

Number of Miles in One Degree of Longitude on Certain Lines of Latitude	
Latitude	*Miles*
Equator	70
10°N or S	69
20°N or S	65
30°N or S	60
40°N or S	53
50°N or S	45
60°N or S	35
70°N or S	24
80°N or S	12

180° 165° 150° 135° 120° 105° 90° 75° 60° 45° 30° 15° 0° 15°

West ← → East

© 1996 by The Center for Applied Research in Education

The table next to the map tells how many miles there are in each one-degree length on certain lines of latitude. As the lines of latitude become shorter in circumference, the distance per degree becomes less.

Because all of the lines of longitude are the same length, the number of miles in each degree remains the same; that is, there are approximately 70 miles in each degree.

1. How many miles is it from

a. A to B? _____   d. G to H? _____

b. C to D? _____   e. I to J? _____

c. E to F? _____   f. K to L? _____

2. How many miles is it from

a. C to G? _____

b. F to J? _____

c. J to L? _____

Challenge

Use only lines of latitude and longitude to determine the approximate total number of miles from A to B to E to F to J to I.

Hint: Remember that miles per degree of latitude change from one latitude line to another.

Your answer: _____ miles

North America on the Map

MAJOR PHYSICAL FEATURES OF NORTH AMERICA

A study of the major physical features of North America should prove useful for future in-depth studies of the United States, Canada, and Mexico. The labeled map on the following page of North America will be helpful in accomplishing this objective.

Procedure

1. Photocopy the map and distribute.

2. Photocopy the table below and have your students complete the columns with data from the map.

3. Now would be an opportune time for your students to start building a place name repertory. The suggestions in the "About This Resource" section of *American Continents* should prove helpful.

One of the steps in acquiring a place name repertory is that the places to be memorized should be met in contextual situations; then, during practice, learners should be asked to offer some information about the places identified. Following are some suggestions related to the map on the facing page that could be mentioned when the map and the accompanying activity are explained.

a. The vast extent of the Mississippi/Ohio/ Missouri River drainage area lying between the Appalachian Mountains and the Rocky Mountains.

b. The westward flowing Ohio River that was a great help in carrying settlers to the Mississippi Valley.

c. The Great Lakes/St. Lawrence River system that, after development, became a great transportation route into the interior of the continent.

IMPORTANT LOCATIONS IN NORTH AMERICA		
Nations:	**Mountain Ranges:**	**Lakes:**
Rivers:		
	Islands:	**Other Large Bodies of Water:**
Straits:		

© 1996 by The Center for Applied Research in Education

Name: _____ Date: _____

MAJOR PHYSICAL FEATURES OF NORTH AMERICA

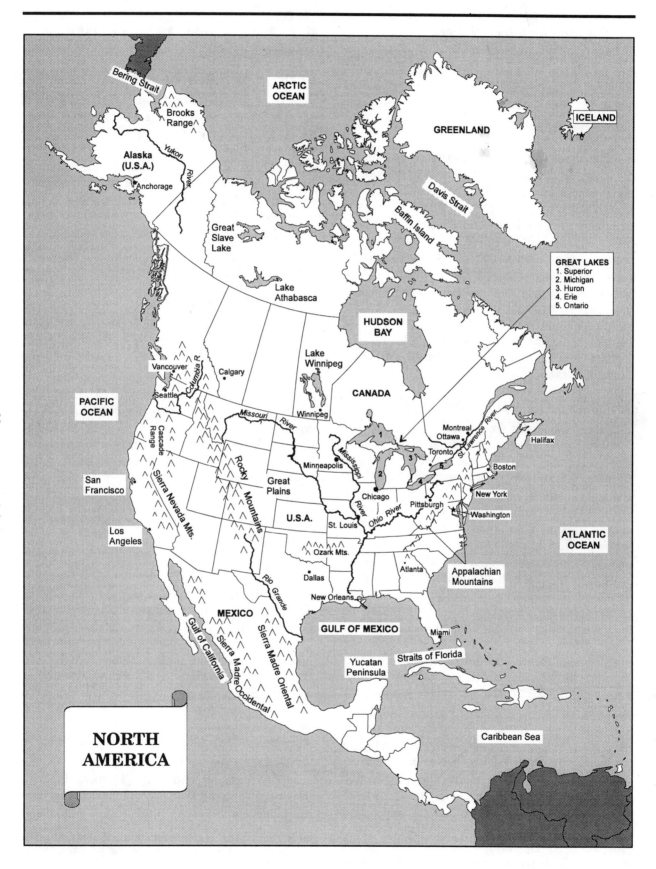

ALL ABOUT RIVERS AND THE MISSISSIPPI VALLEY

Sources and Mouths of Rivers

The point at which a number of rivulets and small streams join together to form one large stream is said to be the *source* of a river. However, there are some rivers that start from one source such as a spring or a lake.

The *mouth* of a river is the place where its water is discharged into another river, a lake, a sea, or an ocean. Sometimes, the mouth of a river may cover a large area over which several smaller streams discharge the river's water—as in a *delta*. The map on the facing page shows the Mississippi River delta with only one stream discharging its water into the Gulf of Mexico. However, if the map were large-scale, numerous small, meandering streams would be shown, all of which are parts of the total mouth of the Mississippi River and all of which are discharging water.

Streams and Direction of Flow

Some students find it difficult to believe that rivers can flow in any compass direction. Especially, they find it incomprehensible that rivers can flow north. This misunderstanding probably comes about because they equate north with "up." They have heard such expressions as "Canada is *up north,*" or "*Down south* in Florida it is warm in the winter." To test if there are students in class who hold this notion, pull down a wall map that shows Egypt. Ask, "In what direction is the Nile River flowing?" It would be unusual if some didn't respond, "South." Of course, the Nile River flows north. It rises in the interior highlands of Africa and flows "downhill" to the Mediterranean Sea, which is sea level.

Once students understand that rivers must flow from high altitudes to lower altitudes, misconceptions they have will disappear. The oceans of the world and other connected bodies of water are at sea level or 0° altitude. Thus, it would be physically impossible for the Mississippi River to flow from the Gulf of Mexico to its source in the interior highlands. It follows, then, that a city such at St. Louis on the Mississippi River must have a higher altitude than a city downstream such as Memphis, Tennessee.

Upstream and Downstream

If a boat is going against the flow or current of a stream it is going *upstream*; whereas, if a boat is going with the flow, it its going *downstream*. At the start of their exploratory trip of the Pacific Northwest, Lewis and Clark were going against the current of the Missouri River; they were going upstream. On their return to the East they were going with the current or downstream. Of course, the downstream journey was much easier than the upstream journey.

Mississippi River Facts

▪ From its source (Lake Itasca, Minnesota) to its mouth (New Orleans, Louisiana, on the Gulf of Mexico) the Mississippi River is 2,340 miles long.

▪ The area drained by the Mississippi River and its tributaries is about 1,250,000 square miles. The drainage area includes the whole or part of 23 states and includes land as far east as Pennsylvania and as far north and west as Montana.

▪ At its widest point (Clinton, Iowa) the Mississippi River is 3½ miles from bank to bank. This exceptional width for a river is the result of a backup from a dam that restricts the river's flow.

▪ The delta of the Mississippi River covers about 13,000 square miles, which is almost twice the size of the land area of New Jersey. The delta was formed from the hundreds of millions of tons of topsoil that eroded from the river's huge drainage area, were carried by flowing waters to the Mississippi's mouth, and were then deposited.

Additional Map Questions and Activities

▪ Use a reference to find the names of the states shown on the map. Then, print the abbreviations of the states' names on the map.

▪ Proceeding from west to east, list all rivers that empty into the Gulf of Mexico.

THE MISSISSIPPI VALLEY

A: _____

1. Put an *S* at the source of each of these rivers: Big Horn, Arkansas, Brazos, Cumberland, Wabash, Tennessee, Alabama, Red (of the South).

2. Put an *M* at the mouth of each of these rivers: Brazos, Muskegon, Rio Grande, Pecos.

3. Put an arrow with its head facing *downstream* beside each of these rivers: Canadian, Arkansas, Tennessee, Ohio.

4. After each river listed at the left below, two cities are named. Which city is farther *upstream*? Check the box before each correct answer.

Arkansas	❏ Tulsa	❏ Wichita
Missouri	❏ Bismarck	❏ Pierre
Ohio	❏ Louisville	❏ Cincinnati
Trinity	❏ Fort Worth	❏ Dallas

5. Check the box in front of each river named below that is a tributary of the Missouri River.

❏ Yellowstone	❏ Platte
❏ Arkansas	❏ Des Moines
❏ Big Horn	❏ Milk

6. What three rivers named on the map are tributaries of the Ohio River?

_____

_____

_____

7. Label the Gulf of Mexico at *A* on the map.

8. How many states does the Mississippi River touch or go through on its journey from Minnesota to the Gulf of Mexico? _____

THE PANAMA CANAL: SHORTCUT THROUGH TWO CONTINENTS

The Importance of the Panama Canal

The activities on the facing page will help your students realize the tremendous savings in miles and time that has resulted from the building of the Panama Canal. Products can be shipped and travelers can travel in less time and at lower cost by using the canal.

The canal has also been an important factor in United States defense. Before the Panama Canal was built, during the Spanish-American War, for example, it took over two months for elements of our Pacific fleet to arrive in the theatre of war in the Caribbean Sea. Now, however, the canal enables our navy to move ships quickly from the Pacific to the Atlantic, and vice versa.

A Trip Through the Panama Canal

The Panama Canal is not a sea-level passage across the Isthmus of Panama. Ships using the canal must, literally, be lifted up and down mountains to get from one side to the other. A transparency of the diagram at the bottom of the page will help your students understand how this is accomplished.

The trip through the canal can be explained sequentially as though a ship were traveling from the Pacific side to the Atlantic side.

1. A ship enters a lock at sea level.

2. The huge gates of the lock are closed and water is pumped into the lock. The ship rises with the water.

3. When the water level of the first lock reaches that of the second, the ship moves forward to the next lock. Locomotives that run on tracks parallel to the locks pull the ships. Water is pumped into the second lock, and once more the ship rises with the water, and, again, the ship is pulled to the next lock.

As can be seen in the diagram, the ship must pass through three locks on the Pacific side of the canal.

4. After passing through the three locks, the ship sails—slowly, it should be emphasized—through Gaillard Cut and Gatun Lake to the set of three locks that will lower the ship to sea level on the Atlantic side. From there the ship will be able to proceed to its destination.

Interesting Facts about the Canal

❑ The locks are similar to a two-way street; that is, they are double, and ships going in opposite directions pass each other in the locks and on Lake Gatun. So, in reality, there are twelve locks, six on each end of the canal.

❑ The transit through the entire canal system is about 50 miles.

❑ As many as 10,000 ships use the canal each year.

❑ In 1978 a treaty between the Republic of Panama and the United States was signed. The treaty provides that by the end of 1999 Panama will take over the ownership and operation of the Panama Canal and all United States troops will be withdrawn. The United States agreed to protect Panama's neutrality after the takeover. In case of any obstruction of the movement of ships through the canal by a foreign power, the United States has the right to intervene militarily.

Panama Canal Locks: This diagram shows a cross section of the locks of the Panama Canal connecting the Atlantic and the Pacific Oceans.

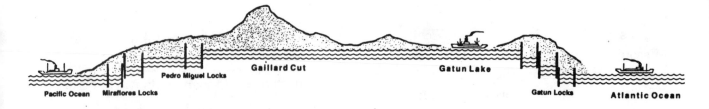

Pacific Ocean • Miraflores Locks • Pedro Miguel Locks • Gaillard Cut • Gatun Lake • Gatun Locks • Atlantic Ocean

THE PANAMA CANAL: SHORTCUT THROUGH TWO CONTINENTS

1. Label the following places on the map. Write on the lines next to the letters. **Note**: It is not necessary to write the name of the country.

A. New York

B. Rio de Janeiro (Brazil)

C. Strait of Magellan

D. Buenos Aires (Argentina)

E. Callao (Peru)

F. Panama Canal

G. San Francisco

2. Use the **Distances by Sea** table below for help in answering the following questions.

a. What is the distance by sea from New York to Callao by way of the Strait of Magellan? _____ miles

b. What is the distance between these two cities by way of the Panama Canal? _____ miles

c. How many miles are saved by using the Panama Canal route? _____ miles

d. Write the distance on each of the two lines from New York to Callao.

3. Use the table to determine how many miles are saved in going from New Orleans to Callao by way of the Panama Canal. _____ miles saved

4. Use the scale of miles and the table to solve this problem.

What is the difference in miles between the San Francisco–Buenos Aires air route and the San Francisco–Buenos Aires Panama Canal route? _____ miles

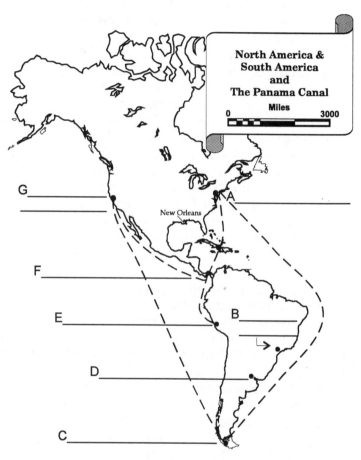

North America &
South America
and
The Panama Canal

Miles

0   3000

G _____
_____

New Orleans

F _____

E _____   B _____

D _____

C _____

A

Distances by Sea	
	STATUTE MILES
New York to Buenos Aires	6,752
New York to Callao,	
via Strait of Magellan	11,061
via Panama Canal	3,873
New York to Rio de Janeiro	5,486
New Orleans to Buenos Aires	7,009
New Orleans to Callao,	
via Strait of Magellan	11,313
via Panama Canal	3,200
San Francisco to Buenos Aires	
via Strait of Magellan	8,719
via Panama Canal	10,075
San Francisco to Rio de Janeiro	
via Strait of Magellan	9,690
via Panama Canal	8,804

THE GREAT LAKES–ST. LAWRENCE SEAWAY

A Cooperative Endeavor

The Great Lakes–St. Lawrence Seaway project was a cooperative effort between the United States and Canada to afford both countries access to the Atlantic Ocean from their interiors, and vice versa. One country could not have built the seaway alone because each country owns portions of each of the Great Lakes, except for Lake Michigan which is entirely within the United States. Moreover, because at least half of the length of the St. Lawrence River is within the borders of Canada, the United States did not have access to the Atlantic Ocean from its Great Lakes cities. All other portions of the seaway are entirely within Canada, for example the Welland Canal between Lake Erie and Lake Ontario.

Considering the enormous amounts of money, labor, planning, materials, and equipment necessary to complete the project, the seaway is a tribute to the friendship that exists between the United States and Canada. Yet, when it is realized that this mutual respect has existed since the end of the War of 1812, more than 180 years, it is not really surprising. The seaway, one of the world's greatest engineering efforts, is simply another manifestation of the spirit that enables the two countries to have an entirely unfortified border.

Gateway to Interior North America

The seaway "opened" the interiors of both the United States and Canada. That is, ocean-going ships could bring in or carry away products from cities more than 2,300 miles from the Atlantic Ocean. Before the seaway was built, products from such places as Minnesota had to be loaded and shipped by rail or truck to ocean ports, unloaded, then reloaded on ships for transportation to world ports. Now such products are simply loaded and shipped by rail or truck to a port city on the Great Lakes.

Similarly, the seaway has eased the expense of importing goods to our interior. Because shipping costs are partly determined by the number of miles products are carried and the extent to which they are handled, any diminishment of the miles and handlings between ports will lower transportation charges. For example, it is less costly for Japan to ship products to Chicago by way of the Atlantic and the seaway than by way of the Pacific to San Francisco and then overland to the Great Lake city. And, since some cities in northern Europe are actually closer to the Great Lake cities than to New York, it is less costly for them to ship products directly to the interior via the seaway.

It should be noted that there are two other routes to the Great Lakes from the East. The New York State Barge Canal System connects New York to Lake Erie by an all-water route that follows the Hudson River to Albany, then west along the Barge Canal to Buffalo. Still another route connects Lake Michigan to the Gulf of Mexico via the Chicago Sanitary and Ship Canal, the Illinois River, and the Mississippi River.

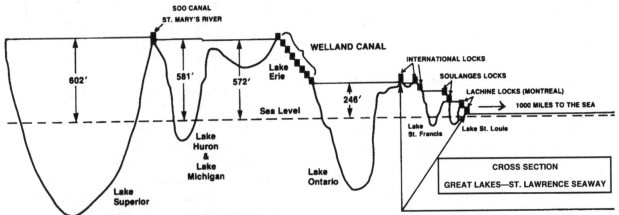

The elevations of the Great Lakes–St. Lawrence Seaway and the locks along the route can be better visualized by cross section. Important to note is the dashed line that denotes sea level.

Name: _____ Date: _____

THE GREAT LAKES–ST. LAWRENCE SEAWAY

1. What states have some border on the Great Lakes?

Lake Superior: _____

_____, _____

Lake Michigan: _____

_____, _____, _____

Lake Huron: _____

Lake Erie: _____, _____ ,

_____, _____

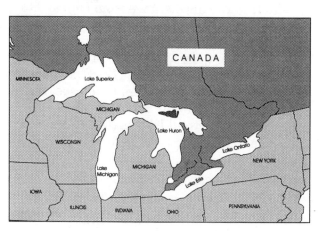

Lake Ontario: _____

2. Study the map/diagram at the bottom of the page for the answers to the following questions:

a. What is the surface elevation of each of the Great Lakes?

Superior: _____' Michigan: _____'

Huron:_____' Erie:_____' Ontario:_____'

b. What is the drop in elevation from Lake Erie to Lake Ontario? _____ '

c. Once a ship enters the St. Lawrence Seaway from the ocean, how many feet does it rise *before* it enters Lake Ontario? _____ '

d. Which of the cities in the listed pairs that follow has the higher elevation? Underline the correct answers.

• Detroit or Montreal? • Montreal or Erie?

• Chicago or Duluth?   • Hamilton or Detroit?

3. The arrows in the lakes and along the sides of the St. Lawrence River show the direction water flows from Lake Superior to the Gulf of St. Lawrence (Atlantic Ocean). Close to each arrow write DOF, for "Direction of Flow."

4. Using a blue pencil or crayon, lightly color the Great Lakes and the St. Lawrence River.

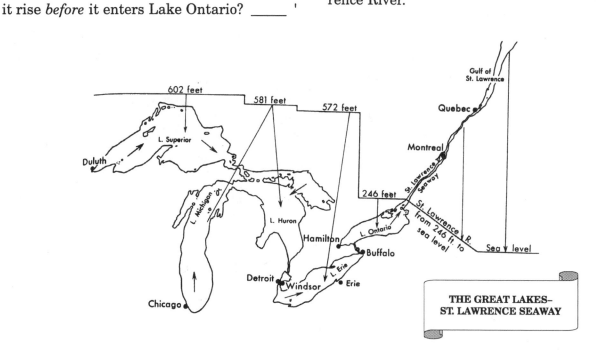

THE GREAT LAKES–
ST. LAWRENCE SEAWAY

19

Name: _____ Date: _____

AIR DISTANCES IN THE UNITED STATES

To find the air distance from Chicago to Boston, place the corner of a strip of paper on the dot for Chicago on the map below, and make a mark where the edge of the paper touches the dot for Boston. Lay the paper along the scale of miles. You can see that Boston is between 800 and 900 miles from Chicago. But it would be better to have a more exact distance. Here is how to find it:

✈ Each space marked off on the scale of miles represents 50 miles.

✈ The measurement you have made should show a little more than one space beyond 800, or about 75 miles.

✈ Add the 75 miles to the 800. The sum is 875; so, it would be more accurate to say that the distance between the two cities is about 875 miles.

1. The map below proposes two air distances between Chicago and each city elsewhere on the map. Which distance is the more accurate? Measure each distance, then write the correct distance in the table in the next column.

2. Approximately how many hours would it take for an airplane to fly from Chicago to Washington, D.C, if it were traveling at

City	Air Line Distance from Chicago
Boston, MA	
Washington, D.C.	
Miami, FL	
St. Louis, MO	
New Orleans, LA	
El Paso, TX	
Los Angeles, CA	
San Francisco, CA	
Salt Lake City, UT	
Seattle, WA	

an average speed of 400 miles per hour? _____ hrs.

Approximately how many hours would it take to fly from Seattle to Chicago, traveling at the same average speed? _____ hrs.

What is the approximate number of hours required to fly cross-country from Seattle to Washington, D.C., via Chicago at the same average speed? _____ hrs.

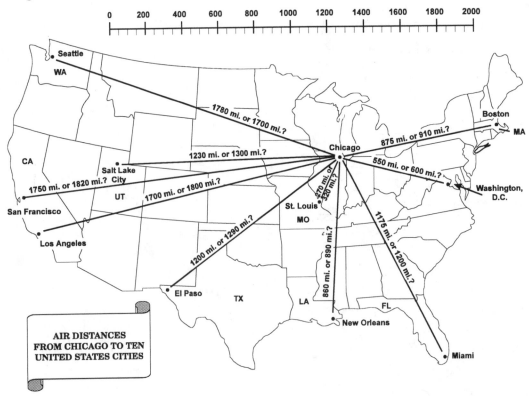

AIR DISTANCES FROM CHICAGO TO TEN UNITED STATES CITIES

Name: _____ Date: _____

THE UNITED STATES OF AMERICA: HOW IT GREW

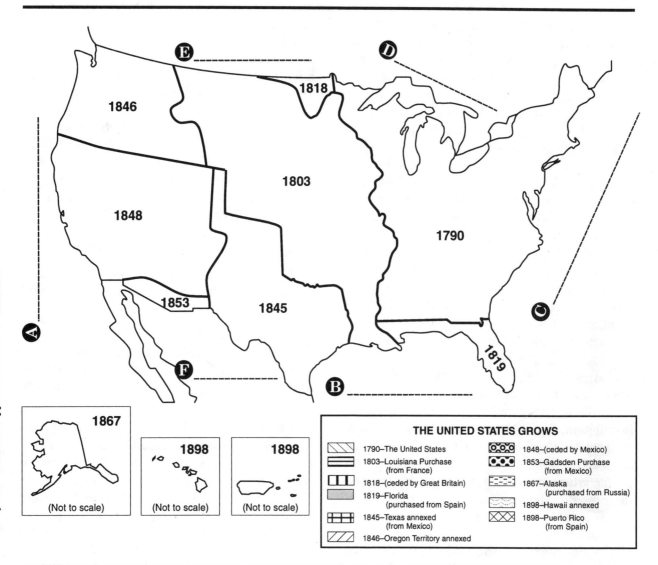

The United States began as a group of English colonies on the eastern coast of North America, crowded between the Atlantic Ocean coast line and the Appalachian Mountains. From that beginning almost 400 years ago there has been tremendous territorial growth. At the completion of the map activity that follows you will have a better understanding of the territory that was gradually added to our country. We now stretch from the Atlantic Ocean to the Pacific Ocean and beyond.

1. Complete the labeling of the map as follows:

   A Pacific Ocean   **C** Atlantic Ocean   **E** Canada

   B Gulf of Mexico   **D** The Great Lakes   **F** Mexico

2. Dates on the map indicate when the territories that now make up our fifty states and the Commonwealth of Puerto Rico were added to the Union. These dates are also shown in the map legend. Carefully shade each territory on the map, using the pattern indicated beside the date in the legend.

3. Carefully color all the waters light blue.

UNITED STATES PLACE NAMES SHOW OUR DIVERSITY

The United States is a country that has been settled by people from all over the world. Some of the groups of people settled in particular parts of the country. It was only natural that they gave their settlements names of places that reminded them of the countries from which they came. Sometimes, they placed "New" at the beginning of the name, as, for example, *New Prague*, which reflects a Czechoslovakian origin. Sometimes, New was not included, as in *Berlin*, New Jersey.

Some places have been given certain names because they resemble other places in the world. *Cairo*, Illinois, at the conjunction of the Mississippi River and the Ohio River, caused settlers to make an association with Cairo, Egypt, which is located on another great river, the Nile. In this case the use of Cairo doesn't mean that the people who settled there were Egyptians.

Another rich source of names of places comes from religious groups that settled in an area. Thus, we have such place names as Bethlehem, Pennsylvania, and Lebanon, New Jersey. Neither of these two places were settled by people from the Middle East. The people who did settle in those places wanted their towns to be associated with the Bible and places mentioned in the Bible, both old and new testaments.

Some places in the United States have names that have no connection with the settlers' country of origin except in language. For example, a town in New Mexico called Tres Piedras (Spanish for "Three Rocks") was so named because the settlement was near such a topographical feature.

Many places have been named after famous people. Lincoln, Nebraska, and Roosevelt, New Jersey, were named after two presidents. Dozens of other places bear such names.

Native American names and language are probably the largest single source of modern American place names. There isn't any state, except Hawaii, that does not have cities, mountains, and other places that have adopted Indian names, including Pontiac,

Michigan; Shawnee, Ohio; and Cherokee, North Carolina.

Some place names are very popular and have been applied in many different places. The *United States Road Atlas*, published by the American Map Corporation, lists 13 Lebanons, 17 Lincolns, and 9 Bethels.

On a drive through the state of New York, one notices dozens of names of foreign cities—for example, Syracuse (Italy), Yorkshire (England), Salamanca (Spain), Damascus (Syria), and Ithaca (Greece).

Suggestions for Teaching Place Names

1. Present some background on place names as told about in the foregoing and/or from other sources.

2. Have your students study road map indexes of their own state for names that most likely have an ethnic, foreign city or country, religious, famous person, or Indian origin.

3. Photocopy and distribute the facing page. Have your students find place names on the map that are also somewhere in the word search puzzle at the top of the page. When they find a place that is named in both the map and the puzzle, they are to draw a neat circle around the word in the puzzle. Note that there are more places labeled on the map than there are places to be identified in the puzzle.

Name: _____ Date: _____

UNITED STATES PLACE NAMES SHOW OUR DIVERSITY

Place Name Word Search Puzzle

A	K	G	L	I	N	C	O	L	N	F
L	P	R	A	T	H	E	N	S	H	K
H	Y	Z	L	I	S	B	O	N	D	L
A	S	U	B	I	T	H	A	C	A	M
M	R	R	L	N	Q	S	P	H	M	T
B	O	I	C	A	I	R	O	E	A	N
R	M	C	U	B	A	W	N	R	S	O
A	E	H	E	G	Y	P	T	O	C	R
P	U	L	A	S	K	I	I	K	U	W
B	E	T	H	A	N	Y	A	E	S	A
L	E	B	A	N	O	N	C	E	R	Y

United States Place Names

As groups settled in the United States they sometimes applied the names of the country or city from where they came to the new settlement. They also used the names of Indian tribes and chiefs. Some of the most frequently used names are from the Bible. Many places were named after famous people.

There are 16 towns and cities listed in the Place Name Word Search Puzzle. Each place is shown on the map, along with five extra places. First select a city from the map; then, look for the city in the puzzle. When you find it, draw a circle around the name.

The name of one city, *Pulaski*, has been circled to help you get started.

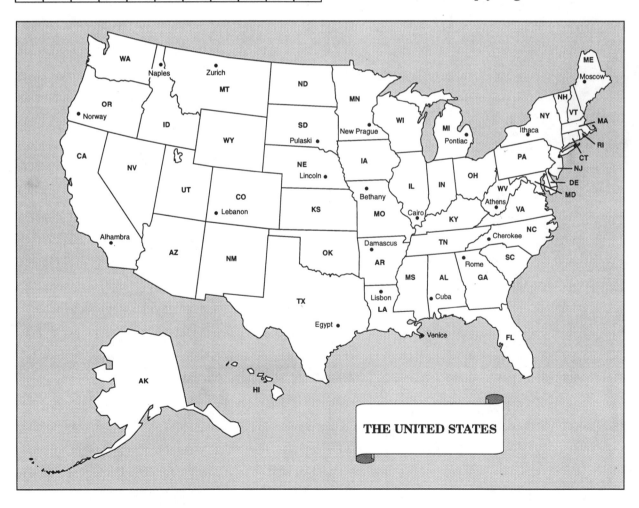

THE UNITED STATES

Northeastern States

NORTHEASTERN STATES: A TABLE OF FACTS

Obtaining information from tables is one of the skills that make up the *ability* to read. But, even the skill of reading a table has a number of subskills, e.g., understanding and utilizing the row and column headings, finding a particular cell, and so on. When reading a narrative paragraph, students should first "get" the facts, and then make inferences. Likewise, in reading a table the first task is to get the facts, and then make comparisons and infer patterns and relationships that the facts suggest.

Note: An *ability* can be thought of as the "umbrella" that covers (encompasses) a number of subskills. For example, the *ability* to read maps would include, among many others, the following subskills: reading direction, reading scale, interpreting colors and contour lines as indicators of elevation.

Procedure for Utilizing the Next Two Pages

1. Make photocopies of the two following pages. Distribute.

2. Have your students answer the questions from facts gleaned from the table.

3. After steps 1 and 2 have been completed, present, via a transparency, the uncompleted graph at the bottom of the table page. Then, with the students, complete the graph with information from the "Area in Square Miles" column of the table. The completed graph is shown below.

4. Suggested steps:

❧ Write the title of the graph.

❧ Complete the enumeration of the horizontal axis.

❧ Write the names of the states in order of size with the smallest state at the bottom of the vertical axis.

❧ Determine the end of each bar; this includes interpolation and estimation as to where bars end.

❧ Shade or draw lines within the bars to make them stand out.

State	A Comparison of the Areas of the Northeastern States
New York	54,471
Pennsylvania	46,058
Maine	35,387
West Virginia	24,231
Maryland	12,407
Massachusetts	10,555
Vermont	9,615
New Hampshire	9,351
New Jersey	8,722
Connecticut	5,544
Delaware	2,489
Rhode Island	1,545

0　5　10　15　20　25　30　35　40　45　50　55　60

Square Miles (1000s)

Name: _____ Date: _____

NORTHEASTERN STATES: A TABLE OF FACTS

FACTS ABOUT THE NORTHEASTERN STATES				
State and Capital (North to South)	Population	Area in Square Miles with Rank Shown in Parentheses ( ) *	Highest Point with Elevation Shown in Parentheses ( )	Nickname
Maine (Augusta)	1,239,448	35,387 (39)	Mt. Katahdin (5,267')	Pine Tree State
New Hampshire (Concord)	1,125,310	9,351 (46)	Mt. Washington (6,288')	Granite State
Vermont (Montpelier)	575,691	9,615 (45)	Mt. Mansfield (4,393')	Green Mountain State
New York (Albany)	18,197,154	54,471 (27)	Mt. Marcy (5,344')	Empire State
Massachusetts (Boston)	6,012,268	10,555 (44)	Mt. Greylock (3,487')	Bay State or Old Colony
Connecticut (Hartford)	3,277,316	5,544 (48)	Mt. Frissell (2,380')	Constitution State or Nutmeg State
Rhode Island (Providence)	1,000,012	1,545 (50)	Jerimoth Hill (812')	Little Rhody or Ocean State
Pennsylvania (Harrisburg)	12,048,271	46,058 (33)	Mount Davis (3,213')	Keystone State
New Jersey (Trenton)	7,879,164	8,722 (47)	High Point (1,803')	Garden State
Delaware (Dover)	700,269	2,489 (49)	Elbright Road (442')	First State or Diamond State
Maryland (Annapolis)	4,964,898	12,407 (42)	Backbone Mountain (3,360')	Old Line State or Free State
West Virginia (Charleston)	1,820,137	24,231 (41)	Spruce Knob (4,861')	Mountain State

* Includes total of land and water

State														
Rhode Island														

0   5

Square Miles (1000s)

NORTHEASTERN STATES: A TABLE OF FACTS

1. What state is the largest in area?

    _____

2. What state is the smallest in area?

    _____

3. What two states are the closest in size?

    _____ and _____

4. What state has the highest point of elevation?

    _____

5. A mile is 5,280 feet. What state's highest point is just 13 feet short of a mile?

    _____

6. The figures in parentheses ( ) in the *Area in Square Miles* column tell you the rank in size of the state when compared with *all* the other states in the country. What is the rank of:

    Rhode Island? _____

    Delaware? _____

    Connecticut? _____

7. What is the nickname for each of the following states?

    New York: _____

    New Jersey: _____

    West Virginia: _____

8. How many states in the United States are larger than New York? _____

9. Judging from the nickname for New Hampshire what would be your guess as to one of the *industries* in the state?

    _____

10. The Northeastern States listed below are in alphabetical order. However, they could be ranked in order of population. New York, which has the largest population, would be number "1" as you can see in the table below. Study the large table; then, rank the other eleven states.

NORTHEASTERN STATES RANKED BY ALPHABETICAL ORDER AND POPULATION	
State	**Population Rank**
Connecticut	
Delaware	
Maine	
Maryland	
Massachusetts	
New Hampshire	
New Jersey	
New York	1
Pennsylvania	
Rhode Island	
Vermont	
West Virginia	

Challenge

Alaska is the largest state. Its land and water area totals 656,000 square miles. Rhode Island is the smallest state. Its land and water area totals 1,500 square miles.*

How many times would Rhode Island fit in to Alaska? _____

* *Note*: Alaska's area has been rounded to the nearest 1,000; Rhode Island's area has been rounded to the nearest 100.

© 1996 by The Center for Applied Research in Education

Name: _____ Date: _____

NORTHEASTERN STATES: CAPITALS AND RIVERS

1. On the map, label the states as follows:

A Maine   K Maryland
B New Hampshire L Delaware
C Vermont
D New York
E Massachusetts
F Connecticut
G Rhode Island
H Pennsylvania
I New Jersey
J West Virginia

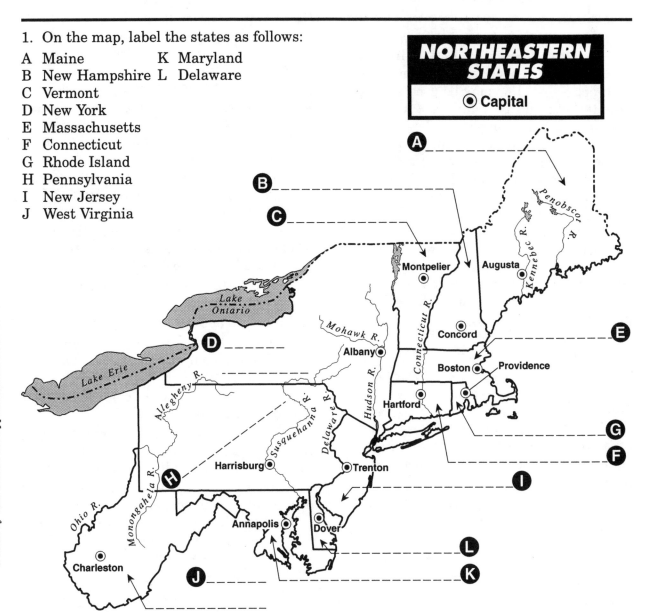

NORTHEASTERN STATES

⊙ Capital

2. Color Lake Erie and Lake Ontario light blue.

3. There are several important rivers in the Northeastern States.

a. What two rivers form the Ohio River?

_____

_____

b. What river separates New Jersey and Pennsylvania? _____

c. What river separates Vermont and New Hampshire and flows south through Massachusetts and Connecticut?

_____

d. What river flows south through New York? _____

e. On what river is Harrisburg located?

_____

f. Which of the two rivers shown in Maine is farther east? _____

NORTHEASTERN STATES: INFORMATION AND SUGGESTIONS

1. Rivers As Boundaries Between States

Your students may not realize that when a river is a boundary between states a dash-dot (–·–·–·–·) line may be used that represents both the boundary and the river. One way to help students understand this convention of maps is to point to the Connecticut River symbol which is a dash-dot line between Vermont and New Hampshire, where it serves as a boundary, but an unbroken line where it flows through Massachusetts and Connecticut.

Another option is to always show a river as an unbroken line, but to indicate when the river is also a boundary by drawing a dash-dot line parallel to the unbroken line.

Boundary
River

2. Capitals

a. A capital is not necessarily the largest city in a state. This is true for New Jersey (Trenton), New York (Albany), Delaware (Dover), Pennsylvania (Harrisburg), Maryland (Annapolis), Maine (Augusta), New Hampshire (Concord), and Vermont (Montpelier).

b. Eight of the 12 capitals in the Northeastern States are on major rivers or bays. One reason for the waterside locations is that early settlements were dependent upon water for transportation and trade; there were very few roads. The list of capitals so situated includes:

◉ Augusta on the Kennebec River
◉ Boston on Massachusetts Bay
◉ Albany on the Hudson River
◉ Hartford on the Connecticut River
◉ Harrisburg on the Susquehanna River
◉ Trenton on the Delaware River
◉ Annapolis on Chesapeake Bay
◉ Providence on Narragansett Bay

3. How to Make a Circle Graph

Circle graphs are relatively easy to read, but are more difficult to make. You may want to teach a lesson on making circle graphs. If so, the following should prove helpful.

A circle graph represents 100% of two or more components. Each component is represented by a segment of the circle that is proportionate to the entire circle.

Example: A lake contains three islands with the area of each as follows: Island A, 5 sq. mi.; Island B, 6 sq. mi.; Island C, 8 sq. mi. The total sq. mi. equals 19.

Question: How can each island's square mileage be depicted on a circle graph? Following are the steps:

1. Find the percent each island is of the whole. Thus, Island A is 26%, Island B is 32%, Island C is 42% (Total: 100%).

2. Convert the percent for each island to degrees, as follows:

a. There are 360° in a circle.

b. For each island multiply its percent × 360°. Thus, Island A equals 94°, Island B equals 115°, and Island C equals 151°.

3. How are the number of degrees for each island arranged on a circle?

a. Draw a radius straight up from the center of the circle to the edge of the circle. This is the beginning line for the segments.

b. With a protractor, measure the number of degrees for Island A and draw a radius. From the radius measure the number of degrees for Island B and draw a radius. Whatever remains is Island C's segment.

c. The completed graph for the three islands:

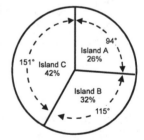

4. Circle Graph on the Facing Page

a. The three-state group represents 54% of the total. 54% translates to 194° (.54 × 360°).

b. The nine-state group represents 46% of the total. 46% translates to 166° on the graph (.46 × 360°).

c. A protractor was then utilized to plot the segments.

Name: _____ Date: _____

NORTHEASTERN STATES: ACRES OF HARVESTED LAND

"Square Area" Graphs

The "square area" graph shows how three Northeastern States (New York, Pennsylvania, Maryland) compare with the other nine combined states of the region relative to the number of acres of land harvested in a recent year. There are 100 squares in the graph and each square represents 1% of the total.

1. What percent of the acres was harvested by the "Big Three?" _____ %

2. What percent of the acres was harvested by the combined other nine states? _____ %

3. What is the percent difference between the two? _____ %

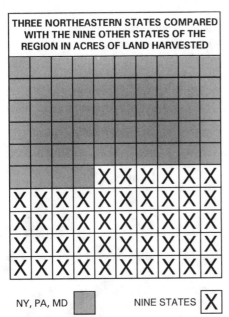

NY, PA, MD ▣   NINE STATES X

"Circle Area" Graphs

1. Circle graphs are sometimes called "pie graphs." This is because they are round and may be divided into "slices."

2. The circle graph in the next column also shows a comparison of the Big Three and the other nine combined states with regard to the number of acres of land harvested. You can see that the largest slice would belong to the Big Three: NY, PA, MD. Neatly print the abbreviations for these states in the larger segment, which represents 54% of the circle.

3. For the smaller segment neatly print abbreviations of the other nine states: ME, NH, VT, MA, CT, RI, NJ, DE, WV. These abbreviations should be written on the lines outside the segment.

4. To make the graph more interesting and easy to read, use two colors to color the segments.

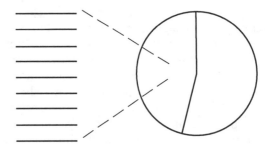

THREE NORTHEASTERN STATES COMPARED WITH THE NINE OTHER STATES OF THE REGION IN ACRES OF LAND HARVESTED

Activity

1. The three combined states (PA, NY, MD) harvest a total of 9,012,000 acres. Pennsylvania's share of that was 45%, New York's share was 38%, and Maryland's share was 17%. Your task is to use the key of the graph to help you know how to show each state's portion of the entire graph; then complete the graph.

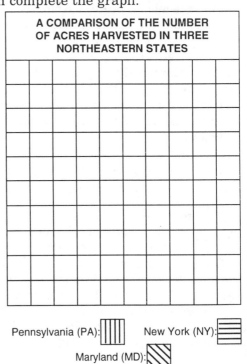

A COMPARISON OF THE NUMBER OF ACRES HARVESTED IN THREE NORTHEASTERN STATES

Pennsylvania (PA): ▥   New York (NY): ▤
Maryland (MD): ▧

MAINE: HIGHLIGHTS IN ITS GEOGRAPHY AND HISTORY

1. Maine Names

The origination of the name "Maine" is somewhat obscure. Most likely, the name derived from the necessity of early seafarers and explorers to distinguish between the many offshore islands of the region and the *mainland*; hence, after a period of time the term "mainland" was shortened and became *Maine*.

Another expression that refers to Maine is *Down East*. This terminology causes confusion because some people might think of Maine as *up north*. However, neither *down* nor *up* are appropriate as compass directions on Earth. Nevertheless, *Down East* is used and has a rational geographical background. It seems that when the old-time sailing ships navigated from Boston, or other points south, to Maine they were sailing *down wind*; i.e., the wind was behind them. And, since the ships were sailing eastward along the coast of Maine it became natural to speak of Maine as *Down East*, and the people who lived in Maine as *Down Easterners* or *Down Easters*.

2. Maine's Forests

It was with good reason that the people of Maine chose the white pine tree to symbolize their state. In the early days of the state white pine was in great demand as masts for sailing ships. However, by 1900, white pine forests were so decimated that the lumber industry turned to the cutting of fir, hemlock, spruce, and birch trees. This kept the manufacturing establishments producing paper for newsprint, bags, cardboard, napkins, and a host of other wood based products such as construction lumber, insulation, and furniture. With all this activity, however, the state is 90% forest covered even today, and the most important manufacturing activity remains centered around forest products.

Over the years the lumber industry in Maine has undergone another significant change. Great log "rafts" are no longer floated down rivers, such as the Penobscot and Kennebec, to the lumber mills. Today, virtually all cut logs are transported to the mills by truck or rail. This change came about for several reasons. One was that it was dangerous for loggers to "ride" the logs down the rivers to the mills for the purpose of preventing log jams; many a logger has been crushed to death or seriously injured while trying to free a log jam. Another reason the rivers were abandoned as transportation routes was that they made the lumber industry too seasonal; that is, when the rivers froze in the winter there was no movement of logs. Lastly, the water-soaked and rotting logs released toxins into the water that polluted rivers, killing fish and vegetation, and contaminating drinking water.

3. Maine Potatoes

More than two billion pounds of potatoes are grown in Maine each year. How many potatoes is that if we assume the average potato weighs one-quarter of a pound? Some eight billion potatoes, and that's a lot of potatoes. In the United States, only Idaho and Washington produce more potatoes than Maine.

Most of Maine's potatoes are grown in Aroostock County, which is in far northern Maine, close to the Canadian border provinces of Quebec and New Brunswick. Why are potatoes so prolific in Aroostock County? The answer lies in the area's cool, moist climate, and its loose, aerated loam (a rich mixture of clay and sand). All these things allow the tubers, which grow on the stem of the plant beneath the surface, to grow freely without the restrictions of clay and rocks. It is the tubers (potatoes) that we actually eat.

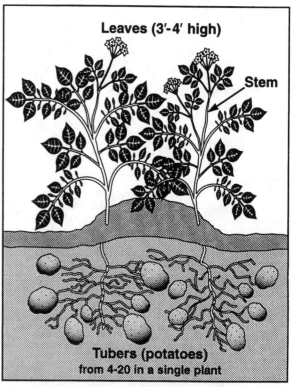

A TYPICAL POTATO PLANT

MAINE: LOCATING PLACES BY QUADRANT

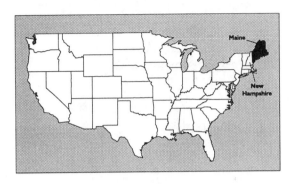

Maine in the United States

1a. Describe Maine's position within the United States. _____

_____

_____

_____

 b. What is the only state that borders on Maine? _____

Maine Map Locations

Notice that the map of Maine in the next column is sectioned into squares. The squares make it easy to find places. For example, if you wanted to help some people locate *Cross Island* on the map you could say, "It's somewhere in section E-5." They would look down the "5" column to where the "E" row intersects. *Cross Island* would be somewhere within that square.

Listed below are some of Maine's interesting locations. Study the map and write the number and letter of the section in which each place is located.

1. *Portland*, Maine's largest city: _____

2. *Augusta*, capital of Maine: _____

3. Town of *Moosehead* on Moosehead Lake: _____

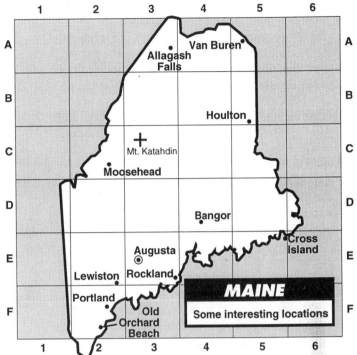

4. *Mt. Katahdin*, Maine's highest mountain (5,267'): _____

5. *Allagash Falls* on the fast-running Allagash River: _____

6. *Bangor* on the Penobscot River: _____

7. *Old Orchard Beach*, summer resort: _____

8. Town of *Van Buren* on the border between Maine and Canada. It holds the record for Maine's lowest recorded temperature of -48°F: _____

9. Bates College, *Lewiston*: _____

10. Town of *Houlton*, close to where United States I-95 crosses the border into Canada: _____

11. Shore Village Museum in *Rockland*, noted for its collection of maritime items: _____

VERMONT: MAPLE TREES AND LAKE CHAMPLAIN

Maple Trees, Maple Syrup, and Maple Sugar

The sugar maple is the state tree of Vermont, and for good reason. No other state produces as much maple syrup or its by-products as Vermont does. Before European settlers invaded their domain, Indians were tapping sugar maples for the flavorful sap they yielded. After being introduced to the sweet treat, it didn't take very long for the colonists to learn Indian procedures for converting the sap of the trees into syrup and candy. Sweets were a scarce commodity in the colonies, so the products of the sugar maple became very popular.

The sugar maple grows as high as 140', almost one-half the length of a football field. A large maple may have a trunk diameter of five feet, or almost sixteen feet in circumference; three average sized men linked hand-in-hand would barely circle such a tree. The sugar maple's bark is gray and its leaves are dark green. People drive to Vermont in the fall of the year to see its leaves, which have turned to brilliant orange, yellow, and red.

The steps in converting the sugar maple's sap to maple syrup and maple sugar are as follows:

1. In the spring of the year "tap" the tree; that is, bore a three-quarter inch hole about three inches into the trunk of the tree. Then, drive a wooden or metal spout into the hole.

2. Hang a bucket on the spout; the sap drips into the bucket. Cover the bucket to keep debris and insects from falling into the sap.

3. Each day collect the sap, pour it into large tanks, and then boil the sap. Boiling rids the sap of excess water. After most of the water has evaporated, that which remains is maple syrup. Boil the syrup a little longer and it thickens into maple cream; a little more boiling and the result is soft maple candy; and, finally, more boiling results in maple sugar. After boiling, one gallon of maple syrup is converted into seven or eight pounds of hard candy.

The cross section that follows illustrates a tap and spout that has been inserted into the trunk of a sugar maple tree.

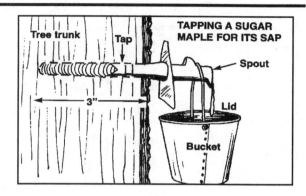

Lake Champlain

Lake Champlain was named after Samuel de Champlain who "discovered" it in 1609. Of course, Indians had lived near or on the shores of the lake hundreds of years before Champlain arrived.

Lake Champlain is some 125 miles long and is shared by the United States and Canada. Within the United States it is shared by New York and Vermont. The lake is narrow, no more than one-half mile wide at it northern and southern ends. The longest east-west distance, at about the middle of the lake, is about fourteen miles. A ferry travels to and from Keeseville, New York, to Burlington, Vermont. The lake empties water into the Richelieu River at its north end; the Richelieu River, in turn, empties its water into the St. Lawrence River.

During the Revolutionary War and the War of 1812, Lake Champlain was of great strategic value. In both wars the British tried to win control of the lake and the Hudson River. By so doing, they would have gained the objective of separating the northern colonies/states from the middle and southern colonies/states. In both cases their efforts failed.

© 1996 by The Center for Applied Research in Education

 Name: ______________________ Date: __________

VERMONT: SKI LOVERS' STATE

Ski Vermont

In the Northeastern States there are hundreds of wonderful ski resorts. Vermont, especially, is noted for great skiing. There are dozens of ski resorts in Vermont; however, the map on this page shows only a few.

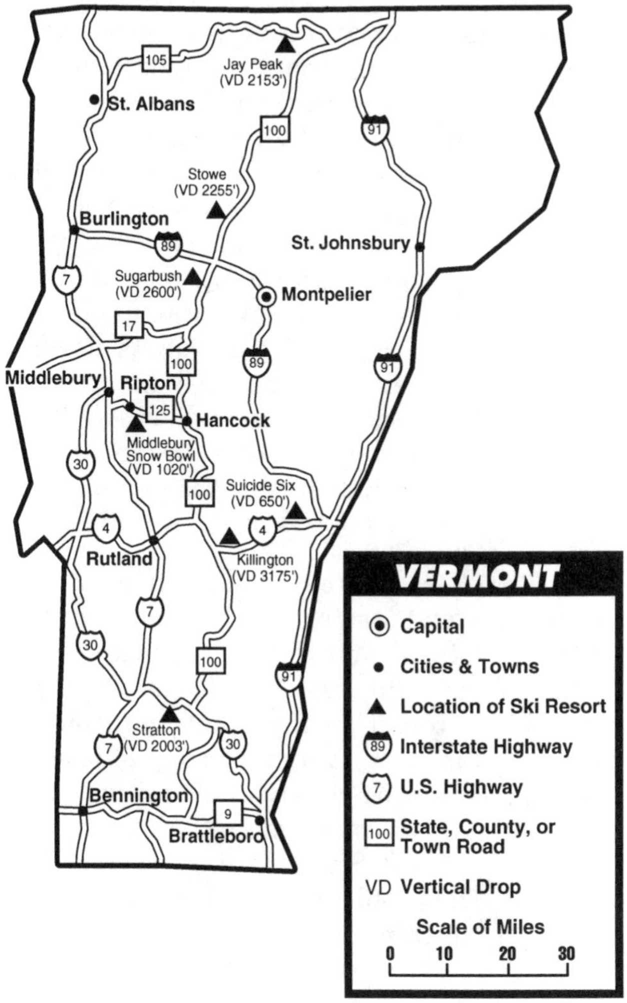
105
Jay Peak
(VD 2153')
St. Albans
100
91
Stowe
(VD 2255')
Burlington
89
St. Johnsbury
7
Sugarbush
(VD 2600')
Montpelier
17
100
89
91
Middlebury
Ripton
125
Hancock
Middlebury
Snow Bowl
(VD 1020')
30
100
Suicide Six
(VD 650')
4
4
Rutland
Killington
(VD 3175')
7
30
100
91
Stratton
(VD 2003')
7
30
Bennington
9
Brattleboro
VERMONT
Capital
Cities & Towns
Location of Ski Resort
Interstate Highway
U.S. Highway
State, County, or Town Road
VD Vertical Drop
Scale of Miles
0 10 20 30

1. Complete the table below with information from the map. On the table you'll see the heading "Vertical Drop." Vertical Drop is abbreviated as VD on the map. Vertical Drop means that from the top of the highest trail to its base there is a drop of so many feet; however, the trail itself would be much longer. For example, a drop may be 1,000', but the trail would be much more, perhaps 5,000'.

Name of Ski Resort	Vertical Drop	Highway Location*
Jay Peak	2,153'	105
Stowe		
Suicide Six		
Killington		
Sugarbush		
Stratton		
Middlebury Snow Bowl		

** Use IS for Interstate, US for United States, and ☐ for other roads.*

2. Imagine that you are in Bennington and you are going to Jay Peak for a ski weekend. Choose a route of travel and list, in order, the highways you would travel.

1st: ____________ 3rd: ____________

2nd: ____________ 4th: ____________

3. Imagine that you are on your way to Sugarbush from Brattleboro. You find that where state road 100 meets US-4 from the west, state road 100 is blocked with snow for three miles north, so you have to take a different route. Name in order all the highways you would travel if you took the shortest alternate route. Complete the blanks.

Take US-4 west to _____; drive north to _____, then east to _____, then north to Sugarbush.

4. What is the difference in length of the vertical drop between:

a. Killington and Suicide Six? __________

b. Stowe and Sugarbush? __________

c. Stratton and Jay Peak? __________

NEW HAMPSHIRE: THE GREAT STONE FACE AND MT. WASHINGTON

Mt. Washington

Mt. Washington, with an elevation of 6288' is the highest mountain east of the Mississippi River. It comes as a surprise to some people to learn that the strongest wind (231 mph) ever recorded on Earth's surface was measured on this mountain. Mt. Washington is so high and situated far enough north that in some years its ski resorts are still operating in June. The snow on the mountain is so deep in the winter that the road to the summit of the mountain is closed and even the cogwheel train shuts down. Drivers who make it to the top of the mountain in the warmer parts of the year are proud to display a bumper sticker which reads "This car climbed Mt. Washington."

Great Stone Face

The "Great Stone Face," sometimes called the "Old Man of the Mountain" or the "Profile," is a well-known natural New Hampshire landmark. Three ledges of granite, one on top of another, protrude from a sheer cliff in such a way that the profile of a man's face can be clearly distinguished. At the foot of the precipice is Profile Lake, over which the Great Stone Face appears to be looking. The profile is about forty feet high from strong chin to broad forehead, its size making the face visible from a great distance. In fact, distance makes the outline all the more distinguishable.

The profile was made famous by Nathaniel Hawthorne, who wrote the short story "The Great Stone Face" in 1851. One of the passages in the story suggests that "It was a happy lot for children to grow up to manhood or womanhood with the Great Stone Face before their eyes, for all the features were noble, and the expression was at once grand and sweet, as if it were the glow of a vast, warm heart that embraced all mankind in its affections and had room for more. It was an education only to look at it."

Hawthorne goes on to tell of a young boy, Ernest, who loved to look at the face. He was told by his mother that legend predicted

"THE GREAT STONE FACE"

that some day a person would grow to manhood who would have a profile very much like that of the Great Stone Face. That person would become the "greatest and noblest personage of his time."

Many great and famous men were said to have a likeness to the Old Man of the Mountain, but to Ernest they all lacked the character that went beyond similar appearances. As the story turns out, Ernest, who was a simple and modest person but who had profound and unusual insights into life and its meaning, is finally realized to be the embodiment of the Great Stone Face in both physical appearance and inner wisdom.

Some New Hampshire Facts

❑ Its Atlantic Ocean general *coastline* is only 13 miles, but its tidal *shoreline* is about 131 miles. Its beautiful shore, along with more than 1,000 lakes nestled in forested mountains, makes the state a major tourist attraction.

❑ Agriculture, including farming, fishing, and forestry, accounts for only one percent of the state's gross product.

❑ The state bird is the purple finch; the state flower is the purple lilac; the state tree is the white birch; and the state motto is "Live free, or die."

NEW HAMPSHIRE: LOCATING PLACES BY QUADRANT

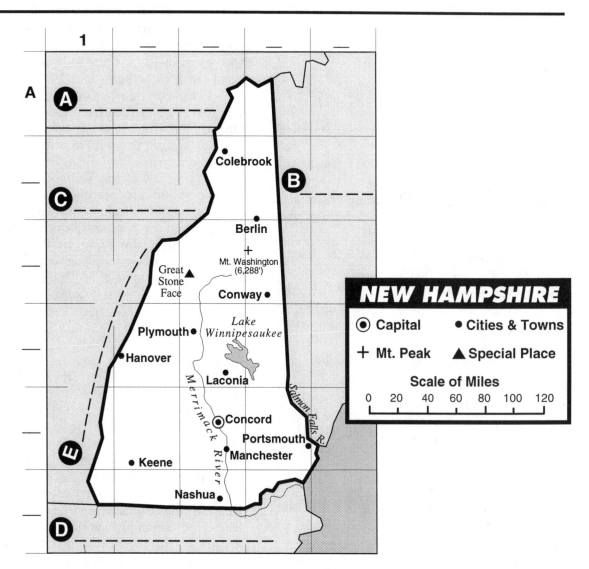

1. On the lines provided on the map label all the places listed below.

Ⓐ Canada   Ⓓ Massachusetts
Ⓑ Maine   Ⓔ Connecticut River
Ⓒ Vermont

2. Note that the map is divided into rectangles or *quadrants*. If a place is listed as being in Quadrant A1, the map reader will more quickly find the place than if there were no quadrants; only part of the map has to be searched. Some maps have hundreds of names!

To Do

a. Along the left vertical line on the map, label the quadrants A through F.

b. Along the top horizontal line on the map, label the quadrants 1 through 5.

c. In which quadrant is each of the following places.

____ Keene   ____ Conway

____ Colebrook   ____ Hanover

____ Concord   ____ Mt. Washington

____ Great Stone Face ____ Portsmouth

____ Laconia   ____ Nashua

NEW YORK: NEW YORK CITY, NIAGARA FALLS

New York City: Some Superlatives

Population: More than 7 million people in its 301 square miles

Population density: An average of about 24,000 people per square mile

Hospitals: About 100 spread throughout its five boroughs

Higher education: Almost 100 colleges and universities

Elementary and high schools: More than 900 public schools and some 1 million students; about 900 private schools

Television stations: 13 at the latest count; also, 117 radio stations

Tall buildings: World Trade Center at 1368' and 110 stories; Empire State Building at 1250' and 102 stories; some 65 buildings 600' or higher

Bridges: Verrazano-Narrows at 4260', the country's longest suspension bridge

Tunnels: The second, third, and fourth longest underwater vehicle tunnels in the United States, in order of length: Brooklyn-Battery, 9,117'; Holland Tunnel, 8,557'; Lincoln Tunnel, 8,216'

Waterfront: Some 500 miles

Ships entering and leaving NY harbor: Some 15,000 yearly

Tourism: Some 20 million visitors yearly

Newspapers: Three of the country's leading daily newspapers including the *Wall Street Journal*, approximate circulation 1,800,000; *New York Times*, approximate circulation 1,150,000; New York *Daily News*, approximate circulation 800,000. Also published: 40 foreign language newspapers in 20 different languages

Niagara Falls

The Niagara River connects Lake Erie and Lake Ontario, but this doesn't mean that there is a smooth passage on the river from one lake to the other. Lake Erie's surface elevation is 572' above sea level while Lake Ontario's elevation is 246' above sea level. These differences in elevation mean that the river falls 326' in its 36 mile length. For any river with that much fall in so few miles there will be a very strong current with lots of "white water." But, the situation is compounded on the Niagara River because most of the drop occurs over cliffs that are called Niagara Falls.

In the early days of our country it was not possible to go by boat from Lake Erie to Lake Ontario or vice versa. It was necessary to portage around the falls and the river. Today, however, boats travel from one lake to the other by means of the Welland Canal, which can accommodate ocean-going ships. By a series of "steps" or locks boats are raised and/or lowered and the Niagara Falls are bypassed.

Although the Niagara Falls were an obstacle to navigation, positive results have come about because of them. One is the awesome power of the falling water which generates hydroelectricity used by both the United States and Canada. Scores of industries use the relatively cheap power to manufacture paper, chemicals, aluminum, steel, and other products. Thousands of homes are furnished with the electricity needed for light, heat, and to run the motors of refrigerators, vacuum cleaners, and other modern appliances.

Another positive resulting from Niagara Falls is that millions of people have visited the area to see them. They may be seen from the air, from outlooks, from bridges, and from sight-seeing boats that sail on the quiet waters at the foot of the great drops. Obviously, tourists must be served, so thousands of Americans and Canadians make their livings directly and indirectly from tourism generated by the Falls and other attractions in the area.

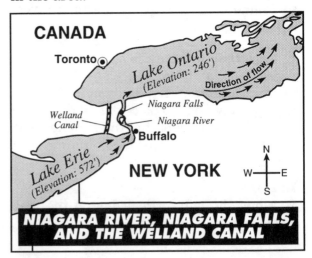

NIAGARA RIVER, NIAGARA FALLS, AND THE WELLAND CANAL

Name: _____ Date: _____

NEW YORK: A BORDER WITH CANADA AND FIVE OTHER STATES

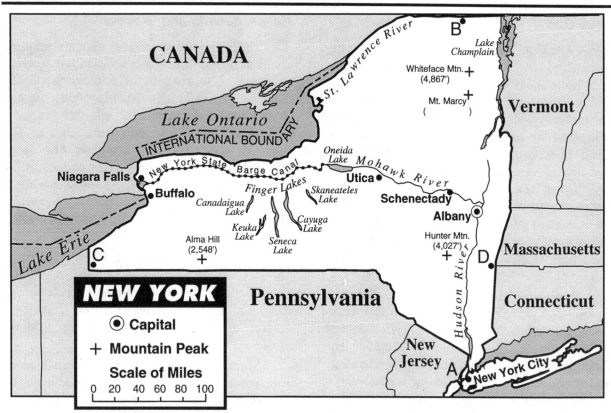

1. What five states border New York?

_____ _____ _____

_____ _____

2. Which two of the five Great Lakes border New York?_____ _____

3. What river flowing out of Lake Ontario serves as a border between New York and Canada? _____

4. Find the "Finger Lakes." List them from *west to east*.

a._____   d._____

b._____   e._____

c._____

5. What lake on New York's eastern border is shared with Canada and Vermont?

_____

6. Mt. Marcy at 5,344' is the highest mountain in New York. Draw a circle around the symbol for Mt. Marcy and neatly print its elevation on the map.

7. On what river or body of water are each of the following cities located?

Albany: _____

Schenectady: _____

Buffalo: _____

Utica:_____

8. Approximately how many miles is it from New York City to the state's northernmost point, that is from point **A** to point **B**?

_____ miles

9. What is the approximate distance from west to east following New York's southern border, that is from point **C** to point **D**?

_____ miles

10. What two cities are at the western end of the New York State Barge Canal?

_____ _____

39

MASSACHUSETTS: HIGHLIGHTS IN ITS GEOGRAPHY AND HISTORY

Cape Cod

Cape Cod may be one of the most easily recognized land features in the United States. It is a classical example of both a peninsula and a cape. The Cape has been described in various ways, for example, "the fishhook in the Atlantic," "an arm bent at the elbow with the hand beckoning one to the Massachusetts mainland," and "an arm flexing its muscle." The "Cape," as it is familiarly called, is aptly named. In the early days cod fish swam in great schools near its shores. Today, however, cod are a threatened species, and laws have been passed limiting the amount of cod that can be netted by commercial fishermen.

The Cape juts so far into the Atlantic Ocean that it was at its tip, where Provincetown is now located, that the *Mayflower* first set anchor in 1620. The next step for the Pilgrims was to cross Cape Cod Bay and go about the business of starting a settlement on the mainland at Plymouth.

Today, both Provincetown and Plymouth have been restored. *Mayflower II*, a replica of the original *Mayflower*, lies at anchor in Plymouth. Across the bay in Provincetown, visitors find a wonderfully preserved colonial town with a town crier, who makes his rounds spreading the news by voice.

Although Cape Cod is a frequently visited place, much of it is unspoiled by human development and is like it was more than 375 years ago. Some 40,000 acres have been set aside as the Cape Cod National Seashore. Now, the grass covered sand dunes, which are very susceptible to destruction by natural forces and humans, are protected. Yet, places are set aside for recreation where visitors can picnic in natural settings.

Massachusetts and Glaciers

Thousands of years ago glaciers scraped and bulldozed the state now called Massachusetts. The results of the work of the glaciers is easily discernible today in the state's rounded mountains, glacial deposits, and stray rocks and boulders. One of the several glaciers that covered the land pushed the sea aside and extended itself far out into the water. When it melted back it left a ridge of debris, called a *terminal moraine*. That ridge of land is now called Cape Cod.

The revered Plymouth Rock, said to be used as a landing dock by the Pilgrims, and now sheltered by a canopy to help preserve it, was a "stray" that was carried there by a glacier and left behind when the glacier melted.

Many of the lakes and ponds in Massachusetts are also legacies of the glaciers. The tremendous weight and scraping power of the moving ice gouged out great depressions in the land. Then, when the glaciers retreated they left ridges of debris that acted as dams at the end of the depressions. Melt from the glaciers filled the depressions or valleys, and lakes were created.

Massachusetts' western mountains, the Berkshires, are rounded at their summits. It was the combined scraping power of the glaciers, thousands of feet thick, plus natural erosion that made the mountains rounded.

Notice in picture 1 that the glacier looks like a river flowing through a valley. As the glacier melts backward, as shown in picture 2, the rocks and stones it carries will be left behind, as in picture 3.

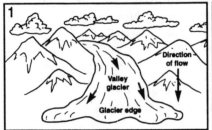
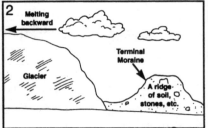

Name: _____ Date: _____

MASSACHUSETTS: MAP/CROSSWORD

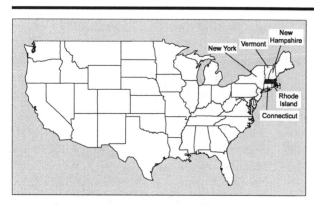

Massachusetts in the United States

1. Describe Massachusetts' position within the United States. _____

_____

_____

_____

2. List all the states that border on Massachusetts. _____

_____

_____

_____

_____

MASSACHUSETTS

- ◉ Capital
- ● Cities and towns

Scale of Miles
0 20 40 60 80

Across

1. City located on Massachusetts Bay
3. City about 13 miles northwest of New Bedford: _____ River
5. City about 12 miles west of the center of Boston
6. Waterway that connects Buzzards Bay and Cape Cod Bay: _____ Cod Canal
9. City about 42 miles west of Quincy
13. City about 8 miles northeast of Northampton
15. City in southern Massachusetts and on the Connecticut River

Down

2. Island south of Cape Cod
4. City on the coast of Massachusetts Bay
6. River that flows from north to south across Massachusetts (abbreviation)
7. City on Cape Cod Bay
8. City in west central Massachusetts
10. Bay on the southern side of Cape Cod
11. Direction one would go from Brockton to Springfield
12. Town in Massachusetts' far northwest: North _____
14. City about 20 miles southeast of Taunton: _____ Bedford

CONNECTICUT: HIGHLIGHTS IN ITS GEOGRAPHY AND HISTORY

1. Tobacco in Connecticut

It comes as a surprise to tourists and others to see tobacco plants growing in Connecticut. Ordinarily, tobacco is thought to be an agricultural product of the southern states. Yet, Connecticut is among the top ten tobacco growing states in the country, and it is Connecticut's most important crop. Connecticut's tobacco is of very high quality and is much in demand for cigars. In fact, it was a Connecticut woman who made the first American cigar in 1801, and ever since then Connecticut has been a leader in producing and manufacturing that tobacco specialty.

2. The Connecticut River

From its source in northern New Hampshire, the Connecticut River flows south and forms the boundary between Vermont and New Hampshire, continues on through Massachusetts, then Connecticut, and finally empties into Long Island Sound. The 407 mile long river divides Connecticut into two roughly equal parts.

The river's mouth is wide and deep, thus permitting ships a means of exit and entrance to the Atlantic Ocean. Large ocean-going ships navigate the river as far north as Connecticut's capital, Hartford. North of Hartford navigation of the river is confined to small craft; there are too many falls and rapids for anything larger. Yet, those very falls and rapids have served Connecticut well in the past. The swift-flowing water furnished the power to turn the paddle wheels that were needed for textile plants, paper plants, and other industries. Today, the water of the Connecticut River is used to produce hydroelectric power to run the hundreds of manufacturing establishments in the Connecticut River Valley.

The Connecticut River and Long Island Sound, which lies between the shore lines of Connecticut and Long Island, provide recreational opportunities for hundreds of thousands of people. Marinas line the banks of the river, and small craft of all descriptions cruise on the outlet waters of the "Sound," as it is called. There are numerous beaches on both the Connecticut and Long Island shorelines. There are interesting places to visit such as Mystic Seaport, which has been restored to what it once was as a leading New England whaling community.

When Indians lived along the Connecticut River, the water was as pure as it could be. Starting in colonial times, however, the river became more and more polluted by municipal and industrial waste. By the 1960s the water was undrinkable, few people would dare swim in it, and fish and plant life had all but disappeared. The river had the dubious distinction of being one of the country's most polluted rivers.

Now for the good news: the conditions described above have been rectified. All the states that share the river met and agreed to cooperate in restoring the river. The states, with the help of the federal government, gradually reduced or entirely eliminated the causes of the river's pollution. Today, the river has been so cleaned-up that even the salmon that once spawned in the headwaters of the river have returned, and little children can once more enjoy splashing in its water.

3. Some Connecticut Facts

State Bird: Robin
State Tree: White Oak
State Song: *Yankee Doodle*
State Animal: Sperm Whale
State Mineral: Garnet

Name: _____ Date: _____

CONNECTICUT: RIVERS AND CITIES

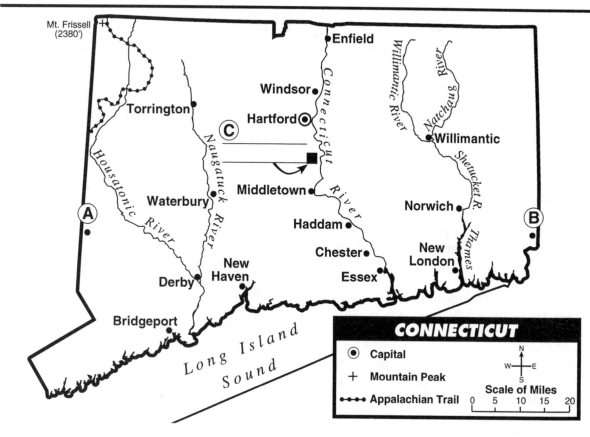

Connecticut Map Locations

1. Which of the following communities are *downstream* from Hartford, the capital of Connecticut?

____ Windsor   ____ Enfield

____ Middletown   ____ Chester

____ Haddam   ____ Essex

2. What town is at the junction of the Housatonic and the Naugatuck rivers?

_____

3. The community of Willimantic is located at the junction of what two rivers?

_____ _____

What river is formed from these two rivers? _____

4. What city is at the mouth of the Thames River? _____

5. In Connecticut, how many times does the Appalachian Trail cross the Housatonic River? _____

6. All the rivers shown on the map finally empty into what body of water? _____

_____

7. How many miles is Connecticut from west (point **A**) to east (point **B**)?

_____ miles

8. If you were hiking north on the Appalachian trail, in which direction would you look to see Mt. Frisell, Connecticut's highest elevation? _____ How high is Mt. Frisell? _____

9. Dinosaurs roamed Connecticut more than 200 million years ago. Exhibits of them can be seen at Dinosaur State Park. Label the park at **C** on the map.

RHODE ISLAND: HIGHLIGHTS IN ITS GEOGRAPHY AND HISTORY

Rhode Island and Religious Tolerance

Rhode Island has the much respected honor of being the first of the British colonies in the New World to be founded on the principle of religious freedom for all. This principle is now embedded in the United States Constitution as the First Amendment. The state's tradition of religious tolerance began when Roger Williams was forced to leave the Massachusetts Bay Colony because he disagreed with the established religion.

Williams left Massachusetts in 1636 and started a settlement at a place that he called Providence. One of the first laws of the new colony was that people would be left to follow their own beliefs in matters of religion. The colony became a haven for many settlers who were not welcome elsewhere, and included Catholics, Jews, Quakers, Protestants, and many others.

The word *Providence* is still part of the official name of the state that the colony became: State of Rhode Island and Providence Plantations. So, even though the state is the smallest in the United States, it has the longest name. Today, however, most people call the state Rhode Island and, sometimes, in affection, "Little Rhody."

Rhode Island Attracts Visitors

A glance at a large scale map shows the great irregularity of Rhode Island's coast. That irregularity, along with 36 islands and the waters of Narragansett Bay and Block Island Sound, all combine to attract vacationers. Numerous beaches and calm waters appeal to swimmers, small boaters, and those who enjoy fishing.

Rhode Island also has attractions for those who find enjoyment in visiting historical sites, museums, restorations, and annual events. Some examples follow:

♟ *The United States' Oldest Jewish Synagogue*

The synagogue is located in Newport, which itself is a favorite vacation spot. The synagogue was built in 1763, but the congregation goes back even further to 1638.

☥ *Block Island and Southeast Lighthouse*

A fifteen minute ferry boat ride from Point Judith on the coast carries tourists to Block Island. Aside from the cool breezes and scenic lighthouse, visitors are fascinated by the modern windmill that looks like a giant propeller. The windmill captures the almost constant winds to generate electricity for the islanders.

⛏ *Slater's Mill In Pawtucket*

Samuel Slater was a pioneer in establishing Rhode Island as a manufacturing state, especially in the textile industry. Slater learned how to operate textile machines while he was in England. He brought his knowledge back to the United States, where he persuaded Moses Brown, a business man, to finance the building of a textile mill. Pawtucket was chosen as the site for the mill because of a plentitude of water power, nearby markets, and capable workers. Slater's enterprise, ingenuity, and mechanical ability have earned him the right to be called the "Father of American Industry." The original mill has been restored and now is a museum open to the public.

Rhode Island and Population Density

Rhode Island, the smallest state, has a higher population density than any other state except New Jersey. If we take Rhode Island's population (1,000,012) and divide it by its area (1545 square miles) we discover that if all the people in the state were evenly distributed over the state, that there would be about 647 people in each square mile.

However, an interesting aspect of the state's population density arises when it is realized that almost 1,000,000 of the state's people live in two metropolitan areas at the head of Narragansett Bay—Providence and Pawtucket. Another aspect to be considered is that two-thirds of the state's acreage consists of agricultural, forested, and undeveloped land. All this means that there are plenty of areas in Rhode Island where few people live. A corollary lesson to be learned is that population density figures can lead to erroneous conclusions if their limitations are not realized.

© 1996 by The Center for Applied Research in Education

Name: _____ Date: _____

RHODE ISLAND: MAP-WORD PUZZLE

Map-Word Puzzle

Fill the empty squares with names from the map. Places that have two parts to their names are separated by a space. When the puzzle is completed every empty square should have a letter, and all the place names should be spelled completely.

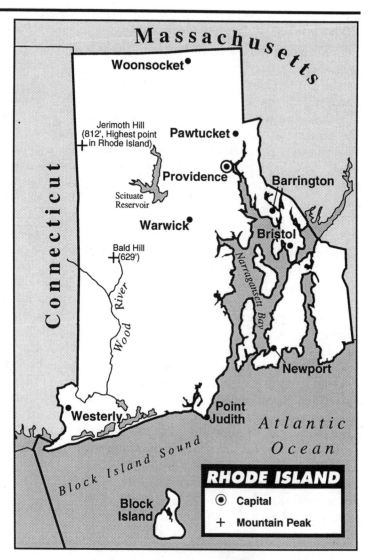

PENNSYLVANIA: HIGHLIGHTS IN ITS GEOGRAPHY AND HISTORY

Philadelphia—A Great City

Philadelphia, with more than 1,600,000 people, is Pennsylvania's largest city, as well as the United States' fifth most populous city. Located on the Delaware River with quick access to the Atlantic Ocean and the ports of the world, and almost directly in line with Washington, D.C.; Baltimore; New York; and Boston, Philadelphia is a great trade center. A car or truck traveling on the several major highways that enter or skirt the city could easily be in Washington in less than three hours, and in New York in two hours. The coastal railroad lines that enter the city allow the trips to be made in even less time.

Philadelphia—a word that mean *brotherly love* in Greek—was founded in 1682 by William Penn and his Quaker followers; hence, Philadelphia is known by two nicknames: "City of Brotherly Love" and "Quaker City." Philadelphia is a most historic city, especially in relation to our early history. It was the capital of the American colonies during most of the American Revolution. The Declaration of Independence was signed in Independence Hall; in that same building the United States Constitution was written and signed, and it was there that the Liberty Bell rang out in celebration of these great events. Betsy Ross is said to have sewn the first official American flag in Philadelphia. Philadelphia was also the chosen home of Benjamin Franklin, one of the founders of the nation's first circulating library and the academy that later became the University of Pennsylvania.

The Ohio River—Waterway to the West

The Ohio River, famous in American history, is formed at Pittsburgh by the confluence of the Monongahela River from the south and the Allegheny River from the north. The Ohio River's southwestward flow carried untold thousands of early American settlers and their possessions to the Mississippi River. However, before reaching the Mississippi River, many settlers disembarked from their barges and rafts at points along the river's route and began their homesteading activities. Unquestionably, the Ohio River hastened the settlement of the entire Mississippi Valley.

The Delaware River

The Delaware River completely separates New Jersey from Pennsylvania. From its "white water" beginnings in New York to its steady and calm flow into Delaware Bay, the river serves useful purposes: it provides water for communities and industries; recreation for fishing, boating, tubing, and swimming enthusiasts; and a transportation route for ocean-going ships from the Atlantic Ocean north to Trenton. In its travel the river flows 390 miles past beautiful scenery including the Delaware Water Gap, Washington Crossing State Park, and the striking skyline of Philadelphia. The Delaware serves large cities (Easton, PA; Trenton, NJ; Philadelphia, PA; and Wilmington, DE) and dozens of smaller communities.

The Delaware is famous in American history for George Washington's crossing of its ice-choked waters at Washington Crossing, eight miles north of Trenton, on Christmas Day, 1776, for the purpose of attacking the British, who held Trenton. The battle that ensued and the capture of Trenton by Washington's troops was one of the turning points of the war favorable to the patriot cause.

Each year thousands of Americans visit the site of the crossing of the Delaware. Each Christmas Day the crossing is reenacted by volunteers dressed in authentic garb, poling their way in "bull boats" from the Pennsylvania shore to the New Jersey shore.

Oil in Pennsylvania

Titusville, Pennsylvania, only a few miles from Erie, Pennsylvania, was the site of the first drilled and commercially successful oil well. Even today, a high grade of oil is pumped from the wells in the area. Some statistics on the early oil industry:

- The first well, drilled under the direction of Edwin Drake in August 1859, was 69½' deep.
- Drake's well pumped 25 barrels of oil on its first day of operation. Before the year was out the well produced 2,000 barrels of oil.
- Drake's oil sold for about $20 a barrel. Three years later so many wells had been drilled in the area that the price of oil dropped to less than 25¢ per barrel.

Name: _____ Date: _____

PENNSYLVANIA: COMPUTING DISTANCES BETWEEN CITIES

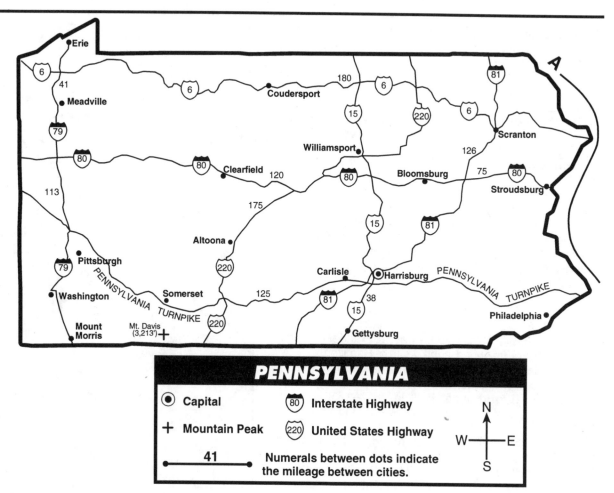

Finding Distances Between Cities

On some road maps a number is printed between two places. That number tells how many miles of road there are between the places. Here is an example:

```
A          B                  C
•   10   •        20         •
```

In the example there are 10 miles of road between **A** and **B** and 20 miles of road between **B** and **C**. By adding the 10 miles to the 20 miles we know there are 30 miles between **A** and **C**.

Use this process for determining mileage in the activities that follow, and at the same time become acquainted with Pennsylvania.

1. On the map what is the distance in road miles between:

a. Washington and Meadville on US-79? _____

b. Washington and Erie on US-79? _____

c. Bloomsburg and Stroudsburg on I-80? ____

d. Coudersport and Scranton on US-6? _____

e. Altoona and Williamsport on US-220? ____

f. Clearfield and Bloomsburg on I-80? _____

g. Clearfield and Stroudsburg on I-80? _____

h. Carlisle and Somerset on the Pennsylvania Turnpike? _____

2. Add to the map by labeling the *Delaware River* at **A**.

3. The highest elevation in Pennsylvania is Mt. Davis, located in the southwest part of the state. What is Mt. Davis' elevation? _____

NEW JERSEY: PLACES OF INTEREST

1. **Kittatinny Mountains**: Millions of years old . . . Worn down by the work of wind, water, glaciers . . . Foothills of the Appalachian Mountains . . .

2. **Delaware Water Gap**: One of the few natural passes through the mountains used by pioneers on their westward treks . . .

3. **Washington Crossing State Park**: Where Washington and his troops crossed the Delaware River on Christmas night (1776) on their march to Trenton and victory . . .

4. **Princeton**: Home of Princeton University, established in 1746 . . .

5. **Trenton**: Capital of New Jersey . . . Important manufacturing center . . .

6. **Delaware Bay**: A great waterway for ships sailing to Wilmington, Delaware, and Philadelphia, Pennsylvania . . .

7. **High Point**: NJ's highest elevation at 1803' . . . Located in High Point State Park, through which hikers follow the Appalachian Trail (Georgia to Maine, 1200 miles) . . .

8. **The Palisades**: Several miles of sheer palisades (cliffs) that edge the Hudson River on the New Jersey side . . .

9. **Hoboken**: Site of the duel between Alexander Hamilton and Aaron Burr that ended in the death of Hamilton . . .

10. **Morristown National Historic Park**: Where Washington's troops spent the winters of 1779 and 1780 . . .

11. **Barnegat Lighthouse**: Built in 1857–1858 . . . A welcome light and warning for ships entering New York Harbor . . .

12. **Atlantic City**: Famous beach resort . . . Home of the Miss America contest . . .

13. **Chatsworth Area**: Area in NJ, a leading cranberry state, where crop is produced . . . Recent annual crop of more than 450,000 barrels . . .

14. **Pine Barrens**: Hundreds of square miles of scrub oak and pine beneath which lies one of the East's greatest aquifers (underground water storage) . . .

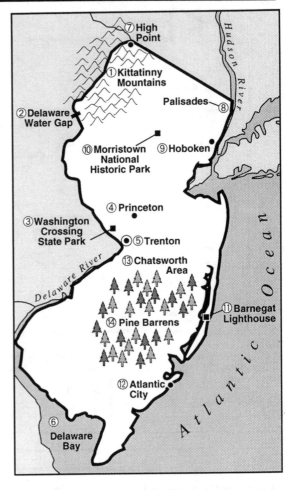

Suggestions For Using This Page

1. Make a transparency and/or photocopies of the upper part of the page.

2. Ask questions that can be answered from the information presented.

3. Some suggested questions:

a. For what crop is the area around Chatsworth noted? (*Cranberries*)

b. If you were a captain of a ship approaching New York harbor from the south, what light would you be looking for? (*Barnegat Lighthouse*)

c. Where do the beauty and talent winners from all the states go to compete for the Miss America title? (*Atlantic City*)

d. On Christmas Day every year a great crowd gathers at Washington Crossing to watch a reenactment of an important historical event. What do you think the event portrays? (*Washington and his troops crossing the Delaware*)

e. Suppose you were sailing north on the Hudson River and looked west just before you reached the northern boundary of New Jersey. What high cliffs would you see? (*The Palisades*)

f. Why did the settlers who were traveling west go through the Delaware Water Gap? (*It was a natural opening through the mountains.*)

g. What kinds of trees would you most likely see in the forests around Chatsworth? (*Scrub oak and pine*)

h. What three forces worked to wear down the Kittatinny Mountains? (*Wind, water, glaciers*)

i. What event took place in Hoboken that took the life of one of our country's great leaders? (*Alexander Hamilton was killed in a duel with Aaron Burr.*)

j. Suppose you could hike an average of fifteen miles a day on the Appalachian Trail. How many days would it take you to hike the entire trail? (*80 days*)

Name: _____ Date: _____

NEW JERSEY: GAINING INFORMATION FROM MAPS

New Jersey in the United States

1a. Describe New Jersey's position within the United States. _

_____

_____

b. List all the states that border on New Jersey. _____

_____ _____

New Jersey on the Map

1. What state is on New Jersey's northern border? _____ Its western border? _____

2. What river separates New Jersey from Pennsylvania? _____ Into what bay does the river flow? _____

3. What ocean is on New Jersey's east? _____

_____

4. What river forms part of New Jersey's northeastern border? _____

5. What is New Jersey's capital? _____

6. How many miles is it from High Point to Cape May? _____ miles. How many miles is it from Trenton to Asbury Park? _____ miles

7. What three rivers whose sources are in New Jersey flow into the Atlantic Ocean? _____

_____ _____

8. What river flows from Lake Hopatcong into the Delaware River? _____

9. What river other than the Delaware flows into Delaware Bay? _____

10. On what river is New Brunswick located?

_____ Newark? _____

11. What direction is Atlantic City from Trenton?

____ East ____ Northwest ____ Southeast ____ West

12. What direction is Newark from Trenton?

____ Northeast ____ Northwest ____ West ____ East

13. The New Jersey Turnpike is one of our country's busiest and most important highways. What two states does it connect? _____ and _____

14. If you were to take the ferry from Cape May to Cape Henolopen, what bay would you cross? _____

_____ What state would you land in? _____

DELAWARE: ORIGINATIONS, DELMARVA, AND INTERESTING FACTS

Delmarva Peninsula

Delaware is part of the Delmarva Peninsula. The name is derived from the states that share the peninsula—the DEL in Delaware, the MAR in Maryland, and the VA of Virginia. It seems strange that such a small peninsula is divided into three parts with two of the parts separated from the mainland by a large body of water, Chesapeake Bay. The rationale for the division is that in colonial times the borders of the colonies were arbitrarily set according to rivers, bays, and lines of latitude.

Another unusual feature of Delaware's conformation is the neat arc that serves as part of the border between Pennsylvania and Delaware. The arc is the only such type boundary in the United States.

The history of the arc is interesting. In William Penn's time the people of the three southernmost counties of Penn's grant felt they were being ignored by the more populous north. The three counties asked to be separated from Pennsylvania. A peaceful separation was arranged and the counties became the crown colony of Delaware. As part of the boundary settlement between the two colonies the arc of a circle with a twelve-mile radius was drawn from the courthouse in New Castle as the center point.

Interesting Facts about Delaware

❑ Log cabins, which became the most typical type of frontier dwelling, were introduced in the New World in the early 1800s by Swedes who settled in what is now Delaware

❑ Delaware was the first state to ratify the United States Constitution, hence, the nickname *The First State*. Delaware's motto, "Liberty and Independence" is a true reflection of the spirit of independence that existed from its very beginnings as a part of Pennsylvania, then to its status as an independent colony, and then to statehood.

❑ Chemicals, Delaware, and the name du Pont are closely related. A powder mill started by a French immigrant, Eluthere Irenee du Pont, in 1802 was the beginning of Delaware's chemical industry. Today, the original du Pont enterprise is greatly expanded and is known as the E. I. du Pont de Nemours and Company. Other chemical companies, such as Hercules, Inc., have also made Delaware their headquarters. The manufacture of chemicals and related products such as nylon, plastics, and drugs is Delaware's leading industry.

❑ Delaware's second largest industry is food production, especially the raising and processing of chickens. Broilers, which range in age from seven to twelve weeks, are a Delaware specialty. Approximately two-thirds of Delaware's farm income is derived from the poultry industry. Most of the remaining one-third of its farm income is from the sale of crops such as soybeans, barley, wheat, and corn.

❑ Delaware's ocean coastline extends about thirty miles between its southern boundary with Maryland and the entrance to Delaware Bay. The coast is actually a narrow dune-covered reef. Behind the reef are two bays—Rehoboth Bay and Indian River Bay. The bays are entered through an inlet that divides the reef. Vacationers can enjoy boating and swimming in the quiet bay waters or the more challenging ocean-side surf.

Name: _____ Date: _____

DELAWARE: TRANSPORTATION CROSSROAD

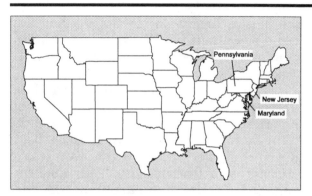

Delaware in the United States

1a. Describe Delaware's position within the United States. _____
_____
_____

b. List the states that border Delaware.
_____ _____
_____

    Delaware is a small state, but in many ways it is an important state, especially in relation to highway and water transportation routes.

Cape May–Lewes Ferry

1a. Connect Cape May and Lewes with a line. Label the ferry line with the abbreviation CM-L.

b. Approximately how many miles is the ferry route across Delaware Bay? _____

c. If you were driving south on the Garden State Parkway in New Jersey and crossed Delaware Bay on the Cape May–Lewes ferry, with what US highway could you connect? _____

Intracoastal Waterway

    The Intracoastal Waterway provides a safe passage for small boats sailing north-south along the Atlantic coast.

    Follow the waterway north in Delaware Bay. What is the name of the canal that connects Delaware Bay with the Elk River? _____

Note: The Elk River leads into Chesapeake Bay.

United States Highway 13 and Distances

1a. Notice the highway that runs north-south from Wilmington to Maryland. In the blank shields along the highway carefully print **13**, the number of the highway.

b. Use the scale of miles to determine Delaware's greatest north-south distance. Measure from point **A** to point **B**. _____

c. What is Delaware's greatest east-west distance? Measure from point **C** to point **D**. _____

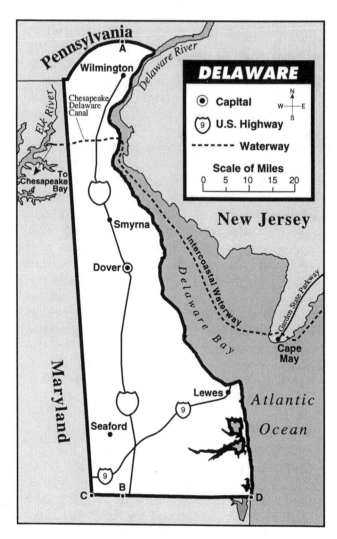

MARYLAND: HIGHLIGHTS IN ITS GEOGRAPHY AND HISTORY

Chesapeake Bay

Maryland is noted for its odd shape and its varied topography, which includes a low-land east and a mountainous west. However, its most notable feature is, perhaps, Chesapeake Bay. The bay divides the state into two distinct parts—the east shore and the west shore. At the northern head of the bay, the Susquehanna River empties all the water it has collected from its tributaries in its 450-mile journey from its source in northern New York. Other significant rivers that pour their waters into the Chesapeake Bay include the Patuxent and the Potomac.

From its northern head to its southern entrance, Chesapeake Bay is some 200 miles long. The bay is spectacularly irregular and provides more than 3,200 miles of shoreline; that is more than the distance across the United States from New York to San Francisco. Innumerable pleasure craft, hundreds of commercial fishing boats, and the largest ocean-crossing boats ply the waters of the bay.

The people of the eastern shore and those of the western shore of Chesapeake Bay had, in former times, little to do with each other. Too many miles of open water separated them. However, in 1952 the world's longest all-steel bridge over salt water—that is, Chesapeake Bay—was constructed. The bridge had the immediate effect of bringing the two sections together. Marylanders from the west shore crossed the bridge to enjoy Maryland's Atlantic coast beaches, and Easterners gained easy access to Baltimore and even Washington, D.C. So popular was the bridge and so clogged with two-way traffic that Maryland has since built a second bridge across the bay.

Maryland and American History

Books have been written about the part that Maryland and Marylanders have played in American history. Such events as the colony's first settlement in 1632, the 1649 act of the Maryland Assembly that proclaimed religious freedom throughout the colony, the battles fought there in the American Revolution, Annapolis serving as a capital for the Continental Congress, and the battles fought on the state's land and bay during the Civil War have given Maryland a respected and honored place in American history.

The special event that occurred on Chesapeake Bay and that has moved Americans ever since was the writing of the "Star-Spangled Banner" by Francis Scott Key during the War of 1812. Key was a prisoner on a British man-of-war that was engaged in the bombardment of Fort McHenry on the western shore of the bay. If the British could subdue the fort the planned invasion of Baltimore would be facilitated. As night fell, Key watched bombs from the ship falling on the fort. He wondered if the American flag he had seen waving over the fort would survive the battle. When he saw the flag still waving "by the dawn's early light" he was inspired to write the words that became our national anthem.

United States Naval Academy

In 1845, when James K. Polk was President of the United States, he realized there was a need for an academy to train young men to be officers in the Navy and Marine Corps. George Bancroft, Secretary of the Navy at that time, carried through on Polk's authorization and arranged for the establishment of the United States Naval Academy. Annapolis, Maryland, was chosen as the site for the Academy. The capital city's location on the west shore of Chesapeake Bay, its proximity to the waters of both the Bay and the Atlantic Ocean, and its central location on the nation's east coast were factors in determining the site.

In 1861, during the Civil War, the Academy was temporarily moved to Newport, Rhode Island; the Annapolis location was too close to the battles being fought. In 1865 the training of officers for the Navy was resumed at Annapolis.

Today both men and women are eligible to apply for admission to the school. Upon graduation successful candidates receive a bachelor of science degree. They then are commissioned as ensigns in the Navy or as second lieutenants in the Marine Corps.

MARYLAND: POINTS OF INTEREST

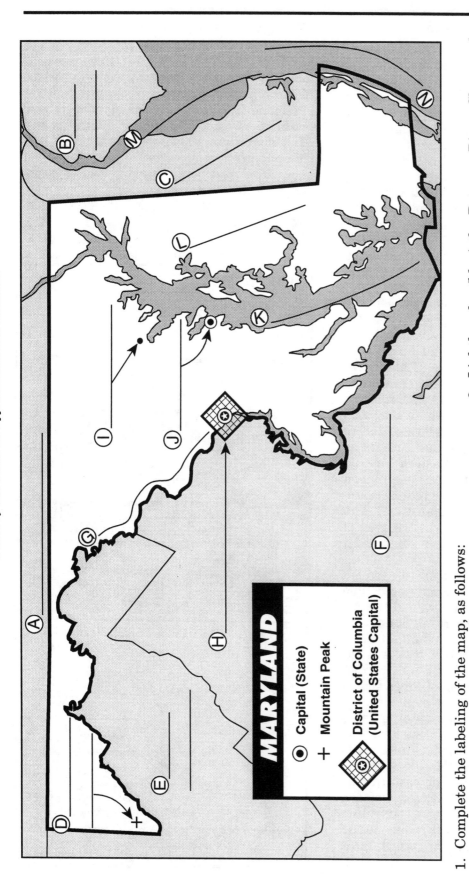

© 1996 by The Center for Applied Research in Education

1. Complete the labeling of the map, as follows:

Ⓐ Pennsylvania **Ⓔ** West Virginia **Ⓙ** Annapolis

Ⓑ New Jersey **Ⓕ** Virginia **Ⓚ** Chesapeake Bay

Ⓒ Delaware **Ⓖ** Potomac River **Ⓛ** "East Shore"

Ⓓ Backbone Mtn. **Ⓗ** Washington, D.C. **Ⓜ** Delaware Bay

(Highest point **Ⓘ** Baltimore **Ⓝ** Atlantic Ocean

in Maryland)

2. Lightly color (blue) the Potomac River, Chesapeake Bay, Delaware Bay, and the Atlantic Ocean

3. Draw light diagonal (/ / /) lines in all the land that is not a part of Maryland.

Legend:
⊙ Capital (State)
+ Mountain Peak
◈ District of Columbia (United States Capital)

MARYLAND

WEST VIRGINIA: ITS BEGINNINGS AND COAL PRODUCTION

West Virginia Becomes a State

Originally, West Virginia was a part of Virginia. However, there was never a close relationship between eastern Virginia and western Virginia. Important reasons for the lack of commonality between the two sections are based in geography—distance and mountains. Western Virginia has some of the most rugged terrain in the United States. In the days before 1900, there were few good east-west roads, and rivers connecting the sections were not easily navigable except by small boats and many portages. A glance at a physical map will show that West Virginia's mountains are northeast-southwest oriented. Few rivers cut through all the mountains to the Atlantic Ocean coast of Virginia.

The differences in terrain between the coastal plains east and the highlands west led to differences in economic, social, and political life. Westerners developed small farms with relatively few slave workers. Easterners developed large plantations that were worked by slaves. Plantation social life was different from small farm social life, where long and difficult distances had to be traveled before people could join together in such events as balls and elaborate parties. Eastern Virginia had a greater population than western Virginia; thus, the east had greater representation in the state legislature. The consequences were that the western part of the original state received less government support.

Easterners developed trade with foreign countries because they had easily accessible ports on several navigable rivers and the Atlantic Ocean coast. Westerners, all but denied trade with the east because of mountain barriers, developed trade relations to the west. Westerners had the Ohio River that carried their products to the Mississippi River and as far as New Orleans on the Gulf of Mexico.

When the Civil War began the differences between eastern Virginia and western Virginia came to a head. A choice had to be made as to whether Virginia would side with the Union or the Confederacy. For eastern Virginia it was the Confederacy; for western Virginia it was the Union. After a convention in 1861, western Virginia voted to become the independent state of Kanawha, which later became West Virginia.

Coal

Although most people today do not use coal to heat their homes, it is still widely used for other purposes. Chemical products such as plastics, insecticides, and wood preservatives are made from coal, and about 40% of coal produced is used to generate electric power. After more than 200 years of coal production this important mineral still underlies about one-half of West Virginia's land and is extensively mined.

For coal that is far below the earth's surface **drift mines** and **shaft mines** are dug. The drawings below show the basic steps in these two kinds of mining operations.

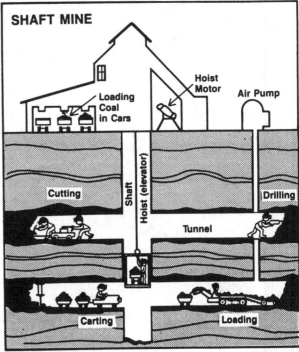

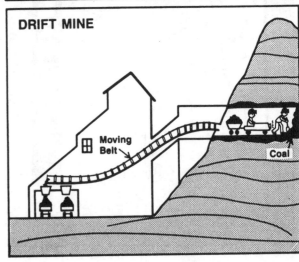

Name: _____ Date: _____

WEST VIRGINIA: MOUNTAIN PEAKS AND RIVERS

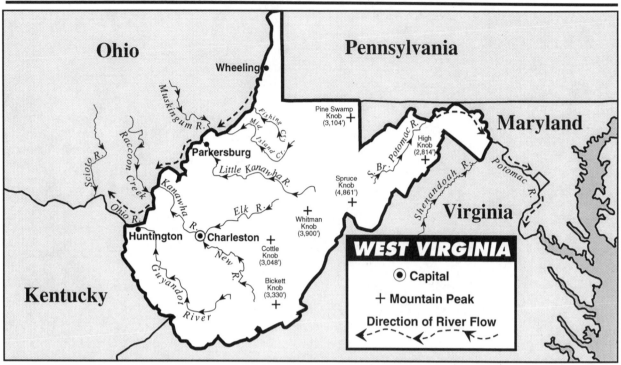

1. Six of West Virginia's high mountain peaks are shown on the map. Their altitudes are shown in parentheses ( ).

In the table below arrange the mountain peaks in order from the highest to the lowest.

Mountain Peak	Altitude in Feet

2. The Ohio River forms most of West Virginia's western border. West Virginia and Ohio's smaller rivers pour their waters into the Ohio River making it ever greater.

Starting from the north and following the Ohio River's flow toward the southwest, list the rivers feeding into the Ohio River.

a. _____ e. _____

b. _____ f. _____

c. _____ g. _____

d. _____ h. _____

3. Much of West Virginia's northern and eastern border is formed by the Potomac River. What two rivers are shown as feeding into the Potomac? _____

_____

4. What two rivers join at Charleston, the capital of West Virginia, to form the Kanawha River? _____

5. Rivers begin at high altitudes and flow to lower altitudes. Using this bit of information, where is West Virginia's highest land, in the eastern or western part of the state? _____

Southeastern States

SOUTHEASTERN STATES: A TABLE OF FACTS

The statistics on the following page present an opportunity for students to gain skill in completing a picture graph. By so doing, they will also develop a reasonable understanding of the populations of the Southern States.

Procedure

1. Help your students round the population of each state to the nearest 500,000. The rounded numbers can be written below the states' populations in the "Population" column of the table.

2. Refer to the uncompleted graph at the bottom of the following page. Call attention to the graph's title and key.

3. In the column labeled "States" on the graph, have them list the states from that with the greatest population to that with the smallest, with the most highly populated state at the top of the column.

4. Help your students determine the number of symbols for each state. Next, have them draw the symbols on the graph to represent each state's population. Be sure they realize that each half symbol represents 500,000 people.

Note: The population figures were rounded to the half-million to make it easier for your students to draw a fraction of a symbol. Students should realize that graphs sometimes do not show exact figures and proportions. Nevertheless, graphs are useful for quick, visual comparisons that are reasonably accurate.

Populations of the Southern States Compared		
States		
Florida	☺ ☺ ☺ ☺ ☺ ☺ ☺ ☺ ☺ ☺ ☺ ☺ ☺ ⌣	13½
Mississippi	☺ ☺ ☺ ☺ ☺ ☺ ☺ ☺ ☺ ⌣	9½
North Carolina	☺ ☺ ☺ ☺ ☺ ☺ ☺	7
Georgia	☺ ☺ ☺ ☺ ☺ ☺ ☺	7
Virginia	☺ ☺ ☺ ☺ ☺ ☺ ⌣	6½
Tennessee	☺ ☺ ☺ ☺ ☺	5
Louisiana	☺ ☺ ☺ ☺ ⌣	4½
Alabama	☺ ☺ ☺ ☺	4
Kentucky	☺ ☺ ☺ ☺	4
South Carolina	☺ ☺ ☺ ⌣	3½
Arkansas	☺ ☺ ⌣	2½
Key: ☺ = 1,000,000 people ⌣ = 500,000 people		

Roundings

Florida: 13,500,000 = 13½ symbols

Mississippi: 9,500,000 = 9½ symbols

North Carolina: 7,000,000 = 7 symbols

Georgia: 7,000,000 = 7 symbols

Virginia: 6,500,000 = 6½ symbols

Tennessee: 5,000,000 = 5 symbols

Louisiana: 4,500,000 = 4½ symbols

Alabama: 4,000,000 = 4 symbols

Kentucky: 4,000,000 = 4 symbols

South Carolina: 3,500,000 = 3½ symbols

Arkansas: 2,500,000 = 2½ symbols

© 1996 by The Center for Applied Research in Education

SOUTHEASTERN STATES: A TABLE OF FACTS

FACTS ABOUT THE SOUTHERN STATES				
States and Capitals (North to South)	Population	Area in Square Miles* (Rank Shown in Parentheses)	Highest Point (Elevation Shown in Parentheses)	Nickname
Virginia (Richmond)	6,377,000	68,139 (20)	Mt. Rogers (5,729')	Old Dominion
Kentucky (Frankfort)	3,755,000	40,410 (37)	Black Mtn. (4,139')	Bluegrass State
Tennessee (Nashville)	5,024,000	42,144 (34)	Clingmans Dome (6,643')	Volunteer State
North Carolina (Raleigh)	6,843,000	52,669 (28)	Mt. Mitchel (6,684')	Tar Heel State or Free State
Arkansas (Little Rock)	2,399,000	53,187 (27)	Magazine Mtn. (2,753')	Land of Opportunity
Mississippi (Jackson)	9,437,000	47,689 (32)	Woodall Mtn. (806')	Magnolia State
Alabama (Montgomery)	4,136,000	51,705 (29)	Cheaka Mtn. (2,405')	Heart of Dixie or Camellia State
Georgia (Atlanta)	6,751,000	58,910 (21)	Brasstown Bald (4,784')	Empire State of the South or Peach State
South Carolina (Columbia)	3,603,000	31,113 (40)	Sassafras Mtn. (3,560')	Palmetto State
Louisiana (Baton Rouge)	4,287,000	47,752 (31)	Driskill Mtn. (535')	Pelican State
Florida (Tallahassee)	13,488,000	58,664 (22)	Walton County (345')	Sunshine State

* Total of land and water

Populations of the Southern States Compared	
States	
	Key: ☺ = 1,000,000 people ☺ = 500,000 people

Name: _____ Date: _____

SOUTHEASTERN STATES: STATES, CAPITALS, CITIES

1. On the map print the name of each state, as follows:

Ⓐ Kentucky: _____

Ⓑ Virginia: _____

Ⓒ Arkansas: _____

Ⓓ Tennessee: _____

Ⓔ North Carolina: _____

Ⓕ Mississippi: _____

Ⓖ Alabama: _____

Ⓗ Georgia: _____

Ⓘ South Carolina: _____

Ⓙ Louisiana: _____

Ⓚ Florida: _____

2. On the blank lines next to the names of the states above, write the names of their capitals.

3. Label the following on the map:
Ⓛ Gulf of Mexico
Ⓜ Atlantic Ocean
Ⓝ Mississippi River

4. In which state is each of the following cities:

New Orleans: _____

Mobile: _____

Miami: _____

Savannah: _____

Tampa: _____

Charleston: _____

Birmingham: _____

Charlotte: _____

Louisville: _____

Memphis: _____

Norfolk: _____

SOUTHEASTERN STATES

◉ Capital

Name: _____ Date: _____

THE SOUTHEASTERN STATES AND THE APPALACHIAN MOUNTAINS

SOUTHEASTERN STATES
Appalachian Mountains
enclosed within the
dash-dot line

The illustration and the map above will help you understand how difficult it was in early times to cross the Appalachian Mountains.

1. According to the map, what four Southeastern States were not partly covered by the Appalachian Mountains?

_____ _____

_____ _____

2. The illustration shows a group of early pioneers crossing the mountains to get to the inexpensive, fertile land west of the mountains.

From what you see in the picture complete the sentences that follow. The words at the end of the story will give you some clues as to what should be written in the blank spaces.

The pioneers' belongings were carried

on the backs of _____ or in _____

pulled by _____. The tools the horses

carried on their backs included a _____,

a _____, a _____, and an _____.

The men carried _____ for _____

or to shoot _____ for food.

The pioneers had to cross _____,

_____, and _____. The mountains

appear to be covered with _____. In

the background along the river is a steep

_____.

game	rivers	axe	oxen	valleys
shovel	carts	horses	protection	trees
cliff	hoe	rake	mountain	guns

Answer the following questions on the reverse side of this page.

3. Take a guess: On the horse, what is the object to the left of the axe? For what would it be used?

4. Imagine that the pioneers could travel an average of six miles each day and that it was a 240 mile trip through the mountains. How many days would they be on the trail?

5. What reasons can you think of that might explain why the pioneers are not floating to their destination on a flatboat in the river?

COTTON PRODUCTION IN THE SOUTHEASTERN AND OTHER STATES

The cotton production map on the facing student application page tells how many bales of cotton were produced in various states in a recent year. And, that is a helpful way to present information. But, there are other useful ways to treat information of a statistical nature. For example, the states could be listed alphabetically in a table. This arrangement makes it easy to find a particular state's production.

Still another way to arrange the data on the map would be to list the states according to the amount of cotton they produced with the highest producer listed first, the next highest, second, and so on.

There is no reason why both alphabetical order and rank order can't be listed in the same table. It would be helpful to the development of your students' work-study skills if they had such an experience. Of course, the manipulation of the facts related to cotton will also bring a better understanding of cotton as an extremely important southern states' crop.

The following suggests a way that students might go about reorganizing this information in order to increase their understanding of it.

1. Explain that the numbers in the states tell the amount of cotton produced in the various states. Each bale of cotton weighs 500 pounds. The number of bales produced is in itself impressive. To make it more impressive, translate Texas' bales into pounds—2,574,000,000 pounds.

2. Suggest that the information can be taken from the map and reorganized into a table.

3. Have your students list the states alphabetically under the column headed STATES.

4. Have your students transfer the numbers for each state to the column headed AMOUNT.

5. In the column headed RANK, have your students rank the states in order of production. Of course, Texas is number 1.

Note: The uncompleted student application page can be made into a transparency to be projected. As you complete the table on the transparency, have your students complete their tables at their seats.

You may want to show another way to arrange the cotton production information, that is, via a bar graph. The completed bar graph below can be made into a transparency and projected. It would be interesting to poll your students to find out which of the three means of arranging information they like best. You may help them to understand that there is no one "best" way; each approach has its merits.

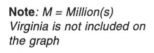

Cotton Production

in the

Southeastern

and

Other States

Note: *M = Million(s)*
Virginia is not included on the graph

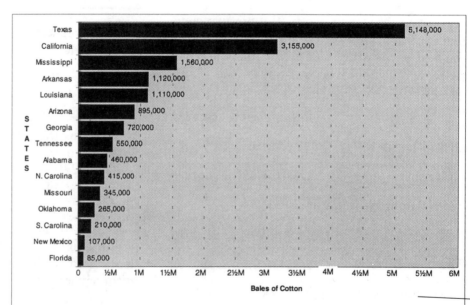

State	Bales of Cotton
Texas	5,148,000
California	3,155,000
Mississippi	1,560,000
Arkansas	1,120,000
Louisiana	1,110,000
Arizona	895,000
Georgia	720,000
Tennessee	550,000
Alabama	460,000
N. Carolina	415,000
Missouri	345,000
Oklahoma	265,000
S. Carolina	210,000
New Mexico	107,000
Florida	85,000

Name: _____ Date: _____

COTTON PRODUCTION IN THE SOUTHEASTERN AND OTHER STATES

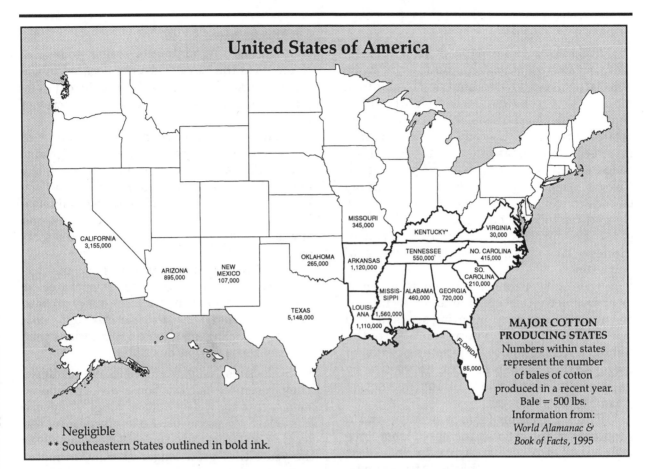

© 1996 by The Center for Applied Research in Education

MAJOR COTTON PRODUCING STATES

STATE	AMOUNT*	RANK	STATE	AMOUNT	RANK

* Number of bales of cotton produced in a recent year. One bale = 500 lbs.

VIRGINIA: INTERESTING FACTS ABOUT TOBACCO AND CAVES

Tobacco in Virginia

Tobacco was introduced as a colonial crop in Virginia by John Rolfe—the Rolfe who later married Pocahontas. He obtained high quality tobacco seeds from the West Indies, cultivated them at the Jamestown settlement, and, thereby, saved Virginia from economic disaster. The tobacco those seeds produced became very popular in Europe, especially Great Britain. To supply the demand, thousands of acres were cleared for tobacco culture. Demand was so great and profits so large that, initially, tobacco was planted in the streets of Jamestown.

The cultivation of tobacco is a labor-intensive activity. A great amount of "hands-on" work is necessary: planting seeds in seed beds, transplanting young plants to the fields, cultivating soil, pinching ends of leaves so that they spread out, harvesting by hand-cutting, and the culminating act of curing tobacco leaves.

The increase in tobacco acreage and a simultaneous need for an increased labor force influenced growers to turn to the least expensive labor supply, that is, Africans who were forced into involuntary servitude or slavery. Thus, each year, beginning in 1619, the year "indentured servants" were introduced to the colony, more and more Africans were captured, enslaved, and transported to Virginia and other colonies. It was the beginning of a problem—slavery—that was to plague the country for almost 250 years until the problem was resolved by the Civil War.

Today, Virginia is still one of the leading tobacco growing states; in fact, tobacco is the state's leading agricultural product. The following statistics, which may be presented in a bar or picture graph, show where Virginia stands among the six leading tobacco states:

State	Pounds of Tobacco Produced (in a recent year)
North Carolina	596,285,000
Kentucky	471,825,000
Tennessee	129,140,000
South Carolina	110,760,000
Virginia	101,405,000
Georgia	96,320,000

Luray Caverns of Virginia

One of Virginia's interesting geological elements is the Luray Caverns, located in the Appalachian Mountains in northwest Virginia. The caverns underlie some 65 acres of land.

The caverns were formed millions of years ago by underground rivers which gradually eroded away the soft limestone of the region. When the rivers stopped flowing they left huge open areas and lengthy hallways. There are several "rooms" in the caverns, one of which is 300 feet high (the length of a football field).

Acid water from above seeps into the caverns. After the seeping water evaporates, it leaves mineral deposits that gradually grow to become *stalactites*, *stalagmites*, and *columns*. Following are simple explanations that tell how these formations differ.

1. Stalactites hang from the cave's ceilings. They resemble icicles. Some are enormous; some are only a few inches long. They are formed when some of the materials in the seeping water stick to the cave's ceiling. Over the years they grow longer as mineral materials accumulate.

2. Stalagmites grow upward from the floor of a cave. Dripping water strikes the floor, evaporates, and leaves mineral deposits that harden. Over a long period of time the mineral deposits accumulate.

3. Columns are formed when a stalagmite and a stalactite grow to the extent that they join to form a column.

In the Luray Caverns electric lightning has been installed to enhance and dramatize the colorful formations. Even more, an organ that utilizes the limestone formations as "pipes" plays specially selected music that evokes a variety of emotions in visitors.

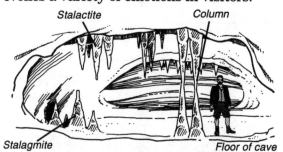

Diagram of a Limestone Cave

Name: _____ Date: _____

VIRGINIA: A GEOGRAPHY HISTORY TOUR

Virginia in the United States

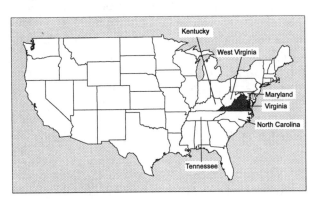

1a. Describe Virginia's position within the United States. _____

_____

_____

b. List all of the states that border on Virginia. _____

_____

_____

Population Growth of Virginia

On the line graph below show the growth of the population of Virginia.

Year	Population	Year	Population
1800	808,000	1920	2,300,000
1840	1,000,000	1960	4,000,000
1880	1,500,000	1992	6,400,000
		2000	?

POPULATION GROWTH OF VIRGINIA

Millions of People

7
6
5
4
3
2
1
0

1800 1840 1880 1920 1960 2000
1992

Year

Famous Places in Virginia

On the numbered lines surrounding the map write the following titles of six of Virginia's geographical and historical attractions.

❶ Natural Bridge
❷ Chimney Rocks
❸ Yorktown
❹ Williamsburg
❺ Appomattox Court House
❻ Cumberland Gap

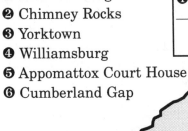

❶ _____

An arch through a mountain carved out by running water

❷ _____

Rock towers resembling chimneys, each more than 100′ high

❸ _____

Where the British surrendered to Washington, thus ending the American Revolution

❻ _____

A natural opening in the mountains

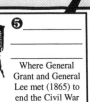

❺ _____

Where General Grant and General Lee met (1865) to end the Civil War

❹ _____

Colonial capital of Virginia, beautifully restored

65

KENTUCKY: GEOGRAPHY AND HISTORY FACTS

The Ohio River

On its journey from Pittsburgh, Pennsylvania, to its ultimate destination, Cairo, Illinois, the Ohio River forms more than two-thirds of Kentucky's boundaries with other states. The river first meets Kentucky at the junction of West Virginia, Ohio, and Kentucky. Then, in its westward/southwestward journey, it twists and curves hundreds of times as it finds ways to circumvent the numerous mountains in its path. Along Kentucky's border the river flows past important cities—Cincinnati, Ohio; Louisville, Kentucky; Owensboro, Kentucky; Evansville, Indiana; Paducah, Kentucky—until, finally, it empties its water into the Mississippi River.

The flow of the Ohio along Kentucky's border has not always been smooth. Early westward-migrating pioneers found their rafts and flatboats alternating between lazy drifting and frightening speed. Upon reaching the site of present day Louisville, both pioneers and commercial riverboat persons had to unload their precious cargo and carry it overland around the dreaded Falls of the Ohio. Any large and unwieldy craft attempting to shoot the falls was almost certain to be wrecked.

In 1830 a canal was dug around the notorious Falls of the Ohio. Boats going upstream or downstream could safely proceed. Louisville, which had its start as the loading/unloading place to avoid the falls, continued to grow after the canal was built and is Kentucky's largest city today.

Some facts about the Ohio River before and after its travels along Kentucky's boundaries are interesting. From its beginning at the confluence of the Allegheny River and the Monongahela River at Pittsburgh, it flows for 981 miles to the Mississippi River. It passes through or along the borders of seven states: Pennsylvania, Ohio, West Virginia, Indiana, Kentucky, Illinois, and Missouri. Since the building of the canal at Louisville, many other dangerous shallows, rock ledges, and rapids have been eliminated. Today, the Ohio River is a water highway for every conceivable kind of freight. Powerful tugboats push barges—sometimes as many as twenty barges in a string—loaded with coal, petroleum, steel, grain, chemicals, soybeans between Pittsburgh and Cairo. From Cairo, cargo continues to be carried on the Mississippi River to New Orleans and from there, perhaps, to ports on the Atlantic and Pacific coasts and foreign lands.

Kentucky Geography and History Facts

❑ Present-day Kentucky was a part of Virginia until 1792, when it became an independent state. It is one of only four states—Massachusetts, Pennsylvania, and Virginia are the others—that have **Commonwealth** as part of the states' official name.

❑ Kentucky's nickname is the **Blue Grass State**. The term **blue grass** refers to a type of grass, the blooms of which have a bluish tint in the spring. Of course, the grass is green when it has matured. The Bluegrass region of Kentucky, in the north-central part of the state, is noted for the racing and riding horses bred in the region.

❑ Fort Knox, on the Fort Knox Military Reservation, is where most of the United States gold bullion, some $6 billion dollars in value, is stored.

❑ Both Abraham Lincoln, President of the United States, and Jefferson Davis, President of the Confederacy, were born in Kentucky. By a twist of fate, both of these men were presidents during the Civil War.

❑ Other famous Americans born in Kentucky include Daniel Boone, frontiersman; Zachary Taylor, general and president; Carry Nation, crusader against alcohol; James Audubon, naturalist; and Muhammad Ali, world heavyweight boxing champion.

❑ Kentucky, a "border state" between the Union and the Confederacy, was officially a Union state during the Civil War. Even so, of the some 110,000 Kentuckians who were soldiers during the conflict, approximately one-third fought for the Confederacy.

Name: _____ Date: _____

KENTUCKY: MAP/CROSSWORD

ACROSS

1. State on Kentucky's southwest border (abbr.)
3. Military reservation
7. City at junction of Rt. 75 and Rt. 64
8. Town east of Lexington (abbr.)
9. Leave Kentucky any place on its southern border and you enter the state of _____. (abbr.)
10. City in southwestern Kentucky
11. City in south central Kentucky (abbr.)
13. Capital of Kentucky
16. City on the Ohio River
17. Town in Kentucky's most northern section (abbr.)
19. The name of a river and the name of a state on Kentucky's northern border
20. City on Kentucky's eastern border

DOWN

2. Cross the Ohio River from this city and you're in Indiana.
4. River that flows into the Ohio River
5. Kentucky is wider from east to west than from north to _____.
6. Cross the Mississippi River from Louisville and you're in the state of _____. (abbr.)
12. City at the meeting of the Ohio River and the Mississippi River
14. Town on Rt. 64
15. State on Kentucky's eastern border (abbr.)
18. State on Kentucky's southeastern border (abbr.)

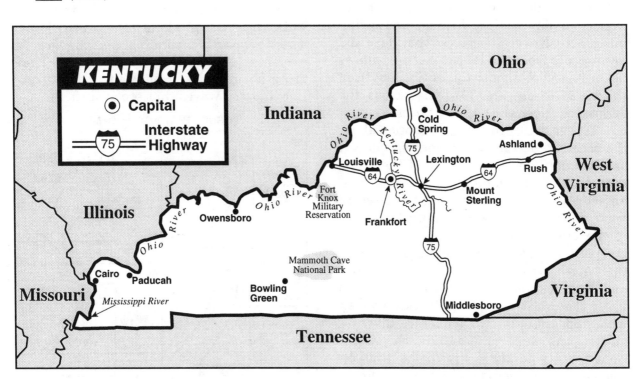

TENNESSEE: THE TENNESSEE RIVER AND DAMS

The Tennessee River

The Tennessee River has its sources high in Tennessee's eastern mountains. Starting at about 3,000' above sea level, the river flows swiftly over rocks, shallows, and steep drops. Adventurous boaters and rafters enjoy the thrills of riding the "white water" of the Tennessee River and its rushing tributaries. But, as the river wends its way southwestward, it slows down. One important reason for this is that numerous dams that act as "brakes" have been built across it. The dams back up the water and, in so doing, create a number of narrow lakes.

There are several other helpful results of the dams that cross the Tennessee River. First, in times of heavy rains and melting snows, which at one time would have caused devastating floods, excess water can be stored behind the dams and released gradually after the rains have slackened. Second, the water stored behind the dams can be directed through openings (flumes) in the dams. The falling water turns huge wheels that generate electric power for homes and industries. Third, the backed-up water behind the dams creates lakes that are wonderful for boating, fishing, and swimming. Fourth, a series of locks that raise and lower boats from one lake to another allows boats to travel almost the entire length of the river. There are 39 dams across the Tennessee River and its tributaries.

It is easy to form a misconception about the path of the Tennessee River, especially if one has only an isolated map of the state, that is, a map that does not show Tennessee's connecting states. The river begins north of Knoxville, flows southwestward out of the state into Alabama, across all of northern Alabama into Mississippi, and then north across Tennessee into Kentucky and, finally, dumps its water into the Ohio River. It seem strange, then, to see on a map what appears to be two Tennessee Rivers— one in the east and one in the west. Contributing to the confusion is that on some maps the river is not shown as a single line, but as two somewhat parallel lines; this gives the impression of a long series of narrow lakes rather than a river.

More About Dams

The diagrams at the bottom of the page illustrate some of the ways that natural forces can adversely affect dams.

Figure 1 shows that water pressure can weaken a dam. The water pressure against a strip one foot wide and 200 feet high is 624 tons.

Figure 2 illustrates how movement of the earth, as in an earthquake, can crack dams.

Figure 3 illustrates that the weight of dams can cause them to sink.

Figure 4 shows four elements that can work together or alone to weaken dams: water seepage; expanding ice; changes in weather, especially temperatures that bring about quick expansion and contraction; lapping waves that erode surfaces.

FORCES THAT ACT ON DAMS

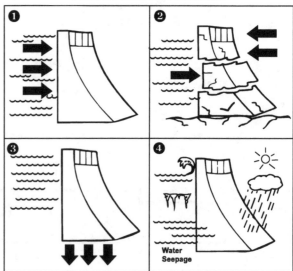

© 1996 by The Center for Applied Research in Education

Name: _____ Date: _____

TENNESSEE: AN AERIAL SURVEY

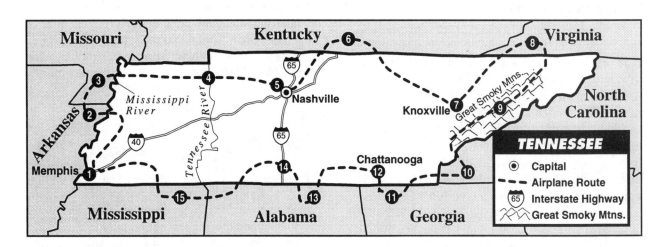

1. Imagine that you are making an aerial survey of Tennessee and the states that surround it. You have a map in your lap, and as you look down on earth you identify some of the most important physical and cultural features. You start and end your flight at number ❶ on the map.

❶ _____ : Tennessee's largest city

❷ _____ : Neighboring state

❸ _____ : Neighboring state

❹ _____ : Flows north and joins the Ohio River

❺ _____ : Tennessee's state capital

❻ _____ : Neighboring state

❼ _____ : Home of the University of Tennessee's largest campus

❽ _____ : Neighboring state

❾ _____ : Part of Great Smoky Mountains National Park

❿ _____ : Neighboring state

⓫ _____ : Neighboring state

⓬ _____ : Tennessee's fourth largest city

⓭ _____ : Neighboring state

⓮ _____ : North-south route connecting Alabama through Nashville to Kentucky

⓯ _____ : Neighboring state

2. Use the map at the top of the page to help you label the states that surround Tennessee as shown in the map that follows.

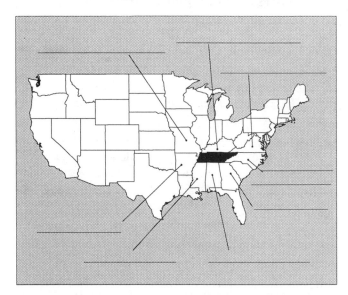

3. On the reverse side tell how you would describe Tennessee's location within the United States.

NORTH CAROLINA: TEXTILES AND THE OUTER BANKS

Textiles and North Carolina

North Carolina's most important industry in terms of money value is tobacco. But, close behind is the state's second most important industry—the manufacturing of textiles of all kinds. From its small beginnings 200 years ago, the number of textile manufacturing plants has grown to more than 1,100. These factories are busy producing hosiery, carpets, sheets, towels, denim and other products made from cotton, and synthetic fabrics such as nylon and rayon.

There are several reasons why North Carolina's textile industry, which is greater than that of any other state, took hold. First, North Carolina has an abundance of water power that was necessary in early times to turn the wheels of the cotton mills. Second, raw cotton was easily available from the fields of North Carolina and neighboring states. Third, there was a plenitude of workers, many of whom had had experiences working in textile mills in Scotland and England.

North Carolina's coastal location and excellent ports allowed it to ship its products north and south along the Atlantic coast and, also, to foreign countries. Later, the growth of railroads and roads made it even easier to reach markets not only along the coast, but also inland. As the country grew, the market for cotton, of course, grew with it.

The four "necessaries" for the textile industry to grow and that are present in North Carolina—power, workers, materials, and markets—are symbolized below.

power

materials

workers

market

North Carolina's Outer Banks

The term "Outer Banks" refers to a chain of narrow islands—really sandbanks—along North Carolina's coast. They are well known for several reasons, including the following:

❑ The banks act as protective barriers for the mainland of North Carolina. The force of the huge waves, high tides, and strong winds that result from Atlantic storms is considerably lessened before they meet the mainland.

❑ It was on one of the Outer Bank islands that Orville and Wilbur Wright launched the first successful propeller-driven airplane. This event occurred in early December 1903 at Kitty Hawk, located on one of the northernmost islands, Bodie Island. It was the constancy of the winds and the lack of obstacles such as trees on the island that influenced the brothers to use Kitty Hawk for their experiment. A monument at Kitty Hawk now commemorates the event.

❑ Roanoke Island, located between an extreme eastward outer island and the North Carolina mainland, was the site of the first attempt by the English to establish a colony in the New World (1585). The attempt failed and the would-be group of settlers sailed back to England. Again, in 1587, another group braved the dangers of the New World and sailed to Roanoke. This attempt was even more disastrous. In 1591, four years later, ships from England arrived to supply the colony, but not a living person was found. No one really knows what happened to the group of 91 men, 17 women, and nine children of the "Lost Colony."

NORTH CAROLINA: AIRLINE DISTANCES

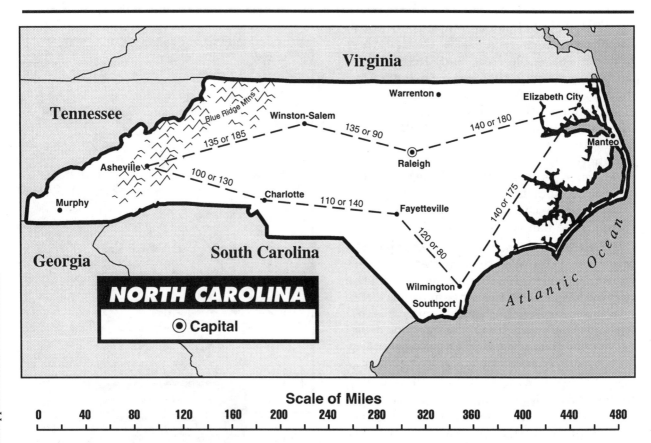

Scale of Miles

| 0 | 40 | 80 | 120 | 160 | 200 | 240 | 280 | 320 | 360 | 400 | 440 | 480 |

To find the airline distance from one point (place) to another point (place), lay the corner of a strip of paper on the first point and make a mark where the edge of the paper touches the second point. Then lay the paper along the scale of miles. Read the mileage at the place where the second point touches.

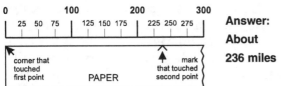

Answer: About 236 miles

1. About how many miles long is the southern boundary that North Carolina shares with South Carolina and Georgia? Place a check before the best answer.

_____ 300 _____ 350 _____ 400 _____ 450

2. About how many miles long is the northern boundary that North Carolina shares with Virginia?

_____ 260 _____ 300 _____ 335 _____ 395

3. Manteo, in extreme eastern North Carolina, is about how many miles from Murphy, in extreme western North Carolina?

_____ 450 _____ 500 _____ 550

4. The distance between Southport, in southern North Carolina, and Warrenton, in northern North Carolina, is about how many miles? _____ miles

5a. Raleigh, Winston-Salem, Asheville, Charlotte, Fayettsville, Wilmington, and Elizabeth City are eight of North Carolina's important cities. On the lines between the cities draw a circle around the number that best tells the distance between the two places.

b. What is the total distance from Raleigh through all the places named in 5a. above and then back to Raleigh?

_____ miles

71

SOUTH CAROLINA: THE PIEDMONT BELT AND THE FALL LINE

The Appalachian Mountains in South Carolina's northeast have been both a problem and a blessing, and this could be said of every state that has a portion of the mountain chain within its boundaries. The chief problem the mountains presented in the past was how to get over them to the lands to the west. Passes such as the Cumberland Gap and westward flowing rivers such as the Ohio River were of great help. But, sometimes it was necessary for emigrants to the west to chop their way through the heavily forested hills.

One of the benefits of the Appalachian Mountains chain is that numerous rivers have their sources in them, especially on the eastern slopes. As the streams and rivers join and approach the Atlantic coastal regions they broaden and become navigable.

The earliest settlements were almost always located on one of the rivers that began in the Appalachians. Charleston, South Carolina's second largest city, is an example. The city is located at the mouths of two small rivers that are connected to other rivers that originate in the hills of western North Carolina. Thus, the rivers give the city access to the interior and to other ports in both the United States and the world.

Columbia, South Carolina's capital, located in the center of the state, also got its start because of the state's rivers, but not for the same reason as Charleston. The first settlement of Columbia was at a place where the Broad River meets the "fall line." The fall line is an imaginary line that connects the waterfalls of the many rivers that flow eastward from the more-than-1,200-mile-long Appalachian Mountains chain. The fall line is also the place beyond which boats can no longer go upstream unless a canal has been built around the falls.

On the map also notice the term "Piedmont Belt." Piedmont is a foreign word that means "The land at the foot of the mountains." As you can see, the piedmont is the land that separates the Appalachian Mountains from the coastal plains. The fall line lies on the eastern edge of the piedmont. Think of the Piedmont Belt as land varying

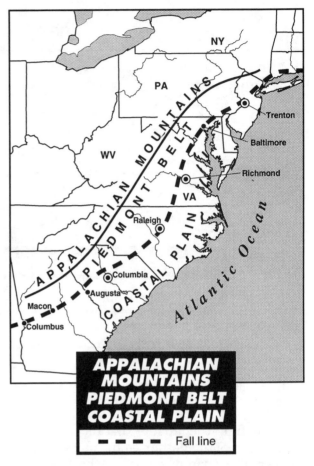

APPALACHIAN MOUNTAINS
PIEDMONT BELT
COASTAL PLAIN

– – – – – Fall line

© 1996 by The Center for Applied Research in Education

in width from a few miles to perhaps 100 miles. If you were to travel throughout the Piedmont Belt you would see hills, valleys, plains, rivers, small farms, towns and, on the eastern edge, large fall-line cities.

Dozens of east coast cities are located on the fall line because they are the last interior ports on rivers and because their waterfalls provide power. At first, the falling water was used to turn the wheels that ground grain into flour, sawed logs into lumber, and powered the complex machinery that turned cotton yarn into cloth. Today the power of the falling water is still used, but in another way; the energy from the falling water turns the turbines that generate hydroelectric power. Columbia, South Carolina's largest city, for example, owes much of its growth and prosperity to the hydroelectric plants in its vicinity. The map on this page shows several such fall-line cities.

Name: _____ Date: _____

SOUTH CAROLINA: LOCATING PLACES BY QUADRANT

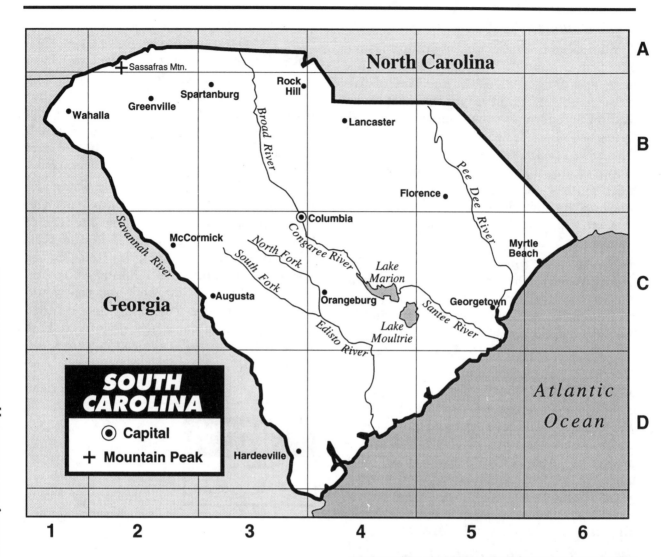

The map of South Carolina above is divided into partitions called **quadrants**. Quadrants make it easy to locate places. Instead of trying to find a place among hundreds that may be named on a map, all one has to do is find the quadrant in which the place is located. Finding a place in a small quadrant is a lot quicker than searching an entire map.

In the empty column in the opposite chart, write the letter and number of the quadrant in which each place is located.

Place	Quadrant
Columbia	
McCormick	
Rock Hill	
Lancaster	
Myrtle Beach	
Wahalla	
Georgetown	
Sassafras Mtn.	
Lake Marion	
Florence	
Augusta	
Spartanburg	
Greenville	
Orangeburg	
Hardeeville	

GEORGIA: STONE MOUNTAIN AND THE APPALACHIAN TRAIL

Stone Mountain

Imagine a solid chunk of granite rising out of the ground. It is 700 feet high, 2 miles long, and 1 mile wide. On one face of the stone visualize a giant carved mural of three of the Confederacy's most famous historical figures—Robert E. Lee, Jefferson Davis, and "Stonewall" Jackson—all of whom are mounted on clearly detailed horses. The figures are so large that thirty people once stood on the shoulder of Lee.

Now, picture yourself being carried in a skylift to the top of the stone. After you arrive at the top you look down on a beautiful park. People are sitting in lawn chairs, children are playing games, and swimmers are splashing in the lake at the foot of the great stone.

After you return to the base of Stone Mountain, you decide to play a round of golf on the park's golf course. Some of your group have other thoughts; they decide that they will take a walk to a restored plantation, while others visit one of the park's museums. After these activities you all meet once more at the foot of the stone. You spread some blankets on the lawn, open picnic baskets, and have an enjoyable lunch. All in all, everybody had a wonderful time.

The Appalachian Trail

Do you enjoy walking and camping out, and do you like to be challenged? If so, you might want to take a hike on the Appalachian Trail. But, be prepared to be away from home for a long time if you walk the trail's entire length of some 2,000 miles when all the twists, turns, and up-and-downs are considered. If you are a strong and determined hiker who can average fifteen miles a day, it will take you about 133 days! That's about 4½ months.

You would have to think carefully about when and where you are going to start the hike. The best time of the year to start might be late spring, and the best place to start might be at the trail's northern end at Mt.

Katahdin, Maine. Why? The answer is that if you started in early June from Mt. Katahdin, and if everything went well, you would be at Springer Mountain, Georgia, by the beginning of October, before the weather starts getting cold. If, on the other hand, you started at Springer Mountain in August, you'd probably be hiking in snow by the time you got to Maine at the end of November.

The map below shows the route of the Appalachian Trail. You can see that you would go through or along the borders of fourteen states. You would find the trail well-maintained by the United States Forest Service and private hiking clubs. The Trail would be well-marked, and you would find special places with camping facilities. And, if it is ever necessary, usually a short walk off the trail will take you to a road and small towns.

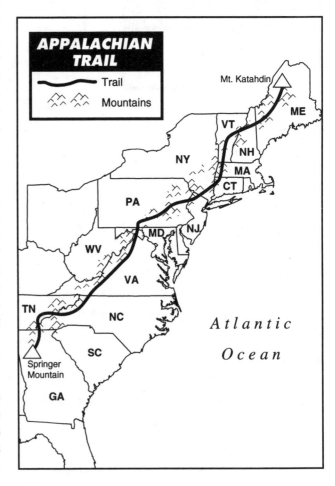

Name: _____ Date: _____

GEORGIA: MATCHING PLACES AND DESCRIPTIONS

Each of the items in the *Places* column can be matched with one of the items in the *Descriptions* column. Write the number of the *Places* items on the line in front of the matching item in *Descriptions*. There are two extra items in the *Places* column.

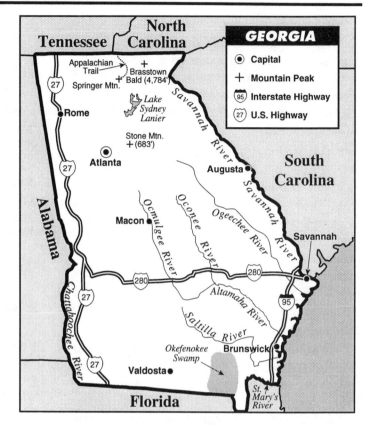

Places

1. Atlanta
2. Savannah River
3. Tennessee
4. Rome
5. Okefenokee
6. Saltilla River
7. Chattahoochee River
8. Brunswick
9. Macon
10. City of Savannah
11. Augusta
12. St. Mary's River
13. Lake Sydney Lanier
14. Brasstown Bald
15. Springer Mountain
16. Stone Mountain
17. Altamaha River
18. Valdosta
19. Ogeechee River

Descriptions

_____ Southern end of the Appalachian Trail

_____ Georgia's highest point, 4,784' high

_____ Forms border with Alabama

_____ City on Georgia's South Carolina border

_____ Coastal city

_____ Seaport, and US-280 ends/begins there

_____ City on US-27

_____ Formed by the Ocmulgee River and the Oconee River

_____ Crossed by I-95 as the highway enters Florida

_____ Capital

_____ River that enters Atlantic Ocean south of Brunswick

_____ World's largest single piece of granite, 683' high

_____ Forms border with South Carolina

_____ Lake southeast of Springer Mountain

_____ Swamp in southeast Georgia

_____ Large city in central Georgia

_____ State on Georgia's northwest border

FLORIDA: ITS KEYS AND ITS SPRINGS

Florida Keys

Alaska and Florida don't have much in common as far as climate goes, but they do have a geographic similarity—both states have a long and curving series of islands trailing off their coasts. Alaska has the Aleutian Islands, and Florida has the Florida Keys.

A map would show the Florida Keys to be about 180 miles from end to end. The map would have to be quite large to show all the *keys*, as they are called from the Spanish word *cayo* which means small island, for there are many islands. Some islands are no larger than a football field; others may be as much as thirty miles long. Cuba is quite close to some of the keys; only about 100 miles of open water separates them.

The Keys, which have been called "Florida's Necklace," can be subdivided into three groups: those islands closest to the Florida mainland, the middle islands in the string known as the Marquesa Keys, and the distant Dry Tortugas.

The last named group, the Dry Tortugas, are not a vacationer's paradise, for they are very dry and barren and have few trees. Also, the only ways to reach them are by boat or small airplane. The "Tortugas" part of the name is the Spanish word for turtles. When Ponce de Leon, the Spanish explorer who gave them their name, first landed on the islands he was astonished to see hundreds of turtles. However he and his men were pleased to find the turtles because they made nourishing soup, and their eggs, which were buried in the sand, were delicious.

An overseas highway, 128 miles long, takes inhabitants and visitors from the Florida mainland to Key West. About 25,000 people live in the city as residents, but each year tourists by the thousands drive over the island roads and connecting bridges for visits. The attractions of the Keys are many: great fishing, swimming, boating, scuba diving, and bird watching.

Florida's Springs

Florida has more than 30,000 lakes and ponds, seventeen large springs and thousands of smaller ones, and one of the largest underground water storage areas in the United States. Do not think of underground water as being contained in a huge lake; rather, think of the water as being stored in a "sponge" made up of porous rock and sand.

As you may know, a spring is a natural opening in the earth's surface through which underground water bubbles. Most springs have small openings, but some openings are very large.

How does one know whether a spring is "large" or "small"? Size is determined by measuring how many cubic feet of water flow from a spring each second. A spring with a flow of 100 cubic feet per second is large and is known as a spring of "first magnitude." To understand how much water that is, think of a swimming pool 40' long, 30' wide, and 5' deep. Such a pool could be filled with water in less than one minute if it were fed by a first magnitude spring!

From where does Florida's water come? From the state's heavy rainfall of more than fifty inches a year. Much of that rain, a yearly average of thirty-two inches, falls between May and October. The rain readily sinks into the sandy soil and is stored until a natural spring or driven well brings it to the surface.

© 1996 by The Center for Applied Research in Education

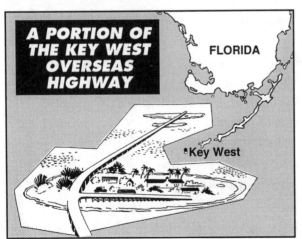

A PORTION OF THE KEY WEST OVERSEAS HIGHWAY

FLORIDA

Key West

FLORIDA: SOME OF ITS TOURIST ATTRACTIONS

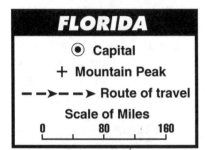

FLORIDA
- ⊙ **Capital**
- ✛ **Mountain Peak**
- – –➤– –➤ **Route of travel**
- **Scale of Miles**
- 0   80   160

We started our trip on Florida's "panhandle" at the old city of ❶_____. We headed east and drove past Florida's highest point, which is only ❷_____ feet high. We crossed the ❸_____ River, and about 180 miles from Pensacola, we arrived in Florida's capital city, ❹_____. After a brief tour we started for Florida's largest city, ❻_____. However, before we got to the city we crossed the ❺_____ River. We stayed overnight, and in the morning we boarded a train for ❼_____, the oldest city in the United States. It was founded by people from Spain in ❽_____.

We rented a car and drove to the next place on our tour, ❾_____. We heard it was permissible to drive on the hard-packed sand of Daytona's beach—so that's what we did! Of course, every once in a while we stopped for a quick dip in the ocean.

Next, we headed for ❿_____. We were hoping to see a spaceship launched, but we were too late. However, we did have a guided tour of the Kennedy Space Center.

⓫_____ was the next stop. We spent two days visiting Disney World. Everybody in our group said they liked "It's a Small World" the best. Close to Disney World is Sea World. We sat in the first row of the seaquarium and got splashed and soaking wet when the whales flipped their tales in the pool. We didn't mind; it was fun.

Next, we took a plane from Orlando to ⓭_____. On the way we flew over ⓬_____. The flight attendant told us that the lake is the second largest lake in the United States, after Lake Michigan. She also said there were 30,000 lakes in Florida. Miami was interesting, but so many tourists! Would you believe Florida has 14 million visitors each year?

On our way to ⓯_____ from Miami we flew over the ⓮_____ region, which covers more than 5,000 square miles; that's about the size of Connecticut.

Tampa was interesting, but best of all was when we went to see the manatees, commonly called sea cows, swimming in the Manatee River. They were so gentle and adorable. We felt sad when we learned that many had been maimed and killed by the propellers of motorboats. But, we felt much better when we were told that steps were being taken to protect them.

From Tampa it was a long flight across the ⓰_____ to Pensacola. About 100 miles before Pensacola we could see ⓱_____ City to the northeast.

77

ALABAMA: GEORGE WASHINGTON CARVER AND PEANUTS

All about Peanuts

Georgia is the United States' greatest grower of peanuts and is followed by Alabama. However, it was a research scientist from Alabama, George Washington Carver, who first studied peanuts and found more than 300 uses for both the plant and its fruit. The fruit is what we commonly call "peanuts."

Before Carver's discoveries, the southern states relied on cotton as their main crop; it was the crop that put cash into farmers' pockets. But there were negative sides to reliance on cotton. When the market for cotton was not good, farmers realized smaller incomes in spite of an equal amount of effort. Also, the cotton-eating boll weevil infested cotton fields in the early 1900s and all but destroyed cotton production. Finally, cotton takes much out of the soil and puts nothing back. The consequence of this was that each year the same fields produced less and less cotton.

But Carver's work rescued cotton growers; they turned to growing peanuts when Carver's newly developed uses for peanuts created great demand for them. Not only did farmers gain a reliable source of income, but also those who learned ways to turn raw peanuts into useful products found employment.

It should also be mentioned that Carver, who was born as a slave in 1864 and who did not know how to read until he was twenty years old, was determined to become educated. He progressed so rapidly that in his thirties he became a professor at the highly respected Tuskegee Institute in Alabama. While there, in addition to finding new uses for peanuts, he developed 100 uses for sweet potatoes, 75 uses for pecans, and numerous uses for clay, wood shavings, cotton plant stalks, and other agricultural products. Here is a partial list of some of the products that come from peanuts and sweet potatoes: plastics, lubricants, dyes, soap, paint, ink, face creams, shoe blackening, candy, flour, paper, and, of course, peanut butter.

Many people would be surprised to learn that the peanuts they love to eat are not grown above ground; they are grown below the ground's surface. The illustration below shows this in a cross-sectional view of a peanut plant. Notice that the above-ground part of the plant is very leafy. The plant can grow as high as 30", and as wide as 48". The leafy part of the plant is also useful; it can, for example, be used as a rich animal feed.

The leafy part of the peanut plant also serves to reproduce the plant. It grows flowers which, as they wither, droop to the ground. The ends of the withered flowers, *stalks*, contain seeds. The stalks begin to grow downward into the ground. Eventually, the seeds become peanut pods. Usually, a pod contains two peanuts, which are not really "nuts," but seeds.

Peanuts are exceptionally good food. A pound of roasted peanuts has at least as many calories as a pound of beef. About 25% of a peanut is protein, which makes it an important part of the diet of people around the world who don't have access to beef. Fifty percent of a peanut is oil. You may not realize it, but it is quite possible that the oil you put on your salad is really peanut oil, and you can even buy bread made of peanuts on which you can spread your peanut butter and jam.

Name: _____ Date: _____

ALABAMA: CITIES, RIVERS, AND MOUNTAINS

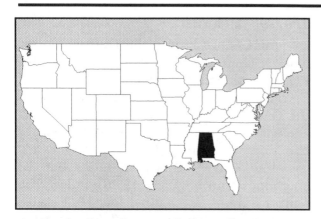

1. Study the maps and then decide if the following statements are **True** or **False**. Circle your choice—T or F.

a. Alabama shares a border with four other states.   T   F

b. The Tennessee River flows in and out of Alabama.   T   F

c. Alabama is larger than Florida. T   F

d. The Perdido River forms part of the border between Alabama and Mississippi.
                                                      T   F

e. Mobile is located on the eastern side of Mobile Bay.   T   F

f. The Tallapoosa River and the Cahaba River join to form the Alabama River.
                                                      T   F

g. The Chattahoochee River is part of the boundary between Alabama and Florida.
                                                      T   F

h. Tuscaloosa is between 100 and 130 miles northwest of Montgomery   T   F

i. The highest mountain in Alabama is Logan Peak.   T   F

j. Tennessee is closer to Huntsville than Georgia is.   T   F

k. Alabama's northern border is between 140 and 155 miles long.   T   F

l. The Black Warrior River is a tributary of the Tombigbee River.   T   F

m. The Perdido River empties into the Gulf of Mexico.   T   F

n. A direct airplane flight between Selma and Mobile would not be more than 175 miles.
                                                      T   F

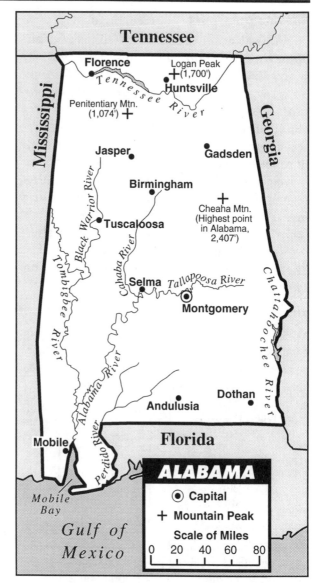

2. Carefully study the map of Alabama. Then write two statements (sentences) that should be answered either true or false. With your teacher's permission, ask one of your classmates to respond to your statements.

a. _____

_____

_____   T   F

b. _____

_____

_____   T   F

MISSISSIPPI: ITS RELATIONSHIP TO THE GULF OF MEXICO

Mississippi Coast

Mississippi's share of the Gulf of Mexico's **coastline** is about 44 miles. However, its **shoreline** is about 360 miles. The difference between coastline and shoreline is important. Coastline is the general outline of a coast, and only large indentations are considered a part of the coastline. Shoreline is much more detailed; all the small "dents" (coves, inlets, etc.) and "points" (peninsulas, promontories, etc.) are included. A country or state may have a long coastline but not have many harbors, or it may have a short coastline with many good harbors. The sketches below show the differences between shoreline and coastline.

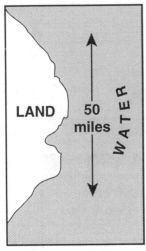 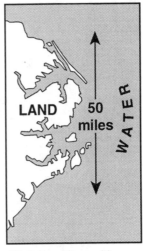

A) A coastline with very little shoreline

B) A coastline with a long shoreline (includes islands)

As you can see, both A and B show the same length coastline, but B has a much greater shoreline. A's coast is **regular**; B's coast is **irregular**.

So, Mississippi is fortunate; its irregular shoreline has several indentations that make fine harbors and ports of trade such as Biloxi and Pascagoula. According to the 1995 *World Almanac and Book of Facts*, Pascagoula handled more than 29 million tons of freight in a recent year. Of the fifty busiest ports in the United States it is number 22, and growing fast.

The Gulf of Mexico

Mississippi shares the Gulf of Mexico and its shoreline with four other states—Florida, Alabama, Louisiana, and Texas. Florida enjoys a special relationship with the Gulf; the Gulf's waters lap on the west shore of the peninsula and the south shore of the state's panhandle. The five-state coastline of the Gulf is 1,631 miles, but the shoreline is an amazing 17,461 miles. The Gulf coastlines of the other four Gulf states are Louisiana, 397; Texas, 367; Alabama, 53; and Florida, 770.

Numerous rivers empty their waters into the Gulf of Mexico. Of course, the greatest water contributor is the Mississippi River, which carries the water from dozens of rivers of the interior plains. Along with the Mississippi River there are many rivers that pour water directly into the Gulf, including the Rio Grande, Colorado (Texas), Brazos, Tombigbee, Alabama, and Chattahoochie.

There are hundreds of bays and inlets along the Gulf's irregular coastline. These arms of the Gulf provide shelter from the open sea for large and small boats. However, there is additional protection from the storms that strike Gulf coast lands. That protection is provided by a thousand-mile long link of bays, canals, and constructed sea walls called the **Gulf Intracoastal Waterway**. The force of winds and waves sweeping in from the south is lessened before it reaches the ships that are sailing through the Waterway's safe "aisle."

The Gulf of Mexico provides several other benefits for Gulf states. The catches of shrimp and oyster boats contribute millions of dollars to the states' economies. Probably more important to the economy is the fact that thousands of vacationers, especially in winter, enjoy the warm water and sunshine of the coast. Taking care of vacationers provides thousands of jobs for workers in the tourist industry.

MISSISSIPPI: RIVERS, RESERVOIRS, CITIES

1. List in *alphabetical order* all the cities shown on the map.

🐭 _____

🐭 _____

🐭 _____

🐭 _____

🐭 _____

🐭 _____

🐭 _____

🐭 _____

🐭 _____

2. List from *north to south* all the rivers shown on the map that empty into the *Mississippi River*.

🐭 _____

🐭 _____

🐭 _____

3. List from *east to west* all the rivers that empty into the *Gulf of Mexico*.

🐭 _____

🐭 _____

🐭 _____

4. List from *south to north* all the reservoirs shown on the map.

🐭 _____

🐭 _____

🐭 _____

🐭 _____

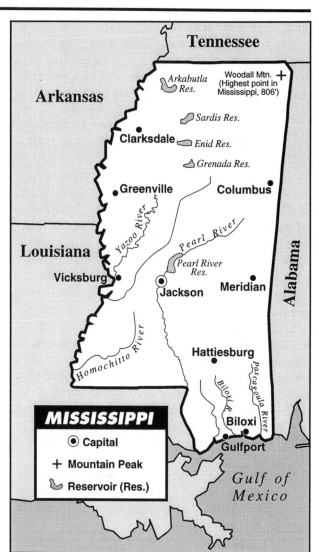

5. Describe the location of Mississippi's highest point as you would to someone who is not familiar with Mississippi.

_____

_____

_____

_____

_____

6. Draw a star after the capital of Mississippi in your list of cities in item 1 above.

LOUISIANA: THE MISSISSIPPI RIVER AND ITS DELTA

The Mississippi River

The Mississippi River has played a most significant part in American history since 1539, when the Spanish explorer de Soto and his men stepped on the land that has since become part of the state of Louisiana. It was 143 years later, 1682, that the French explorer Sieur de La Salle completed the exploration of the Mississippi River from Canada, south and downstream, to the Gulf of Mexico. Based on La Salle's explorations, France laid claim to the entire Mississippi River Valley. La Salle named the region *Louisiana* in honor of the ruling French king, Louis XIV. Although many states have been formed from the region, today's state of Louisiana has kept the original name.

The Mississippi River has been, and still is, both a blessing and, in some ways, a problem to Louisiana. The river is a ready-made highway to the interior plains of the continent. This was especially important in the early days of our history for there were no highways, railroads, or airplanes. The lack of good transportation meant that New Orleans became the beginning or ending point for people and products being carried up and down the river. Of course, this led to a steady growth of the city itself and the entire state.

One major problem the river presented in early times was getting east-west traffic across its wide water. The problem was first solved by utilizing ferry boats. Later, with advances in engineering and construction materials, bridges were built to span the river. Even so, it wasn't until 1935 that a bridge over the Mississippi River—completely contained within Louisiana—was completed.

A second problem that the Mississippi River presented was controlling the floods that occurred as the result of spring rains and melting snow. This problem was solved, although not completely because even today Louisiana experiences floods, by building high banks or *levees* (sometimes called *dikes*) along the course of the river. The levees contain the rising water and keep it from flooding the land. But, sometimes the levees break or the water rises so much that it overflows the levees. When this happens the resulting loss of lives and damage to property can be very extensive.

Other ways have been devised to control the flooding Mississippi. One method is to dig channels that funnel water to lakes or even the Gulf of Mexico. Another method of control is to build dams across rivers that feed water into the Mississippi River. The dams hold back the water until such times that the river and its dikes can contain it; then, the water is gradually released.

The Delta of the Mississippi River

Imagine an area that . . .

☞ is a great peninsula that is made up of a number of smaller peninsulas;

☞ is as large as Massachusetts and Connecticut combined;

☞ is criss-crossed by hundreds of small streams;

☞ is as flat as a table top;

☞ has a body of water, Lake Pontchartrain, that is 40 miles long and 25 miles wide;

☞ has fertile soil that is often more than a foot thick;

☞ is growing larger each year.

The delta of the Mississippi River, which is part of the state of Louisiana, is all of these things and more.

From where has all the delta soil come? The answer is that for thousands of years the rivers that entered the Mississippi River from the east and west carried huge amounts of topsoil, gravel, and mud washed off millions of square miles of land. Some of the material was dropped in the channel of the Mississippi River, but most of it was deposited at the river's mouth. To better understand just how much soil has been "delivered," think of a building 100' wide, and 100' high or 1 million cubic yards. That's how much soil is estimated to be deposited **each day**. Now, think how much that would be in a year, then a thousand years, then ten thousand years, or more.

Name: _____ Date: _____

LOUISIANA: PLACE NAMES ON A MAP AND IN A PUZZLE

P	E	A	R	L	K	T	R	V	W	G	K	L	Z	N	N
F	O	H	J	B	A	T	O	N	R	O	U	G	E	E	E
A	D	N	M	N	P	O	U	L	X	Z	Y	K	L	W	W
T	R	K	C	S	A	B	I	N	E	A	C	B	A	O	I
C	I	D	E	H	F	H	J	K	W	D	R	T	F	R	B
H	S	A	R	K	A	N	S	A	S	F	O	W	A	L	E
A	K	U	V	C	A	R	L	M	P	Q	R	B	Y	E	R
F	I	A	D	K	N	A	T	C	H	E	Z	Y	E	A	I
A	L	A	K	E	C	H	A	R	L	E	S	P	T	N	A
L	L	B	O	G	A	L	U	S	A	G	F	H	T	S	D
A	K	T	E	X	A	S	M	P	F	I	A	B	E	R	C
Y	C	Y	D	G	H	J	K	R	M	O	N	R	O	E	O
A	C	A	L	C	A	S	I	E	U	M	P	U	Z	D	K

Louisiana Word Search Puzzle

There are seventeen cities, rivers, etc., listed in the puzzle. All of the names are shown on the map, but not all the names in the map are listed in the puzzle.

The places are listed either *across* or *down*, except for two that are listed *diagonally* from left-to-right.

Here is an effective way to proceed:

1. Select a name from the map.

2. Search for the name in the puzzle.

3. If you find the name in the puzzle, draw a neat line around all the letters in the name.

4. If you don't find a name, select another name from the map.

Note: Only the names of rivers, reservoirs, and mountains are listed in the puzzle; the words *river*, *reservoir*, *mountain,* and, in one case, *lake* are omitted.

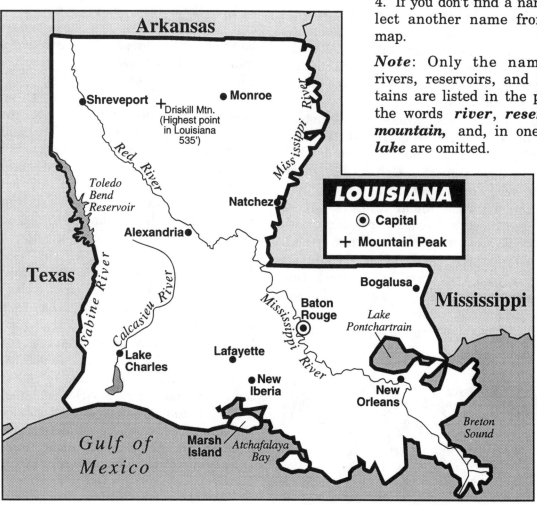

ARKANSAS: DIAMONDS AND ALUMINUM

Diamonds in Arkansas

You can imagine the surprise of an Arkansas farmer who was plowing his field, turning up soil, when, suddenly, he spied a peculiar shining stone. On picking it up he saw that it was not an ordinary "stone." What was it? He had a suspicion that it might be a diamond, but he couldn't tell for sure. He took his find to experts who told him it was a genuine diamond. The diamond was found in the only diamond field in all of North America. Many thousands of years ago an erupting volcano had spilled diamonds over the area. Earth and vegetation covered them, and there they remained until farmer John Huddleston came along in 1906.

Professional miners brought in mining machinery and went to work. They dug out more than 50,000 diamonds before the precious gems became so scarce that it was no longer profitable to mine them commercially. The largest diamond they found, called the "Uncle Sam," weighed 40.23 carats and, at that time, was worth more than $250,000.

In 1972, the area where the diamonds were found was made into a state park called "Crater of Diamonds State Park." Visitors are welcome to search for diamonds in a 35-acre section set aside for digging. After the eager diamond hunters pay a small fee, digging tools are provided and park employees help them to know when they've found the "real thing." Whatever searchers find they may keep. Since the park was opened, more than 17,000 diamonds, an average of about two a day, have

been dug up. And they say that not all the diamonds have yet been found.

Mining for Bauxite

Almost all of the bauxite mined in the United States comes from Arkansas. What! You don't know what bauxite is? Well, it's fairly safe to say that hardly a day goes by without you using the materials extracted from bauxite. Bauxite is the basic mineral from which alumina (aluminum) is obtained. There are other materials in bauxite, but it is the alumina that is most important.

Bauxite is easier to mine than many other minerals. That's because it isn't necessary to dig shafts and tunnels to get it; it is obtained through **strip mining** and **open-pit mining**. These are methods of mining that, as a first step, "strip" the top soil, rocks, trees, and subsoil from the earth's surface. This procedure exposes the bauxite. Then, deeper holes are dug as the mineral is taken out of the ground; this is where **open-pit mining** begins.

Bulldozers and other earth-moving machines pick up the bauxite and dump it into trucks or freight cars. The bauxite is taken to refining and smelting plants where the alumina is separated from other materials in the bauxite. After being smelted, the alumina is taken to factories where it is made into useful things such as window frames, pots, pans, airplane parts, and automobile parts.

The area in Arkansas where bauxite is found is in the central part of the state, south of Little Rock. Bauxite has been, and is, so important to the area that there is a town located there named Bauxite.

Much of the alumina extracted from the bauxite mined in Arkansas is made into aluminum products in Arkansas factories. Unfortunately, Arkansas cannot supply all of the alumina needed for aluminum products. The United States must import from other countries such as Suriname in South America and Jamaica in the Caribbean Sea.

ARKANSAS: CITIES, RIVERS, PLACES OF INTEREST

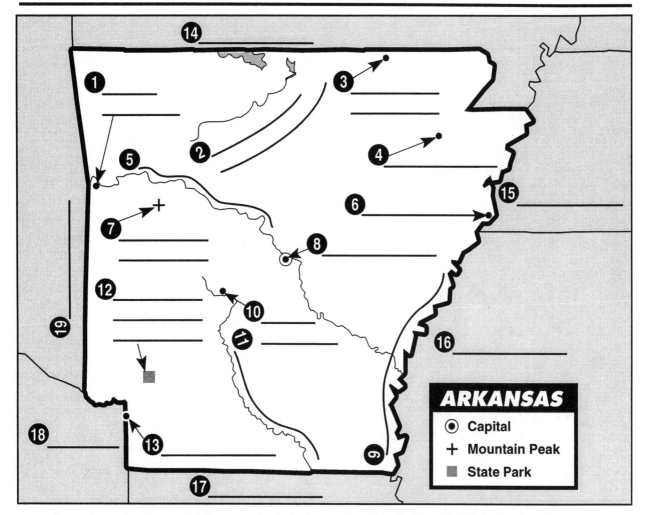

Complete the map of Arkansas by labeling the following places.

1. **Fort Smith**: Arkansas' second largest city

2. **Buffalo National River**: Only major river in Arkansas without a dam . . . Protected from development by the United States government

3. **Mammoth Spring**: Clear water gushes from one of the world's largest single springs

4. **Jonesboro**: One of only seven Arkansas cities with more than 30,000 people

5. **Arkansas River**: A major tributary to the Mississippi River

6. **West Memphis**: River port

7. **Magazine Mountain**: Arkansas' highest point (2,823')

8. **Little Rock**: Capital of Arkansas

9. **Mississippi River**: Forms almost all of Arkansas' eastern boundary

10. **Hot Springs**: Warm mineral water for bathing and soothing aches and pains

11. **Sabine River**: Flows south to become a boundary between Louisiana and Texas

12. **Crater of Diamonds State Park**: North America's only diamond field

13. **Texarkana**: A town divided between Texas and Arkansas

14. Missouri

15. Tennessee

16. Mississippi

17. Louisiana

18. Texas

19. Oklahoma

North Central States

Name: _____ Date: _____

NORTH CENTRAL STATES: RIVERS AND LAKES

THE NORTH CENTRAL STATES WITHIN THE UNITED STATES

NORTH CENTRAL STATES

- ◉ **Capitals**
- –·– **State Boundaries**
- –···– **International Boundary**

© 1996 by The Center for Applied Research in Education

The questions that follow are concerned with the North Central States.

1. Which states border Lake Superior?

_____ _____

_____

2. Which states border Lake Michigan?

_____ _____

_____ _____

3. Which state borders Lake Huron?

_____

4. Which states border Lake Erie?

_____ _____

5. Which lake is the only one completely within the United States?

_____

6. Which state has the Mississippi River as its *entire* western border?

_____

7. What states have the Mississippi River as their *entire* eastern border?

_____ _____

8. Which state is the only state with the Mississippi River running *through* it?

_____

9. The Ohio River forms all or a part of the borders of which states?

_____ _____

_____

10. What river and what two lakes form part of the border between Minnesota (United States) and Canada?

_____ _____

_____

11. Which state has the Mississippi River as a complete eastern border and the Missouri River as a *complete* western border?

_____

NORTH CENTRAL STATES: MAP PUZZLES

Each map on this page has clues that will help you identify the names of the places or things that are shown by question marks (?) and letters. "C" before a ? means *city*; "R" means *river*; "S" means *state*; "L" means *lake*. Maps in this book, your basic history textbook, encyclopedias, and other sources will be of help to you.

City:

_____

State:

_____

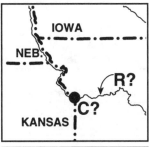

City:

_____

River:

_____

City:

_____

Lake:

_____

City:

_____

River:

_____

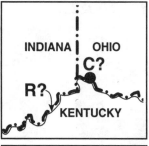

City 1:

_____

City 2:

_____

City:

_____

River:

_____

City 1:

_____

City 2:

_____

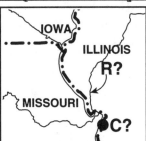

City:

_____

River:

_____

City 1:

_____

City 2:

_____

City 1:

_____

City 2:

_____

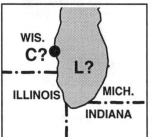

City:

_____

Lake:

_____

Name: _____ Date: _____

NORTH CENTRAL STATES: TABLE OF FACTS

FACTS ABOUT THE NORTH CENTRAL STATES				
State and Capital (North to South)	**Population**	**Area in Square Miles with Rank Shown in Parentheses ( )**	**Highest Point with Elevation Shown in Parentheses ( )**	**Nickname**
Minnesota (St. Paul)	4,517,416	86,943 (12)	Eagle Mountain (2,301')	North Star State or Gopher State
Wisconsin (Madison)	5,037,928	65,499 (23)	Timms Hill (1,951')	Badger State
Michigan (Lansing)	9,477,545	96,705 (11)	Mt. Curwood (1,979')	Great Lakes State or Wolverine State
Iowa (Des Moines)	2,814,064	56,276 (26)	(Not named) (1,670')	Hawkeye State
Missouri (Jefferson City)	5,233,849	69,709 (21)	Taum Sauk Mtn. (1,772')	Show Me State
Illinois (Springfield)	11,697,736	57,918 (25)	Charles Mound (1,235')	The Prairie State
Indiana (Indianapolis)	5,712,799	36,420 (38)	(Not named) (1,257')	Hoosier State
Ohio (Columbus)	11,091,301	44,828 (34)	Campbell Hill (1,549')	Buckeye State

Note: **Area** is the total of land and inland waters such as lakes.

CROSS-NUMBER PUZZLE

A "Cross-Number Puzzle" is solved in the same way an ordinary word puzzle is solved. The only difference is that numbers are used instead of words. Be careful in reading the numbers in the table and then transferring them to the puzzle.

Across
1. Minnesota's population
5. Minnesota's rank in area
6. Minnesota's highest elevation
9. Illinois' area
10. Ohio's highest elevation
11. Wisconsin's rank in area
14. Michigan's rank in area
15. Illinois' population
17. Missouri's population

Down
2. Illinois' highest elevation
3. Wisconsin's area
4. Ohio's population
7. Indiana's rank in area
8. Ohio's rank in area
9. Wisconsin's population
12. Missouri's rank in area
13. Iowa's highest elevation
16. Illinois' rank in area

NORTH CENTRAL STATES: SOLVING AND MAKING PUZZLES

Some of the application pages in *American Continents* have required learners to read maps, to utilize skills involving direction and distance, and to interpret symbols in order to complete a crossword puzzle. In so doing, they became familiar with a region or state's general conformation and some specifics such as rivers, mountains, and cities. The puzzles also provided practice in reading brief definitions and descriptions, and in spelling place names precisely. They also provided a challenge and an interesting way to become acquainted with new information and review previously encountered facts.

The puzzle on the facing page provides opportunities to read a table for information and to reorganize numerical information in another form, that is, the puzzle. In reading the table, learners are required to read row and column headings, scan the columns for the appropriate "cell," and then transfer their findings to the puzzle. Through these activities, learners are acquiring specific facts and developing work-study skills.

It may be that your learners have not encountered cross-number puzzles; however, it is unlikely that they will have difficulty with the number variety. A brief explanation and one or two examples should be enough to get them started.

As provision for quick reference, the completed puzzle is reproduced below.

CROSS-NUMBER PUZZLE

Developing a Crossword Puzzle

It's a challenge to solve a crossword puzzle, but it's even more of a challenge to make one. The following suggestions will place your students in the latter position.

1. Provide sheets of graph paper for your students. Have them rule off a portion of the paper within which their puzzle will fit. Suggested number of spaces across and down: 12 to 15.

2. Have your students make a list of proper names derived from the last two columns on the facing page. Such a list could include Hoosier, Badger State, Campbell Hill, and others.

3. Print one of the names in the middle of the puzzle, either horizontally or vertically. Use the word as a base that other words interjoin.

4. Try to provide for a balanced number of UPs and DOWNs.

5. After all the names are on the puzzle, number them.

6. Write brief descriptions of the selected words. An entire name does not have to be in the puzzle, for example:

ACROSS

1. Springfield is its capital. _____

DOWN

2. Minnesota is called the _____ State.

NORTH CENTRAL STATES: LEADERS IN AGRICULTURE

The North Central States are noted for their agricultural production. The northern states in the region—Minnesota, Wisconsin, Michigan—are part of what is known as the "Dairy Belt." The southern states in the region—Iowa, Missouri, Illinois, Indiana, Ohio—are part of the "Corn Belt." The table indicates how much corn is grown in the Corn Belt states and how many cows are in the Dairy Belt states.

Following is a suggested use of the table's data.
1. Enlarge the map on this page, photocopy, and distribute.
2. Make a transparency of the table. Explain the table and the footnotes.
3. Have your students draw symbols on the map that represent how many cattle are in each of the Dairy Belt states and how many bushels of corn are produced in each of the Corn Belt states.

NORTH CENTRAL STATES

 Each represents 100,000 cows

Each represents 100,000,000 bushels of corn

ABBREVIATIONS
IA = Iowa
IL = Illinois
IN = Indiana
MI = Michigan
MN = Minnesota
MO = Missouri
OH = Ohio
WI = Wisconsin

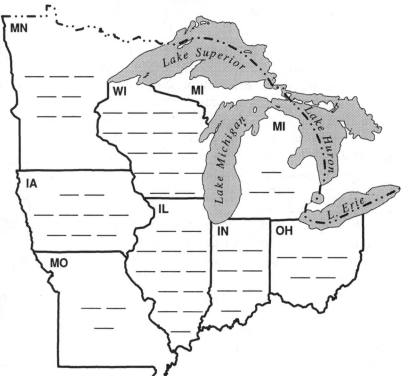

NORTH CENTRAL STATES					
State	**Number of Dairy Cattle[1]**	**Symbols[2]**	**State**	**Bushels of Corn[3]**	**Symbols[4]**
Wisconsin	1,600,000	16	Illinois	1,300,000,000	13
Minnesota	700,000	7	Iowa	900,000,000	9
Michigan	300,000	3	Indiana	700,000,000	7
(1) Rounded to nearest 100,000			Ohio	500,000,000	5
(2) Each symbol represents 100,000 cows			Missouri	300,000,000	3
			(3) Rounded to nearest 100,000,000. (One bushel of corn equals 56 lbs.)		
			(4) Each symbol represents 100,000,000 bushels of corn		

NORTH CENTRAL STATES: RESEARCH QUESTIONS

The questions on this page are brief and specific and are concerned only with the North Central States. The answers to the questions can be found in almanacs, encyclopedias, textbooks, and maps. By searching out the answers to the questions your students will become acquainted with various sources of information and will gain skill in reading to find the answers to specific questions.

Suggestions

1. This activity provides an opportunity for two students to work together.
2. Photocopy the bottom portion of this page and distribute.
3. Gather various reference books as mentioned above and place them in a particular place in your classroom.
4. An entire period can be devoted to research or the activity can be an out-of-school assignment.
5. Answers may be written on the reverse side of the photocopy; number from 1 to 25.

1. Which state has the longest Great Lakes shoreline?
2. On what river is Cincinnati located?
3. Which is Missouri's largest city, St. Louis or Kansas City?
4. In what state would you find Bowling Green State University?
5. What line of latitude is the northern border of Minnesota?
6. What is the name of Wisconsin's largest city?
7. On what two Great Lakes does Wisconsin border?
8. How many states share a border with Indiana?
9. For which one of these products are Detroit, Flint, Pontiac, Jackson, and Racine noted: computers, automobiles, television sets?
10. What mineral is mined in great quantities in northeastern Minnesota, northern Michigan, and Wisconsin?
11. Chicago is the largest city in the North Central States. What city is the second largest?
12. What two cities are known as the "Twin Cities"?
13. In which state would you find the "Pro Football Hall of Fame"?
14. In which state was former President Hoover born?
15. What is the state bird of Michigan?
16. What is the state tree of Missouri?
17. Which one of our presidents was from Missouri?
18. What is the state motto of Wisconsin?
19. What was the date of Indiana's entrance into the Union?
20. In what city is the United States' tallest building? How tall is it? What is its name?
21. Which state has the lowest recorded temperature? What is that temperature?
22. On what river is Peoria, Illinois, located?
23. Which two of the North Central States do not have shorelines on any of the Great Lakes?
24. Which of the North Central States has the shortest shoreline along any of the Great Lakes?
25. In what state is the University of Notre Dame?

MINNESOTA: LAND OF LAKES AND IRON

Open-Pit Iron Mines

Picture a hole in the earth about three miles long, one mile wide, and some 400' deep. The sides of the pit are ringed with "giant steps," actually roads, that spiral down to the bottom of the pit. The steps have been gouged out by giant earth moving machines. Such an excavation is the world's largest open-pit iron ore mine. It is located in Minnesota's northeastern hills, the Mesabi Range.

At the bottom of the pit, ore is dug out of the ground, then loaded on a conveyor belt that carries it to the top of the pit. Then, the ore is loaded onto railroad cars that transport it to Duluth or some other port city. Finally, the ore is loaded on huge barges, each barge capable of transporting as much ore as could be carried on 400 railroad cars. From the ports on Lake Superior the ore is delivered to steel mills on the southern shores of the Great Lakes or to the area around Pittsburgh, Pennsylvania.

There are many open-pit mines in the Mesabi Range; the one described above happens to be the largest. All of the mines are developed and operated in much the same way although there are some differences. In some open-pit mines railroad cars are loaded directly on the floor of the pit. In other operations huge trucks capable of carrying up to 125 tons transport the ore to the top of the pit.

There have been some changes in the quality and quantity of ore obtained from the Mesabi Range. In the early days of the mining industry in Minnesota, about 1900, the ore taken out was rich and plentiful. But, the demand for iron was so great that the supply gradually decreased. The future didn't look good for Minnesota's mining industry. The situation was saved, however, when mining engineers found ways to extract iron from low-grade ore called *taconite*. Today, Minnesota is still the greatest iron producing state in the country. About 65% of the iron we need for thousands of products originates in Minnesota.

Note: In this brief article the word *ore* has been used several times. Just what is ore? It is a deposit of materials in the earth, especially in rock, that contains minerals such as iron. To obtain the mineral, the ore must be treated in various ways to separate the desired mineral from the rock. It may take several tons of ore to produce a ton of iron.

Interesting Facts about Minnesota's Lakes

Cars bearing Minnesota license plates proudly proclaim that the state has 10,000 lakes. However, if a lake is defined as being over ten acres in size, there are 11,842 lakes, according to the pamphlet published by the Minnesota Office of Tourism. If lakes smaller than ten acres are taken into account, there are some 15,000.

The state's lakes are a great source of enjoyment for the people of Minnesota. In a recent year more than 2,000,000 individuals— that's one out of every two people—in the state had fishing licenses. Fishing takes place not only in warm weather, but also in the winter when the lakes are frozen over. The hardy fishers build small "fish houses" on the ice, cut holes in the ice, and drop their lines into the frigid water.

The tourism pamphlet mentioned above tells the reader that Minnesota has 201 lakes called Mud Lake, 154 Long Lakes, and 123 Rice Lakes. One of the lakes is called Mugwump Lake; another, Bologna (Pronounced "Baloney") Lake; and then there is a Diddle de Woddle Lake.

MINNESOTA: FINDING PLACES WITH LATITUDE AND LONGITUDE

This activity will give you practice in locating places using latitude and longitude, and it also will help you become better acquainted with Minnesota.

Complete the sentences below with information gained from the map.

1. St. Paul and Minneapolis are located just south of the _____ line of latitude.

2. Mankato is located just east of the _____ line of longitude.

3. All of Upper Red Lake is north of the _____ line of latitude.

4. La Crosse, which is in Wisconsin, lies between 43°N and _____N.

5. The latitude of Eagle Mountain is almost _____N, and its longitude is about 90½°W.

Note: Another way of writing 90½° is 90° 30'. This is because each degree is divided into 60 minutes or, as it is written, 60'. So, if a place is halfway between 90°N and 91°N, it is said to be 90° 30'N.

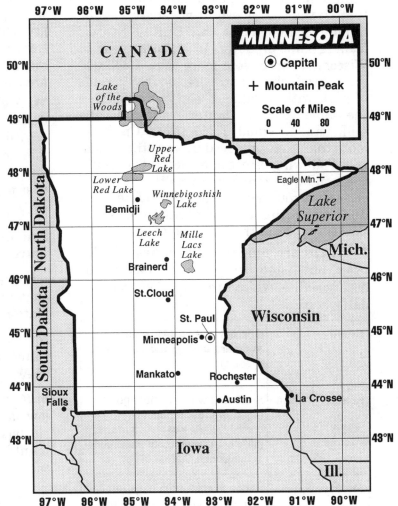

6. You may remember that each degree of latitude on a line of longitude is equal to about 70 miles. Here is an example:

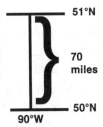

With this knowledge you can easily determine north-south distances on maps that have lines of latitude and longitude. Here is a problem:

Minnesota is about 6° in length from its most southern boundary to its most northern boundary (Lake of the Woods). What would that number of degrees be equal to in miles? _____ miles

7. Here is a map of Mille Lacs Lake in central Minnesota. If you were to tell someone where the lake is located, you could say, "The lake is in the rectangle between 46°N and 47°N, and 93°W and 94°W.

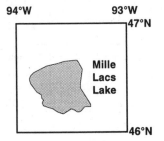

Using this same method how would you locate the rectangle within which Leech Lake and Lake Winnibigoshish are located? Complete the following:

These two lakes lie between _____°N and _____°N, and _____°W and _____°W.

WISCONSIN: ALL ABOUT MILK

America's Dairyland

Wisconsin is known as the Badger State*, but it also has another nickname, that is, the title above. It well-deserves the name because it is the United States' leading milk producer. In a recent year in Wisconsin there were more than 1,645,000 cows, producing almost 24,103,000 pounds of milk with a value of $3,175,000,000. In the same year, the butter made from the milk (cream) equaled 357,452,000 pounds, more than that produced by any other state.

Following are some facts about milk cows, milk, and milk products that apply to our entire country and that contribute to an understanding of those North Central States that form the Dairy Belt.

🐄 There are numerous varieties of milk cows, but listed below are the four major breeds—all of which are part of Wisconsin's dairy herds.

Breed	Characteristics (All comparisons are among the four listed breeds)
Holstein-Friesian	Black and white spotted; good producers, but product is comparatively low in butterfat; the most numerous of the breeds in the United States.
Jersey	Range in color from gray, tan, and brown; smallest of the four major breeds; produce less milk than the three other breeds, but more than make up for this with the high butterfat content of their milk (butterfat—important to the production of cream).
Guernsey	Tan with white markings; greater milk producers than the Jerseys; rich milk with high butterfat content, but not as great as the Jerseys'.
Brown Swiss	Light to dark brown; second to Holstein-Friesian in milk production; product rich in minerals, nonfat solids, and sugar—great for cheese production.

🐄 In a recent year the milk from Wisconsin's cows made 2,052,913,000 pounds of cheese.

🐄 Those who use certain brands of thick, white paste may not realize it but the basic ingredient of the sticky-stuff—casein—comes from milk. Other widely used products that may be partly composed of by-products of milk are paint and plastics.

🐄 A glass of milk is a kind of mini-mineral deposit. Some of the minerals found in milk are calcium, potassium, copper, zinc, iron, aluminum, and manganese. Calcium is the most important mineral because it helps the growth of strong bones and teeth.

🐄 A milk glossary:

raw milk: milk as it comes from the cow; untreated

whole milk: milk that has a certain percent of cream, as specified by federal or state laws

fortified milk: milk that has had certain things added to it, for example, vitamins D or A

buttermilk (cultured): sweet milk with a low fat content to which unharmful bacteria has been added. After a period of fermentation the milk takes on a sharper taste.

pasteurized milk: milk that has been heated to the point that all harmful bacteria have been destroyed

🐄 Cow's milk is, by far, the most widely used milk in the United States. However, milk from other mammals is a part of some people's diets. Perhaps the most popular alternative is goat's milk, used in special diets. It is easier to digest than cow's milk, so it is helpful to some young children; it also contains more fat and protein than cow's milk does.

---

* The badger is the state animal of Wisconsin. Some say the name derived from the fact that the first lead miners in Wisconsin found shelter in caves for themselves and their families, much as some badgers do; hence, the name.

Name: _____ Date: _____

WISCONSIN: CODED PLACE NAMES

Solving the Map Puzzle

1. Twelve places on the map are identified by numerals. What are the names of those places? You can answer this question by doing the following:

a. Choose a numeral from the map.

b. Find the numeral in the list below.

c. Translate the dots and dashes that follow that numeral into letters according to the International Code.

d. Write the letters above the dots and dashes.

e. Carefully print the name of the place on the map.

Note: Number 1 has been done to help you get started.

International Code			
A •—	H ••••	O ———	V •••—
B —•••	I ••	P •——•	W •——
C —•—•	J •———	Q ——•—	X —••—
D —••	K —•—	R •—•	Y —•——
E •	L •—••	S •••	Z ——••
F ••—•	M ——	T —	
G ——•	N —•	U ••—	

1 — A •— S ••• H •••• L •—•• A •— N —• D —••

2 — _ — •• —— —— ••• | •••• •• | •—• •—•• •—•

3 — • •— ••— —•—• •—• •— | •• •—• • •

4 — •—— •— ••— ••• •— ••—•

5 — ——• •—• • • —• | —••• •— | —•——

6 — •— •——• •——• •—•• • — ——— | —•

7 — ——— ••• •••• —•— ——— ••• ••••

8 — •—•• •— —•— • | •—• •• | —• | —• | • | —••• | •— | ——• | ———

9 — •—•• •— —•—• •—• ——— ••• | ••• •

10 — ••• •••• • —••• ——— —•— —— | •— —•

11 — —— •— —•—• •• ••• ——— —•

12 — —— •• •—•• •—— •— ••— —•— • | •

97

MICHIGAN: PIONEER IN MOTOR VEHICLE PRODUCTION

🚗 Michigan is, by far, the United States' greatest automobile/truck manufacturing state. One reason for this is that Michigan gained an early start in the industry through the efforts of such inventors as Henry Ford. Ford organized the Ford Motor Company in 1903. After a period of experimentation he started mass production of his famous Model T, affectionately called the "Tin Lizzie." Other pioneers of the motor vehicle industry recognized his success and decided to locate in Michigan.

News of the growing automobile manufacturing industry attracted small businesses that supplied materials and parts for the vehicles. This, in turn, brought into the state people employed by such businesses and people seeking work. Workers and their families needed housing, food, clothing, and other products and services; so, supporting industries were established. This, of course, brought even more people into the region. The population of Michigan soared. In the period between 1910 and 1930, the number of people in Michigan grew from 2,810,000 to 4,842,000.

Michigan was also greatly helped in becoming the "Automobile Capital of the United States," as some call the state, because of its location. The mines that produced iron were located in nearby Minnesota and in Michigan itself. Iron was converted into steel in mills along the shores of the Great Lakes and Pittsburgh. The proximity of basic materials and the presence of local factories that could fashion the materials into parts and assembly plants where the parts could be put together into automobiles reduced production costs and fostered the industry.

Michigan's location on four of the Great Lakes; its central position within the United States; the rivers, railroads, and roads in the region; and, later, the establishment of the St. Lawrence Seaway—all decreased the potential cost of transporting the finished product to markets. All this helped to keep the prices of vehicles low so that average Americans could afford to buy them.

🚗 How many vehicles are on the roads in the United States, and what states have the most vehicles?

In a recent year, there were 190,362,000 automobiles, trucks, and buses in the United States. If these motor vehicles were distributed among the entire population of the United States, there would be one vehicle for every two people—including men, women and children. With the approximately 60,000,000 vehicles left over after such a distribution, we could give every person in Canada three vehicles—and there would still be some remaining.

The following table tells what states have the most vehicles.

State	Automobiles, Trucks, Buses
California	22,202,000
Texas	12,767,000
Florida	10,232,000
New York	9,780,000
Ohio	9,030,000
Pennsylvania	8,179,000
Illinois	7,982,000
Michigan	7,311,000

🚗 What countries are the leaders in motor vehicle production? It may surprise you to see that the United States is no longer number 1.

WORLD MOTOR VEHICLE PRODUCTION	
Country[1]	Automobile, Commerical Vehicles[2] Manufactured (1993)
Japan	11,227,545
United States	10,864,203
Germany	3,990,650
France	3,155,717
Canada	2,237,733
South Korea	2,050,058
1: Six leading countries	2: Trucks, buses, etc.

MICHIGAN: LAKES, CITIES, DISTANCES

1. Michigan is the only state that borders on four of the Great Lakes. Carefully label the lakes on the map.

A. Lake Superior
B. Lake Michigan
C. Lake Huron
D. Lake Erie

2. What three states border on Michigan?

_____

_____

_____

3. What is the name of the narrow strip of water that separates the southern part of Michigan from the northern part?

_____

4. Into what lake does each of the following rivers flow?

Au Sable R. _____

Kalamazoo R. _____

Muskegon R. _____

Manistee R. _____

5. What is the air distance in miles between each of the following cities?

Lansing–Saginaw _____

Lansing–Chicago _____

Lansing–Detroit _____

Lansing–Madison _____

Lansing–Ironwood _____

Lansing–Escanaba _____

6. Imagine you are in an airplane flying over Mt. Curwood. You are at an altitude of 5,000'. How many feet are there between you and the top of the mountain? _____ feet

7. Here is a challenge opportunity to practice using distance and direction on maps.

Draw a light line beginning at Detroit to Flint, southwest to Kalamazoo, north to Traverse City, northwest to Escanaba, northwest to Ironwood, east to Sault Ste. Marie, and south to Detroit.

How many miles is the entire round trip? _____

© 1996 by The Center for Applied Research in Education

IOWA: CORN FOR PEOPLE AND ANIMALS

Iowa is usually first or second in the amount of corn grown in a state. It switches positions with Illinois, although recently Illinois seems to be first more often. Of course other Corn Belt states—Indiana, Michigan, Minnesota, Missouri, Nebraska, Wisconsin, Ohio—are also great corn producers. People all over the world eat corn grown in the Corn Belt. The greatest importers of corn, such as Japan, are countries that have large populations but do not have enough land to grow the crops necessary to feed all their people.

Not all corn is the same; there are numerous varieties. **Sweet corn** is the variety that most people eat at the dinner table. **Dent corn** is the variety of corn that is fed to animals such as cows and hogs. It's not that humans couldn't eat dent corn; some do, but it doesn't have the tenderness or flavor of sweet corn.

Flint corn is a variety of corn that grows well in northern lands where the growing season is short. The kernels of flint corn are round and hard, much harder than those of dent corn or sweet corn. Flint corn can be eaten off the cob, but more often it is processed in some way and used in a variety of foods or made into various kinds of products. Because flint corn kernels have a variety of colors from white to red, it is often used as decoration, especially in the fall at Halloween. A common name for flint corn and other kinds of corn that have colored kernels is **Indian corn**.

It was the Indians of Middle America, chiefly the Mayans and Aztecs of what is now Mexico and Guatemala, who first grew and ate corn. The knowledge they gained by studying and experimenting with corn and the skills they developed in growing it gradually, over a period of hundreds of years, spread to all parts of North America. Corn, more than any other crop, helped the people of pre-Columbus America become less dependent upon hunting, fishing, and gathering (seeds, berries, roots) for their food supply.

Today, corn is one of the world's most important crops. It is grown in almost all parts of the world. You can gain an

LEADING CORN GROWING COUNTRIES	
Country	Tons* of Corn Grown in a Recent Year
United States	189,867,000
China	93,350,000
Brazil	22,604,000
Mexico	13,527,000
France	12,780,000
* Metric ton (2,204 lbs.)	

appreciation of just how important corn has become by studying the table above.

The total amount of corn grown throughout the world in a recent year was about 478,775,000 metric tons. As you can see in the table, the United States' share of that total was approximately 25%.

When people think of corn, very often they think of corn-on-the-cob with a spreading of butter and a sprinkling of salt. Or perhaps, they see corn as coming out of a can ready to be heated and served. But, there are dozens of by-products that are made from corn. Here are a few:

☞ Food for farm animals, which, after they have eaten it, becomes another form of food: milk from cows, beef from steers, pork from hogs, eggs from chickens, and so on

☞ Medicines such as penicillin, vitamins, and antibiotics

☞ Plastics, paper, textiles

☞ Alcohol used as an additive to gasoline

☞ Cornstarch for puddings, cakes, pie fillings

☞ Synthetic rubber

☞ Cosmetics, explosives, glue

In northern climates in winter cows cannot graze in fields, so they eat ground up corn plants—stalks, leaves, cobs, and kernels—all mixed together. The mix is called **silage**, and it is stored in tall, cylindrical, windowless towers, called **silos**, seen on farms. During the winter months when the cows are sheltered in a barn, farmers draw silage from the silo and feed it to their cows.

Name: _____ Date: _____

IOWA: RIVERS AND CITIES

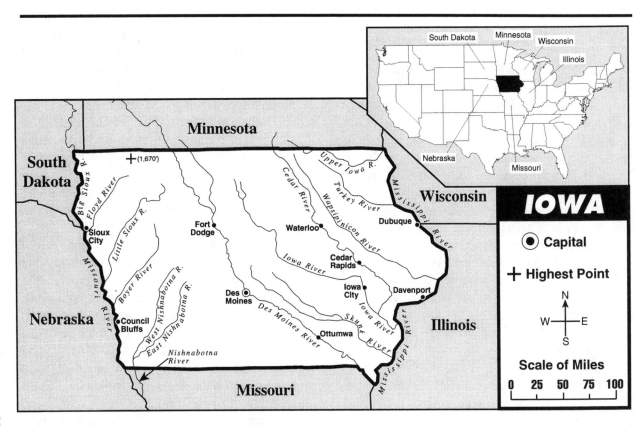

1. What state borders Iowa on the south?

_____

On the north? _____

2. What two states border Iowa on the east? _____ _____

On the west? _____

_____

3. Number the rivers listed below in the order from **north to south** in which they flow into the Mississippi River.

___ Skunk River   ___ Upper Iowa River

___ Turkey River   ___ Wapsipinicon River

___ Iowa River   ___ Des Moines River

4. Number the rivers listed below in the order from **north to south** in which they flow into the Missouri River.

___ Floyd River

___ Boyer River

___ Little Sioux River

___ Nishnabotna River

5. On what rivers are the following cities located?

Des Moines _____

Dubuque _____

Fort Dodge _____

Ottumwa _____

Davenport _____

Iowa City _____

Council Bluffs _____

Waterloo _____

Cedar Rapids _____

ILLINOIS: TRANSPORTATION HUB, HOME OF THREE PRESIDENTS

Transportation Hub

Chicago is the United States' third largest city, following New York and Los Angeles. The latest figures available (1994) tell us that there are approximately 2,784,000 people living in Chicago. This means that about one of every four people in the state live in the city. As in many large United States cities, the population of Chicago has decreased considerably in the past few years. In 1970, Chicago's population was 3,369,000; thus, the city has lost more than 585,000 people over a 24-year period.

Chicago has been called "The Crossroads of America" because it is such an important transportation center. Its Chicago-O'Hare International Airport is the busiest in the world in the number of passengers who use it: 65,091,168 in a recent year.

Chicago also has one of the most active ports in the United States. Ships enter and leave Chicago by means of the Great Lakes and St. Lawrence Seaway, or they can use the system of rivers and canals that lie between Chicago and the Gulf of Mexico's port of New Orleans, Louisiana. In a recent year more than 22,000,000 tons of cargo entered and left Chicago via ships.

Along with being the United States' number one air center, Chicago is also the country's busiest rail center. The city's location explains why this is so; it is in the center of a tremendous agricultural and manufacturing region. Beef, grain, steel, machinery, chemicals, and other products too numerous to mention are transported on Chicago's spiderweb of railroad tracks that spread out from the city. More than 25,000 freight cars and 1,200 passenger trains enter and leave the city every week.

Three Presidents from Illinois

Abraham Lincoln was born in Kentucky in 1809, but his family moved from his birthplace to Indiana. After a few years in Indiana the family moved to Illinois. Abe was 21 years old at the time. Illinois is very proud that Lincoln lived most of his life there. In fact, Illinois is often called "The Land of Lincoln." After Lincoln was assassinated in 1865, just a short time after the Civil War ended, his body was returned to Illinois and buried in a cemetery in Springfield.

There are many reminders of Lincoln in Illinois. His home in Springfield has been declared a national historic site. Another reminder of Lincoln is the restored village of New Salem, where Lincoln lived before he was married and where he managed the village store and was postmaster.

It was only four years after the death of Lincoln that another person who made his home in Illinois, Ulysses S. Grant, was elected President. Grant knew Lincoln well, for it was Lincoln who gave him command, toward the end of the Civil War, of all the Union armies. It was Grant who brought the war to a successful conclusion for the Union and who accepted General Robert E. Lee's surrender in April 1865.

Grant's home in Galena, Illinois, was made a state memorial in 1932. The house has been preserved and looks very much as it did, inside and outside, when Grant lived there. In 1881 Grant and his family moved to New York, where he died in 1885. Grant's body now lies in a beautiful tomb in New York City overlooking the Hudson River. The money to build the tomb was donated by thousands of people who respected his part in two wars, the War with Mexico and the Civil War, and his two terms as president.

A third president, Ronald Reagan, was born in Illinois in 1911. He spent his boyhood in Illinois and graduated from Eureka College. After graduation he became a sports announcer in a Des Moines, Iowa, radio station. In 1937 he moved to California, where he became a popular movie star. During World War II he served as a captain in the Army Air Force.

Reagan was interested in politics. He ran for governor of California and was elected in 1966. In 1980 he ran for the presidency and was elected. In 1984 he ran again and was reelected.

ILLINOIS: CITIES, RIVERS, AND LAKES

Print on the dashed lines the name of each place described.

1. Capital of Illinois:

_ _ _ _ _ _ _ _ _ _ _

2. Highest point in Illinois:

_ _ _ _ _ _ _

_ _ _ _ _

3. City approximately 40 miles east of Springfield: _ _ _ _ _ _ _

4. Rivers in order from north to south that join the Mississippi River:

_ _ _ _ _ _ _ _ _ _ _,

_ _ _ _,

_ _ _ _ _ _ _ _,

_ _ _ _ _ _ _ _,

_ _ _ _ _ _ _ _,

_ _ _ _ _

5. Two cities on Lake Michigan north of Chicago:

_ _ _ _ _ _ _ _,

_ _ _ _ _ _ _

6. City on Mississippi River opposite to St. Louis, Missouri:

_ _ _ _ _ _ _ _ _ _ _ _

7. Two states on Illinois' east boundary:

_ _ _ _ _ _ _,

_ _ _ _ _ _ _ _

8. River on which Peoria is located:

_ _ _ _ _ _ _ _

9. City approximately 80 miles north-west of Chicago:

_ _ _ _ _ _ _ _

Wisconsin
+ Charles Mound (1,235')
Waukegan
Rockford
Evanston
Aurora • Chicago
Iowa
Moline
Kankakee
Peoria
Bloomington
Champaign • Danville
Quincy Springfield ⊙
Decatur
Lake Shelbyville
Missouri
Missouri R.
St. Louis   E. St. Louis
Carlyle Lake
Rend Lake
Kaskaskia River
Little Wabash R.
Wabash River
Indiana
Mississippi River
Ohio R.
Metropolis **Kentucky**
Ohio R.
Lake Michigan

ILLINOIS
⊙ Capital   + Mountain Peak
Scale of Miles
0   40   80

10. Two lakes connected by the Kaskaskia River:

_ _ _ _ _ _ _,

_ _ _ _ _ _ _ _ _ _ _ _

11. Two states on Illinois' west boundary:

_ _ _ _ _ _ _ _,

_ _ _ _

INDIANA: A GUIDE TO ITS STATE PARKS

The facility chart to the right lists 19 of Indiana's state parks. The map shows where the parks are located. Do you enjoy paddle boating? If you do, the chart will tell you which state parks have that accommodation, and many other things, as well.

The information below tells more about six of the parks.

INDIANA STATE PARKS FACILITY CHART

Park	Nearest Town	Acreage	Bicycle Rental	Camping	Canoe Rental	Cross Country Ski Rental	Cultural Arts Program	Dumping Station	Family Housekeeping Cabins	Fishing	Group Camp Buildings	Hiking	Inn	Inn Accommodations	Museum or Visitors Center	Naturalist Service	Paddle Boat Rental	Picnicking	Playground Equipment	Recreation Building Rental	Rowboat Barn (horseback riding)	Saddle Barn (horseback riding)	Swimming	Tennis and Other Games	Toboggan	Water Skiing	Wildlife Exhibit
Bass Lake	Knox	22		•						•								•					•				
Brown County	Nashville	15,543	•(H)	•				•	•	•		•	•	•	•	•		•	•	•	•		•			•
Chain O' Lakes	Albion	2,678	•	•	•			•	•	•		•				•		•	•	•			•			
Clifty Falls	Madison	1,360		•				•		•		•	•	•	•			•	•	•			•			
Harmonie	New Harmony	3,465	•	•				•	•	•					•			•	•	•			•	•		
Indiana Dunes	Chesterton	2,182		•			•	•		•		•			•	•		•	•	•			•			
Lincoln	Lincoln City	1,747		•	•			•		•		•			•	•		•	•	•			•			
McCormick's Creek	Spencer	1,833		•				•	•	•		•	•	•	•	•		•	•	•			•			
Mounds	Anderson	259		•	•			•		•		•			•	•		•	•	•			•			•
Ouabache	Bluffton	1,065	•(H)	•	•			•		•		•				•		•	•	•	•		•			•
Pokagon	Angola	1,203	•(H)	•	•	•		•		•		•	•	•	•	•		•	•	•	•		•	•		
Potato Creek	North Liberty	3,840	•(H)	•				•	•	•		•			•	•		•	•	•	•		•			
Shades	Waveland	3,084		•				•		•		•				•		•	•	•						
Shakamak	Jasonville	1,766	•	•	•			•	•	•		•				•		•	•	•			•		•	
Spring Mill	Mitchell	1,319		•				•	•	•		•	•	•	•	•		•	•	•			•			
Tippecanoe River	Winamac	2,761	•(H)	•	•			•		•		•			•	•		•	•	•	•					
Turkey Run	Marshall	2,382		•				•	•	•		•	•	•	•	•		•	•	•	•		•			
Versailles	Versailles	5,903	•(H)	•	•			•		•		•				•		•	•	•	•		•			
Whitewater	Liberty	1,710	•(H)•	•	•			•		•		•			•	•		•	•	•			•		•	

H= denotes additional horsecamp available

Indiana Dunes: Winds cause the dunes to slowly change positions. Sometimes interesting things are uncovered as, for example, buried forests. But the park is not all sand dunes. There are forests, and it offers a variety of activities, including swimming in Lake Michigan.

Mounds: Thousands of years ago burial mounds were created by Indians of the region. Many remnants of the Indians' civilization have been uncovered, for example, smoking pipes, bracelets, and tools.

Clifty Falls: Hikers can view beautiful falls and a deep canyon. On warm days one can sit amid the many rapids and enjoy cool water.

Spring Mill: There is plenty to see in this park, including a restored pioneer village, caves, and a memorial that honors astronaut Gus Grisson.

Lincoln: Abe Lincoln lived in Indiana from the time he was seven to twenty-one years old. Those who want to know more about Lincoln can sit in a 1,500 seat amphitheater and learn much about his early life by watching an interesting presentation.

Turkey Run: If one's interests include covered bridges, fast running water, or a specially developed nature center, Turkey Run is the place to go. Why *Turkey* Run? Indiana is famous for turkeys; in a recent year farmers raised some 288,000 pounds of the Thanksgiving bird. Indiana also has many wild turkeys in its woods and fields.

INDIANA: RIVERS, HIGHWAYS, AND CITIES

Most of the items in the **Places** column can be matched with one of the items in the **Descriptions** column. Write the number of the **Places** item on the line before the matching item in **Descriptions**. There are two extra listings in the **Places** column.

Places

1. New Albany
2. Eel River
3. Vincennes
4. Bloomington
5. US Highway 30
6. Chicago
7. Gary
8. Richmond
9. Interstate Highway 64
10. Ohio
11. Kentucky
12. Ohio River
13. Illinois
14. Indianapolis
15. Terre Haute
16. Lake Michigan
17. Anderson, Muncie
18. Lafayette
19. Wabash River
20. Kankakee River

Descriptions

___ City northwest of Gary on Lake Michigan

___ City at intersection of Interstate Highways 65 and 64

___ Two cities on the White River as it approaches Indianapolis

___ State to Indiana's west

___ Forms Illinois' southern boundary

___ A tributary river to the White River

___ City about ten miles northwest of Monroe Lake

___ City at eastern end of US Highway 40

___ Indiana state capital

___ City at the northern end of Interstate Highway 65

___ City about 40 miles west of Kokomo

___ Lake on Indiana's northern boundary

___ US Highway on which Fort Wayne is located

___ Southernmost city on Wabash River

___ State to Indiana's south

___ East-west Interstate Highway in southern Indiana

___ State to Indiana's east

___ City where US Highway 40 crosses the Wabash River

OHIO: THE OHIO RIVER AND ITS WATERSHED

The Ohio River

The Ohio River and its tributaries have been and still are among the most important geographical elements in the United States. The role the river played in helping pioneers move westward for some 1,000 miles is well-known. Its present use as a waterway to transport as much as 175,000,000 tons of products a year between Pittsburgh and Cairo, Illinois, where it joins the Mississippi River, makes it one of the busiest "highways" in the country.

Following are some interesting facts about the Ohio River:

❑ If the Allegheny river, which joins with the Monongahela River at Pittsburgh to form the Ohio River, is added to the Ohio's length, the total flow of the two rivers is more than 1,300 miles.

❑ The Ohio River flows through or along the borders of six states—Pennsylvania, Ohio, West Virginia, Kentucky, Indiana, and Illinois.

❑ Numerous cities, centers of population and industry, are located on or close to the river, including Pittsburgh, PA; Wheeling and Cincinnati, OH; Huntington, WV; Louisville, KY; and Evansville, TN.

❑ The navigability of the Ohio River has been considerably improved since Indian canoes and pioneer flatboats floated on its waters. Shallow stretches have been dredged deeper, and numerous canals and locks have been constructed to accommodate large tugboats and barges.

❑ Prior to the early 1900s, the Ohio River caused considerable flood damage to cities, towns, and farms along its banks. People dreaded the coming of heavy spring rains because the danger of floods was always present. Finally, the federal government decided that something had to be done to control the river. Dams were constructed on the rivers that flowed into the Ohio River. The dams hold back water; then, when the danger of flooding is over, the backed-up water is gradually released.

Other helpful flood control measures included building dikes along low places in the river's banks, and clearing and deepening channels so that more water could be accommodated and helped to flow freely. Today, the annual flood damage has been all but eliminated, although the threat still exists.

❑ A **watershed** can be described as an area bounded by high land within which most of the precipitation that falls drains into a stream. A small watershed may be part of a larger watershed or, as it is sometimes called, a **basin**. A watershed takes its name from the stream which serves as the main drain. Thus, the Ohio River Watershed has the Ohio River as its final conduit or "drain pipe." This watershed is made up of thousands of small rivulets, brooks, and streams, and large rivers. The Wabash River, the Cumberland River, and the Tennessee River—all of which are themselves major watersheds—are part of the Ohio River Watershed. In all, this watershed is spread over parts of fourteen states and some 200,000 square miles of land.

As large as the Ohio River Watershed is, it is part of the Mississippi River Watershed. This huge basin includes streams and rivers between the Appalachian Mountains to the east, the Rocky Mountains to the west, Canada to the north, and the eventual receiver of the Mississippi's water, the Gulf of Mexico, to the south.

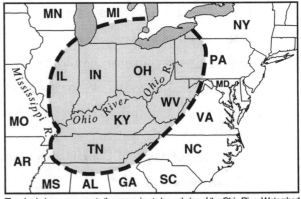

The shaded area represents the approximate boundaries of the Ohio River Watershed.

OHIO: LOCATIONS ON THE MAP

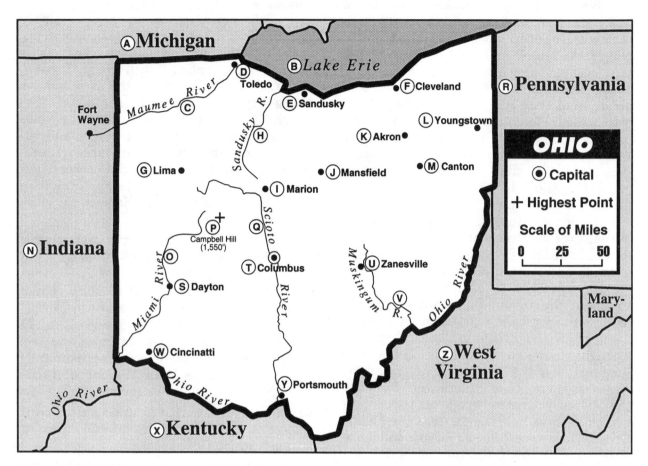

The places and things shown on the map have a circled letter near them. On the line or lines before each description below write the letter from the map that best fits the description.

__ City northwest of Campbell Hill

__ State on Ohio's west

__ River connecting Fort Wayne and Toledo

__ Capital of Ohio

__ __ __ Three states, not including Ohio, that have the Ohio River on their borders

__ City on the Muskingum River

__ State to Ohio's north

__ Ohio's highest point

__ City located close to where the Miami River leaves Ohio

__ __ __ Three cities on Lake Erie's shore

__ City about 53 miles east of Columbus

__ River that flows southwest out of Ohio and joins the Ohio River

__ River flowing north into Lake Erie

__ City northwest of Canton and west of Youngstown

__ State to Ohio's southwest

__ __ Two cities that end with "ton"

__ City about 215 miles south of Toledo

MISSOURI: THE MISSOURI RIVER

Before 1800, little was known about the Missouri River and the land through which it flows. However, when the United States bought the land from France—a transaction that became known as the Louisiana Purchase—Americans wanted to know more about what they had purchased. Questions were asked: Was there good farm land to be had? Was there gold in the hills? Were the Indians friendly? Was the river navigable? Was it possible that a safe overland route connecting the Atlantic Ocean to the Pacific Ocean could be built?

Thomas Jefferson, who was President at that time and who was mainly responsible for the Louisiana purchase, wanted answers to these questions and others. He arranged for an expedition to explore the Missouri River and the surrounding country. The men he chose to lead the expedition were Meriwether Lewis and William Clark. They were to begin their journey from St. Louis near the junction of the Mississippi River and the Missouri River. Their orders were to follow the Missouri River to its sources and, if possible, continue on to the coasts of the Pacific Ocean. They were to keep a journal and make a record of all the things they observed.

Lewis and Clark and their carefully chosen companions began their long journey in the spring of 1804. Some 18 months later, November 1805, they had crossed the Rocky Mountains and reached the Pacific Ocean. After a short stay during the worst months of the winter they began their return journey. This time they were traveling downstream, so their progress was much faster. They arrived in St. Louis in September, 1806—much to the surprise of many people who thought they had perished.

Their work had many positive results. Most important, perhaps, was that the knowledge and experience they gained encouraged others to settle in the new land. So many settlers entered the Louisiana Purchase that in a few years several new states were formed. In 1821, 15 years after the Lewis and Clark expedition, Missouri became the twenty-first state to enter the Union.

The mighty Missouri River, second in size only to the Mississippi River, divides Missouri into two distinct parts. The southern part, which makes up approximately two-thirds of the state, is a region of plateau, high hills and narrow valleys. And, as is often found in places with rough terrain, there are numerous caves, the most famous being Crystal Caverns in southeast Missouri. The northern one-third of the state consists of rolling hills, wide plains, and numerous streams small and large (Platte River, Chariton River, and Salt River). Jefferson City, Missouri's capital, is located on the Missouri River, as is Kansas City, the state's largest city.

Following are some interesting Missouri River facts:

❏ The river is 2,315 miles long. From where the Missouri River joins the Mississippi River to the Gulf of Mexico is 1,171 miles; so, the combined length of the two rivers is 3,486 miles. This is approximately 1,000 miles more than the air distance from New York to San Francisco.

❏ The Missouri River has significant effects on the seven states around which or through which it flows.

Flows Within	Forms Part of the Border Between
Montana (source)	Nebraska & South Dakota
North Dakota	Nebraska & Iowa
South Dakota	Nebraska & Missouri
Missouri	Kansas & Missouri

❏ Four state capitals are located on the Missouri River: Helena, Montana; Bismarck, North Dakota; Pierre, South Dakota; Jefferson City, Missouri.

❏ The Missouri River is a wonderful highway for products to and from the farms and industries along its path. But, the river is more than a highway. The waters stored behind the numerous dams on the Missouri and its tributaries are sources of hydroelectric power, flood control, and irrigation. Fort Peck Dam on the Missouri is the world's largest earth-filled dam. It stretches almost four miles across the river.

Name: _____ Date: _____

MISSOURI: FINDING RIVERS, CITIES, AND STATES ON A MAP

All the places required to complete the crossword puzzle are shown on the map. Wherever there are two words that tell the name of a place, a single space has been left open between the first and second word.

ACROSS

1. City in southwest Missouri

3. River that joins the Missouri River north of Kansas City

5. City in southeast Missouri: Poplar _____

9. State on Missouri's southwest border (abbreviated)

10. Tulsa is a city in the state of _____

11. State east of Missouri and north of Kentucky (abbreviated)

13. State east of Missouri and south of Kentucky

14. City close to where the Missouri River joins the Mississippi River: St. _____

DOWN

1. Capital of Missouri

2. State west of Missouri and north of Kansas

4. City about 25 miles north of where the Ohio River joins the Mississippi River

6. State on Missouri's southern border

7. River that joins the Missouri River about 90 miles east of Kansas City

8. Mountain that is Missouri's highest point

12. State west of Missouri and south of Nebraska

MISSOURI CROSSWORD PUZZLE

Great Plains States

GREAT PLAINS STATES: CAPITALS, MAJOR CITIES, AND RIVERS

1.   On the map print the names of the states, as follows:

A North Dakota _____

B South Dakota _____

C Nebraska _____

D Kansas _____

E Oklahoma _____

F Texas _____

2.   On the blank lines next to the names of the states above, print the names of their capitals.

3.   On the map, label the following:

G Gulf of Mexico

H Canada

I Rio Grande

J Mexico

K Platte River

L Arkansas River

M Red River

N Brazos River

Note: Arrows on rivers indicate direction of flow; dashed (---) lines are for printing.

4.   In which state is each of the following cities?

Wichita: _____

San Antonio: _____

Sioux Falls: _____

Omaha: _____

Houston: _____

Fargo: _____

Dallas: _____

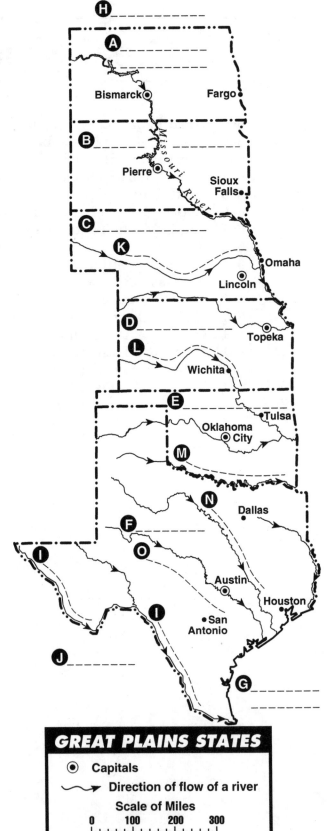

© 1996 by The Center for Applied Research in Education

GREAT PLAINS STATES

◉   **Capitals**

⌇→   **Direction of flow of a river**

Scale of Miles

0   100   200   300

Name: _____ Date: _____

GREAT PLAINS STATES: A TABLE OF FACTS

FACTS ABOUT THE PLAINS STATES				
State and Capital (North to South)	**Population**	**Area in Square Miles with Rank Shown in Parentheses ( )***	**Highest Point with Elevation Shown in Parentheses ( )**	**Nickname**
North Dakota (Bismarck)	638,000	70,704 (19)	White Butte (3,506')	Peace Garden State
South Dakota (Pierre)	696,004	75,896 (17)	Harney Peak (7,242')	Coyote State or Mount Rushmore State
Nebraska (Lincoln)	1,578,385	77,358 (16)	Johnson Township (5,426')	Cornhusker State
Kansas (Topeka)	2,477,574	82,282 (15)	Mount Sunflower (4,039')	Sunflower State
Oklahoma (Oklahoma City)	3,145,585	69,903 (20)	Black Mesa (4,973')	Sooner State
Texas (Austin)	16,986,510	268,601 (2)	Guadalupe Peak (8,749')	Lone Star State
* Includes total of land and water				

1. Fill the blank squares with names from the table. Notice that before each line is an abbreviation that gives you a hint as to the kind of words that should be printed in the spaces. **M** stands for the name of the **highest point** in a state; **S** stands for the **name** of a state; **N** stands for the **nickname** of a state.

2. **Numbers Challenge**

a. How many more people does Texas have than all of the other Plains States put together? _____

b. Three states have elevations (height above sea level) of more than one mile (5,280'). How much more than a mile above sea level is the highest point in

South Dakota? _____

Nebraska? _____

Texas? _____

GREAT PLAINS STATES: MEASURING DISTANCES WITH LATITUDE

The activity on this page will help your students:

☑ gain a better understanding of the immense distances in the Plains States,

☑ practice using latitude as a means of measuring distances,

☑ become better acquainted with place names in the Plains States.

Procedure

1. Explain that one degree of latitude on any line of longitude equals about 70 miles. Example:

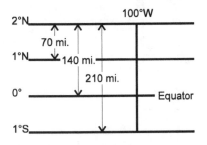

2. ***Practice Problems***

a. From the southernmost city in the Plains States—Brownsville, (approx. 26°N)*—to the 49°N line of latitude (boundary between Canada and United States) is how many miles?

Solution:

(1) Subtract 26° from 49°, or 23°.

(2) Multiply 23° × 70 miles, or 1,610 miles.

3. ***Additional Problems***

a. What is the distance in miles between:

✎ Houston (30°N) and Kansas City (39°N)? _____ miles

✎ Austin (30°N) and Fort Worth (33°N)? _____ miles

✎ Lincoln (41°N) and Sioux City (44°N)? _____ miles

✎ Wichita (38°N) and Oklahoma City (35°N)? _____ miles

---

* All latitudes have been rounded to the nearest degree.

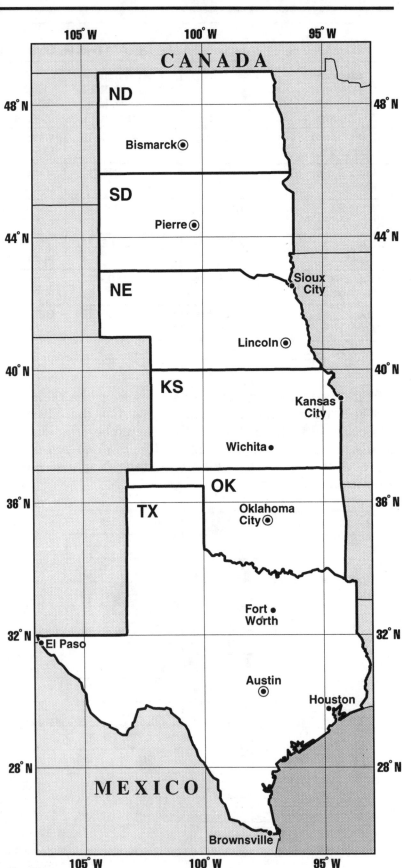

GREAT PLAINS STATES: INTERESTING FACTS

The activity on this page has been designed to help your students learn some basic facts about the Great Plains States and, concomitantly, practice the work-study skill of classifying/categorizing information under specific headings.

Procedure: 1. Photocopy the bottom portion of this page and distribute.

2. Students read the facts and then decide in which category they best belong. Then, they write the numbers of the facts in the spaces below the headings. Number 1 has been categorized to help students get started.

3. You may want to have your students work in cooperative groups of two.

Facts about the Great Plains States

1. The tallest structure—not a building—in the Great Plains States is a TV tower in North Dakota: 2,063' high.

2. Texas has a shoreline on the Gulf of Mexico that is 3,359 miles long.

3. The deepest oil well in the United States is in Oklahoma: 31,441' deep.

4. Texas is the greatest cotton-producing state in the United States: 5,148,000 bales in a recent year; each bale weighs 460 lbs.

5. Of all the Great Plains States, North Dakota has the lowest average annual precipitation (rain, snow): about 16".

6. The lowest temperature recorded in the Great Plains States: -44°F, Bismarck, ND.

7. Oklahoma has more Indian reservations than any other Great Plains State: 36. It has a greater Indian population than any other state in the United States: 252,000.

8. Kansas grew more wheat in 1993 than did any other state: 388,000,000 bushels.

9. "Dakota," as in South Dakota and North Dakota, is an Indian word meaning "friend."

10. North Dakota produced more barley, a grain, than any other state: 117,600,000 bushels in a recent year.

11. The state flower of Nebraska is the goldenrod.

12. Two United States Presidents were born in Texas: Dwight D. Eisenhower and Lyndon B. Johnson.

13. The highest peak in the United States *east* of the Rocky Mountains is in south Dakota: Harney Peak, 7,242'.

14. Jim Thorpe, a Native American, thought by some to be the world's greatest athlete ever, was born in Oklahoma.

15. Omaha, Nebraska, was the starting point, in 1865, of the eastern end of the Union Pacific railroad.

16. North Dakota is said to be located exactly in the center of North America.

17. There are only three states—Alaska, Vermont, and Wyoming—that have fewer people than North Dakota, which had a 1993 population of 634,935.

18. Texas produces more oil than does any other state: in a recent year 651 million barrels.

19. On their exploratory expedition of the Louisiana Purchase, Lewis and Clark spent their first winter with the Mandan Indians in west central South Dakota, 1804–1805.

20. The first Europeans to explore what is now Kansas were Spaniards led by Francisco de Coronado in 1541.

21. The growing season in the Great Plains States varies from south to north: 210–240 days in south Texas, 150–180 days in Kansas, 90–120 days in most of North Dakota.

GREAT PLAINS FACT CLASSIFICATION TABLE							
History	Geography	Population	Personalities	Agriculture	Mining	Climate	Miscellaneous
							1

Name: _____ Date: _____

NORTH DAKOTA: ROAD DISTANCES

The table below will help bring more understanding of distances within North Dakota, as well as from four major cities to North Dakota. The distances shown in the table are road distances. Roads go up and down hills, around curves, around large bodies of water, and so on. Distances by air from one place to another are generally much shorter because they are "as the crow flies," that is, over all obstacles.

Here is an example: The distance by road from Seattle, Washington, to Fargo, North Dakota, is 1,427 miles; by air it is 1,312 miles, a difference of 115 miles.

Distances Within North Dakota

Following are some practice problems in using the table:

What is the road distance between:
- Minot and Fargo? _____ miles
- Williston and Grand Forks? _____ miles
- Bismarck and Grand Forks? _____ miles
- Fargo and Williston? _____ miles
- Bismarck and Minot _____ miles
- Devils Lake and Fargo? _____ miles

Distances to and from North Dakota

What is the road distance between:
- New York and Bismarck? _____ miles
- Chicago and Bismarck? _____ miles
- Los Angeles and Bismarck? _____ miles
- Seattle and Bismarck? _____ miles

© 1996 by The Center for Applied Research in Education

ROAD DISTANCES INSIDE AND OUTSIDE NORTH DAKOTA						
	Bismarck	**Devils Lake**	**Fargo**	**Grand Forks**	**Minot**	**Williston**
Bismarck		180	191	276	114	243
Chicago	837		646			
Fargo	191	163		78	260	400
Grand Forks	276	89	78		210	338
Los Angeles	1669		1839			
Minot	114	121	260	210		126
New York	1659		1468			
Seattle	1236		1427			
Williston	243	249	400	338	126	

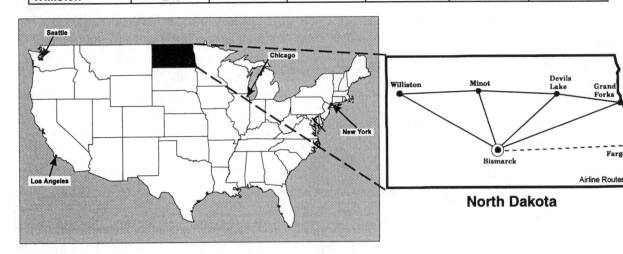

North Dakota

Name: _____ Date: _____

NORTH DAKOTA: RIVERS, LAKES, CITIES

Study the map to find the answers to the questions that follow. Circle either "Yes" or "No" to answer each question.

1. Is Bismarck, the capital of North Dakota, located on the Missouri River?   **Yes**   **No**

2. Does the Yellowstone River join the Missouri River from the north?   **Yes**   **No**

3. Is South Dakota the only state that borders North Dakota on the south?   **Yes**   **No**

4. Is the northern border of North Dakota more than 275 miles from east to west?   **Yes**   **No**

5. Does the Maple River first flow south and then make a turn toward the northwest?   **Yes**   **No**

6. Is the highest point in North Dakota more than one-half mile above sea level?   **Yes**   **No**

7. Is Garrison Dam at the eastern end of Garrison Reservoir?   **Yes**   **No**

8. Does the Red River of the north form all of North Dakota's eastern boundary?   **Yes**   **No**

9. Is Sentinel Butte more than 800' lower in elevation than White Butte?   **Yes**   **No**

10. Is South Dakota's western boundary longer than its northern boundary?   **Yes**   **No**

11. Is Jamestown at the southern end of Jamestown Reservoir?   **Yes**   **No**

12. If you were using the Missouri River to go to Williston from Bismarck would you be going downstream?   **Yes**   **No**

13. Could you sail a boat on the Missouri River from Bismarck to Williston without taking the boat out of the water?   **Yes**   **No**

14. Does the Red Lake River flow into the Red River of the North?   **Yes**   **No**

15. Is the distance from north to south in North Dakota between 180 and 200 miles?   **Yes**   **No**

16. Does the Province of Alberta (Canada) border North Dakota?   **Yes**   **No**

SOUTH DAKOTA: LAND DIVISIONS, SPECIAL ATTRACTIONS

South Dakota Divided by the Missouri River

The Missouri River, flowing from north to south through South Dakota, divides the state into two roughly equal parts. The parts are quite different in most regards.

The eastern part:

❑ is made up mostly of rolling plains;

❑ is dotted with numerous glacial ponds and lakes as well as huge artificial lakes created by backing up river water behind dams;

❑ has tall grasses wherever they are allowed to grow wild;

❑ has great fields of wheat, barley, corn, and soy beans;

❑ has large herds of beef and dairy cattle;

❑ has flocks of sheep producing wool and mutton;

❑ has some two million hogs;

❑ has few forested areas (however, trees can be found along the banks of rivers and streams);

❑ has mostly small towns, with the exception of Sioux Falls, which has a population of 100,000 people. Even the capital, Pierre, has only about 13,000 people.

The western part:

❑ is much rougher land with numerous ravines, steep hills, and flat-sided buttes that stand out like shoe boxes on top of a table;

❑ has some rolling plains, which are much higher than those in the east;

❑ has high mountains, including Harney Peak, which has an elevation of 7,242' above sea level;

❑ has some forests, mostly in the Black Hills in the west central part of the state, which are composed mainly of coniferous (cone bearing) trees—including spruce, pine, and juniper;

❑ has small towns and only one large city, Rapid City, which has a population of about 45,000.

Perhaps the most remarkable region of South Dakota is in the southwestern part of the state, an area known as the "Bad Lands." The land well-deserves the title— not because outlaws, gunfighters, and "bad" people lived there—because of the nature of the land formations and, especially, the poor soil. Winds, rains, and floods have washed out the topsoil leaving clay, subsoil, rock, and gravel. The area has been called "wild," wild and arid enough to fit the expression **semidesert**. It's difficult to make a living in the region by growing crops, so the most important form of agriculture is concerned with herding animals.

South Dakota's Black Hills

South Dakota's most important industry is agriculture. Its second most important industry is tourism. Its numerous state and national parks attract hundreds of thousands of visitors each year.

One of the most popular of South Dakota's attractions is a hilly, mountainous region in the western part of the state, the Black Hills, named by the Indians who lived there. When the Indians looked westward from the plains, especially in the early evening when the sun was behind the mountains, the forested mountains appeared very dark; hence, the name Black Hills.

The Black Hills are famous for several things, including gold mines. The Homestake mine located there is the largest gold-producing mine in North America or South America. Even today, after more than 115 years of extracting gold, the Homestake mine produces about one-third of all the gold mined in the United States.

The Mount Rushmore National Memorial in the Black Hills is another place tourists enjoy visiting. The heads of four great Americans—George Washington, Thomas Jefferson, Abraham Lincoln, and Theodore Roosevelt—have been carved on the side of a solid granite mountain. The heads are about sixty feet high from chin to the top of the head. To gain a better idea of the immensity of the heads, the largest statues in the entire world, imagine the statues as complete from head to toe. Such statues would be more than 350' tall, or more than the length of a football field stood on end.

SOUTH DAKOTA: RIVERS, BORDERING STATES, MOUNTAINS

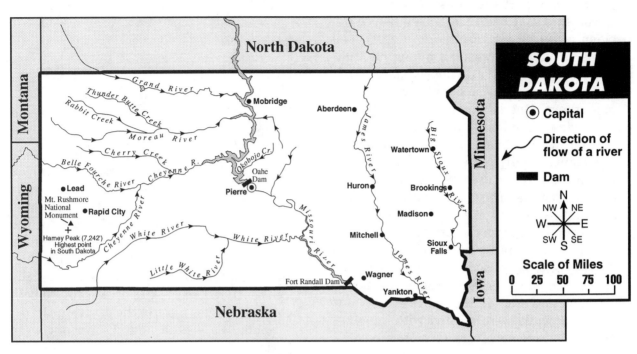

© 1996 by The Center for Applied Research in Education

1. Complete each of the following sentences by drawing a circle around the word in parentheses that best completes the sentence. *Note*: The arrows on the rivers indicate *downstream*.

a. The Moreau River flows in a general (**westward, eastward**) direction.

b. The Little White River first flows (**eastward, westward**), and then runs toward the (**north, south**).

c. The Cheyenne River is joined by the Belle Fourche River and Cherry Creek, both of which flow (**eastward, westward**).

d. The James River is a (**north-to-south, south-to-north**) flowing river.

2. What two streams contribute water to the Moreau River? _____

_____

3. What community on the James River most likely has the highest elevation? ____

_____

4. If you were in a boat at the source of the Big Sioux River, could you float without

oars or power to Watertown?

_____ Yes _____ No

Explain your answer: _____

_____

5. What is the name of the dam north of Pierre on the Missouri River that holds back river water and widens the river?

_____

6. What is the name of the dam on the Missouri River just west of the town of

Wagner? _____

7. What is Harney Peak's elevation?

_____

8. Starting at the north and proceeding in a *clockwise* direction, write the names of the states that surround South Dakota.

a. _____ d. _____

b. _____ e. _____

c. _____ f. _____

NEBRASKA: SETTLING THE PLAINS—A SCARCITY OF WOOD

The Great Plains presented a number of problems that had to be solved before the region could be settled and developed. The problems were so great and numerous that, at first, pioneers were anxious to go through the plains as quickly as possible rather than settle there. One of the most difficult problems was providing shelter from the weather, wild animals, and human enemies such as unfriendly Indians and outlaws.

In the East, houses were constructed of wood and stone. Those two materials were extremely scarce on the plains. But, American ingenuity provided substitutes. The only raw material that was thick, tough, and plentiful was grass sod. So, the settlers dug out the sod, cut it into rectangles about two feet long, and stacked the sod row upon row until four walls were created with openings left for windows and doors. (Fig. 1)

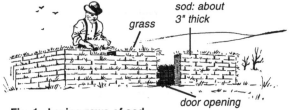

Fig. 1. Laying rows of sod

For a roof the builders took the stoutest limb available and used it as a ridge pole. Then, they put rafters in place and laid branches across the rafters. Then, sod was laid on the branches. (Fig. 2)

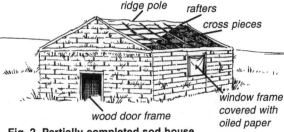

Fig. 2. Partially completed sod house

The result was a snug house, or "soddie," that was warm in winter and cool in summer. And, as a reward for all the backbreaking work, in the spring of the year prairie flowers would blossom from the roof and side walls, making the soddie a kind of "flower-house."

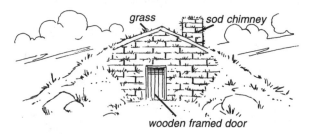

Fig. 3. Dugout house

Another way to provide shelter was to dig a hole in a hillside, making a kind of cave. The sides of the hole became the walls of the shelter. The front of the hole was walled with sod with an opening left for the door. A roof was provided in much the same way as for a sod house. The door of the dugout, as that kind of shelter was called, usually faced south where the sun could provide both light and heat for most of the day. (Fig. 3)

Both the soddie and the dugout were considered temporary homes. After the railroads from the East penetrated the region, they brought materials such as lumber, stone, and nails, so that permanent homes could be built. But, in the time between the early 1800s and the end of the Civil War (1865), the soddies and dugouts provided very satisfactory housing.

Another problem resulting from the scarcity of wood was fencing. Fencing was needed to keep animals from wandering away from the farms and to prevent animals, especially buffalo and free-ranging beef cattle, from trampling field crops and gardens. A really satisfactory answer to this problem was not found until the invention of barbed wire in 1874. The wire, stretched from post to post, limited the movement of animals into or out of prohibited areas.

Finding fuel for cooking food and providing heat in winter was another problem caused by the lack of wood. Sometimes food could be cooked by burning tightly wrapped and tied bundles of grass. Still another method of providing fire was to burn dried buffalo dung or "chips." Chips not only burned steadier and longer than grass, but also were plentiful in the plains, which was once the home of millions of buffalo.

NEBRASKA: ROAD MILEAGE AND AIR DISTANCE

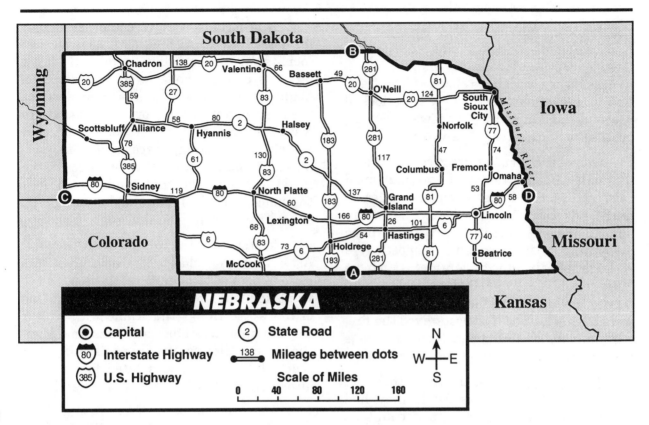

1. What is the distance in road miles on US-20 from

🖎 Chadron to Valentine? _____ miles

🖎 Valentine to Bassett? _____ miles

🖎 Bassett to O'Neill?_____ miles

🖎 O'Neill to So. Sioux City? _____ miles

What is the total distance on US-20 from Chadron to So. Sioux City?_____ miles

2. What is the total distance in road miles on I-80 from

🖎 Omaha to Lincoln? _____ miles

🖎 Lincoln to Lexington?_____ miles

🖎 Lexington to North Platte? _____ miles

🖎 North Platte to Sidney? _____ miles

What is the total distance in road miles on I-80 from Omaha to Sidney? _____ miles

3. Follow the route outlined below, then answer the final question.

a. Start at Hastings and drive north to Grand Island.

b. From Grand Island drive west to the last labeled city on SR-2.

c. Turn south on US-385 and drive to the next labeled city.

d. Turn east and drive to the next labeled city.

e. Where are you?_____

4. What is the air distance from south (Point A) to north (Point B) in Nebraska?

_____ miles

5. What is the air distance from west (Point C) to east (Point D) in Nebraska?

_____ miles

6. In what two cities would you expect to find bridges over the Missouri River from

Nebraska to Iowa? _____

KANSAS: DANGERS OF THE PLAINS

Pioneers who settled in what is now Kansas and other Great Plains states had to have exceptional courage and resourcefulness if they were to be successful settlers. The natural environment may have looked peaceful—and in many ways it was—but the possibility of disaster was always present.

One of the greatest dangers was fire. It took only a spark to start a blaze that would rage across hundreds of square miles of grassland. Aided by the winds, which were almost always present, a fire could burn everything in its path until stopped by a river or a rain storm. Animals such as buffalo and antelope fled before searing flames, trying to run faster than the fields were burning. Even if they survived the fire, the problem of finding grass to eat was present; the fire may have consumed it all.

As for the farmers, the crops they had so carefully planted, the cattle they had raised, and even their homes could be destroyed in a matter of minutes. What did the farmers do when they saw smoke on the horizon and the wind blowing toward them? They hitched their oxen or horses to plows and then plowed furrows around their homes and crops as quickly as possible. Their hope was that when the fire reached the plowed ground it would not be able to leap over it and would either die out or go around. (Fig. 1)

Swarms of locusts were another danger farmers faced. Every few years, as in a cycle, locusts by the millions might fly to a farmer's corn or wheat crop, settle on the blades of wheat or stalks of corn and eat them down to nothing but stubble. There wasn't much that could be done to prevent locusts from coming except, if time permitted, to build smoky fires on edges of the fields. The hope was that winds would blow the smoke over the fields and discourage the swarm from settling on the crops. (Fig. 2)

Winters on the plains were severe. Aside from the cold itself, which often was close to zero in temperature, there were the winds to make the cold feel even colder. One of the worse things that came with winter was blinding snow storms or blizzards. More than one settler caught in a blizzard never reached home and was later found dead after warmer weather melted the deep snow.

Venturing out of the house in a blizzard to perform a chore, such as milking cows, could also lead to death. To prevent getting lost in the blinding snow, settlers tied ropes to themselves and their homes; they could always follow the rope back to the entrances of their soddies or dugouts. Another method used to ensure against getting lost was to tie ropes from the house to outbuildings such as barns. By hanging onto the ropes they could guide themselves to safety. (Fig. 3)

Fig. 1 The plains farmer fights to keep his farm from burning.

Fig. 2 Locusts by the million could easily eat a field of wheat

Fig. 3 A blizzard on the plains could kill many animals and people

Name: _____ Date: _____

KANSAS: COMMUNITIES AND QUADRANTS

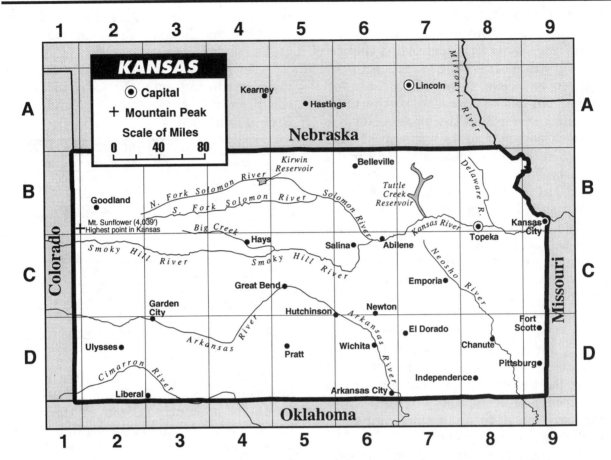

The map of Kansas is divided into sections called *quadrants*. Places on maps can be more easily found if their locations are narrowed down to a quadrant. For example: Abilene, Kansas, is located in quadrant C6. Notice that the letter of the quadrant is listed first and is followed by the number of the quadrant.

Imagine that you are making an index of Kansas cities and their quadrants for a map. The communities listed in the table are alphabetically arranged. In the blank space before each place, write the quadrant in which it is located. Follow the sample for Abilene given above.

INDEX OF KANSAS COMMUNITIES AND THEIR QUADRANTS			
Quadrant	Community	Quadrant	Community
	Arkansas City		Independence
	Belleville		Kansas City
	Chanute		Liberal
	El Dorado		Newton
	Emporia		Pittsburg
	Fort Scott		Pratt
	Garden City		Salina
	Goodland		Topeka
	Great Bend		Ulysses
	Hays		Wichita

OKLAHOMA: PETROLEUM AND WHEAT IN THE GREAT PLAINS

Oil in the Great Plains States

Ordinarily, motorists do not ask gas station attendants for a "petroleum change" when they think it is time to replace the oil in their vehicles; they ask for an "oil change." Oil has become a popular term for the thick, brown fluid the ancient Romans observed seeping from the earth, most often between rocks. The Romans already had a word for oil, *oleum*, and a word for rock, *petras*. The combination of the two Latin words resulted in a new word—*petroleum*.

The Romans and other ancient people made use of petroleum; for example, the Egyptians greased the axles of their chariots and carts with oil. Some ancients believed that "rock oil" had medicinal value so they used it as an ointment or salve.

It wasn't until gasoline-powered automobiles and trucks were invented that oil came to be in great demand. The main reason for the demand is that gasoline is made from petroleum. Also, huge quantities of oil are used to keep the engines of automobiles operating smoothly.

The increased use of oil meant that more efficient and productive ways had to be developed to get the oil out of the earth. Why not dig holes (wells) deep into the earth and pump oil out in the same way that water was brought to the surface? The method was tried and it worked. The first person in the United States to dig a commercially productive well was Edwin L. Drake. This significant event took place near Titusville, Pennsylvania, in 1859. Since that time thousands of wells have been drilled. At the present time there are almost 600,000 wells in the United States pumping oil on a daily basis.

Huge quantities of oil were discovered in the Great Plains states. Oklahoma became one of the leading oil-producing states and remains so today. It is not possible to travel very far in central Oklahoma without seeing oil derricks. Sometimes it is a single derrick in a field; at other locations dozens of derricks are operating as a part of large oil companies. Oil is so important in Oklahoma

that on the front lawn of the capital building in Oklahoma City, oil is pumped out of the ground on a daily basis.

The table that follows lists the ten leading oil-producing states. Notice in the listing the prominence of Oklahoma and other Great Plains States.

| LEADING PETROLEUM PRODUCING STATES* ||
State**	Millions of Barrels
Texas**	651,000,000
Alaska	627,000,000
California	305,000,000
Louisiana	143,000,000
Oklahoma**	102,000,000
Wyoming	97,000,000
New Mexico	70,000,000
Kansas**	54,000,000
North Dakota**	33,000,000
Colorado	30,000,000
* In a recent year	** Great Plains State

Wheat—Millions of Bushels

Wheat—the grain most often ground into flour to make bread and other baked goods—is a principal crop of the Great Plains states. Of the eight leading wheat-growing states, five are in the Great Plains. The amount of wheat grown by the leaders is very great: 1,489,496,000 bushels, each weighing 60 pounds, for a total of more than 89 billion pounds in a recent year. The bar graph below compares the eight leading states in the amounts of wheat each grows.

| EIGHT LEADING WHEAT GROWING STATES ||
State	
Kansas	389
North Dakota	335
Montana	204
Washington	178
Oklahoma	162
Texas	118
South Dakota	112
Idaho	110

0   50 100 150 200 250 300 350 400
Millions of Bushels

© 1996 by The Center for Applied Research in Education

Name: _____ Date: _____

OKLAHOMA: LATITUDE AND LONGITUDE, RIVERS AND CITIES

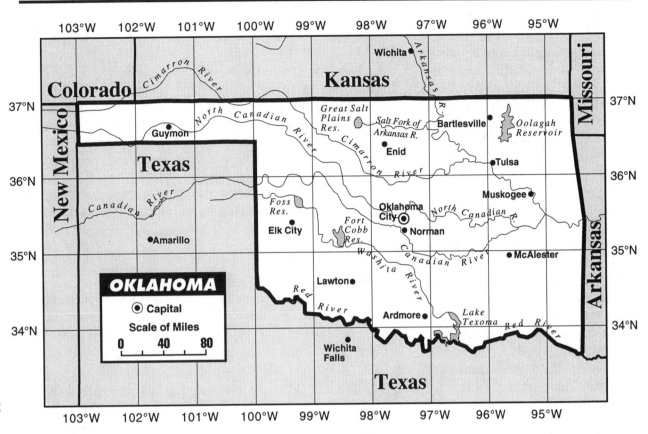

© 1996 by The Center for Applied Research in Education

Latitude and Longitude Quadrants

1. Name all the cities located in each of the following latitude and longitude quadrants.
   The quadrant bounded by

🖎 34°N and 35°N; 95°W and 96°W:

_____

🖎 36°N and 37°N; 97°W and 98°W:

_____

🖎 35°N and 36°N; 95°W and 96°W:

_____

🖎 35°N and 36°N; 97°W and 98°W:

_____

🖎 36°N and 37°N; 101°W and 102°W:

_____

🖎 35°N and 36°N; 99°W and 100°W:

_____

Rivers and Cities

2. Name the river that

🖎 flows from west to east through the capital of Oklahoma: _____

🖎 joins the Arkansas River about 15 miles west of Tulsa:_____

🖎 flows out of New Mexico into Oklahoma, out of Oklahoma into Colorado, out of Colorado into Kansas, out of Kansas into Oklahoma, out of Oklahoma into Kansas, out of Kansas into Oklahoma: _____

_____

🖎 flows into and out of Foss Reservoir, then into Lake Texoma: _____

🖎 forms part of Oklahoma's boundary with Texas:_____

3. If you were to go all the way by boat from Tulsa to Oklahoma City, on what three rivers would you sail? _____,

_____, _____

TEXAS: TORNADO COUNTRY

The nickname for Texas is "Lone Star State," but another appropriate name could well be "The Tornado State." In a 30-year period ending 1991, Texas experienced 4,174 tornadoes for a yearly average of 139, far more than any other state.

Texas is first in the country when it comes to tornadoes, but Oklahoma, Kansas, Nebraska, South Dakota, and North Dakota also have serious tornado problems. One of the reasons tornadoes occur so often in these states is that there are great stretches of level land and high temperatures in late spring and summer. These two conditions make it more likely for tornadoes to develop than, for example, in mountainous lands.

What is a tornado? It is a violent, swiftly rotating column of air. Its appearance, when viewed from a distance, is that of a funnel. The narrow part of the funnel is in touch with the ground; the wide part is high in the air and seems to hang from a dark cloud. Tornadoes can not only be seen, for they are usually black, but also heard—their roar is terrifying. Adding to the terror of a tornado is that it may be accompanied by flashes of lighting, booming thunder, heavy rain, and hailstones that pelt the earth like small bombs.

Tornadoes, also called "twisters," develop when a layer of cold, dry air pushes itself over a layer of moist, warm air. Because warm or hot air rises, it tries to break through the cold air and escape. Its manner of escaping is to go upward. As it rises the air starts whirling, not un-like a spinning top. The escaping, rapidly twirling and rising hot air causes a loss of air pressure at ground level.

The upward movement in the center of a tornado lifts objects such as houses, barns, trees, automobiles, animals, and people, not unlike a house vacuum cleaner sucks up dirt and crumbs from a rug. Sometimes objects will be carried for miles before a tornado weakens and releases the objects. Tornadoes destroy property in other ways. The loss of air pressure at ground level outside a house or barn results in air pressure within the building being greater than the outside pressure. The result? The building could explode, just as a balloon explodes if too much air is blown into it.

Diagram of a Tornado

There is great variety among tornadoes relative to size, wind velocity, nature of their paths across the land, and their speed of travel. The diagram below will provide information about these things and others, as well.

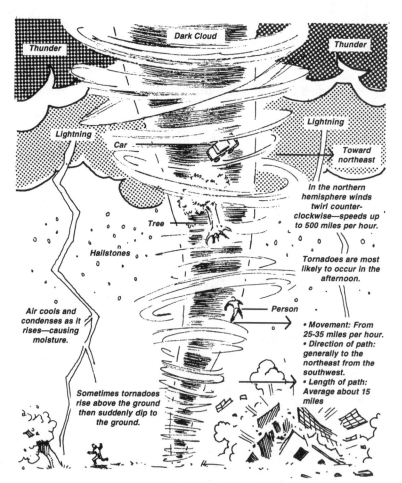

A FULL-BLOWN TORNADO

© 1996 by The Center for Applied Research in Education

Name: _____ Date: _____

TEXAS: CODED PLACE NAMES

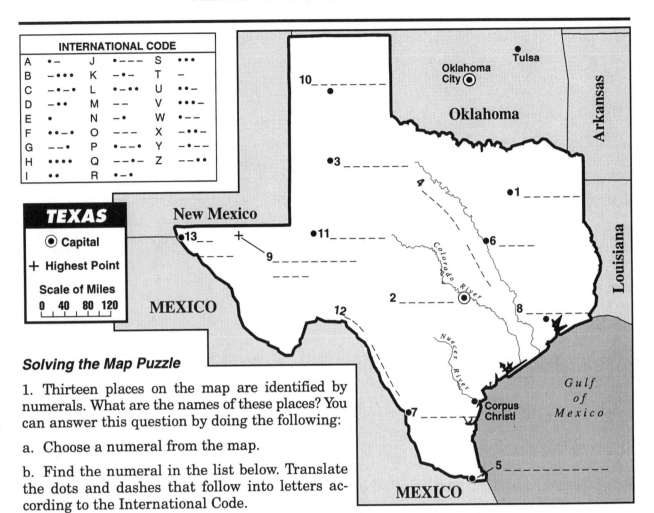

INTERNATIONAL CODE

A	•—	J	•———	S	•••
B	—•••	K	—•—	T	—
C	—•—•	L	•—••	U	••—
D	—••	M	——	V	•••—
E	•	N	—•	W	•——
F	••—•	O	———	X	—••—
G	——•	P	•——•	Y	—•——
H	••••	Q	——•—	Z	——••
I	••	R	•—•		

Solving the Map Puzzle

1. Thirteen places on the map are identified by numerals. What are the names of these places? You can answer this question by doing the following:

a. Choose a numeral from the map.

b. Find the numeral in the list below. Translate the dots and dashes that follow into letters according to the International Code.

c. Write the letters above the dots and dashes.

d. Carefully print the name of the place on the map.

① —••/•—/•—••/•—••/•—/•••

② •—/••—/•••/—/••/—•

③ •—••/••—/—•••/—•••/———/—•—•/—•—

④ —•••/•—•/•—/——••/———/•••
   •—•/••/•••—/•/•—•

⑤ —•••/•—•/———/•—/—•/•••/̄
   •••—/••/•—••/•—••/•

⑥ •——/•—/—•—•/———

⑦ •—••/•—/•—•/•/—••/———

⑧ ••••/———/••—/•••/—/———/•

⑨ ——•/••—/•—/•—•/•—/•••/••—/•——•/•
   •——•/•/•—/—•—

⑩ •—/——/•—/•—•/••/•—••/•—••/———

⑪ ———/•••/•/•••/•••/•—

⑫ •—•/••/———/ ——•/•—•/•—/—•/••/•

⑬ •/•—•• •—•/•—/•••/———

127

Western States

Name: _____ Date: _____

WESTERN STATES: CAPITALS, RIVERS, AND BOUNDARIES

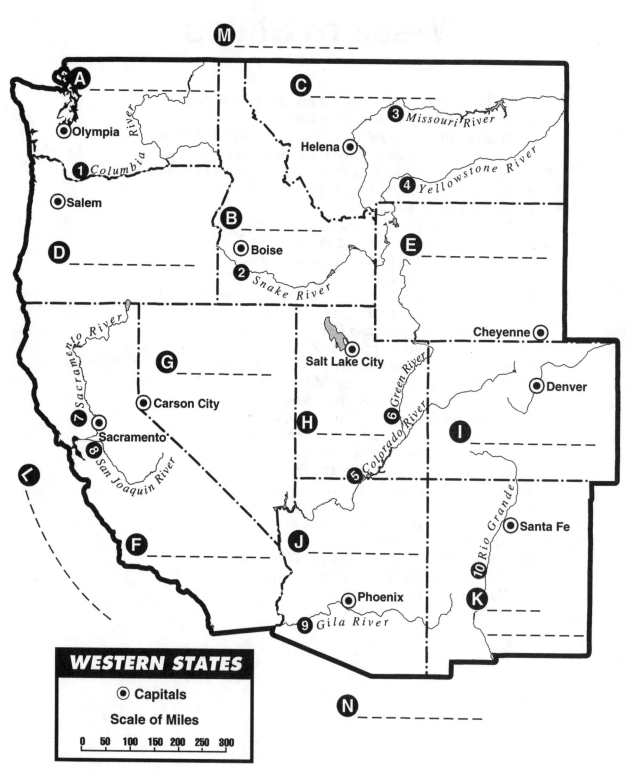

Name: _____ Date: _____

WESTERN STATES: CAPITALS, RIVERS, AND BOUNDARIES

1. Label the states as follows:

A Washington   **G** Nevada

B Idaho   **H** Utah

C Montana   **I** Colorado

D Oregon   **J** Arizona

E Wyoming   **K** New Mexico

F California

2. Name the rivers shown by the circled numbers on the map.

1 _____

2 _____

3 _____

4 _____

5 _____

6 _____

7 _____

8 _____

9 _____

10 _____

3. Name the capital of each state as shown on the map.

a. Washington: _____

b. Idaho: _____

c. Montana: _____

d. Oregon: _____

e. Wyoming: _____

f. California: _____

g. Nevada: _____

h. Utah: _____

i. Colorado _____

j. Arizona: _____

k. New Mexico _____

4. Label the Pacific Ocean at L, Canada at M, Mexico at N.

5. What four states join and make four perfect right angles (+)?

_____

_____

_____

_____

6. What three states border on the Pacific Ocean?

_____

_____

_____

7. What three states border on Canada?

_____

_____

_____

8. What three states border on Mexico?

_____

_____

_____

Name: _____ Date: _____

WESTERN STATES: WATER IN THE WEST

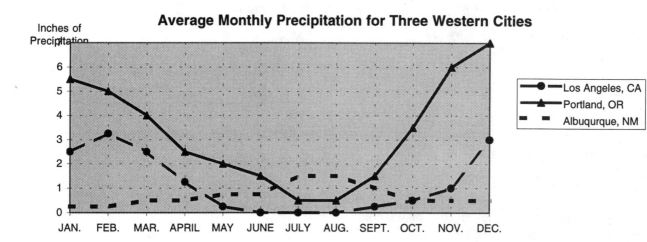

Average Monthly Precipitation for Three Western Cities

Inches of Precipitation

Los Angeles, CA
Portland, OR
Albuqurque, NM

JAN. FEB. MAR. APRIL MAY JUNE JULY AUG. SEPT. OCT. NOV. DEC.

1. *Precipitation* includes all the forms of water that fall to earth—rain, mist, snow, sleet, hail.

The graph above shows the average precipitation, by months, in Portland, Los Angeles, and Albuquerque. The numbers used were rounded to the nearest one-fourth inch.

Use the graph to finish the table below. In the table, *T* stands for trace (less than one-fourth inch of precipitation) and is not to be counted in finding the total recorded for that month. When you have written the figure for each month, add and write the average *yearly* precipitation for each of the three cities.

Average Monthly Precipitation (in inches)												
	J	F	M	A	M	J	J	A	S	O	N	D	TOTAL
Los Angeles	2½	3¼	2½	1¼	¼	T	T	T	¼	½	1	3	
Portland													
Albuquerque													

2. How many more inches of precipitation per year does Portland have than the other two cities combined? _____

3. Does Portland have more precipitation in winter or in summer? _____

4. Does Albuquerque have more precipitation in winter or in summer? _____

5. Which three months are the driest in Los Angeles? _____

_____

To go ahead: Make a vertical bar graph to show the average yearly precipitation in the three cities. Color the bar for Portland green, the bar for Los Angeles yellow, and the bar for Albuquerque red.

© 1996 by The Center for Applied Research in Education

Name: _____ Date: _____

WESTERN STATES: A TABLE OF FACTS AND A NUMBER PUZZLE

FACTS ABOUT THE WESTERN STATES

States and Capitals (North to South)	Population	Area in Square Miles with Rank Shown in Parentheses ( )*	Highest Point with Elevation Shown in Parentheses ( )	Nickname
Washington (Olympia)	5,255,276	71,302 (18)	Mount Rainier (14,410')	Evergreen State
Idaho (Boise)	1,099,096	83,574 (14)	Borah Peak (12,662')	Gem State
Montana (Helena)	839,422	147,046 (4)	Granite Peak (12,799')	Treasure State
Oregon (Salem)	3,031,867	98,386 (9)	Mount Hood (11,239')	Beaver State
Wyoming (Cheyenne)	470,242	97,818 (10)	Gannett Peak (13,804')	Equality State
California (Sacramento)	31,210,750	163,707 (3)	Mount Whitney (14,494')	Golden State
Nevada (Carson City)	1,388,910	110,567 (7)	Boundary Peak (13,140')	The Silver State or Sugarbush State
Utah (Salt Lake City)	1,859,582	84,904 (13)	Kings Peak (13,528')	Beehive State
Colorado (Denver)	3,565,954	104,100 (8)	Mount Elbert (14,433')	Centennial State
Arizona (Phoenix)	3,936,142	114,006 (6)	Humphreys Peak (12,633')	Grand Canyon State
New Mexico (Sante Fe)	1,616,483	121,598 (5)	Wheeler Peak (13,161')	Land of Enchantment

* Total of land and water

The Cross Numbers Puzzle is solved in the same way an ordinary crossword puzzle is solved. Read the descriptions, find the correct number in the table, and then carefully fill in the blanks with the numbers.

ACROSS
2. Population of Washington
3. Area of the Gem State
6. Idaho's rank in size
7. Beehive State's area
9. Population of the state that has Sacramento as its capital
11. Washington's rank in size
13. Height of the third highest mountain listed in the table
14. Area of Wyoming
16. Height of Kings Peak

DOWN
1. Population of the Centennial State
4. Area of the state that has Denver as its capital
5. Height of Colorado's highest mountain
8. Height of the Treasure State's highest mountain
10. Area of the fifth largest state in the USA
11. Height of Humphreys Peak
12. Equality State's rank in size
15. Utah's rank in size

133

WASHINGTON: GRAND COULEE DAM, NORTHWEST INDIANS

Grand Coulee Dam

The Grand Coulee Dam across the Columbia River was completed in 1942. At 555' high it is one of the highest dams in the United States; the highest is the Oroville Dam on the Feather River in California–754'. The reservoir that resulted from the construction of the dam is known as Franklin Delano Roosevelt Lake. Roosevelt was President of the United States when the Grand Coulee was completed. The lake, 151 miles long, holds 9,552,000 acre feet of water (one acre foot is equivalent to one acre of water 1' deep).

A study of the illustration below shows some interesting things. The Grand Coulee is not only a dam, but also a bridge across the Columbia River. The buildings at the two ends of the dam are hydroelectric plants that produce electricity for three states: Washington, Idaho, and Oregon. The lake behind the dam is used for recreational purposes such as swimming, boating, and fishing. During times of heavy rain the dam holds back water to prevent downstream flooding. Also, during dry seasons water can be released from the lake to irrigate farms that lie below the dam.

Grand Coulee Dam

Northwest Indians

The native American Indians who lived in what is now northwestern United States and British Columbia in Canada can be classified under various tribal names: Haida, Kwakiutl, Nootka, Tsimishian, and Chinook. Regardless of tribe, these Indians all lived in very much the same way. This was because their environments were similar: an ocean front; a "back yard" of high, heavily forested mountains; copious rainfall; four distinct seasons; and plentiful wildlife.

It was the Chinook who made their home in what is now Washington along the shores of the Pacific Ocean. Representative of Indians of the American northwest, Chinook lived differently than Indians of the dry southwest, the open plains, and semitropical Florida. One difference was in the way the Chinook constructed their homes. They made axes and wedges from stone, which enabled them to cut down large trees and to split logs into planks. As a next step they framed their houses with stout corner posts, ridge poles, and rafters. Finally, they covered their frames with planks and decorated them elaborately with carvings and paintings. The houses were sturdy, kept out heavy rains, and were snug and warm in winter.

Obtaining food was not a great problem for the Chinook. Because these people lived close to the sea, fish were an important part of their diet. They were skillful fishermen, who caught fish with bone hooks, spears, and nets. Fish were eaten immediately or dried on racks and then stored for food in the winter months.

Birds' eggs, rabbits, deer, elk, roots, and berries were all easily obtained from the forests that covered the mountains. The ocean shores provided these people with shell fish, sea turtles, and clams.

The Chinook even learned how to take their large, strong canoes out to sea and catch whales. One whale with all its meat could feed a whole encampment for weeks; plus, careful never to waste, the Chinook put the oil and bones of whales to good use.

Name: _____ Date: _____

WASHINGTON: MOUNTAINS, RIVERS, CITIES, AND A COASTLINE

What appears to be a jumble of meaningless letters on each line of the list that follows really isn't a jumble; it's a puzzle. Here's how to solve the puzzle:

a. Starting with the first letter, every other letter on the line helps spell the name of a place or thing in or close to Washington. Here's an example:

C V A J N P A R D K A is CANADA.

b. After you solve a puzzle, find the place or thing on the map; then, look for its number which will be close by its name. Write its number in the blank circle at the beginning of the line.

◯ TYAPCKOMMCA: _____

◯ CMOGLSURMPBZIQA RGISVDETR: ____

_____

◯ MKT RVAJIWNDITEZR: _____

◯ SBPGOFKTAUNWE: _____

◯ SJNYATKCE RAIPVOEWR: _____

_____

◯ ODLNYMMKPGISA: _____

◯ VJAKNFCSOTUPVWEVR: _____

◯ WDASLELTA WNABLCLZA: _____

_____

◯ BAOSNDNFEGVJIKLVLBE DPATM: ____

_____

◯ YPAYKTIRMBA: _____

◯ GTRRAENWD CAOSUDLFEKE DBAFM:

_____

◯ OPKUATNROVGSAJN RFIDVSENR: ____

_____

◯ CPAUSTCEACDDE RYATNCGME: _____

_____

◯ BPEULTLFIENDGGHKABM: _____

◯ SQEWAETRTTLYE: _____

◯ LLOKNJGGVFISEPW: _____

135

IDAHO: POTATOES AND TOURIST'S PARADISE

There are dozens of ways to prepare potatoes—French fried, mashed, scalloped, chips, boiled. But if you like your potatoes baked, you can't go wrong if you use "Idaho's," as they are popularly called. There is something about Idaho's soil that seems to make its potatoes well-suited for baking. Of course, *Idaho*'s can be prepared in any of the other ways mentioned above.

Idaho is the country's leading potato-growing state. Washington follows in second place, and Colorado is third. It is interesting to note that the three leading potato-growing states are all in the northwestern United States. The leading potato-growing state east of the Mississippi River is Maine.

Following are some facts about potatoes:

The average potato is about 75%–80% water, but the solid parts of potatoes are very nutritious. Potatoes contain important vitamins, protein, and iron. Contrary to popular opinion, potatoes do not have excessive calories, perhaps 75 to 100 for an average potato. It is how they are cooked (fried in grease or oil) and what is put on them after they are cooked (butter, sour cream) that adds the calories.

Potatoes are grown throughout the world. It was the former Soviet Union, now broken into fifteen separate republics, that led the world in potato production. Poland, Germany, China, and France all grow more potatoes than the United States does.

Potatoes are used mainly as food for humans and such animals as hogs and cattle.

Various by-products are made from potatoes, including alcohol, flour, and starch.

Potatoes have played an important part in history, especially in Ireland. The Irish people were, and still are, very dependent upon potatoes. The failure of the Irish potato crop in 1845 and 1846 led to many deaths by starvation. Thousands of Irish people migrated to the United States to escape starvation and poverty.

Idaho Tourist Attractions

Tourists are attracted to Idaho by the hundreds of thousands. Serving the needs of tourists is one of Idaho's major industries. In a recent year tourists spent almost $2 billion to see and experience the wonders of Idaho. What are some of those wonders? Following are brief descriptions of only a few of them.

Hell's Canyon National Recreation Area: 52,000 acres . . . Site of North America's deepest canyon; deepest point from canyon floor to rim, 7,900' . . . Flowing through the canyon—the Snake River; great white water rafting . . .

Shoshone Falls: Falls on the Snake River with a drop of 212' (compare with the greatest drop of Niagara Falls, 176') . . .

Balanced Rock: Huge boulder 40' high and weighing forty tons resting on a small rock only a few feet in diameter . . .

Craters of the Moon National Monument: 80 square mile area resembling the surface of the moon; volcanic craters, stray rocks, lava cones resulting from tremendous volcanic activity thousands of years ago . . . Apparently barren as in a desert, but many unusual plants flourish . . .

Sun Valley: Located in south central Idaho . . . Year-round resort, best known for its winter sports, especially skiing . . . Resembles an Alpine village . . . Pioneered in the use of chair lifts on ski slopes . . .

Wallace District Mining Museum, and Sierra Silver Mine Tour: Museum—photographs of old-time mining methods, displays of mining techniques, slide show . . . Mine Tour—a trolley ride into a real silver mine . . . Silver ore souvenirs, perhaps containing traces of silver . . .

IDAHO: MAP PUZZLE

There are 23 cities, rivers, etc., spelled out in the word puzzle. The places are printed either across or down.

If a place or thing has two words in it—such as Flathead Lake—there is no space between the words.

Here is an effective way to proceed:

1. Select a name from the map.

2. Search for the name in the puzzle. When you find the name, draw a neat line around all the letters in the name. All the names in the puzzle are somewhere on the map.

T	W	I	N	F	A	L	L	S	E	A	I	N	B	S	M
W	Y	E	F	S	C	A	N	A	D	A	D	E	O	A	F
A	O	S	L	E	W	I	S	T	O	N	A	V	R	N	P
S	M	N	A	S	M	I	L	V	J	R	H	A	A	D	O
H	I	A	T	M	O	R	E	G	O	N	O	D	H	P	C
I	N	K	H	A	N	R	Y	S	A	L	F	A	P	O	A
N	G	E	E	E	T	B	O	I	S	E	A	R	E	I	T
G	M	R	A	S	A	L	M	O	N	N	L	O	A	N	E
T	O	I	D	E	N	A	M	P	A	D	L	I	K	T	L
O	S	V	L	W	A	L	L	A	C	E	S	T	H	U	L
N	C	E	A	L	B	U	R	L	E	Y	O	R	N	T	O
A	O	R	K	B	O	Z	E	M	A	N	J	E	A	A	N
M	W	I	E	C	W	E	I	S	E	R	H	E	A	H	L

MONTANA: INDIAN WARS, AGRICULTURE, AND MINERALS

Custer's Last Stand

It was near the Little Rig Horn River in southeastern Montana that one of the best-known battles in American history occurred. The engagement, known as the Battle of the Little Big Horn, or more popularly as Custer's Last Stand, resulted in a crushing defeat of a segment of Lieutenant Colonel George A. Custer's Seventh Calvary Regiment.

Custer had been given the objective of collecting all the Sioux and Cheyenne Indians who were encamped along the Little Big Horn River. The Indians were to be removed to reservations. His plan for meeting his objective called for two separate columns of soldiers—one of which was to be led by himself—to attack the main Indian encampment. A third column was given the task of scouring the area to round up any Indians who were not in the main encampment.

The Indians, however, led by Chief Crazy Horse, were determined to defend the land they occupied. They drove back one column of soldiers who were attacking from across the river. Chief Crazy Horse then turned his attention to Custer's column. The fighting was fierce. Custer's force was outnumbered by the Indian warriors. When the smoke of the battle was cleared and the last bullet and arrow had been expended, all of Custer's men, and Custer himself, lay dead on the field.

Eventually, the Indians were defeated and they were forced to live on reservations. Today, the Custer Battlefield National Monument serves to remind visitors of the terrible ordeal, suffered by both the American soldiers and the American Indians, that occurred there in 1876.

Montana's Agriculture

Montana is the United States' third largest grower of wheat—after Kansas (389 million bushels) and North Dakota (335 million bushels)—with 204 million bushels in a recent year.

Montana harvested 64 million bushels of barley in 1993. The state was second to North Dakota, which saw a harvest of 113 million bushels.

Montana's plains, which cover approximately two-thirds of the state, enable its farmers to grow such large quantities of wheat and oats. Both of these crops flourish on level or rolling land and require less rain than, for example, corn. Fortunately, although the plains receive less than fifteen inches of precipitation annually, at least one-half falls within the three-month growing season from May through July. Another source of the all-important water needed for crops such as sugar beets or mustard seed is a well-developed irrigation system that serves some two million acres of Montana's land.

Montana's Minerals

Montana well deserves the nickname "Treasure State." Within its borders vast quantities of coal, gold, silver, lead, oil, and copper have been mined, and vast quantities of minerals remain to be uncovered. In 1993, almost $500 million of nonfuel minerals (excludes coal, oil, and natural gas) were taken from the ground.

It was the lure of quick riches from gold and silver that first attracted miners to Montana in the 1860s. And in those days Montana was truly a part of the "wild west" often depicted in motion pictures—complete with outlaws, sheriffs, gun battles, and hangings. Those days have passed away, but gold is still there in the hills. Individual gold seekers have been replaced by large companies that use modern machinery to extract the ore.

The world's largest copper mine is in Montana. Most of the mining done is the "open pit" variety, which utilizes huge earth-crushing, earth-moving equipment. In a recent year Montana ranked fourth in the nation in the output of copper, lead, and silver, and fifth in gold, phosphate, and zinc production.

Name: _____ Date: _____

MONTANA: A MOUNTAIN AND PLAINS STATE

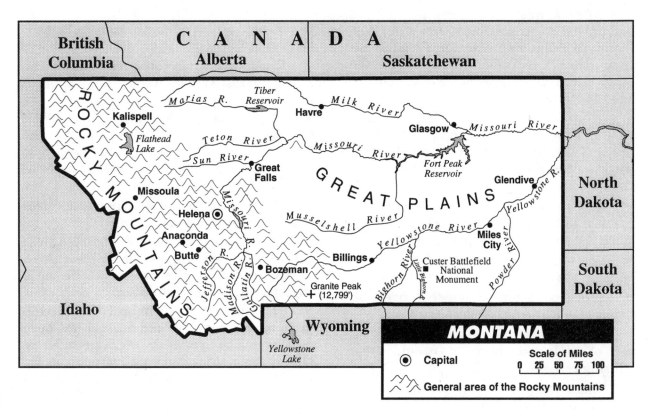

True or False

Circle the correct choice.

1. North Dakota is the only state on Montana's eastern border.　　T　　F

2. Custer Battlefield National Monument is located on the eastern side of the Little Bighorn River.　　T　　F

3. The Musselshell River first flows eastward, then northward until it joins the Missouri River.　　T　　F

4. Granite Peak, Montana's highest peak, is more than two miles above sea level. *Note*: Length of a mile–5,280'.　　T　　F

5. The capital of Montana—Helena—is east of the Missouri River.　　T　　F

6. Flathead Lake is almost directly north of Missoula.　　T　　F

7. Approximately one-third of Montana is covered by the Rocky Mountains.　T　　F

8. The Yellowstone River flows in a southwesterly direction.　　T　　F

Complete the Sentences

1. _____ River joins the Yellowstone River at a point northeast of Miles City.

2. Three rivers come together to form the Missouri River; they are the _____ River, the _____ River, and the _____ River.

3. The Sun River joins the Missouri River from the _____.

4. Bozeman is approximately _____ miles south of Great Falls.

5. The three Canadian provinces on Montana's northern boundary are _____, _____, and _____.

139

OREGON: THE WILLAMETTE RIVER AND VALLEY

After Marcus and Narcissa Whitman had proved it was possible to cross the Rocky Mountains in a wagon and had established their mission in Walla Walla, Washington, other adventurous Americans were encouraged to follow.

It could be asked, "Why did those would-be settlers cross more than 1,000 miles of the Great Plains? Why didn't they settle on the plains?" Following are some of the reasons:

☞ Few people believed it was possible to make a good living on the plains. For one thing the sod was too tough to plow.

☞ The summers were very hot, and the winters were severe.

☞ There were few streams or rivers for drinking or for transportation.

☞ Every few years great droughts—periods of little precipitation—would occur, causing crops to fail.

☞ There were no forests to furnish lumber for houses or fuel.

☞ Locusts periodically swarmed over the region devouring everything that was in their path.

Many people called the region "The Great American Desert," and their only interest was to cross it as quickly and safely as possible.

When the pioneers heard there were fertile lands in the Oregon Country that could be purchased cheaply, they packed their belongings, joined a wagon train, and headed west. Beginning about 1840, thousands upon thousands followed the Oregon Trail from Independence, Missouri, to the Oregon Country.

And where in Oregon were many of those hardy pioneers going to settle? The answer is the Willamette Valley in Oregon between the Coast Ranges and the Cascade Range. Following are some of the reasons settlers took great risks to get there.

☞ The northward flowing Willamette River was a natural highway, 190 miles long. It served as a "road" for small boats and rafts.

☞ The valley of the Willamette was broad—30 miles wide in some places—level, and fertile.

☞ Wood was easily obtainable from the heavily forested mountains that ran parallel to the river.

☞ The Willamette emptied into the Columbia River only a few miles from the Pacific Ocean. This meant that the people of the valley had access to foreign ports as well as United States ports.

What part does the Willamette River and Valley play in today's Oregon?

☞ The Valley is still Oregon's most productive farming region. Crops grow easily in the fertile soil and the mild climate with its plentiful rain.

☞ The river has been improved by dredging a deeper channel, and a canal has been constructed to bypass the Willamette Falls. Ocean-going ships can sail upstream as far as Portland, and smaller watercraft can now go as far as Eugene, which is some 125 miles upstream.

☞ Numerous small and large companies are either on the banks of the Willamette or close to it. These manufacturing establishments turn out a diversity of products, including lumber and lumber products, metals, and canned fruits and vegetables.

☞ The capital of Oregon, Salem, is located in the valley, as are four of the state's large cities: Portland, 439,000; Eugene, 113,000; Salem, 108,000; Beaverton, 53,000. These cities plus numerous smaller communties contain more than one-half of Oregon's population.

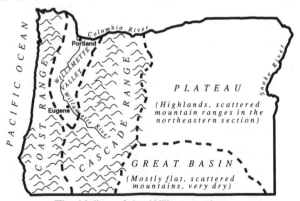

The Valley of the Willamette between
the Cascade Range and the Coast Range

Name: _____ Date: _____

OREGON: MOUNTAINS AND RIVERS

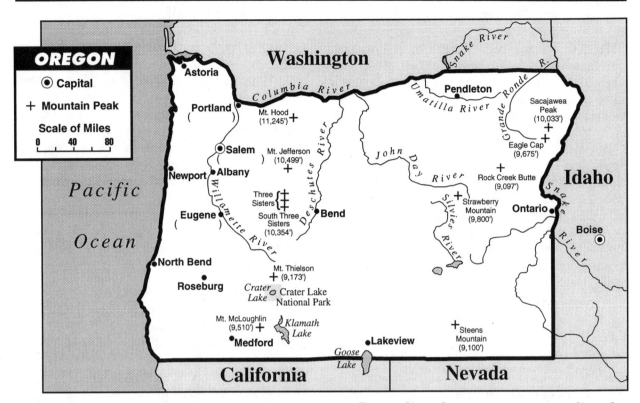

1. Oregon has some very high mountains. The ten shown on the map are all over 9,000' in elevation. Mount Hood, the highest mountain in Oregon, is 11,245' above sea level. This means that a straight line drawn out to the sea from the top of Mount Hood would be more than two miles above the level of the sea.

The table below lists the elevations of the mountains shown on the map. Find the name of the mountain that fits a particular elevation; then write its name in the table.

Mountain	Elevation
	11,245'
	10,499'
	10,354'
	10,033'
	9,800'
	9,675'
	9,510'
	9,173'
	9,100'
	9,097'

2. Proceeding from west to east, list the tributaries to the Columbia River.

_____

_____

_____

3. The Snake River forms part of Oregon's eastern boundary. The river flows northward into Washington, then turns south and joins the Columbia River. From what state does it enter Oregon? _____

4. Proceeding from south to north, list the tributaries to the Snake River.

_____

_____

_____

5. Oregon's three largest cities are:
- Portland (439,000)
- Eugene (113,000)
- Salem (108,000)

On the map and within the parentheses close to the cities, write each city's population.

WYOMING: POPULATION, YELLOWSTONE PARK, OREGON TRAIL

Wyoming and Population

Wyoming has a smaller population (470,000) than any other state, in spite of the fact that it is the tenth largest state. Its capital, Cheyenne, which is also the largest city in the state, has fewer than 55,000 people. In the entire state there only 16 communities with 5,000 or more people. Compare these figures with those of Michigan, the eleventh largest state: population, 9,500,000 with 180 communities of 5,000 or more people. Detroit, Michigan's largest city, has more than 1,000,000 people.

The scarcity of people in Wyoming may be better understood in terms of density of population, the number of people per square mile.

❑ Wyoming: 4.7 people per square mile
❑ New Jersey: 1,042 people per square mile
❑ California: 190.8 people per square mile
❑ Washington: 73.1 people per square mile
❑ Alaska: 1 person per square mile

Yellowstone National Park

☞ **Founded**: 1872 . . . The first national park in the United States . . .

☞ **Location**: Mostly in northwest Wyoming; western edge in Idaho, northern edge in Montana . . .

☞ **Size**: 2,220,000 acres or 3,472 square miles, about one-half the size of New Jersey . . .

☞ **Features**: Several thousand hot springs and geysers, Old Faithful being the most famous and popular . . . Lower Falls of the Yellowstone River, a 308' fall . . . Yellowstone Lake, about 1½ miles above sea level, the highest large lake in North America . . . Many kinds of animals, including elk, bison, deer, cougar, bighorn sheep, moose, and at least 35 smaller animals; tremendous variety of birds, at least 200 different kind . . .

The Old Faithful geyser is one of Yellowstone's most famous and popular attractions. Its name can be attributed to the fact that year after year it continues to erupt an average of about 11 times in a 24-hour period. During an eruption a fountain of water can rise as high as 100 feet into the air.

The water is boiling hot; parents are warned to tell their children not to go close to the spraying water; they could be seriously scalded.

What causes Old Faithful and the other geysers to spray boiling water? Many theories have been offered. The one that is most generally accepted is that as water seeps into the ground it comes into contact with hot melted rock (magma). The heat converts the water to steam. Because steam exerts great pressure when confined, it expands into the nearest openings. The steam heats the water above it and drives it out into the air in the form of a jet, spray, or overflow.

The Oregon Trail and Wyoming

Wyoming was an important part of the Oregon Trail. After leaving Nebraska, hundreds of Conestoga wagons, similar to the one illustrated below, made their slow trek across Wyoming for more than 400 miles.

There are some interesting things to observe in the illustration.

❑ The foremost wagon is being pulled by oxen; the wagon immediately in front of it is being pulled by horses.

❑ A water barrel is lashed to the side of the wagon.

❑ Broad wheels help keep the wagon from sinking into mud and soft sod.

❑ The canvas top offers protection from the sun and rain.

❑ The mountains in the background have to be crossed.

❑ One man is riding a horse, another is walking, and a woman is riding in the wagon.

Settlers Follow the Oregon Trail

WYOMING: MOUNTAIN PEAKS AND DISTANCES

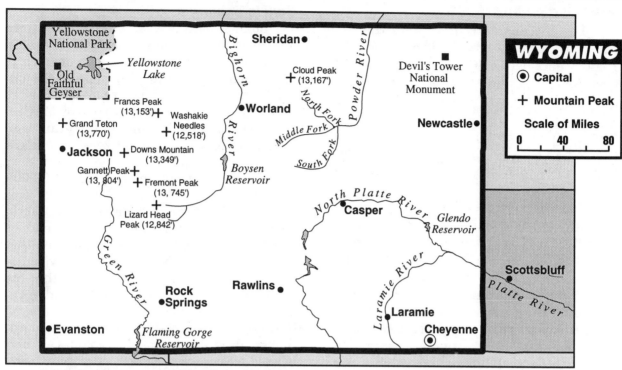

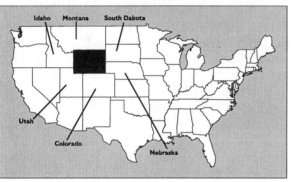

a. Cheyenne - Laramie

____ 30 mi. ____ 45 mi. ____ 60 mi.

b. Cheyenne - Jackson

____ 275 mi. ____ 300 mi. ____ 355 mi.

c. Cheyenne - Evanston

____ 280 mi. ____ 330 mi. ____ 380 mi.

d. Cheyenne - Sheridan

____ 270 mi. ____ 320 mi. ____ 350 mi.

1. The outline map of the United States shows Wyoming's location. Starting at the north and proceeding clockwise, list all the states that border on Wyoming.

a _____ d. _____

b. _____ e. _____

c. _____ f. _____

2. In Wyoming it is sometimes much quicker and easier to travel by small airplane than by automobile.

Use the scale of miles to find the distances between the following places.

Check (✓) the best answer.

3. The mountain peaks listed below are in order of elevation, but their heights in feet have been omitted. Write their elevations in the table as given on the map.

Mountain	Elevation in Feet
Gannett Peak	
Grand Teton	
Fremont Peak	
Downs Mountain	
Cloud Peak	
Francs Peak	
Lizard Head Peak	
Washakie Needles	

CALIFORNIA: MISSIONS AND GOLD

Spain in California

The Indians, of course, were the first people in what is now California, possibly 10,000 years before Spanish intrusions. The first Spaniards were explorers and discoverers. Some 250 years after Cortes landed in what is now Mexico, Father Juniper Serra, in 1769, founded the first permanent mission in San Diego. This mission was followed by 18 other missions scattered throughout California.

The missionaries' first objective was to convert the native American Indians to Christianity. The missions they established were designed to help them accomplish their objective. Each mission was self-sustaining with regard to providing food, clothing, and shelter for the missionaries and Indians who chose to live there. In a typical mission there was always a church, living quarters for missionaries and Indians, vegetable gardens, fields for growing large crops, a blacksmith shop, a carpenter shop, and a bakery. The missionaries helped the Indians increase their knowledge of farming, herding, building, spinning, weaving, leathermaking, soap-making and other useful crafts. Some missions also taught the Indians reading and writing.

The illustration below shows some interesting aspects of a typical mission:

❑ A robed priest
❑ Grapes on vines and in baskets
❑ A church with a bell tower
❑ Indian workers
❑ A fenced garden

Spaniards Establish Missions

Gold in California

John A. Sutter was an immigrant from Switzerland who had a dream—obtain a grant of land in California and develop it into a beautiful estate. But, one of the obstacles to carrying out his dream was that at that time California was a part of Mexico. The only way he could obtain the grant was by becoming a Mexican citizen—and that's exactly what he did.

After Sutter obtained a grant of 50,000 acres and built a fortress-like home, employed scores of servants and other workers, and began raising some 18,000 head of horses, cattle, sheep, mules, and oxen, his dream was shattered. In 1848 gold was discovered on his land. Sutter believed that his estate would soon be overrun by gold seekers. And, he was right. Once the news of gold in California reached the eastern seaboard, thousands of people got the "gold fever" and headed west.

How the gold seekers got to California was a matter of geography. They could take passage on a ship from the United States' east coast, sail south around the southern tip of South America, then north to California. This was a four-to-five month journey and very hazardous.

Another way to reach the west coast was to take passage on a ship, sail to the Isthmus of Panama, cross it by foot, then board another ship and sail north to California. But, this route also presented problems, particularly getting across the narrow, mountainous, snake-infested strip of land without contracting malaria, which was carried by mosquitoes and often led to death.

A third way was to cross the United States on horseback or wagon. There were several overland routes. One of the most popular was to follow the Oregon Trail to Great Salt Lake (Utah), then branch south and west on the California Trail. All overland routes presented the same kinds of problems: a journey of six to eight months, hostile Indians, crossing hot grasslands and deserts, and finally the Sierra Nevada Mountains. One report states that more than 80,000 "forty-niners," as they were called, arrived in California in 1848 and 1849.

CALIFORNIA: PLACES ON THE MAP

Map-Word Puzzle

The objective of this activity is to complete the word puzzle with the names of places and things that are on the map of California. Here are the guidelines for reaching the objective:

1. All the names that have a place in the puzzle are on the map.

2. Places should fit within the number of spaces allotted. *Note*: In the case of a river, omit the word "River."

3. One of the letters in the place name should match one of the letters in CALIFORNIA USA.

4. If a place name consists of two words, a space should be left between the words. An example of how a name should fit the spaces is shown on the puzzle.

Map Questions

1. How high above the floor of Death Valley is the top of Mt. Whitney? _____ feet

2. Part of the names of two places were joined together to make the name of the town in Mexico opposite El Centro, California. What are the two places?

_____

_____

3. In Spanish, the words "San" and "Santa" mean *Saint*. List all the places that include either of these two words.

_____   _____

_____   _____

_____   _____

NEVADA: THE PONY EXPRESS AND HOOVER DAM

The Pony Express: Delivering the Mail

"Pony Express" was the name given to the 1,800 mile cross-country mail route that connected St. Louis, Missouri, and Sacramento, California. The route crossed through what is now eight states. Of those states, Nevada may have been the most difficult to cross; there were 350 miles of trail, long stretches of desert, and rugged mountains. "Stations" where mail was transferred from one rider to another were about fifteen miles apart. At the stations riders could get fresh horses, food, and water.

The route was necessary because communications between the eastern and the western United States were so poor. The cross-country railroads had not been built, there were no roads, and telegraph service had not reached beyond the Mississippi River. To send a letter from Boston, Massachusetts, to Sacramento, California, by ship would take as much as five or six months.

However, it was possible for a team of Pony Express riders to deliver a letter from Missouri to California in about ten days—weather conditions permitting. The record for delivering a letter to California from Missouri was six days. It cost one dollar to deliver a half-ounce letter.

Pony Express riders had to be courageous for there were risks of all kinds: robbers, hostile Indians, storms, accidents. One advertisement for riders stated that riders should be young (not over 18), skinny, wiry, expert riders, willing to face death, and that orphans would be given preference.

The Pony Express operated from April 1860 through October 1861, eighteen months. It died a "sudden death" only four days after the first transcontinental telegraph was completed.

The illustration shows some interesting details and conveys some impressions of a transfer of mail and horses at a station. The "keeper," or person who took care of the horses and other matters, is on the left; the rider is mounting a fresh horse. Notice the speed at which the transfer is being made; there was no time for chatting and visiting. Most stations were very isolated, lonely, and vulnerable to attack.

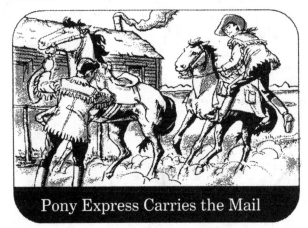

Pony Express Carries the Mail

© 1996 by The Center for Applied Research in Education

Hoover Dam: Questions and Answers

1. **Where is it?** In Black Canyon on the Colorado River, about 30 miles southeast of Las Vegas, Nevada.

2. **How high is Hoover Dam?** 726.4' from foundation rock to the roadway on the crest.

3. **How much concrete is in the dam?** 4,360,000 cubic yards, or enough to pave a highway 16' wide from San Francisco to New York City.

4. **How long did it take to build the dam?** Five years

5. **How many workers were employed?** An average of 3,500, and a maximum of 5,218.

6. **What benefits are derived from the dam?** Among the many, here are a few:

❑ Flood control

❑ Water for irrigating more than a million acres of formerly unproductive land

❑ Water for industries, municipalities

❑ Elimination of sediment that clogged canals and irrigation ditches

❑ Pollution-free, low-cost hydroelectric power

❑ Fish and wildlife conservation; recreation (swimming, fishing, boating) on beautiful Lake Mead

Name: _____ Date: _____

NEVADA: PLACES AND THINGS OF INTEREST

1. Nevada is in many ways a beautiful state; even the dry areas—deserts—have a beauty of their own. Also, the high Sierra Nevada Mountains in the southeastern corner of the state are breathtaking, especially in the summer when they are still capped with snow.

One of the most beautiful places in Nevada is Lake Tahoe, at an elevation of 6,000'. Label **Lake Tahoe** at **A** on the map. Write its elevation on the line below its name.

2. Most of the rivers in Nevada do not end in another river or in a large body of water. Instead, at the end of their flow such rivers either dry up or sink into the sand. Some of the rivers flow only in the "wet season," from the end of November to June.

Label the following "sink hole" rivers as follows:

B Humboldt R.

C Duck Creek

D White R.

E Quinn R.

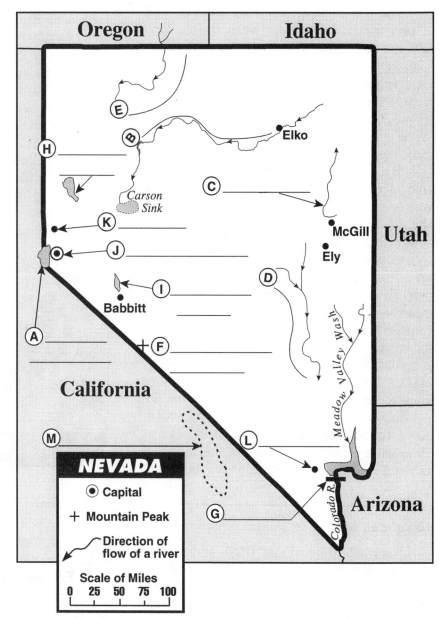

3. Label Nevada's highest point, **Boundary Peak**, at **F** on the map. Its elevation is 13,145'. Write its elevation on the line below its label.

4. Hoover Dam backs up the Colorado River and forms Lake Mead. Label **Hoover Dam** at **G** on the map.

5. Label **Pyramid Lake** at **H**, **Walker Lake** at **I**.

6. Label **Carson City**, Nevada's capital, at **J**; **Reno** at **K**; **Las Vegas**, Nevada's largest city, at **L**.

7. Death Valley, in California, is very close to the Nevada boundary. Very little vegetation grows in Death Valley. It is given that grim name because many animals and humans have died while trying to cross it. Label **Death Valley** at **M** on the map.

UTAH: GREAT SALT LAKE, THE TRANSCONTINENTAL RAILROAD

Completing the Transcontinental Railroad

The United States was very much in need of fast communication between the eastern and western parts of the country. The cross-country telegraph, completed in 1861, was a vast improvement over the land and sea routes. But, the telegraph system was limited to sending and receiving word messages. What was also needed was an efficient and swift means of transporting goods and people.

By 1860 railroads were well developed east of the Mississippi River. The next task was to extend tracks across the Great Plains, the Rocky Mountains and other mountain chains to the Pacific Ocean. This proved to be a tremendous undertaking, but American workers—Irish Americans, Chinese Americans, recently emancipated African Americans, and others—were equal to the job. The plan for completing the cross-country railroad called for western work crews to start from Sacramento, California, and eastern work crews to start from Omaha, Nebraska. The two lines were to join "somewhere" along the route, depending on the progress made in construction. As it turned out, the meeting place was at Promontory, Utah, near the northern end of Great Salt Lake. The day, May 10, 1869, that the Union Pacific line met the Central Pacific line was an occasion that called for ceremony and celebration.

The illustration below, which is based on photographs and word descriptions, conveys some of the spirit and detail of the joining. Notice the two train engines, one of which is still belching smoke. Top hats indicate the dignitaries that were present; workers are in work clothes, and onlookers are fashionably dressed. A United States soldier, a corporal, is standing on the left. The man in the center is holding a golden spike which will be driven into the last railroad tie; another official is reading a proclamation.

Railroads Cross the Continent

Great Salt Lake

Located in northern Utah and almost touching the southern border of Idaho is Great Salt Lake, the largest lake west of the Mississippi River. If ever there was an appropriate name for a lake, Great Salt Lake is it. Depending upon the time of the year, the lake is from five to six times saltier than the oceans. It is virtually a "salt mine"; each year thousands of tons of salt are taken from the lake, refined, and then sold for commercial and domestic (household) use. It is almost impossible to drown in the lake because salt increases the buoyancy of the water. And, don't try to fish in the lake; there aren't any fish; there is too much salt for them to live.

Why is Great Salt Lake so salty? The answer is that the rivers that drain into the lake carry salt that has been washed out of the land. Because the lake has no outlets, the salt accumulates year-after-year; it has no place to go. If salt were not taken from the lake, as mentioned above, the lake would be even saltier.

Here are two more interesting facts about the lake: (1) Railroad tracks laid on a constructed causeway, a kind of dike, cross the lake in an east-west direction, and (2) there are islands in the lake. Antelope Island, the largest, is used for farming. It is easy to recognize the islands from the air because their shores are a bright white from the salt deposited on them.

Name: _____ Date: _____

UTAH: DRY LAND, HIGH MOUNTAINS, AND RIVERS

1. Deserts have been partially defined as areas that receive less than 10" of precipitation in an average year. At least one-third of Utah fits that description.

a. The map shows general outlines of three of Utah's deserts. What are their names?

_____ ,

_____ ,

and _____

b. Study the key to the map and notice that there are dots in the desert symbol. Complete the desert areas on the map with "sand dots."

2. As in Nevada, Utah has numerous streams that do not flow during an entire year. However, there are several year-round flowing rivers.

a. What three rivers contribute water directly to the Colorado River? _____ ,

_____ ,

and _____

b. What two rivers combine to make the Dirty Devil River?

_____ ,

and _____

UTAH

- ◉ Capital
- ✚ Mountain Peak
- ⬭ General outline of desert

Scale of Miles
0   40   80

Idaho

Bear Lake

• Logan

Wyoming

• Ogden

Great Salt Lake Desert

Salt Lake City ◉

Kings Peak (Highest point in Utah, 13,498')

Great Salt Lake

Jordan River

• Provo

Utah Lake

Nevada

Sevier Desert

Green River

Colorado

Sevier Lake

Sevier River

Muddy River

Colorado River

Fremont River

Dirty Devil River

• Moab

✚ Mt. Peale (13,089')

Escalante Desert

Cedar City

San Juan River

• St. George

Arizona

c. Complete the following sentence about the Sevier River by crossing out the incorrect word in the parentheses, and supplying words for the blank.

The Sevier River first flows (north, south), then makes a sharp turn to the (southeast, southwest), and then flows into _____ .

d. What river from the north contributes water (and salt) to Great Salt Lake? _____

e. What river connects Great Salt Lake and Utah Lake? _____

f. What two states share Bear Lake? _____ and _____

3. Use the Scale of Miles to determine Utah's greatest east-west and north-south distances.

East-west: _____ miles   North-south: _____ miles

4. Mt. Peale is Utah's second highest peak. How much higher than Mt. Peale is Kings Peak? _____ feet

COLORADO: THE COLORADO RIVER AND THE ROYAL GORGE

The Royal Gorge

The Royal Gorge is a great canyon carved out of the earth over thousands of years by the flowing action of the Arkansas River. In some places along the gorge, opposite rims are less than fifty feet apart. The water flowing through the gorge is swift; it takes expert boatmen to navigate it. Those who enjoy a more relaxed ride buy tickets for the train that runs through the gorge.

The world's highest suspension bridge, 1,053 feet above the river, spans the gorge. Some people who are afraid of heights are frightened when they cross the bridge and look below. This is especially true if the wind is blowing hard enough to cause the bridge to sway slightly. Of course, the bridge is so constructed that it will sway; a long suspension bridge that is too rigid would not be as safe.

The sketch below will give you a better understanding of the Royal Gorge suspension bridge. Note the two huge supports at the ends of the bridge, the two main suspension cables, which have other vertical cables hanging from them, and the roadbed these cables support.

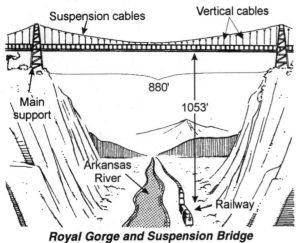

Royal Gorge and Suspension Bridge

The Colorado River

The Colorado River has its beginnings in Colorado at Grand Lake, high in the Rocky Mountains. The river ends its flow when it reaches the Gulf of California in Mexico. In its southwestward journey it cuts through the southeast corner of Utah, the northwest corner of Arizona, and then flows almost directly south along the borders of Nevada, California, and Arizona. The river's journey from beginning to end is 1,450 miles; 90 of those miles are in Mexico.

The Colorado River is one of the United States' most important rivers. Millions of people in the dry Southwest derive benefits from its waters. It supplies water for irrigation, thus enabling land that would be otherwise unproductive to grow crops. The power of its water falling through the penstocks of dams turns turbines that provide electricity for homes, communities, and industries. And, of course, water from the Colorado is used for drinking, swimming pools, and household equipment such as washing machines.

The Colorado River is, perhaps, the most important part of a great Colorado recreational area that has many attractions. Among those attractions is the Grand Canyon. Millions of Americans and visiting foreigners have been drawn to the wonders of this deep cut in the earth one mile deep and in some places more than fifteen miles wide.

At the bottom of the gigantic cleft in the earth the Colorado River rushes on its way. Specially trained and experienced guides take adventurous visitors for a thrilling ride they may never forget. While riding through the "white water" some boaters may have time to look up and see other tourists riding on mules as they make their way to the floor of the canyon.

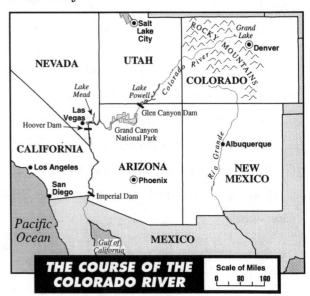

THE COURSE OF THE COLORADO RIVER

Name: _____ Date: _____

COLORADO: CITIES, RIVERS, DISTANCES

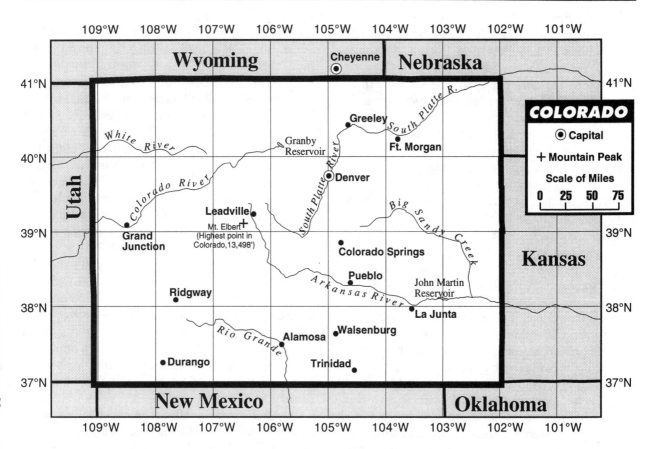

© 1996 by The Center for Applied Research in Education

All of the questions that follow can be answered from information on the map. For each question put a ✓ in either the **Yes** or **No** column.

Questions	Yes	No
1. Is Denver on the South Platte River?		
2. Is the Big Sandy Creek a tributary to the Arkansas River?		
3. Is Colorado bordered by seven other states?		
4. Is Mt. Elbert more than two miles above sea level? Note: one mile = 5,280'		
5. Is the distance between Denver and Colorado Springs more than 70 miles?		
6. On the Arkansas River, is La Junta downstream from Pueblo?		
7. Is Greeley south of the 40°N line of latitude?		

Questions	Yes	No
8. Is Grand Junction located at a higher latitude than Leadville?		
9. Is Colorado Springs west of the 104°W line of longitude?		
10. Does Durango lie in this quadrant: 107°W–108°W, and 38°N–39°N?		
11. Note: A degree of latitude on a line of longitude is approximately 70 miles. Using this knowlege, is Colorado about 280 miles from north to south?		
12. Cheyenne is almost directly north of Colorado Springs. Is the distance between them about 160 miles? Note: Use either degrees or the scale of miles to find the answer.		

151

ARIZONA: PETRIFIED FOREST, THE SAQUARO CACTUS

Petrified Forests

What does "petrified" mean, and what and where is the Petrified Forest National Park? Webster's dictionary tells us that *to petrify* is to "convert into stone or a stony substance." We also find that *petros* is a Latin word that means "rock" and that "petrify" is related to that Latin root. So, petrified wood is wood that has changed in such a way as to become stone or stony.

How does wood become petrified? A part of a tree, such as a limb, falls and eventually becomes buried in the ground. Or, a tree dies and the trunk topples and is buried. During the time the trees are buried, seeping water enters the porous spaces in the branches and trunks and washes away bits of wood. The water carries minerals of various kinds, especially silica. The minerals deposit and harden in the spaces once occupied by wood. Over a period of years the wood in the tree is completely replaced by stone.

The petrified trees are gradually uncovered by erosion and became visible. Some of the stone logs are more than 100' long; some of the logs are complete and some are broken into segments. The petrified logs have such a real appearance that some visitors find it difficult to believe that what they are looking at are no longer real trees.

Several states have "forests" of petrified wood. They are not really forests for forests are composed of live, standing trees.

Arizona's Petrified Forest National Park is in the northeastern part of Arizona near the town of Holbrook. Actually, there are six separate petrified forests in the park. Each year thousands of tourists visit the park. Of course, the tourists are a great help to Arizona's economy. The goods and services they require make for many jobs for Arizonians.

A Desert Cactus and a Desert Bird

In Arizona in May and June a waxy white flower appears on the ends of the "arms" of the Saquaro Cacti. It is a welcome sight on the sandy deserts of southwest Arizona. And, there aren't just one or two blossoms on an arm; the flowers are in clusters. Since a Saquaro Cactus may have as many as 50 arms or branches arranged on its up-to-sixty-feet height, the sight could even be called spectacular. Arizonians so love the flower of the Saquaro, they have declared it to be the official state flower.

The Saquaro Cactus can live as long as 200 years. Some of the plants now living were small plants shortly after the United States won its independence from England.

The state bird of Arizona is called, appropriately, the Cactus Wren. It is the largest of all wrens. Some of them are seven inches in length as compared to most wrens, which are five inches or less. And, guess where many Cactus Wrens build their nests? If you answered, "In the Saquaro Cactus," you would be correct. The thorns of the cactus are sharp, and few enemies of wrens want to risk getting stuck by them. The wrens have another trick to protect themselves and their young from predators; they build several nests and use only one of them for home. Enemies don't want to risk the thorns of a cactus only to find a nest empty.

Another way that the wrens are well-adapted to desert life is that they have long bills. With such bills they are able to reach deep inside cracks and crevices in the cactus plants to find insects and dig them out. This means of obtaining food is important because food for birds is not plentiful in deserts.

The Saquaro (Sah-war-oh) Cactus with Flower Blooms

Name: _____ Date: _____

ARIZONA: MAP-WORD PUZZLE

Word Search

There are seventeen cities, rivers, states, etc., spelled out in the word puzzle. The places are printed either across or down.

If a place is made up of two words—such as Las Vegas—a black space is between the two words.

Here is an effective way to proceed:

1. Select a name from the map.

2. Search for the name in the puzzle.

If you find the name, draw a neat line around all the words in the name. All the names in the puzzle are somewhere on the map.

C	O	L	O	R	A	D	O	K
A	M	E	X	I	C	O	V	W
L	A	S	■	V	E	G	A	S
I	F	P	H	O	E	N	I	X
F	L	A	G	S	T	A	F	F
O	C	N	I	P	U	Y	N	P
R	O	E	L	R	C	U	E	K
N	O	V	A	E	S	C	W	L
I	L	A	■	S	O	C	■	N
A	I	D	R	C	N	A	M	O
Z	D	A	I	O	U	G	E	G
M	G	R	V	T	T	Y	X	A
E	E	M	E	T	A	U	I	L
S	H	V	R	K	H	M	C	E
A	R	I	Z	O	N	A	O	S

NEW MEXICO: RIO GRANDE, CARLSBAD CAVERNS, NUMBERS

Rio Grande

Sometimes people refer to the Rio Grande as the "Rio Grande River." This is incorrect because "Rio" is the Spanish word for *river*. If people say, "Rio Grande River," they are really saying "River Grande River." The *Grande* part of the river's name means "large or great." Mexicans have a different name for the river; they call it *Rio Bravo del Norte*. Bravo means "brave," which, in a sense, means "great." The phrase "del Norte," means "of the North," that is, *The Brave River of the North*.

The Rio Grande *is* a large river, some 1,900 miles long. Its beginning is in Colorado; then, it flows north to south through New Mexico. After the Rio Grande leaves New Mexico it becomes a 1,300 mile border between the United States and Mexico; at the same time it is also the border between Texas and Mexico (see map).

Although it is true that the Rio Grande is a long river, it is also true that for long stretches of its route it is a shallow river. In the dryer parts of its journey, and especially in the dry months of the summer, the river becomes a mere trickle. Near its ending in the Gulf of Mexico even small boats cannot go very far upstream. Tributaries such as the Pecos River (Texas) are helpful in maintaining the Rio Grande's flow.

The importance of the Rio Grande lies not only in the part it plays as a boundary, but also in its being a source of water for irrigation. Dams have been built along its course that, in times of heavy rains, store water in backup reservoirs. This water is released in dry months. The results are that thousands of acres of land that otherwise would be useless for crops produce large quantities of oranges and other citrus fruits, vegetables, and even cotton.

Both the United States and Mexico have worked together to make the Rio Grande useful, and both countries are the beneficiaries of that cooperation.

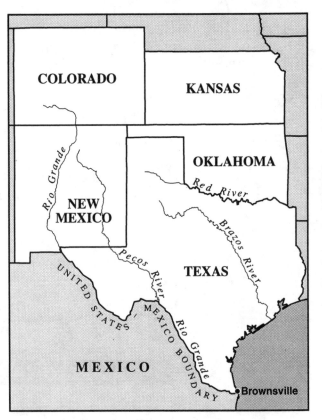

Interesting Facts about New Mexico

Carlsbad Caverns in New Mexico's southeast has the largest "room" of any caverns in the world. The room is 1,500 feet long, 300 feet wide and 300 feet high. The area of the floor of the room is 450,000 square feet; this is about ten acres of floor space. Ten full-sized football fields could be laid out in the room with space left over for bleachers.

Counting in Spanish

Many of the people in New Mexico speak both Spanish and English. Here are the Spanish words for the numbers from one to twenty.

uno – 1	ocho – 8	quince – 15
dos – 2	nueve – 9	dieciseis – 16
tres – 3	diez – 10	diecisiete – 17
cuatro – 4	once – 11	dieciocho – 18
cinco – 5	doce – 12	diecinueve – 19
seis – 6	trece – 13	veinte – 20
siete – 7	catorce – 14	

Name: _____ Date: _____

NEW MEXICO: A TRIP AROUND THE STATE

A Trip through New Mexico

You start your trip at Hobbs in the southeastern corner of New Mexico. Notice that the key to the map tells you that *Interstate* is abbreviated with an I as, for example, I-25. Likewise, *United States* highways are abbreviated with US as in US-70.

1. **What state is a few miles east of Hobbs?** _____

2. **You drive to Carlsbad.** What is the approximate distance from Hobbs to Carlsbad?

_____ miles

3. **At Carlsbad you turn north.** On what highway are you now driving? _____

4. **You drive north on US-285 until you meet US-70. At US-70 you turn northeast and drive to Clovis.** Through what city did you drive before you arrived at Clovis? _____

5. **From Clovis you drive west to I-25. You drive north on I-25 to Albuquerque.** What highway intersects I-25 at Albuquerque? _____

6. **From Albuquerque you drive north on I-25 to Santa Fe. From Santa Fe you drive southeast on US-84.** What highway do you meet? _____

7. **You drive a few miles east on I-40 until you come to Santa Rosa. At Santa Rosa you drive southwest on US-54 toward Alamogordo.** What city do you first meet? _____

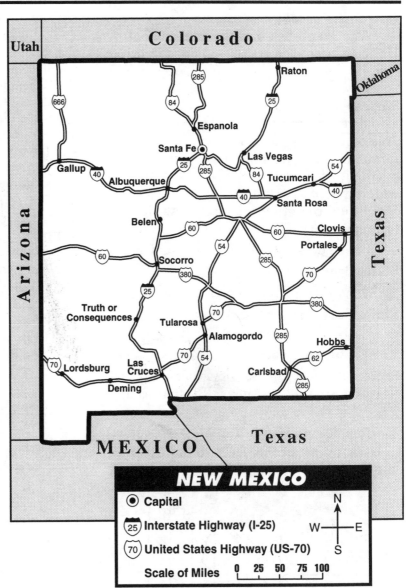

8. **You continue on US-54 to Alamogordo then you turn southwest.** What route are you now traveling? ____

9. **You continue west on US-70 through Las Cruces, Deming, and Lordsburg.** What state do you soon enter? _____

10. Start at Hobbs and draw a line along all the highways you traveled to finally reach Lordsburg. Every inch or so put an arrow on your line that shows the direction you traveled. (>->->-)

11. On the reverse side of this page develop a trip through New Mexico. You could start at Raton on I-25. Use this page as a model.

Name: _____ Date: _____

ALASKA: AREA AND POPULATION

How Big Is Alaska?

The graph below represents the entire United States. The graph is divided into 100 equal sections, and each block represents one percent (1%) of the total of 100 blocks. We can color various blocks to help us visualize and compare the portions of land area occupied by particular states. If a state, for example, takes up five blocks, that means it occupies 5% of the total land and water area of the United States.

Study the graph and complete the following activity.

1. What percent of the land of the United States does Alaska occupy? _____%

2. What percent of the area of the United States does Texas occupy? _____%

3. Compare the Northeast States and Alaska by completing the following sentence: Alaska occupies _____% of the United States and the Northeast States occupy _____% of the area.

4. Complete this sentence: Alaska occupies _____% more of the United States than Texas and the Northeast States together.

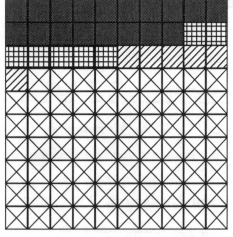

AREA OF THE UNITED STATES

KEY: 1 ☐ = 1%   ▨ Northeast States*

■ Alaska   ⊠ Rest of the U.S.

▦ Texas

---

*   ME, NH, VT, NY, MA, CT, RI, PA, NJ, DE, MD, WV

Alaska's Population

Alaska, is, by far, the largest state in the United States. However, it has fewer people than any other state except Wyoming and Vermont.

How Alaska compares with the two most heavily populated states—New York and California—can be shown on a graph similar to the one in the opposite column. In this example the entire graph will represent the total population of the three states. The number of blocks each state fills will show how the populations of the three states compare.

Follow these steps to complete the graph.

1. Study the key; it will tell you how each state should be represented in the blocks.

2. Carefully fill in the blocks according to the information in the table below.

3. Think of a title for your graph and write it on the lines above the graph.

State	Each State's Percentage of Total Population	Boxes
California	63%	63
New York	36%	36
Alaska	1%	1

Title: _____

_____

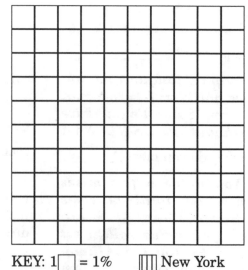

KEY: 1 ☐ = 1%   ▥ New York

■ Alaska   ▨ California

Name: _____ Date: _____

ALASKA: THE USA'S LARGEST AND MOST NORTHERN STATE

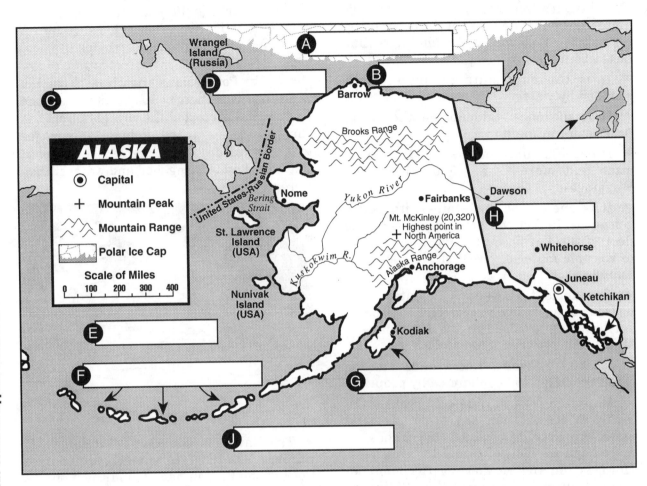

1. Complete the labeling of the map of Alaska, as follows:

A Polar Ice Pack

B Arctic Ocean

C Russia

D Chukchi Sea

E Bering Sea

F Aleutian Islands

G Kodiak Island

H Canada

I Great Bear Lake

J Pacific Ocean

2. Mt. McKinley is the highest mountain in North America. What is its elevation?

_____

3. What city is the capital of Alaska?

_____

4. To which country does St. Lawrence Island belong? _____

5. Approximately how many miles is it from Anchorage to Barrow (Alaska's northernmost community)?

__675 miles   __1,325 miles   __1,600 miles

6. Why would it be difficult for a ship to sail in the area you labeled at **A** on the map? _____

_____

_____

_____

HAWAII: GEOGRAPHY AND HISTORY FACTS

Hawaii's geography and history are quite different from those of the other forty-nine states. Following are some interesting facts about Hawaii.

☞ It is the only state completely surrounded by water.

☞ It is the only state not on the North American continent.

☞ It is 2,400 miles southwest of San Francisco and more than 4,500 miles from Washington, D.C.

☞ It is one of the few states with active volcanoes. In fact, volcanic eruptions on the floor of the Pacific Ocean and the build-up of volcanic materials created the Hawaiian Islands.

☞ The ancient Hawaiians invented surfboards. Even today, world competitions in surfboarding are held in the Hawaiian Islands.

☞ Most of Hawaii's 132 islands are too small or barren to be inhabited by people.

☞ More rain falls on Waialeale Peak on the island of Kauai than any other place on earth. An average of about 460 inches, or more than 38 feet, of rain falls each year. However, on the smallest of the main islands, Kahoolawe, no more than 25 inches of rain falls in a year; it is so dry, windswept and barren that no one lives there.

☞ Hawaii is known as the *Aloha State;* "aloha" translates to *love*, *welcome*, or *greetings*.

☞ The location of Hawaii, midway between North America and Asia and north of numerous South Pacific islands, has helped it to have a diversified population. Six of every ten Hawaiians have an Asiatic (such as Japanese, Chinese, Korean, Filipino) or Polynesian background.

☞ Some 2,000 years ago what is now the Hawaiian Islands were uninhabited. Polynesians, people from the numerous islands to the south, first found the islands and settled them. The Polynesian voyages of discovery were remarkable for they had only the stars and their knowledge of Pacific Ocean currents to guide them.

Some of the Polynesian canoes were double, that is, two canoes tied together. A platform between the canoes helped to prevent capsizing. As the illustration below shows, the Polynesians knew how to use the wind to power their boats. Notice, also, the shelter that protected the voyagers from the sun and storms. Often, Polynesian voyages took several days and nights. This meant that they had to bring food and water if they were to survive.

Polynesian Double Canoe

☞ The Hawaiian Islands were unknown to Europeans until 1778, when Captain James Cook of the British navy found them on one of his voyages of discovery.

Soon after Cook's discovery, Americans and Europeans sailed to the islands. Whaling ships found them a convenient place to obtain food and water. Colonists established pineapple and sugar plantations. Missionaries went there to convert the Hawaiians to Christianity. Then, in 1887, the United States obtained permission to establish a naval base at Pearl Harbor on the island of Oahu.

American influence in Hawaii led to the annexation of the islands in 1898. Two years later the islands were declared a United States territory. Following the defeat of the Japanese in World War II, the Hawaiian people campaigned to have Hawaii become a state. Their efforts were successful; Hawaiians voted 17 to one for statehood. The United States Congress then voted in favor of statehood, and President Dwight Eisenhower signed the papers that, in 1959, made Hawaii the fiftieth state.

Name: _____ Date: _____

HAWAII: THE ISLAND STATE

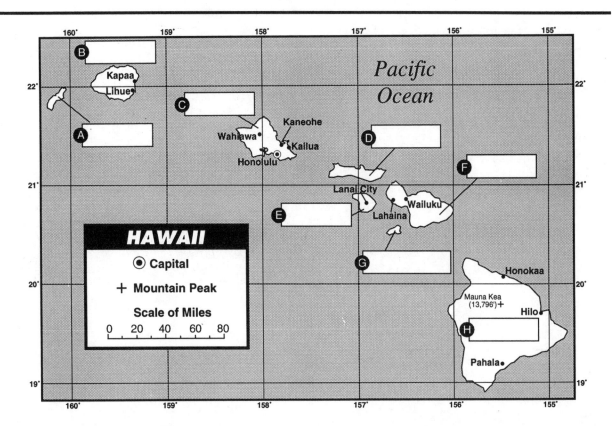

1. Label the eight main islands that make up the state of Hawaii. Use capital letters and print in the boxes.

Ⓐ NIIHAU

Ⓑ KAUAI

Ⓒ OAHU

Ⓓ MOLOKAI

Ⓔ LANAI

Ⓕ MAUI

Ⓖ KAHOOLAWE

Ⓗ HAWAII

Note: The *island* of *Hawaii* is only one of the islands of the state of Hawaii. In all there are 132 islands in the state.

2. Oahu is Hawaii's most populated island. Eight of every ten Hawaiians live on Oahu. And, the capital of Hawaii—Honolulu—is on the southern shore of Oahu.

Learn more about Oahu by studying the map and answering the following questions.

a. What line of longitude crosses over the center of Oahu? _____ °W

b. Between what two lines of latitude does Oahu lie? _____°N and _____°N

c. What island shown on the map is *completely* within the 20°N-21°N–156°W-157°W quadrant? _____

3. Mauna Kea is Hawaii's highest peak.

a. On what island is it located? _____

b. What is its elevation? _____ feet

4. What two consecutive islands shown on the map have the longest stretch of water between them?

_____ and _____

Use the scale of miles to determine the distance between the two islands. Approximately _____ miles

159

Canada

CANADA: READING AND COMPLETING A MAP AND TABLE

The map on the opposite page offers opportunities for your students to become acquainted with the location, conformation, and place names of Canada. Also, several map reading skills can be practiced in the context of Canada.

Following are some suggested procedures.

1. Photocopy the page and distribute.

2. Make a transparency of the page, which will be used throughout the lesson. As you label the transparency, students should label their maps.

3. Label the following:

☞ 49°N: The boundary line for approximately one-half the distance of the United States/Canada border

☞ 141°W: The line of longitude that separates Alaska from Canada

☞ 66½°N: The latitude of the Arctic Circle

4. Canada extends north from approximately 44°N (Windsor on Lake Erie) to 85°N (northern tip of Ellesmere Island). Using 70 miles as the length of one degree of latitude, have your students determine the greatest north-south distance of Canada (41° × 70 miles = 2,870 miles).

5. Canada is made up of ten provinces and two territories. The territories are already labeled on the map. Have your students label the provinces as follows, using the abbreviations provided.

Ⓐ British Columbia (B.C.)
Ⓑ Alberta (ALTA)
Ⓒ Saskatchewan (SASK)
Ⓓ Manitoba (MAN)
Ⓔ Ontario (ONT)
Ⓕ Quebec (QUE)
Ⓖ Newfoundland (NEWF)
Ⓗ New Brunswick (N.B.)
Ⓘ Prince Edward Island (P.E.I.)
Ⓙ Nova Scotia (N.S.)

6. They should also label these significant water features:

❶ Hudson Bay

❷ Pacific Ocean

❸ Atlantic Ocean

Note: The following are already labeled on the map and should be pointed out: Great Bear Lake, Great Slave Lake, Lake Athabasca, Lake Winnipeg.

7. Aspects of Canada on the map:

❑ Canada stretches from approximately 63°W to 143°W; from extreme east to extreme west it is 3,426 miles.

❑ Canada shares four of the Great Lakes (Superior, Huron, Erie, Ontario) with the United States. The fifth lake, Lake Michigan, is entirely within the United States.

❑ Canada's western coastline is considerably shortened by the "pan handle" of Alaska.

The table, "Areas of Canada's Provinces," may be completed as follows:

Province	Area in Square Miles
Quebec	594,860
Ontario	412,581
British Columbia	365,947
Alberta	255,287
Saskatchewan	251,866
Manitoba	250,947
Newfoundland	156,949
New Brunswick	28,355
Nova Scotia	21,425
Prince Edward Island	2,185

Name: _____ Date: _____

CANADA: READING AND COMPLETING A MAP AND TABLE

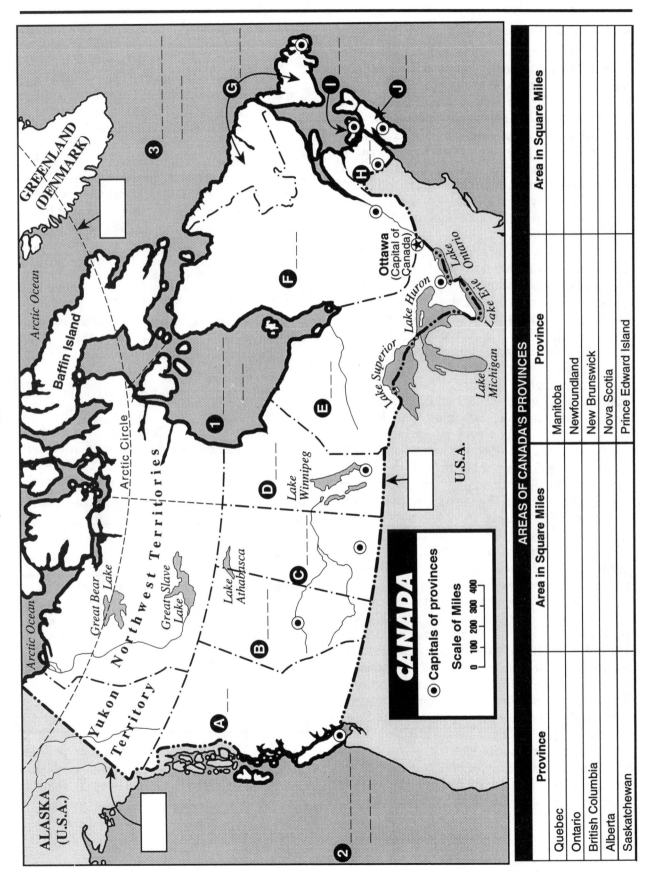

© 1996 by The Center for Applied Research in Education

CANADA
- ⊙ Capitals of provinces
- Scale of Miles
- 0 100 200 300 400

AREAS OF CANADA'S PROVINCES

Province	Area in Square Miles	Province	Area in Square Miles
Quebec		Manitoba	
Ontario		Newfoundland	
British Columbia		New Brunswick	
Alberta		Nova Scotia	
Saskatchewan		Prince Edward Island	

CANADA: ESKIMOS AND LEARNING CENTERS

Learning Centers

A "learning center" is a place set aside in a classroom where various activities on a particular topic are available for students in the class. The activities should differ in difficulty and complexity to better accommodate the levels of ability and interest that are present in a typical class. In most cases activities at a center should be of such a nature that they can be done independently. And, the activities should be designed to expand and enrich the basic subject matter of a unit of study.

Learning centers can be effective in developing skills such as locating and organizing information; map, picture, graph, table, and diagram interpretation; and critical thinking. Activities that are "hands on," such as creating a model, can develop manual dexterity, the ability to plan, and self-reliance.

Canada lends itself well to the learning center approach to teaching. The country has many unique geographical and historical aspects. For example, Eskimos who live in Canada's far north would be of interest to many students. An effective way to capitalize on such interest would be through the use of pictures. The activity on page 166 shows how one picture could be used as the main instructional element in a learning center activity. Carrying out the activity should increase students' understandings of the subject matter facts and thier abilities to make inferences based on those facts.

The picture reading activity also serves one of the objectives of the "Whole Language" movement: Language activities should be included in all subjects across the curriculum. Students gathering information and drawing inferences from a visual stimulus are required to communicate these facts and inferences through language. Thus they utilize language skills while acquiring subject matter knowledge.

The Eskimo drawing on page 166 is an example of the kind of picture that offers many opportunities for inferencing. It contains numerous details about Eskimo life and environment, and it would be easy to state the main idea or ideas of the picture. This, in a sense makes the picture a "paragraph," which should also have a main idea and supporting detail. The picture is simple, yet eloquent; it has appeal to young students because there are children present. From the affective point-of-view the picture shows family life in a positive atmosphere. Activities are clearly discernible and have the capacity to evoke thoughts such as, "That looks interesting. I'd like to be there."

Here is a suggested procedure for making the picture a learning center activity:

1. Photocopy the student page.

2. Place a number of photocopied pages in a folder with the number and title of the activity printed on the tab of the folder and on the activity page.

3. Briefly explain what is to be done in the activity.

4. Prepare a chart that lists the various activities in the center. As students complete activities they should put checks besides their names as listed on the chart.

Note: This procedure eliminates paper work for instructors; the instructor can quickly determine how each student is progressing.

LEARNING CENTER ACTIVITY RECORD: CANADA			
Name	#1: Eskimo	#2: Fishing Banks	(Etc.)
Susan	✔		
Tom		✔	
Pat	✔		

5. Instruct students that they are to keep all papers in a personal folder and that they are to return all activity folders to their proper storage space.

CANADA: ESKIMOS AND LEARNING CENTERS

6. Following is a suggested list of details that the Eskimo picture reveals.

❑ Dogs, a big one and a small one

❑ A small boat with an opening for one person

❑ A fish

❑ A man, a woman, three children ranging in age

❑ A shelter, dome shaped, possibly covered with skins

❑ A platform raised on stilts, something stacked on top

❑ Animals, possibly reindeer or caribou

❑ Warm clothing of skins and furs

❑ An absence of visible snow and ice

7. Here is a story that is simply written, much as a typical student might write. Note the inferential thinking.

The picture shows an Eskimo family. The man by the boat is the father. He has just returned from fishing. His wife and three children are admiring the fish he caught. The dogs are excited. They probably would like to eat the fish.

The animals in the rear of the picture are probably reindeer or caribou. They furnish food for the family. The animals can be milked or they could provide meat. Maybe the milk can be made into cheese. The dogs could eat the meat, too.

There is no snow on the ground, and the animals are eating something on the ground, probably grass. Even though the family members are dressed in warm clothing made of skins and furs, they don't look cold. This is probably a picture of Eskimos in the summer time.

The shelter is probably covered with skins from the reindeer. The domed shape of the shelter would make it difficult for winds to catch hold of it and blow it away.

The raised platform in back of the shelter may be used for storing food. The platform is raised so that dogs or wild animals such as coyotes and polar bears can't get at the food.

Eskimo Background

❑ Eskimos today live in northern North America (Alaska, Canada, Greenland) and in northern Asia, chiefly Siberia. There are an estimated 115,000 Eskimos living in northern lands. Canada has about 25,000 Eskimos; Greenland, 50,000; and Alaska, 40,000.

❑ Eskimo migration from Asia occurred long after the people from Asia, erroneously called "Indians," entered the continent. The early Indians walked across the land bridge, now the Bering Strait, that connected North America and Asia. The Eskimos most likely came across the strait, which replaced the land bridge, in small boats.

❑ Students may be under the impression that Eskimos all live in ice houses or skin tents; this is, of course, incorrect. Some Eskimos do live in such homes and make their livings and enjoy social patterns much as the earliest Eskimo settlers. The majority of Eskimos, however, live in permanent homes in small communities. They very likely may use snowmobiles or four-by-four trucks for transportation as compared to dog sleds. They make their livings as miners, store keepers, tourist guides, government workers , and so on. In other words they are wage earners as compared to hunters, trappers, or whalers going out to sea in small boats.

A typical Eskimo family living in town will buy their food at a grocery store, clothes in a clothing store, and, sometimes, eat in a restaurant. Their homes will have electricity to run sewing machines and vacuum cleaners. The children will attend school and, perhaps, when they are at home, play computer games.

Nevertheless, some of the old ways persist. In more outlying communities, Eskimos may follow ancient spiritual beliefs, whereas most Eskimos are Christians. For entertainment, television shows may utilize Eskimo actors who speak in the Eskimo language. Thus, many Eskimos are in a state of transition—they enjoy modern ways, but, at the same time, they don't want to lose all of the old ways.

ACTIVITY: ESKIMOS AND THEIR ENVIRONMENT

To Do:

1. List all the facts or details you see in the picture.

Fact:_____

Fact:_____

Fact:_____

Fact:_____

Fact:_____

Fact:_____

Fact:_____

Fact:_____

Fact:_____

Fact:_____

2. Write a short story that you think explains the picture. Use the facts you have listed. (Use the back of this page, if necessary.)

_____

_____

_____

_____

_____

_____

_____

_____

_____

_____

_____

_____

_____

_____

_____

Name: _____ Date: _____

CANADA: MAP PUZZLE

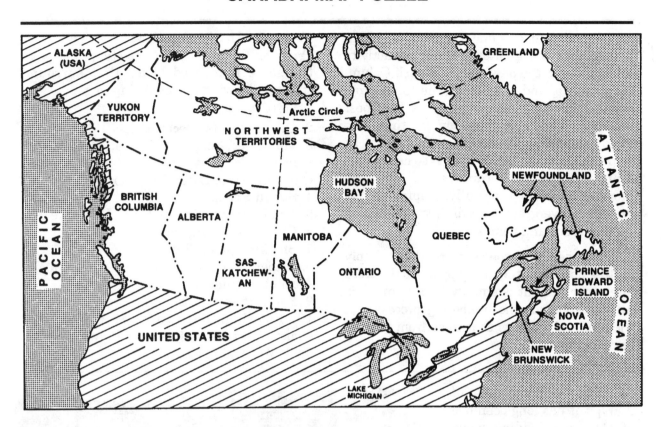

CANADA ON THE MAP

1. Fill the blank squares with names from the map. If a name has more than one word, a blank space separates the words.

2. Answer each question by checking either YES or NO.

a. Do any Canadian *provinces* extend north of the Arctic Circle?

___ YES ___ NO

b. Does Ontario border four Great Lakes?

___ YES ___ NO

c. Does Alaska border any of the Canadian *provinces*?

___ YES ___ NO

d. Do more than three *provinces* border on Hudson Bay?

___ YES ___ NO

167

CANADA: LUMBERING AND WOOD PRODUCTS

One of Canada's major industries is lumbering, and the greatest lumbering activity takes place in the provinces of British Columbia, Ontario, and Quebec. Of the three provinces, British Columbia produces the most lumber. There is good reason for that. The yearly rainfall on British Columbia's western slopes of the Rocky Mountains is so heavy that some areas are true "rain forests." The cool, moist climate is especially helpful to the growth of evergreen ("needle") trees such as spruce, cedar and hemlock.

Lumbering involves more than simply cutting down trees. What happens to the trees after they are cut is equally important. This activity concerns the lumbering process and the kinds of products that come from various parts of trees.

To Do On The Facing Page:

Transfer the listings in the items below to the same numbered boxes that surround the tree drawing on the facing page.

1. Nuts, Fruit
2. Oils, Extracts, Decorations
3. Varnishes, Soaps, Medicines, Waxes, Turpentine, Crayons, Insecticides, Perfumes, Chewing Gum, Latex (rubber)
4. Sugar, Syrup
5. Tannin (for curing leather), Oils, Dye
6. Charcoal, Rosin, Pine Oil
7. Smoking pipes, Tea, Oil
8. Paper, Fuel, Charcoal, Plastics, Rayon, Alcohol, Insulation
9. Poles, Piles, Posts
10. Flooring, Furniture, Shingles, Construction Lumber, Baskets, Plywood, Sawdust, Wood Chips

The manufacture of newsprint has long been one of Canada's leading wood products industries. The sentences that follow describe the main steps in the manufacture of paper, but they are out of order. Study the diagram on this page, and number the sentences to tell the correct sequence.

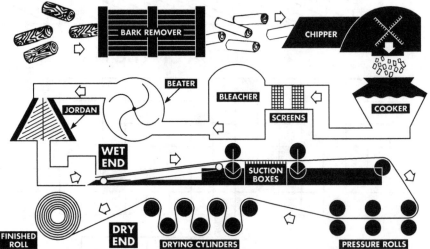

___ After the logs arrive at the paper mill, they are fed into a machine that removes the bark.

___ The logs then go into the chipper, which cuts them into small pieces.

___ Then the pulp goes to the Jordan machine, where the fibers are cut to the proper length.

___ As the wet mass passes through the last machines, the water is removed by suction, by pressure rolls, and by heated drying cylinders.

___ The finished paper comes off the dry end of the machine and is wound in huge rolls.

___ The soggy fibers enter the papermaking machine at the wet end.

___ In the "cooker," chemicals are added to the chips and the mixture is heated until it becomes a soft pulp.

___ Next the pulp passes through the beater, in which the wood fibers are frayed to make them cling together.

___ This pulp is then screened to remove impurities, and bleached by chemicals to make it white.

Name: _____ Date: _____

CANADA: LUMBERING AND WOOD PRODUCTS

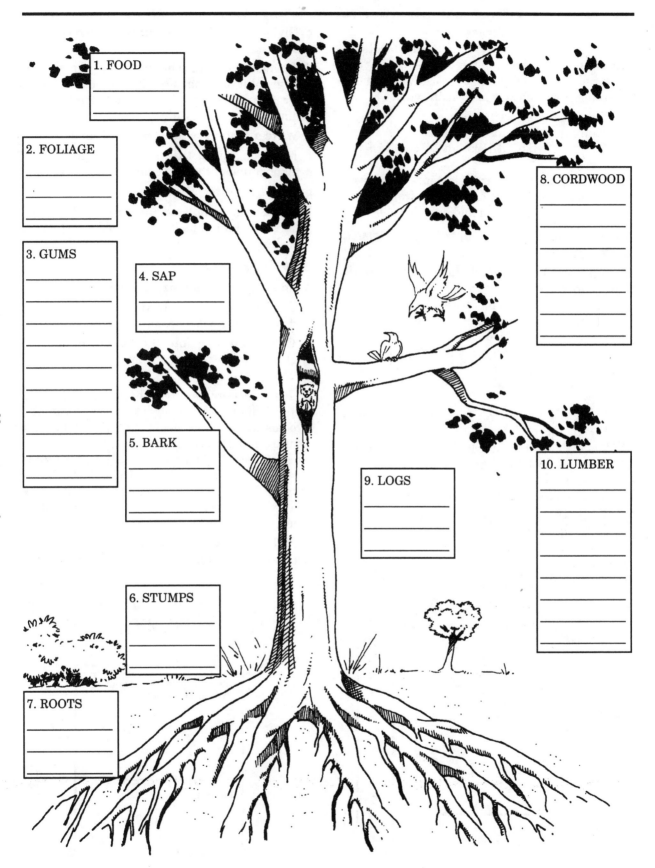

1. FOOD

2. FOLIAGE

3. GUMS

4. SAP

5. BARK

6. STUMPS

7. ROOTS

8. CORDWOOD

9. LOGS

10. LUMBER

CANADA: TOPICS OF INTEREST ON "TV" FILMSTRIPS

1. Canada Research Topics

Some of the many interesting facets of Canada may be depicted on student-created "TV" filmstrips. There are numerous positive outcomes for students who engage in such an activity.

❑ Researching a specific topic

❑ Planning a sequence of "frames"

❑ Working with others on a cooperative endeavor

❑ Utilizing language arts elements on a geography topic, including captioning frames and presenting the strip to an audience

Following Are Some Suggested Topics Related to Canada:

❑ Wild Animals of Canada (polar bears, Arctic foxes, caribou, etc.)

❑ Early European Explorers of Canada

❑ Canada's First Settlement at Quebec

❑ Royal Canadian Mounted Police

❑ Crossing Canada on the Trans-Canada Highway

❑ The Great Lakes and the St. Lawrence Seaway

❑ Salmon Fishing in Canada (salmon life cycle, endangerment)

❑ Canada's National Parks (unique features)

❑ The Hudson's Bay Company

❑ Soo Canals

❑ Gold Strikes in Canada (Yukon)

2. Suggested Steps in Planning and Developing a TV Filmstrip:

a. Select a topic.

b. Research the topic.

c. Divide the topic into subtopics. Each subtopic becomes a frame.

d. Develop the frames on 8½" × 11" paper. Various graphic approaches should be utilized—drawings, photographs, maps, graphs, diagrams, tables, charts, etc.

e. Write a caption or title for each frame.

f. Make an initial title frame that includes a symbolization of the film's main topic.

g. Tape frames together.

h. Attach the completed filmstrip to the dowel rollers. Masking tape is a firm holder, yet easily detached.

3. Making a TV Box

a. An appropriate box size is about 14" × 8½".

b. The box flaps should be tucked inside the box and then taped with masking tape.

c. Cut an opening into the bottom of the box slightly smaller than the frame paper. This will be the TV screen.

d. Insert rollers through the sides of the TV. Rollers should be at least ½" in diameter. Broomstick handles make suitable rollers. To insure a tight fit, the holes for the rollers on the sides of the TV should be slightly smaller than the diameter of the rollers. It should be necessary to force the rollers through the openings. This ensures that the rollers will not wobble when rotated.

e. Make the box attractive by decorating it with wallpaper, coloring, etc.

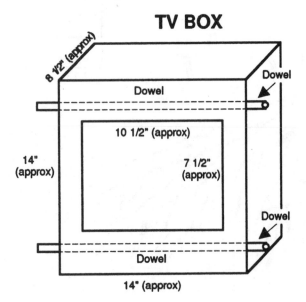

TV BOX

8 ½" (approx)

Dowel

Dowel

10 1/2" (approx)

14" (approx)

7 1/2" (approx)

Dowel

Dowel

14" (approx)

TV FILMSTRIP

Frame 1 (attached to dowel with masking tape)

Tape on back of frames

Frame 2

Roll

Name: _____ Date: _____

CANADA: FISHING AND THE GRAND BANKS

An early explorer of Canada's coast—John Cabot, an Italian sailing for France—was astonished at the huge schools of fish he saw off the coast of what is now Newfoundland. He carried the news back to France, and, soon after, courageous captains and crews of fishing boats sailed to the Grand Banks, as they came to be called. The risks were numerous, but so were the rewards, for the demand for fish in Europe was great. Cabot found the banks in 1497; today, some 500 years later, Canadians and other nationalities are still pulling large catches of fish out of the Grand Banks' waters.

The map shows the location of the Grand Banks and the kinds of fish that are caught there.

The diagram shows a cross-section of a typical fishing bank. Fish are attracted to the bank because there is

plenty of food for them. Sunlight penetrates the shallow waters, and the heat energy from the sun encourages the growth of small plant and animal life upon which the fish feed.

Map and Fishing Bank Activity

1. Complete the following sentences by drawing a line under the best choice in the parentheses: The Grand Banks are off Newfoundland's (southeast, south, southwest coast). The area covered by the banks appears to be (much smaller than, about the same size as, much larger than) the island of Newfoundland.

2. What three provinces, not including Newfoundland, would probably have easy access to the banks?

_____, _____, and _____

3. What are two kinds of fish caught at the Grand Banks? _____ , _____

4. a. Two fishing banks are shown at numbers ① and ② on the diagram. Write **Bank** on the lines provided.
b. Fish are also attracted to the **Continental Shelf**, which is also shallow and receives the sun's heat and energy. Label **Continental Shelf** at ③.
c. Banks are often found far out in the ocean. In the diagram each vertical line marks fifteen miles' distance. The first line is labeled 0; the second line is 15. Continue this number pattern to label the remaining lines.

5. How deep is the water beneath the fishing boat? _____

6. Complete the diagram by drawing schools of fish (◂▸) in the waters above banks one and two.

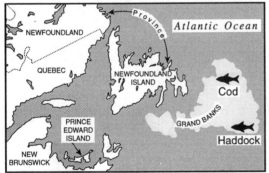

Typical Fishing Bank

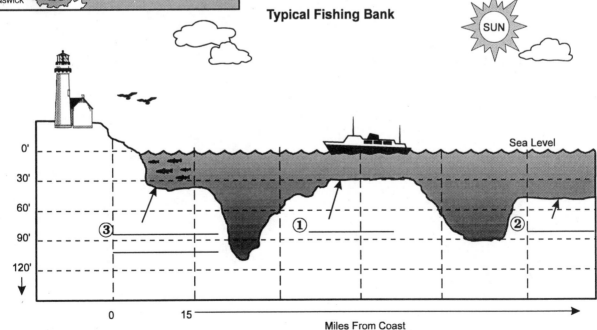

Latin America
(Mexico, Central America,
West Indies)

LATIN AMERICA ON THE MAP

Latin America is a general term for the lands south of the United States. Included in Latin America are the subdivisions of Middle America, the West Indies, and South America. The term "Latin America" suggests that all the people who settled there and live there are of Spanish and Portuguese descent. Although this is in large part true, it is not entirely true. For example, a number of countries in the West Indies have had significant amounts of British, Dutch, and French influence in their histories and developments. Nevertheless, the term "Latin America" is useful, provided its limitations are realized.

Following are some suggestions for introducing students to Latin America. Later in *American Continents* wider and more specific coverage will be included.

1. Make a transparency for your use, and photocopies for students, of the facing page.

2. Notice that each place listed on this page is numbered and there are corresponding numbers on the map. However, the list on the students' page is not numbered.

3. As you use this page's list to identify each country by number and name, have your students write the name of the country in their list. In this way students obtain a map of Latin America with all the countries identified.

Note: All the places listed are independent countries except Puerto Rico (USA) and French Guiana (France).

4. As you identify a country it would be helpful to give some background information. For example, "Country number 2 is Belize. Formerly, it was a British colony known as British Honduras." Another example, "Bolivia, number 31, is a landlocked country. Paraguay, number 32, is the only other land-locked country in South America." Also, you may want to ask your students to mention something they notice about the location of the countries.

Latin American List of Countries*

Middle America
1. Mexico
2. Belize
3. Guatemala
4. Honduras
5. El Salvador   — Central America
6. Nicaragua
7. Costa Rica
8. Panama

West Indies
9. Cuba
10. Jamaica
11. Haiti
12. Dominican Republic
13. Puerto Rico (USA)
14. The Bahamas
15. St. Kitts & Nevis
16. Antigua & Barbuda
17. Dominica
18. St. Lucia
19. Barbados
20. St. Vincent & the Grenadines
21. Grenada
22. Trinidad & Tobago

South America
23. Colombia
24. Venezuela
25. Guyana
26. Suriname
27. French Guiana (France)
28. Ecuador
29. Peru
30. Brazil
31. Bolivia
32. Paraguay
33. Chile
34. Uruguay
35. Argentina

* Exceptions: Puerto Rico and French Guiana

© 1996 by The Center for Applied Research in Education

Name: _____ Date: _____

LATIN AMERICA ON THE MAP

Countries and Other Places of Latin America

Middle America

1. _____

2. _____

3. _____

4. _____

5. _____

6. _____

7. _____

8. _____

West Indies

9. _____

10. _____

11. _____

12. _____

_____

13. _____

_____

14. _____

15. _____

_____

16. _____

_____

17. _____

18. _____

19. _____

20. _____

_____

21. _____

22. _____

_____

South America

23. _____

24. _____

25. _____

26. _____

27. _____

_____

28. _____

29. _____

30. _____

31. _____

32. _____

33. _____

34. _____

35. _____

UNITED STATES

WEST INDIES

MIDDLE AMERICA

SOUTH AMERICA

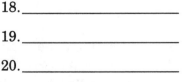

LATIN AMERICA
- Middle America
- West Indies
- South America

MEXICO: A MAP OF ITS HIGHWAYS

Reading a road map of Mexico can be an interesting and helpful way to become familiar with the country. Study the map and key on the facing page to find the answers to the questions that follow.

1. On the line before the name of a United States border city write the number of the Mexican city that is across the border from it.

United States	Mexico
____ El Paso	1. Piedras Negras
____ Calexico	2. Nuevo Laredo
____ Eagle Pass	3. Ciudad Juarez
____ Laredo	4. Reinosa
____ Brownsville	5. Mexicali
____ McAllen	6. Matamoros

2. What is the first Mexican city you would meet after leaving each of the following border cities?

a. Piedras Negras: _____

b. Mexicali: _____

c. Nogales: _____

d. Ciudad Juarez: _____

e. Reinosa: _____

3. What is the number of the highway that connects:

a. Mexico City to San Luis Potosi? _____

b. Torreon to Monterrey? _____

c. Tampico to Vera Cruz? _____

d. Guadalajara to Mexico City? _____

4. How many miles is the drive from:

a. Nogales to Mexico City on highway 15?

_____ miles

b. Mexico City to Ciudad de las Casas on highway 190? _____ miles

c. What is the total number of miles from Nogales to Mexico City to Ciudad de las Casas? _____ miles

5. A road map may give the impression of a smooth and level drive with no hills, mountains, or valleys. However, much of the driving in Mexico can be quite the opposite for there are three main mountain ranges, all with twisting roads that require careful driving.

a. What is the name of the range of mountains between highways ⑮ and ㊺?

_____

b. What is the name of the range between highways ㊗ and ㊇?

_____

c. What is the name of the range south of highways ⑮ and ⑲⓪?

_____

Note: *Occidental* means "West," *Oriental* means "East," and *del Sur* means "of the South." *Sierra Madre* means "Mother Mountain Range"; so, *Sierra Madre del Sur* translates to "Mother Mountain Range of the South."

6. Sometimes it may be more convenient to fly across Mexico and the waters around it. What is the air distance from:

a. Merida to Matamoros? _____ miles

b. Merida to Tampico? _____ miles

c. La Paz to Culiacan? _____ miles

7. You can complete the road map of Mexico by labeling the following:

A Pacific Ocean

B Gulf of California

C Gulf of Mexico

D Gulf of Campeche

To Go Ahead

Notice the mileage chart on the map. Complete the chart with your own city-to-city choices. One line has been completed as an example.

Name: _____ Date: _____

MEXICO: A MAP OF ITS HIGHWAYS

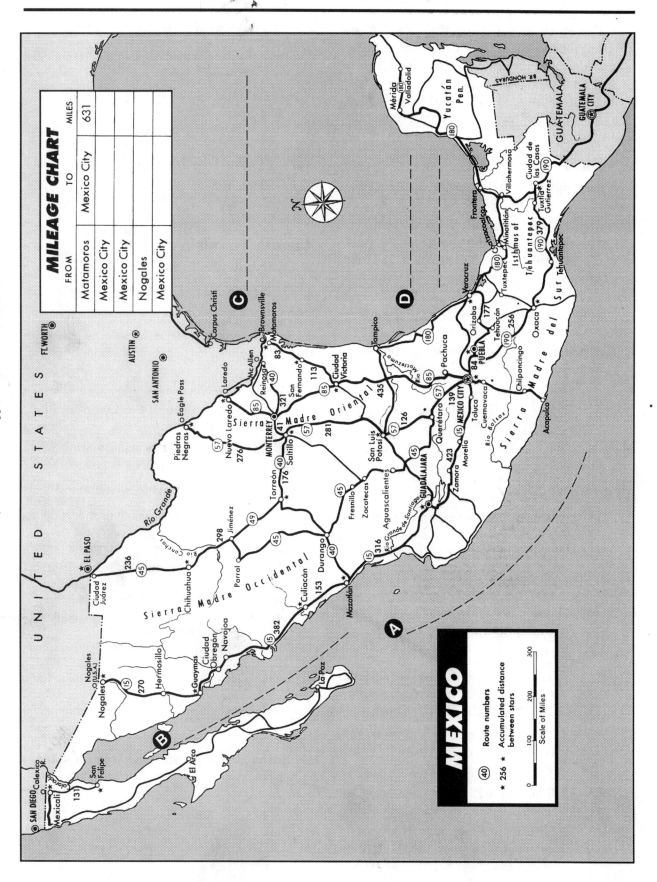

MILEAGE CHART

FROM	TO	MILES
Matamoros	Mexico City	631
Mexico City		
Mexico City		
Nogales		
Mexico City		

MEXICO

⊕40 Route numbers

★ 256 Accumulated distance between stars

Scale of Miles
0 100 200 300

© 1996 by The Center for Applied Research in Education

177

MEXICO: TERRITORIAL ADJUSTMENTS IN ITS NORTH

The story and map on the facing page offer an opportunity for your students to learn how the boundaries of the United States and Mexico were set. Also, the activity accompanying the story and map applies "whole language" to the study of geography and history.

Procedure

1. Photocopy the facing page and distribute.

2. Tell your students that they are employees of a company that devises tests. As part of their job they are to develop a 15-item true-false test (10 questions on the story, 5 questions on the map).

Some guidelines for developing such a test:

✓ The items should be statements that are simple and direct.

✓ Avoid the use of clauses.

✓ Items should be provable by reference to the story and/or map.

✓ Items should not be copies of sentences in the story.

✓ An answer key should be provided.

Note: It would be interesting to have students read one or more items from their tests to their classmates or to "take" each other's tests.

Alternate Procedure

1. Distribute the facing page.

2. Direct students to read/study the material.

3. Administer the true-false and completion test below.

T F 1. Texas declared its independence in 1836.

T F 2. Mexico never agreed to having Americans settle in Mexico.

T F 3. Gold led settlers to Texas.

T F 4. When Texas became a state, there were fewer than thirty thousand people living there.

T F 5. Twenty-seven states were in the Union before Texas was admitted.

T F 6. Texas was an independent nation for nine years.

T F 7. The Mexicans refused to pattern their constitution after the Constitution of the United States.

T F 8. Texas became an independent country after the United States went to war with Mexico.

T F 9. The war with Mexico started in 1846.

T F 10. The Gila River was the northern boundary of the Gadsden Purchase.

T F 11. The mouth of the Colorado River is in Mexico.

T F 12. The Mexicans easily established a strong democratic government.

Complete the following sentences:

A. One thing that hindered democracy in Mexico was a lack of _____.

B. Many Americans went to Texas to grow _____ and raise _____.

C. The Mexican government limited the number of settlers in Texas because _____

_____

_____

_____

D. Both Mexico and the United States claimed the land between the _____ _____ and _____.

© 1996 by The Center for Applied Research in Education

MEXICO: TERRITORIAL ADJUSTMENTS IN ITS NORTH

In 1821 the newly independent government of Mexico granted permission for Americans to settle in the northern part of the country. This territory is now known as Texas. The land was fertile and was well suited for growing cotton. The vast open grazing lands were ideal for cattle ranching. By 1836 more than 30,000 Americans had moved into this territory.

During the years that Texas was being settled and developed by Americans, the Mexican people were struggling to establish a satisfactory government. The constitution they adopted was based on many of the ideas of the Constitution of the United States. Unfortunately, the Mexican people lacked the experience necessary to make a democratic government work. As a result, revolution after revolution swept the country. One dictator after another took over the government.

Most of the dictators were unable to maintain a strong government. Private citizens were often left without protection. Money that was supposed to be used for the benefit of the people sometimes was taken by government officials for their own use. The Texans were especially unhappy with Mexican rule.

The Mexicans were becoming alarmed at the thousands of Americans who were settling their lands. New taxes were imposed on the Texans. Laws were passed that limited the number of new settlers who could come to Texas. The Mexican government failed to protect the lives and property of Americans.

Starting about 1832 there were frequent clashes between Texans and the Mexican authorities. After several early losses, including the famous Battle of the Alamo, the war ended with the defeat of the Mexicans at the Battle of San Jacinto. Then, in 1836, a few months after the San Jacinto victory, Texas declared its independence from Mexico and became the Republic of Texas. In 1845 after nine years as an independent nation, Texans asked to be annexed

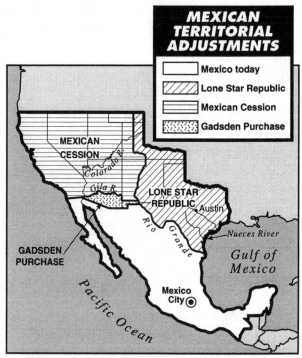

(joined to) the United States. The offer was accepted; Texas then became the twenty-eighth state.

Mexicans were resentful that Texas joined the United States. Furthermore, the new boundary lines were not clear. Both the United States and Mexico claimed the land between the Nueces River and the Rio Grande. War broke out between the two countries in 1846 when General Zachary Taylor's troops, who were in the disputed territory, were attacked by Mexicans. Two years later, Mexico's armies were badly defeated.

In the peace treaty that followed, Mexico gave up its claims to the land between the Nueces River and the Rio Grande. However, the really big land gain was that for $15 million, Mexico gave the United States what has since become the states of California, Nevada, Utah, most of Arizona, and parts of Wyoming, Colorado, and New Mexico.

The United States gained its last piece of Mexican territory in 1853. The United States paid $10,000,000 to Mexico for the land shown on the map as the Gadsden Purchase.

MEXICO: SIZE AND POPULATION

This page offers an opportunity for skill development in making and reading graphs.

Procedure

1. Make a transparency of the six graphs; make photocopies for your students.

2. Present the first pairs of statistics, which show how the United States and Mexico compare in size and population.

Size

USA: 79% (79 squares)
Mexico: 21% (21 squares)

Population

USA: 64% (64 squares)
Mexico: 36% (36 squares)

3. Have your students fill in the blocks of the first pair of graphs with symbols as shown in the keys below them.

4. Use the same approach for the next two pairs of graphs.

Size

Mexico: 74% (74 squares)
Central America: 26% (26 squares)

Population

Mexico: 66% (66 squares)
Central America: 34% (34 squares)

Note: Central America is a region of Latin America that contains seven countries—Belize, Honduras, Guatemala, El Salvador, Nicaragua, Costa Rica, and Panama.

Size

South America: 89% (89 squares)
Mexico: 11% (11 squares)

Population

South America: 69% (69 squares)
Mexico: 31% (31 squares)

5. After the completion of the graphs ask questions that emphasize facts and comparisons.

COMPARING THE UNITED STATES AND MEXICO

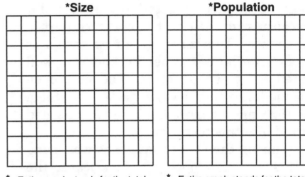

*Size   *Population

* Entire graph stands for the total area of the United States and Mexico.

* Entire graph stands for the total population of the United States and Mexico.

|||| USA   79 squares |||| USA   64 squares

/// Mexico   21 squares   /// Mexico   36 squares

COMPARING MEXICO AND CENTRAL AMERICA

*Size

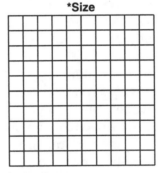

*Population

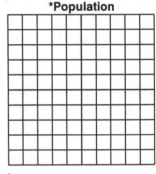

* Entire graph stands for the total area of Mexico and Central America.

* Entire graph stands for the total population of Mexico and Central America.

/// Mexico   74 squares   /// Mexico   66 squares

≡ Central America   26 squares   ≡ Central America   34 squares

COMPARING SOUTH AMERICA AND MEXICO

*Size

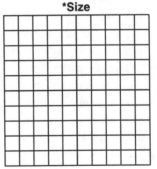

*Population

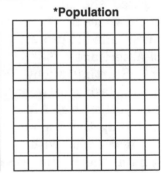

* Entire graph stands for the total area of South America and Mexico.

* Entire graph stands for the total population of South America and Mexico.

⊞ South America   89 squares   ⊞ South America   69 squares

/// Mexico   11 squares   /// Mexico   31 squares

© 1996 by The Center for Applied Research in Education

Name: _____ Date: _____

MEXICO: SPANISH AND ENGLISH WORDS

Spanish is the official language of Mexico and all the countries of Central America. You can gain some understanding of basic Spanish nouns by studying the glossary and then relating words in it with the illustrations.

1. The picture at the right shows a typical northern Mexico farm scene. After each Spanish word below, write the English word with the same meaning.

Spanish	English
agua	
casa	
maiz	
mujer	
cabra	
huerta	
hombre	
puerta	
muchacho	
montaña	
sombrero	
cacto	

2. By identifying objects in the picture and then translating their Spanish names into English you learned several things about farming in northern Mexico. Now, the questions below will give you an opportunity to think about the facts. Write your answers to the questions on the back of this page.

a. What is the purpose for the **muchacho** having such a broad-brimmed **sombrero**?

b. Why isn't it necessary to have a steep roof on the **casa**?

c. Why isn't the **montaña** covered with trees?

d. What are five kinds of food the people on the farm could eat?

e. Why does the farmer have a herd of **cabra(s)** rather than a herd of cows?

f. From where is the **agua** coming? What could it be used for beside drinking, washing, and cooking?

ENGLISH/SPANISH GLOSSARY					
English	**Spanish**	**English**	**Spanish**	**English**	**Spanish**
automobile	coche	door	puerta	mountain	montaña
boat	barco	garden	huerta	pencil	lapiz
book	libro	goat	cabra	table	mesa
boy	muchacho	hat	sombrero	tree	arbol
cactus	cacto	house	casa	water	agua
cloud	nube	lamp	lampare	window	ventana
corn	maiz	man	hombre	woman	mujer

CENTRAL AMERICA: COUNTRIES AND CAPITALS

Word Search/Map Puzzle

The activity on this page will help you become better acquainted with Central America. All of the countries and most of the capitals of Central America are both on the map and listed in the word search. In addition there are other places on the map that are also in the puzzle. Places with two parts to their names have a space between the parts.

A helpful approach to completing the activity is to first find a place name on the map, then look for the name in the word search. When you find a name, draw a neat circle around it.

C	A	R	I	B	B	E	A	N	■	S	E	A	P
L	B	G	E	R	E	C	M	P	E	C	T	M	A
S	E	L	■	S	A	L	V	A	D	O	R	E	C
A	L	E	K	N	L	A	R	N	O	S	A	X	I
N	I	C	A	R	A	G	U	A	E	T	X	I	F
■	Z	F	E	I	V	P	N	M	I	A	W	C	I
S	E	M	M	E	R	I	D	A	Y	■	I	O	C
A	L	A	U	D	H	O	N	D	U	R	A	S	■
L	A	N	B	C	O	L	O	M	B	I	A	D	O
V	S	A	N	■	J	O	S	E	A	C	L	R	C
A	N	G	U	A	T	E	M	A	L	A	I	B	E
D	Q	U	T	E	G	U	C	I	G	A	L	P	A
O	H	A	W	S	A	J	B	E	L	O	P	A	N
R	X	Y	U	C	A	T	A	N	I	D	F	N	Y

Merida

Gulf of Campeche

YUCATAN

Caribbean Sea

Belopan ◉

MEXICO

BELIZE

GUATEMALA

Guatemala ◉ City

HONDURAS

Tegucigalpa ◉

◉ San Salvador

EL SALVADOR

NICARAGUA

Lake Managua

◉ Managua

COSTA RICA

Panama Canal

San Jose ◉

CENTRAL AMERICA

◉ Capitals

PANAMA

Panama City

Pacific Ocean

COLOMBIA

CENTRAL AMERICA: LAND OF VOLCANOES

Procedure

1. In a discussion about volcanoes encourage students to think of ways that volcanoes are both helpful and detrimental to humans. List suggestions on the chalk board.

2. Read the information in the article "Volcanoes" to inform students of the part volcanoes play in the lives of humans.

3. Make a transparency for yourself, and photocopies for your students, of the diagram of an erupting volcano.

4. As you read and/or explain the sequences (box next to the diagram) annotate the transparency while students, likewise, annotate their photocopies.

VOLCANOES

Central America could very well be called *Land of Volcanoes,* for volcanoes are very numerous in the region. Some of them are steaming or rumbling; some occasionally erupt.

Volcanoes have played an important part in the formation of land in Central America. Lava that flows from volcanoes helps create soil. Another benefit of volcanoes is that the ash blown out of craters is a natural fertilizer that enriches soil that may have lost its fertility as a result of years of farming.

Of course, volcanoes have been destructive as well as beneficial. Whole towns have been destroyed by their eruptions. Volcanoes are in plain sight and are constant reminders to Central American people that their lives and homes are always in jeopardy.

Another aspect of volcanoes is that their eruptions substantially add to air pollution. Unlike pollutants brought about by human activities (transportation, manufacturing etc.), which can be controlled, volcanic pollutants cannot be controlled. Volcanic pollution, however, is part of nature's way of bringing about balance between plant and animal life and other elements of the earth. It is human contributions to pollution that upset the balance.

Beneath the outer surface of the earth it is very hot. It is so hot that rock is melted into a thick molasses-like liquid called *magma* (1). As the magma becomes heated, it expands. Gases and steam form. The pressure against the rock surrounding the magma is tremendous. If the gases can find a weak spot in the earth's crust they burst out of the opening. Rocks, ashes, sparks, and fire shoot into the air like giant fireworks. The magma flows out of the opening.

The "pipe" that the materials use to escape to the earth's surface is called a *conduit* (2). The hole at the earth's surface is a *crater* (3). The magma that flows into the open air takes a new name—*lava* (4). As the lava flows, it cools and hardens into layers. Over a long period of time, perhaps hundreds or thousands of years, the layers may take the shape of a *cone-like mountain* (5). The cone may reach thousands of feet into the air.

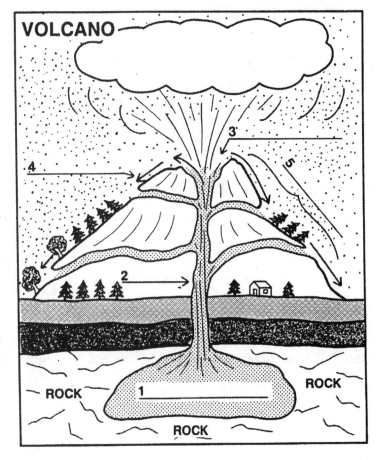

VOLCANO

ROCK

ROCK

ROCK

Name: _____ Date: _____

CENTRAL AMERICA: LAKE NICARAGUA

The information that is necessary to complete this activity is in the story or on the map on the opposite page.

1. The headings below were written to accompany the paragraphs in the story. In front of each heading, write the letter of the paragraph that is related to the heading. If no paragraph relates to a particular heading, leave the line blank.

___ Facts and figures about the lake

___ A means of transportation for local traffic

___ Ocean fish in lake water

___ Water for irrigation

___ A possible canal route

___ Water sports on Lake Nicaragua

___ A lake that was once a bay

2. What are three of the saltwater fish found in Lake Nicaragua?

_____ _____ _____

3. Underline the word or group of words in paragraph **B** that indicates there is more than one explanation as to how saltwater fish came to be in Lake Nicaragua.

4. Draw a circle around the part of the story that tells you that the possibility of a Nicaraguan canal is still discussed.

5. What river connects Lake Nicaragua and Lake Managua? _____

6. What is the elevation of Lake Nicaragua? _____

7. The river flowing from Lake Managua must fall how many feet before it reaches Lake Nicaragua? _____

8. What is the approximate greatest distance from north to south in Nicaragua?

_____

9. What is the widest distance from east to west? _____

10. What natural features could be used in the route of the proposed canal?

_____

11. What is the approximate length in miles of the proposed canal?

☐ 140 miles   ☐ 170 miles   ☐ 195 miles

12. Noting details

a. Weight of some sharks in Lake Nicaragua: _____ lbs.

b. Name of Lake Nicaragua's largest island: _____

c. Two kinds of boats used on Lake Nicaragua: _____

d. Number of islands in Lake Nicaragua:

_____

13. Complete the labeling of the map, as follows:

Ⓐ Gulf of Honduras

Ⓑ Honduras

Ⓒ Caribbean Sea

Ⓓ Pacific Ocean

Ⓔ Costa Rica

Ⓕ Rio Coco (An important part of the boundary between Honduras and Nicaragua)

CENTRAL AMERICA: LAKE NICARAGUA

A If you saw a headline that read "Lake Swimmer Attacked by Man-Eating Shark," you might think that the newspaper had made an error. Sharks ordinarily do not live in freshwater lakes. However, in Lake Nicaragua, sharks weighing as much as 200 pounds have been caught. Other fish, including tarpon and sawfish, which usually live in salt water, are found in this lake.

B Why are saltwater fish thriving in a freshwater lake? Several ideas, or theories, have been suggested. One theory is that Lake Nicaragua and Lake Managua were once a bay on the Pacific side of the isthmus. Then the eruption of volcanoes or earth-quakes changed the land. Earth filled the area around the bay, and lakes were formed. Rivers flowing into and out of the newly formed lakes eventually made the water fresh. The saltwater fish that were trapped when the bay was cut off gradually adjusted to living in fresh water.

C There are many interesting things about Lake Nicaragua. It is about 100 miles long and 45 miles wide. The area of the lake is 3,080 square miles. In some places the lake is more than 200 feet deep.

Travelers on the lake or along its shores may see smoke rising from volcanoes. There are two active volcanoes on Ometepe, the largest island in Lake Nicaragua.

D Lake Nicaragua is an important part of the transportation system of Nicaragua. Steamboats sail from city to city, carrying passengers and cargo. Dugout canoes, sometimes equipped with sails and motors, carry passengers to various places along its shores. The boats also stop at the thousand or more islands that dot the lake waters. New railroads, highways, and airplanes are taking over more and more of the traffic.

E Before the Panama Canal was built, Lake Nicaragua had been considered as a possible link in a canal route across the isthmus. Even today the possibilities of a canal through Nicaragua are mentioned in newspapers and magazine articles. As world trade increases, many countries are hopeful that another canal will be built.

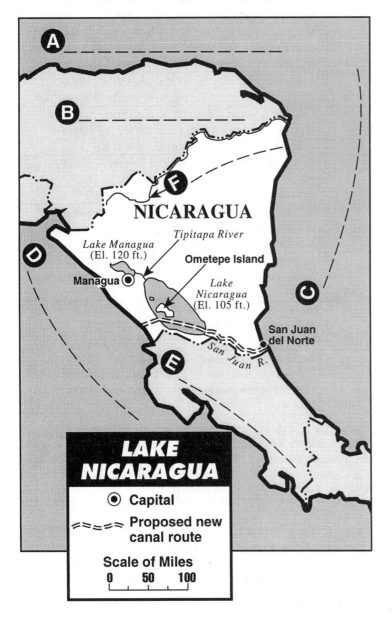

NICARAGUA

Tipitapa River

Lake Managua
(El. 120 ft.)

Ometepe Island

Managua

Lake Nicaragua
(El. 105 ft.)

San Juan del Norte

San Juan R.

LAKE NICARAGUA

⊙ Capital

≈≈≈ Proposed new canal route

Scale of Miles
0   50   100

THE WEST INDIES: GEOGRAPHICAL AND HISTORICAL FACTS

Country and Capital ( )	Population	Area in Sq. Miles	Of Interest
Antigua and Barbuda (St. John's)	65,000	171	Achieved independence from Britain in 1981 . . . Official language: English . . . Inhabitants: mostly of African descent
The Bahamas (Nassau)	273,000	5,382	Achieved independence from Britain in 1973 . . . Made up of some 700 islands and 2,000 islets . . . Most important industry: tourism
Barbados (Bridgetown)	256,000	166	Achieved independence from Britain in 1966 . . . Literacy: 99 of every 100 people . . . Most important industry: tourism
Cuba (Havana)	11,064,000	42,804	About the size of Pennsylvania . . . Gained independence from Spain as a result of the Spanish American War (1898) . . . Chief product: sugar
Dominica (Roseau)	88,000	209	Achieved independence from Britain in 1978 . . . Official language: English . . . Most important products: bananas, citrus, coconuts
Dominican Republic (Santo Domingo)	7,826,000	18,704	Mountains up to 10,000' . . . Language most spoken: English . . . Santo Domingo: oldest European settlement in Western Hemisphere (1496)
Grenada (St. Geroge's)	94,000	133	Achieved independence from Britain in 1974 . . . Principal products: sugar, rum (made from sugar)
Haiti (Port-au-Prince)	6,491,000	10,695	First independent country in the West Indies (1804) . . . Low literacy rate: 53% . . . Frequent revolutions . . . 65% mountain covered
Jamaica (Kingston)	2,555,000	4,244	Achieved independence from Britain in 1963 . . . A major bauxite (aluminum) producer . . . 80% mountain covered . . . Tourism important
St. Kitts and Nevis (Basseterre)	41,000	104	Achieved independence from Britain in 1983 . . . Western Hemisphere's smallest country . . . Sugar production dominates its economy
St. Lucia (Castries)	145,000	238	Achieved independence from Britain in 1979 . . . Chief industries: agriculture (bananas, coconuts, citrus, cocoa), tourism
St. Vincent and the Grenadines (Kingstown)	115,000	150	Achieved independence from Britain in 1979 . . . Most important crop and export: bananas
Trinidad and Tobago (Port-of-Spain)	1,328,000	1,980	Achieved independence from Britain in 1962 . . . Tobago: 116 sq. miles to Trinidad's northeast . . . Important off-shore oil production and oil refining country

© 1996 by The Center for Applied Research in Education

Note: In the 1960s a remarkable increase in the number of new nations began—a total of ten—in the West Indies. The United Kingdom (Britain) guided them through the process of independence and self-rule. British culture and that of the native inhabitants coexist; in fact, several of the new countries have designated English as their official language. It should also be noted that the Central American country of Belize, the former British Honduras, received its independence in 1981.

Procedure:

The large map of the West Indies on the facing page can be made into a transparency and photocopies for students. As you identify the countries and islands of the West Indies and give some basic information, students may annotate their maps. *Note*: Puerto Rico is not included in the fact sheet; however, it should be identified and labeled.

Name: _____ Date: _____

THE WEST INDIES: GEOGRAPHICAL AND HISTORICAL FACTS

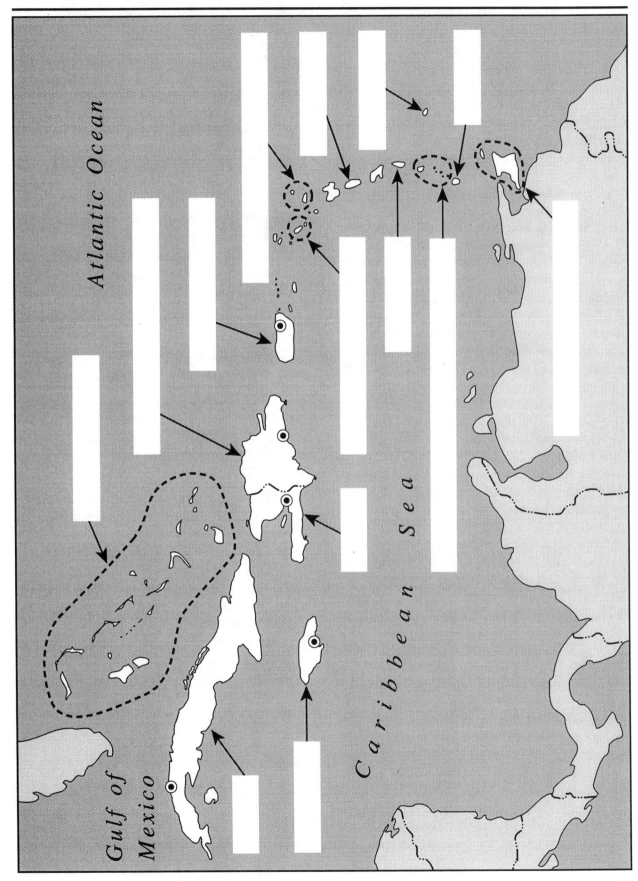

THE WEST INDIES: PUERTO RICO

A Short History of Puerto Rico

The Arawak Indians were the people Columbus met when he discovered Puerto Rico on his second voyage in 1493. The Arawaks were good farmers who grew most of their food. However, they added to their diet by hunting and fishing. Most villages were small, but some had 2,000 or more inhabitants.

Several years after Columbus' discovery, Spaniards began to colonize Puerto Rico. In 1508, Ponce de Leon, who had heard that there was gold on the island, landed there. The Arawaks resisted the invasion, but they were no match for armor-clad, horse-mounted Spaniards who used savage dogs in their attacks. Thousands of Arawaks were either killed or enslaved. Those that survived the fighting soon died from the hardships of slavery or the disease brought to the islands by the invaders. One hundred years after the first Spaniards stepped on the island, it would have been all but impossible to find a pure-blooded Arawak still living.

Ponce de Leon began a settlement in 1508, and from that time on the Spanish population steadily increased. Slaves from Africa were imported to work in the fields, settlements were established in various parts of the island, and fortifications were built to withstand the attacks of the English, Dutch, French, and Carib Indians from neighboring islands.

For almost 400 years Spain ruled Puerto Rico, but the end of its reign came as a result of the Spanish-American War. United States troops landed in Puerto Rico after a severe naval bombardment of the Spanish fort at San Juan. It took only a few weeks to defeat the Spanish forces on the island.

After the Spanish surrender, at a peace conference held in Paris (Treaty of Paris), Puerto Rico was ceded to the United States. In 1917, Puerto Ricans were granted United States citizenship. From that time on, the islanders acquired more and more self-rule. For example, instead of the United States president appointing their governors, the people of Puerto Rico were given the right to elect their governors. Next, Puerto Ricans wrote their own constitution. Finally, in 1952, Puerto Rico became a self-governing commonwealth.

There have been several movements by some Puerto Ricans to have their commonwealth become the fifty-first state. The most recent attempt occurred in November 1993. An election was held; it showed that Puerto Ricans were almost evenly divided on the question of statehood: approximately 49% voted for Puerto Rico to remain a commonwealth, 46% voted for statehood, and 5% for independence.

Some Geography Facts

❑ Puerto Rico is a part of the West Indies group of islands known as the Greater Antilles. The other major islands in the group are Cuba, Hispaniola (Haiti, Dominican Republic), and Jamaica

❑ Puerto Rico consists of a large major island and outlying islands, of which Culebra and Viejes are the largest. The total area of Puerto Rico is 3,430 square miles; New Jersey is about twice its size.

❑ The main island is dominated by a mountain rage, Cordillera Central, which extends east-west from coast to coast. This range, with various subranges, occupies approximately 60% of the land; a narrow coastal lowland ranging up to 12 miles wide and foothills to the Cordillera Central make up the remaining 40% of the land. The main rivers drain northward into the Atlantic Ocean; although they are not navigable, they do great service as sources of hydroelectric energy.

❑ Puerto Rico has a population of about 3.5 million. Its largest cities are San Juan, 437,000; Bayamon, 220,000; Ponce, 188,000; and Carolina, 178,000.

THE WEST INDIES: PUERTO RICO

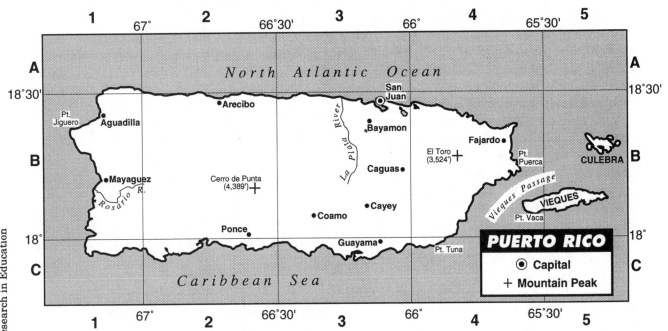

Imagine that you are working in a publishing company. It is your job to arrange all the names on the map in a MAP INDEX that tells in what quadrant a place is found. For example, Guayama is in quadrant C3

1. Before each place listed below, list its quadrant location.

MAP INDEX			
Quad-rant	**Place**	**Quad-rant**	**Place**
	Aguadilla (C)		La Plata (R)
	Arecibo (C)		Mayaguez (C)
	Bayamon (C)		Ponce (C)
	Caguas (C)		Pt. Jiguero
	Cayey (C)		Pt. Puerca
	Cerro de Punta (Mtn)		Pt. Tuna
	Culebra (Is)		Pt. Vaca
	Coamo (C)		Rosario (R)
	El Toro (Mtn)		San Juan (C)
	Fajardo (C)		Vieques (Is)
C3	Guayama (C)		
C: City R: River		Mtn: Mountain	
Is: Island Pt: Point or Cape			

2. A degree of latitude or longitude can be divided into small segments called minutes. A mark similar to an apostrophe (') is used to show minutes. So, 35°40' should be read as *35 degrees, 40 minutes*.

The figure below shows how one degree is divided. Each segment represents 1/60 of a degree of longitude. Line **A** may be read as 59°30'W.

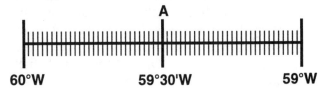

You can see on the map of Puerto Rico that each degree is divided into halves.

Draw a circle around the approximate latitude of

a. Ponce: 18°03'N or 18°27'N

b. Fajardo: 18°20'N or 18°50'N

Draw a circle around the approximate longitude of Caguas.

c. 66°04'W or 65°45'W

189

THE WEST INDIES: TRINIDAD'S ASPHALT LAKE

In Trinidad there is a deposit of asphalt at a place called Pitch Lake. Asphalt is the material that is widely used for such things as road pavements and roof shingles. More than eight million tons of asphalt have been dug out of Pitch Lake, which covers about 115 acres. There is enough of the grayish-black, tar-like material to last at least 50 years.

At one time, the United States imported asphalt from Trinidad. But a less expensive way of making asphalt from petroleum has been developed, so it is no longer necessary to import the material. However, many other countries buy Trinidad's asphalt.

You would not need a boat on Pitch Lake; you can walk on the lake. Of course, with each step you would sink slightly into the blackish surface. As you walk over the lake, you would see workmen chopping and digging out big chunks of asphalt. The chunks are loaded on the small cars of a narrow-gauge railroad.

Do not plan to take the same walk the following week; every few days the railroad tracks are moved. If they were not moved they would sink and disappear. The miners have to pack up their tools and move to another location.

At one place on the lake, a pool of soft, almost liquid asphalt has worked its way to the surface. People call this pool "mother of the lake." Hollows in the lake's surface are filled with rainwater and have formed pools in which small fish live. How they got there no one really knows. One ichthyologist, fish expert, believes that they may have been washed in by floods.

Though asphalt is a good source of income for Trinidad, it is not the most important export of the island. Exports of petroleum and petroleum products are very much greater. Sugar, cocoa, coffee, citrus fruits, and bananas are also more important. However, the value of the asphalt in Pitch Lake cannot be measured by export dollars alone. Thousands of tourists come to see Pitch Lake and other attractions, and they spend money in hotels, restaurants, and shops in Trinidad.

1. What words in the story describe the appearance of asphalt? _____

_____

2. Draw a circle around the sentence in the story that tells two of the uses of asphalt.

3. Why doesn't the United States import asphalt anymore? _____

_____

4. Underline the word in the story that applies to a person who studies fish.

5. What is one explanation of how fish got into the shallow pools of the lake? _____

_____

6. Think of three action verbs that tell what the men in the picture are doing. For example, the man in the top left of the picture is **supervising**.

_____

7. Why wouldn't it be possible to find their tracks one week after a picture of them was taken? _____

8. The inset map in the picture shows the location of Trinidad and Tobago. On the map label **Venezuela** at **A**.

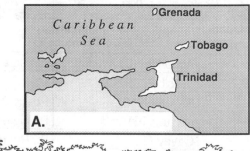

Name: _____ Date: _____

THE WEST INDIES: AN AMERICAN OUTPOST ON CUBA

For almost 100 years the United States has occupied a naval base, called Guantanamo, on the island country of Cuba. Permission to establish the base came as a result of the Spanish-American War of 1898. It was in that war that the United States helped Cuba to free itself from Spain and become an independent country. After the war was won, Cuba agreed to allow the United States to use Guantanamo Bay as a naval station.

The United States' base at Guantanamo has been called the "Key to the Caribbean Sea." From that base armed forces of the United States protect sea and air approaches to the Panama Canal.

1. On the map draw the following:

a. a circle around Guantanamo Bay

b. a line from Guantanamo Bay directly to the Panama Canal

2. What is the approximate distance from Guantanamo Bay to the Canal?

___ 700 mi.　　___ 800 mi.　　___ 950 mi.

3. Imagine that it becomes necessary to protect the Panama Canal. The United States Air Force is called upon to fly armed forces from Miami and New Orleans to the Canal.

a. What is the approximate air distance between Miami and the Canal?

___ 950 mi.　___ 1,150 mi.　___ 1,300 mi.

b. If the airplane flew in a straight line between the two places, over what country would it fly? _____

c. What is the approximate air distance between New Orleans and the Canal?

___ 1,500 mi.　___ 1,350 mi.　___ 1,700 mi.

d. What two countries are separated by the Yucatan Channel? _____

_____

4. To complete the map, you need to label some of the places. Use the abbreviations that follow each name.

1. Guatemala (G)
2. Belize (B)
3. Honduras (HON)
4. El Salvador (ES)
5. Nicaragua (N)

6. Costa Rica (CR)
7. Panama (P)
8. Colombia (COL)
9. Venezuela (VEN)
10. Suriname (SUR)
11. Haiti (H)
12. Dominican Republic (DR)
13. Pacific Ocean (PO)
14. Atlantic Ocean (AO)

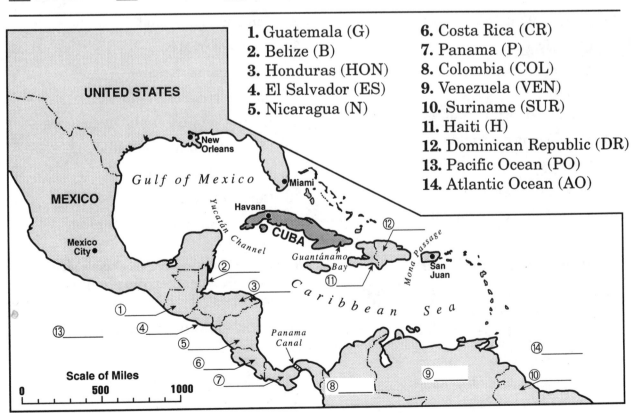

Name: _____ Date: _____

MIDDLE AMERICA AND WEST INDIES: CROSSWORD PUZZLE REVIEW

You have already met most of the words used in the crossword puzzle. However, if you are not sure of the name of a place, check in a textbook or on a map.

Across

1. Mexican port
4. Largest West Indies country
6. Country: Costa _____
7. Mexican mountains: Sierra Madre _____
11. Central American country
13. Managua is its capital
14. Country: _____ Salvador
15. City: _____ Domingo
16. Tegucigalpa is its capital
17. Capital of the Bahamas
21. Mexican peninsula: Lower _____
22. Country that shares an island with Haiti: Domincan _____
23. _____ Juan, Puerto Rico
24. _____ and Tobago
25. Small island country: Saint _____

Down

1. United States possession: _____ Islands
2. San Juan is its capital: Puerto _____
3. Neighbor of Mexico
5. Island group: Greater _____
8. Southeast (abbreviation)
9. Largest country of Middle America
10. City in Yucatan Peninsula
12. Mexican Peninsula
16. Cuba's capital
18. Country west of the Dominican Republic
19. A word that describes Cuba's size as compared to other West Indies countries
20. Trinidad's capital: _____-of-Spain

Name: _____ Date: _____

MIDDLE AMERICA AND WEST INDIES: IDENTIFYING COUNTRIES BY SHAPE

The maps on this page include countries of Middle America, islands of the West Indies, and the Commonwealth of Puerto Rico. The maps are all drawn to the same scale. If you need help in identifying any of the places, refer to a textbook, wall maps, or the maps in other references such as encyclopedias and atlases.

After you have identified a country write its name on the line in its box; then, write the name of its capital close to the black dot that marks its location.

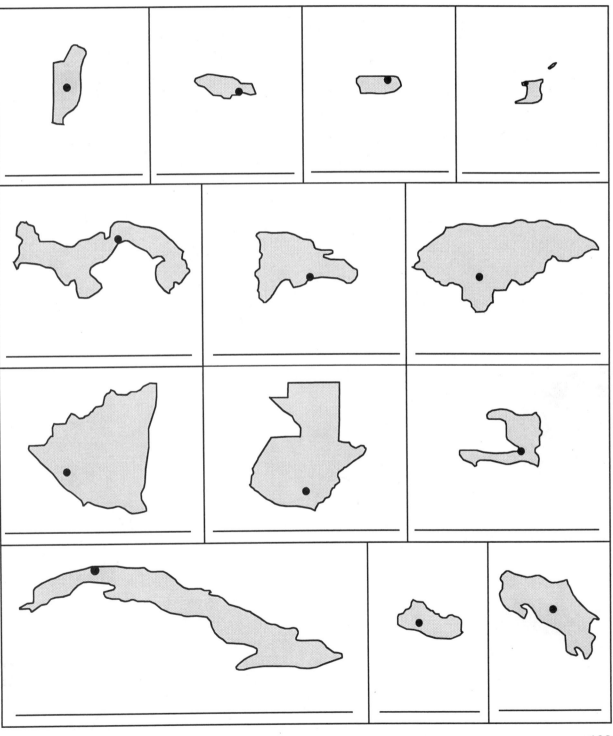

Latin America (South America)

SOUTH AMERICA: TWELVE COUNTRIES AND ONE COLONY

Suggested Instructional Procedure

1. Read the brief introduction below.

2. Distribute photocopies of the map on page 198.

3. Call attention to the information boxes surrounding the map.

4. Students complete the four specifics listed in each box as you dictate. Note abbreviations: Country (CO), Capital (CA), Area (A), Population (P).

5. Students take notes as you mention some of the information in the "Of Interest" sections on these two facing pages. *Note*: Discourage the writing of complete sentences, and encourage stenographic-type notes. Use your own discretion as to what information you dispense because the boxes cannot accommodate all the information about countries.

You may want to use a transparency of the map as you proceed.

South America is composed of twelve independent countries and one colony. The earliest people to inhabit South America were descendants of the Asiatics who entered North America from Asia. The people who followed gradually made their way southward and over the Isthmus of Panama land bridge into South America. This migration took hundreds of years, if not thousands, to complete. The time that it took to populate South America is understandable when it is realized that the trek from northern Alaska to Cape Horn is well over 10,000 miles—and there were no horses or other means of transportation available.

The first Europeans to visit and settle South America were from Spain and Portugal. Columbus did not see any part of South America until his third voyage in 1498. Portugal entered the South American scene in 1500 when Pedro Cabral landed on the coast of South America and claimed what is now Brazil for Portugal.

❶ *Country*: Colombia
Capital: Bogota
Area: 440,831 sq. mi.
Population: 35,578,000
Of Interest: Has coasts on both the Atlantic Ocean (via the Caribbean Sea) and the Pacific Ocean . . . A country rich in natural resources: petroleum, salt, gold, silver, platinum, nickel, iron, salt . . . Agricultural products: coffee (known for its high quality), cocoa (chocolate), bananas . . . Magdalena River: a water highway flowing between mountain ranges and navigable for 750 miles inland

❷ *Country*: Venezuela
Capital: Caracas
Area: 352,144 sq. mi.
Population: 20,562,000
Of Interest: Angel Falls, at 300', the world's highest . . . Orinoco River: extends almost 1,300 miles inland, empties into the Caribbean Sea, navigable for large ships 500 miles inland . . . Petroleum the major source (80%) of export income . . . Lake Maracaibo (really not a lake, but an arm of the Caribbean Sea) and Maracaibo Basin: the country's major oil producing area

❸ *Country*: Guyana
Capital: Georgetown
Area: 83,044 sq. mi.
Population: 729,000
Of Interest: Once known as British Guiana, but now a free and independent nation . . . English the official language . . . Rain forests throughout the entire country leave only 3% of the land suitable for farming . . . East Indians: about 50% of the population, descendants of Asiatic Indians brought to the original British colony to work on sugar plantations

❹ *Country*: Suriname
Capital: Paramaribo
Area: 63,251 sq. mi.
Population: 423,000
Of Interest: Once known as Dutch Guiana, but now a free and independent nation . . . Vast forests to the south covering 75% of the country . . . A flat coastal lowland where dikes are used to permit agriculture, especially rice . . . Arable land: 1% . . . Almost 50% of population Asiatic Indian

SOUTH AMERICA: TWELVE COUNTRIES AND ONE COLONY

❺ *Country*: French Guiana
Capital: Cayenne
Area: 43,740 sq. mi.
Population: 101,000
Of Interest: 90% forest, which is largely unexplored and uninhabited . . . A little more than two people per sq. mi., but, in reality, much less because 40% of the people live in the capital . . . French controlled, although an elected "Council General" (16 members) exists . . . Exports: shrimp, timber, sugar

❻ *Country*: Brazil
Capital: Brasilia
Area: 3,286,470 sq. mi.
Population: 159,000,000
Of Interest: Larger than the USA without Alaska . . . Amazon River flows 2,093 miles within Brazil . . . World's largest coffee grower . . . Only Portuguese speaking country in South America . . . Sao Paulo: world's third largest city, with nearly 19,000,000 people

❼ *Country*: Paraguay
Capital: Asuncion
Area: 157,048 sq. mi.
Population: 5,214,000
Of Interest: Its size greatly reduced as a result of wars in the 1860s . . . The Paraguay River: natural division between east and west . . . East—plains, grasslands, fertile, well-watered; West—part of the Gran Chaco, arid, stunted trees, few resources, few communities, few people, few paved roads, low per person annual income

❽ *Country*: Uruguay
Capital: Montevideo
Area: 68,037 sq. mi.
Population: 3,199,000
Of Interest: Rolling land with low hills (highest point: 1644') and valleys; grassy, well-watered and well-suited to cattle raising and grain farming . . . Population about 90% Spanish, Italian, and Portuguese descent . . . Montevideo: (Spanish for "I see a mountain") contains 40% of the country's population

❾ *Country*: Argentina
Capital: Buenos Aires
Area: 1,073,000 sq. mi.
Population: 33,913,000
Of Interest: Mt. Aconcagua: South America's highest peak at 22,834' . . . Four major regions: Andes Mountains in west; Patagonia in the south—barren, dry, windswept, great

for sheep; Pampa in center—treeless, grassy, fertile, great for cattle and grain; Gran Chaco in northwest, thickly forested, some swamps

❿ *Country*: Chile
Capital: Santiago
Area: 292,135 sq. mi.
Population: 13,951,000
Of Interest: 250 miles maximum east-west width, but some 2650 miles from north to south; about as long as the USA is wide . . . Atacama Desert in north extremely dry, yet agriculturally productive due to irrigation waters from the Andes Mountains . . . Exceptionally irregular southern coast with many islands, fiords, mountains

⓫ *Country*: Bolivia
Capital: La Paz (administrative), Sucre (judicial)
Area: 424,164 sq. mi.
Population: 7,719,000
Of Interest: A landlocked country with the great Andes Mountains to the west and the vast expanse of Brazil to the east . . . One of the world's leading tin producers . . . Lake Titicaca—a notable geographic feature shared with Peru: 12,000' above sea level; 110 miles long, 35 miles wide; about the size of Lake Champlain, Vermont

⓬ *Country*: Peru
Capital: Lima
Area: 496,225 sq. mi.
Population: 23,651,000
Of Interest: 25% of the country covered by the Andes Mountains . . . Great contrasts between coastal Peru (narrow, arid coastal plain) and eastern Peru (tropical jungle) . . . Seat of the ancient Inca Empire, which extended into parts of present day Bolivia, Ecuador, Colombia, Chile, and Argentina . . . One of the world's greatest fishing nations

⓭ *Country*: Ecuador
Capital: Quito
Area: 105,037 sq. mi.
Population: 10,677,000
Of Interest: Takes its name from Spanish for "equator" . . . Possesses the Galapagos Islands some 600 miles off its coast . . . Quito: almost directly on the equator, 9,000' elevation, yet temperatures rarely exceed 75° . . . One-third of the country east of the Andes, mostly jungle . . . Most people: Indians or mestizos (mixed Indian and white), mountain dwellers

Name: _____ Date: _____

SOUTH AMERICA: TWELVE COUNTRIES AND ONE COLONY

CO: _____
CA: _____
A: _____
P: _____

❶

CO: _____
CA: _____
A: _____
P: _____

❷

CO: _____
CA: _____
A: _____
P: _____

❸

CO: _____
CA: _____
A: _____
P: _____

❹

CO: _____
CA: _____
A: _____
P: _____

❶❸

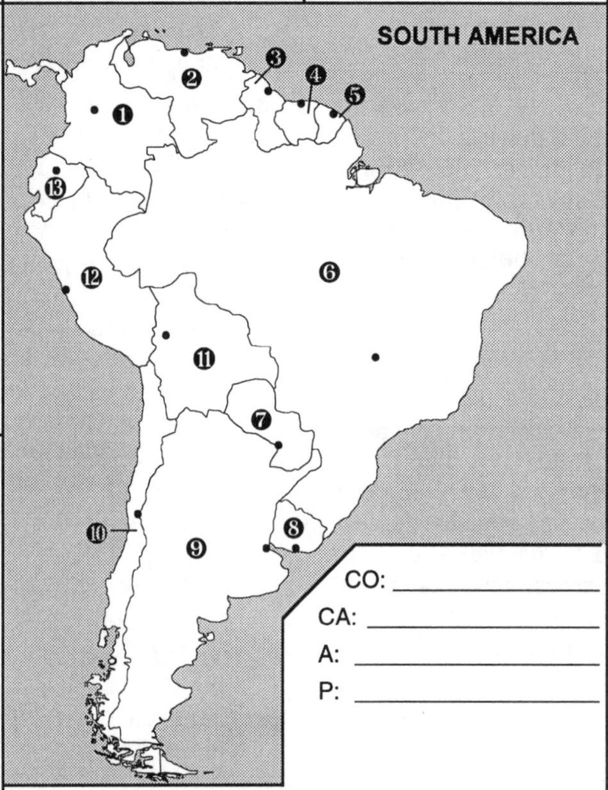

CO: _____
CA: _____
A: _____
P: _____

❺

SOUTH AMERICA

CO: _____
CA: _____
A: _____
P: _____

CO: _____
CA: _____
A: _____
P: _____

❶❷

CO: _____
CA: _____
A: _____
P: _____

❻

CO: _____
CA: _____
A: _____
P: _____

❼

CO: _____
CA: _____
A: _____
P: _____

❶❶

CO: _____
CA: _____
A: _____
P: _____

❶❶

CO: _____
CA: _____
A: _____
P: _____

❾

CO: _____
CA: _____
A: _____
P: _____

❽

Name: _____ Date: _____

SOUTH AMERICA: LATITUDE AND LONGITUDE

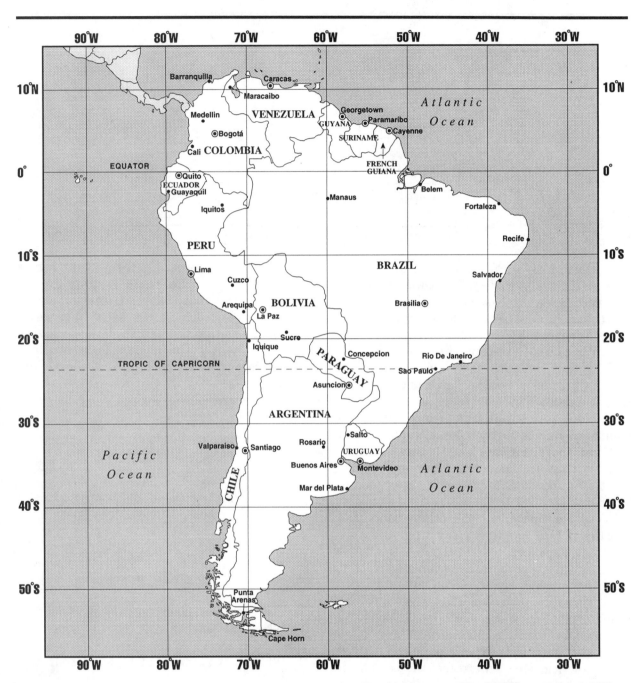

1. What city is located at approximately:

a. 20°S - 70°W? _____

b. 3°S - 60°W? _____

c. 38°S - 57°W? _____

d. 11°N - 75°W? _____

e. 10°N - 66°W? _____

2. Circle the map location that is most accurate for each listed city.

a. Salvador: 13°S - 38°W   27°S - 32°W

b. Georgetown: 6°N - 58°W   8°S - 64°W

c. Punta Arenas: 53°S - 71°W   59°S - 69°W

d. Brasilia: 24°S - 52°W   16°S - 48°W

3. A degree of latitude is equal to approximately 70 miles. Approximately how many miles is it from:

Rosario to Manaus? _____ miles

Punta Arenas to Iquique? _____ miles

SOUTH AMERICA: SEASONS SOUTH OF THE EQUATOR

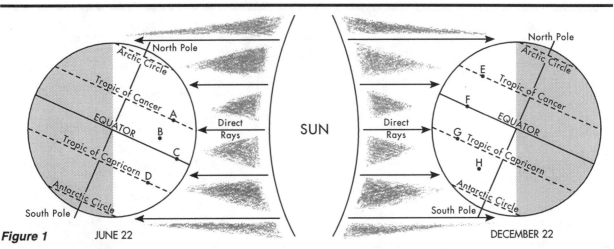

Figure 1   JUNE 22 | DECEMBER 22

If you look at Figure 1, you will see that the earth is tilted 23½°. The tilt is constant all year around. Notice that in June the northern hemisphere is tilted toward the sun. As a result, the northern half of the earth is closer to the sun than the southern half is, and the sun's rays strike the northern half directly. So, the north is experiencing summer.

Now, notice that, at the same time, the southern half is farther away from the sun so that the sun's rays are striking it indirectly; that is, they are glancing off the earth. So, the southern half is experiencing winter.

In December, on the other hand, the northern half is tilted away from the sun, and the southern half is tilted toward the sun. So, the north is experiencing winter, and the south is experiencing summer.

This demonstrates why seasons in the northern hemisphere are opposite seasons in the southern hemisphere. When New York City (north) is experiencing the heat of summer, Rio De Janiero (south) is experiencing the cold of winter. When it is winter north of the equator, people go south for warm vacations; when it is winter south of the equator, people go north for warm vacations.

Figure 2 shows the earth revolving around the sun. The revolution takes one year (365¼ days). Notice that in March the south is enjoying fall, and the north is enjoying spring. Again, the seasons are opposite in the northern and southern hemispheres.

Another interesting result that comes from the tilt of the earth is that for six months of the year the sun shines on one of the poles, but not on the other. Figure 1, June 22, shows the North Pole receiving sunlight, while the South Pole receives none. December 22 in Figure 1 shows just the opposite.

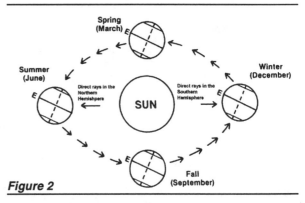

Figure 2

To Do (Write answers on the reverse side.)
1. When it is spring at A (Fig. 1) what season is it at D?
2. When it is summer at H, what season is it at G?
3. Would there be seasons if the earth were not tilted? Explain your answer.
4. In December and January there is a great increase in the amount of fruit and vegetables sent to the northern hemisphere from the southern hemisphere. What might be the reason for this as related to the tilt of the earth?
5. In Figure 2, draw the earth (showing tilt) where it would be on August 1, and February 1.

SOUTH AMERICA: SEASONS SOUTH OF THE EQUATOR

The information you will need to complete this activity can be found on the map and table on this page.

1. Label the following on the map.

A: Tropic of Cancer, 23½°N

B: Equator

C: Tropic of Capricorn, 23½°S

Note: On June 22 the sun is directly over the Tropic of Cancer at noon. The **northern** hemisphere is tilted toward the sun.

On December 22, the sun is directly over the Tropic of Capricorn at noon. The *southern* hemisphere is tilted toward the sun.

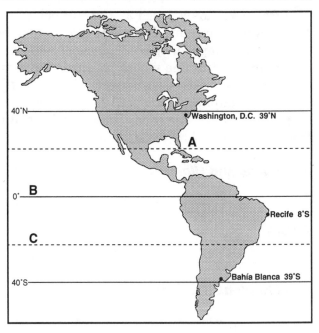

2. What is the latitude of Washington, D.C.? _____

3. What is the latitude of Bahia Blanca, Argentina? _____

4. What is the latitude of Recife, Brazil?

_____

5. What is similar about the locations of Washington, D.C., and Bahia Blanca? ____

_____

6. What are the three winter months in Washington, D.C.? _____,

_____ and _____

7. What are the three winter months in Bahia Blanca? _____

_____ and _____

8. Complete this sentence: When Washington, D.C., is having spring during the months of _____, _____,

and _____, Bahia Blanca is having _____ .

9. The average temperature in Washington, D.C., is how many degrees colder in January than in July? _____

10. The average temperature in Bahia Blanca is how many degrees colder in July than January? _____

11. Notice that there are no seasons shown in the table for Recife. What might be the reason why this is so? *Hint*: Notice Recife's position in reference to the equator and the Tropic of Cancer and the Tropic of Capricorn. Answer on the bottom of this page.

12. In the table find the highest and lowest average temperatures for each city. On the map under the name of each city write its high and low temperatures and the months in which they occur.

AVERAGE TEMPERATURES FOR THREE CITIES IN THE WESTERN HEMISPHERE												
CITY	DEC.	JAN.	FEB.	MAR.	APR.	MAY	JUNE	JULY	AUG.	SEPT.	OCT.	NOV.
Bahia Blanca	71°	73°	72°	65°	60°	52°	47°	46°	48°	53°	59°	65°
Washington, D.C.	38°	37°	37°	46°	56°	66°	74°	78°	76°	70°	60°	49°
Recife	79°	81°	81°	81°	80°	76°	76°	75°	75°	77°	79°	80°

winter months ▨ spring months ▤ summer months ▥ fall months

© 1996 by The Center for Applied Research in Education

Name: _____ Date: _____

SOUTH AMERICA: A PHYSICAL MAP

Physical maps, such as the one below of South America, show natural things such as rivers and mountains. *Political* maps show human-made things such as cities and boundaries. Some maps show both physical and political things. In many cases it is the physical things that determine where political things will be located. And, it should be realized that every event in history was directly or indirectly affected by physical surroundings.

The groupings below will help you gain an understanding of the outstanding physical features of South America. Under each heading fill the blank lines with the names of the features indicated by the heading title.

Mountains and Highlands

a. _____   b. _____   c. _____

Rivers

a. _____   b. _____   c. _____   d. _____

Land Regions (*labeled*)

a. _____   b. _____   c. _____

d. _____   e. _____   f. _____

Oceans and Seas

a. _____   b. _____   c. _____

Ocean Current

_____

Water Passage

_____

Islands

a. _____

b. _____

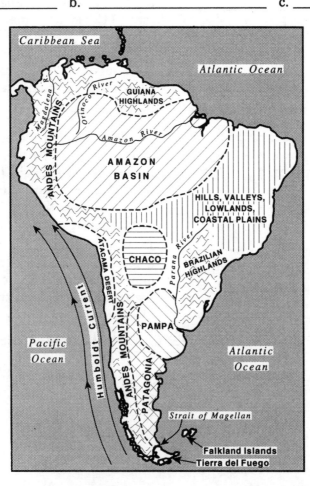

Make the physical features stand out by adding color:

Mountains (Red)

Rivers (Blue)

Land Regions (Green, except yellow for the Atacama Desert)

Surrounding Waters (Wavy blue lines)

Name: _____ Date: _____

SOUTH AMERICA: INTERPRETING ELEVATIONS

The diagram below is a side view, or cross section, showing elevation. In looking at the diagram, imagine that a giant knife has sliced through a portion of land, just as a knife might slice through a layer cake.

The height that land or water is above or below sea level is called elevation, or altitude. All places, including lakes and inland seas, are either below sea level, at sea level, or above sea level.

Elevation affects weather and climate, vegetation and crops, and even people's activities and health. The activities of people in Latin America, especially, are affected by elevation because there is great variety in the land—mountains, highlands, lowlands, and "in-between" lands. Sometimes there is a change of thousands of feet in elevation within a distance of a few miles. In some parts of the Andes Mountains, the land rises above 20,000 feet.

Use the information in the box and the diagram below to do these exercises.

1. What is the elevation of each of these places shown by dots in the diagram?

Place	Elevation	Place	Elevation
A		D	
B		E	
C		L	

2. When a place is below the level of the sea, we use the sign (–) in front of the numeral. Thus, H is –500', or 500 feet below sea level.

What is the elevation of I? _____

H? _____ J? _____

3. Check each place that is:

between 0 and –500' in elevation

____ E ____ J ____ K ____ F

between 500' and 1500' in elevation

____ K ____ M ____ G ____ B

4. How much higher is E than I?

_____

5. What two others words in the box above have the same meaning as *elevation*?

_____   _____

6. On the diagram below, show the "layers" of elevation by drawing the correct symbol for each elevation that is shown in the key. Do not fill in the "air" regions, only the land.

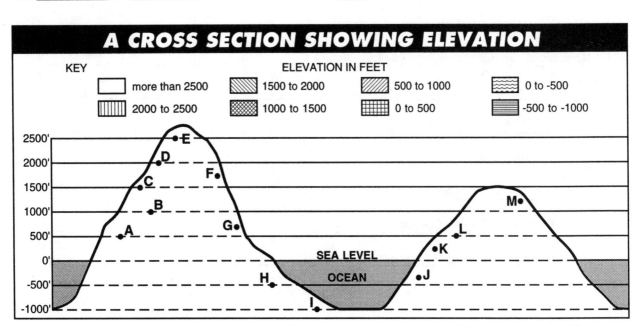

© 1996 by The Center for Applied Research in Education

Name: _____   Date: _____

SOUTH AMERICA: DISTANCES

Imagine that you are a diplomat on a good will tour of South America. Your mission is to develop harmonious relations between your country and the twelve countries you visit.

Procedure

1. On the map notice that there are lines connecting capital cities. On the lines, two mileage distances are listed, but only one is correct.

2. Use the Scale of Miles to determine which listed distance is most accurate. Then, cross out the incorrect distance.

Next, write the correct distance in the table, "Distances Between South American Capitals."

3. After you have completed the table, add the distances to determine the total number of miles you traveled.

4. Finally, determine the north-to-south, and the east-to-west length and width of South America by measuring the distance between points A and B, and C and D.

North-to-South Distance: _____ miles

East-to-West Distance: _____ miles

© 1996 by The Center for Applied Research in Education

DISTANCES BETWEEN SOUTH AMERICAN CAPITALS	
Air Flight	**Distance in Miles**
Caracas, Venezuela to Georgetown, Guyana	
Georgetown, Guyana to Parimaribo, Suriname	
Parimaribo, Suriname to Cayenne, French Guiana	
Cayenne, French Guiana to Brasilia, Brazil	
Brasilia, Brazil to Asuncion, Paraguay	
Asuncion, Paraguay to Montevideo, Uruguay	
Montevideo, Uruguay to Buenos Aires, Argentina	
Buenos Aires, Argentina to Santiago, Chile	
Santiago, Chile to La Paz, Bolivia	
La Paz, Bolivia to Lima, Peru	
Lima, Peru to Quito, Ecuador	
Quito, Ecuador to Bogota, Colombia	
Bogota, Colombia to Caracas, Venezuela	
Total Miles Traveled	

Name: _____ Date: _____

SOUTH AMERICA: DISTANCES

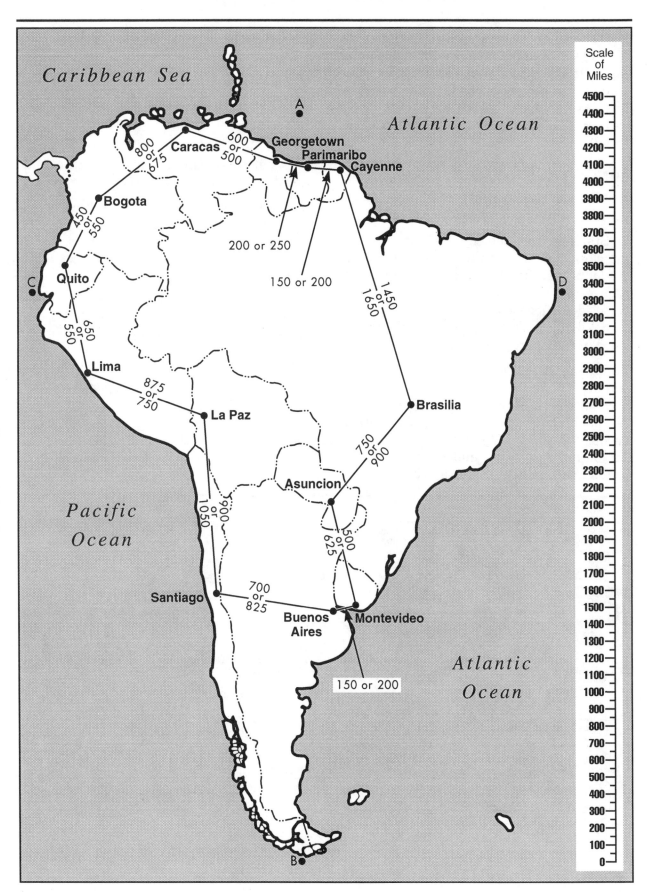

Caribbean Sea

Atlantic Ocean

A

800 or 675

Caracas

600 or 500

Georgetown
Parimaribo
Cayenne

Bogota

450 or 550

200 or 250

150 or 200

1450 or 1650

C Quito

D

650 or 550

Lima

875 or 750

Brasilia

La Paz

Pacific Ocean

750 or 900

900 or 1050

Asuncion

500 or 625

Santiago

700 or 825

Buenos Aires

Montevideo

150 or 200

Atlantic Ocean

B

Scale of Miles

4500
4400
4300
4200
4100
4000
3900
3800
3700
3600
3500
3400
3300
3200
3100
3000
2900
2800
2700
2600
2500
2400
2300
2200
2100
2000
1900
1800
1700
1600
1500
1400
1300
1200
1100
1000
900
800
700
600
500
400
300
200
100
0

SOUTH AMERICA: SPANISH MISSIONS

The illustration shows several aspects of life in a Spanish mission during colonial times. It also offers an opportunity for your students to become more familiar with the Spanish language, which even today prevails in South America with the exception of Brazil.

Procedure

1. Make a transparency of the scene for yourself, and photocopies for students.

2. Starting from the top left and proceeding clockwise around the picture have your students identify, in English, that to which each arrow is pointing. After an object has been identified tell students the Spanish equivalent. Have them write the Spanish word in the appropriate space.

Following are the Spanish and English words:

arco - arch
campana - bell
rueda - wheel
Indio - Indian
azada - garden hoe

planta - plant
padre - priest, father
cruz - cross
mulo - mule
sierra - saw

3. Questions to ask:

a. What might "Toca la campana" mean? (*Ring the bell.*)

b. What might be some of the purposes of the bell? (*call to mass, to work, to lunch; end of work day*)

c. What three kinds of work are the Indians doing? (*gardening, carpentry, carrying*)

d. What might the priest be telling or explaining to the Indians? (*Suggestions: "Be careful when you hoe; the root spread is quite wide." or, "Please load the cart while your friend is hoeing."*)

e. Name things in the picture that the Indians probably did not know about before the coming of the Spaniards.

- saw	- cart	- boards
- bell	- wheels	- stone arches
- metal axe	- harness	- rosary
- metal hoe	- cross	- mule

SOUTH AMERICA: ITS FIGHT FOR INDEPENDENCE

Procedure

1. The story that follows may be read or told as an introduction to the following two pages that highlight the life of Simon Bolivar, known to South Americans as "The Liberator."

2. The geographical elements of South America were significant determiners of why and how the wars there against Spain were fought. Some attention should be given to them before students work on the activity. Following are some points to stress:

a. The remoteness of South America from Spain. This greatly hindered Spain's transportation of armies and supplies. Also, during much of the time that the wars of liberation were taking place, Spain was engrossed in wars in Europe.

b. The Andes Mountains. These served as barriers to transportation and communication within South America as, for example, when San Martin crossed them to liberate Chile after liberating Argentina.

c. The vast forests and swamps of southern Colombia and Venezuela. These were penetrated only as a result of great determination and courage.

For more than 300 years (1500–1824) Spain ruled its colonies in South America with an "iron fist." There was very little, if any, part that the people of South America played in government. All officials were appointed by and sent from Spain, and their first loyalty was to Spain. The main purpose of the colonial governments was to work to enrich Spain; and they were quite successful. Shipload after shipload of gold, silver, and agricultural products left the New World for Spain to increase the Spanish treasury.

Gradually, feelings of resentment towards Spanish rule grew. Indians were forced to work in mines and plantations; thousands of them died from abuse and diseases. Africans were enslaved and transported to Spanish colonies to work on the huge sugar plantations. Mestizos, people who were of mixed Indian and Spanish blood, had little standing as compared to "pure" Spaniards.

Creoles, Spaniards born in the colonies, were considered to be inferior to Spaniards born in Spain. They were restricted in government and commerce. Spain forbade the importation of books because it feared that Creoles might develop "dangerous" ideas from reading about the American colonies' fight for freedom or the internal revolution in France. However, try as it did, Spain was not successful in keeping Creoles from being informed. Books were smuggled into its colonies; moreover, many Creoles had been educated in Europe and were well aware of what was happening in the world.

Several leaders emerged from the great number of people who were no longer willing to endure the autocratic and despotic Spanish rule. One of the first was Francisco de Miranda, a Creole, whose home was in Venezuela. Miranda had had significant experience as a soldier in the Spanish army. However, he began to realize the injustices of Spanish rule, and he came to believe that Venezuela should be free.

Even though he was a South American, he joined with George Washington's colonial army and fought to free the thirteen colonies from Britain. Then he sailed overseas to France to fight on the side of the French who were struggling to rid their country of their king.

Miranda's next objective was to free Venezuela from Spanish domination. In 1811 he declared Venezuela to be independent. He raised an army, of which a Creole named Simon Bolivar was a part, to make his declaration a reality. Eventually, he did succeed in winning control of Caracas, the seat of Spanish authority in Venezuela. However, he could not hold the city in the face of a strengthened Spanish army. After the city was captured, he was seized and transported to Spain, where he spent the rest of his life in a Spanish dungeon.

Bolivar managed to escape capture by the Spanish. He then joined revolutionary forces in Colombia and soon distinguished himself as a leader. From that time on, despite setbacks and disappointments, he successfully fought and freed not only Colombia and Venezuela, but also what is now Ecuador, Peru, and Bolivia. By 1824 he and Jose de San Martin, the liberator of Argentina and Chile, had completely eliminated Spanish rule in every part of South America.

SOUTH AMERICA: SIMON BOLIVAR, "THE LIBERATOR"

Simon Bolivar can, in some ways, be compared to George Washington. Both men were leaders in movements to free their homelands from rule by nations more than 2,000 miles across the Atlantic Ocean. These two pages will help you better understand the life of Simon Bolivar, who has been called "The George Washington of South America."

1. The pictures on the facing page are in correct chronological (time) order. However the descriptions below are not. On the line before each description write the number of the picture it best describes.

___ While visiting Spain, Bolivar was often a guest at the Spanish court.

___ Bolivar, born in 1783 to an aristocratic family, grew up on a Venezuelan ranch, where he became an expert horseman.

___ Bolivar spent twenty years of his life fighting for freedom. He and his men endured extreme hardships when crossing the Andes Mountains.

___ While visiting Rome, Bolivar made up his mind that he would not rest until Venezuela was free.

___ In Bolivar's time there were no public schools, so he studied with a private tutor.

___ After independence was achieved in Venezuela, Colombia, Ecuador, Peru, and Bolivia, Bolivar worked to establish new governments.

___ While in Spain, Bolivar met the woman he married and then brought home to Venezuela.

___ When Bolivar was only 16 years old he sailed for Spain to pursue higher education.

2. Write the number of the picture that shows one of the following details.

___ Monks took part in governmental discussions.

___ Bolivar's armies did not have special uniforms that all the soldiers wore.

___ Visitors to the court of Spain showed respect by kneeling.

3. In picture 3, Bolivar is shown as a young man who is in a thinking mood. Assume he was thinking about his homeland Venezuela, and its relationship with Spain. In a few words tell what his thoughts might have been.

_____

_____

_____

_____

4. Picture 7 shows Bolivar and his men on a campaign.

a. What are some descriptive words that could apply to Bolivar? _____

_____

b. Notice the soldiers' faces and postures. What word can you think of that describes their general attitude toward what they are doing or going to do? _____

5. The numbered countries on the map are the countries that Bolivar liberated. What country is shown by

1? _____

2? _____

3? _____

4? _____

Only a small part of country number 5 is shown. Try to identify it. **Clue**: Lake Titicaca is shown as part of the country.

_____

6. Complete the labeling of the map, as follows:

A and B: Atlantic Ocean
C: Caribbean Sea
D: Pacific Ocean
E: Brazil
F: Guyana
G: Suriname
H: French Guiana

Name: _____ Date: _____

SOUTH AMERICA: SIMON BOLIVAR, "THE LIBERATOR"

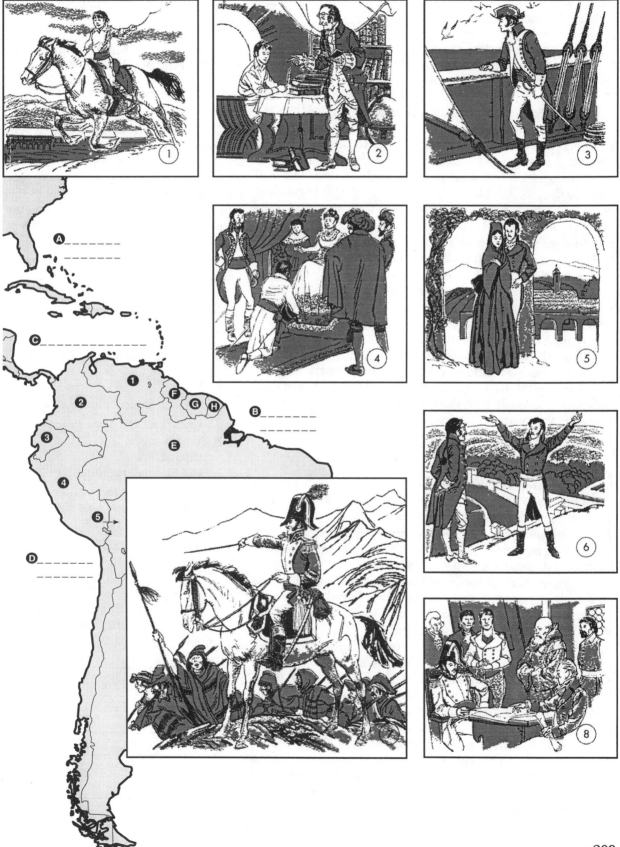

SOUTH AMERICA: SAN MARTIN PREPARES TO FREE CHILE

As you have learned, Simon Bolivar was the liberator of northern South America, and Jose de San Martin was the liberator of Argentina and Chile. The story that follows tells how carefully San Martin prepared before beginning a campaign.

A Much of San Martin's success as a general was due to his careful, step-by-step planning. He also had a keen imagination that helped him find solutions to difficult problems

B For example, one of the problems he had to solve was how to keep his horses and mules from becoming lame on the sharp rocks in the passes over the Andes Mountains. A special horseshoe was needed. He called together those men who understood the problem—blacksmiths, mule drivers, and veterinarians. Together they designed a horseshoe that was well suited to the job. San Martin thought the matter of horseshoes was so important that he instructed the officer who carried the model to Buenos Aires to "Guard it as if it were gold."

C Food was another problem. It had to be nourishing. It had to be light so that it could be transported easily. It had to keep for weeks without spoiling. Was there any such food to be found? The people of the Mendoza region of Argentina ate a food called *charquican*, made of dried beef, fat, and red peppers. These ingredients, mixed with hot water and corn, made a tempting and nourishing meal. A week's supply of this food could easily be carried in a soldier's pack.

D There was very little money to buy shoes for the soldiers. What could be done? A kind of native shoe called *tamango* was made from the pieces of cowhide that butchers ordinarily threw away. For warmth, the shoes were lined with scraps of wool gathered from the people and tailor shops in the towns of Argentina.

E Canteens were needed for carrying water. What would serve better than hollowed-out horns of cows? There was also a great lack of guns and bullets. Why not make them from the metal that could be melted from church bells?

F Bullets could not be fired without gunpowder, but there was no gunpowder. What to do? "Obviously," said San Martin, "we must make our own." An engineer was put in charge of manufacturing the precious explosive. Nitrate, an important ingredient of gunpowder, was found. Soon, barrels of gunpowder were piling up in San Martin's army warehouse.

G As he planned his campaign, San Martin carefully worked out schemes to confuse the Spaniards. False information was given to the enemy. First the attack was going to be at this place, then another place, then still another place. The Spanish commanders frantically moved their forces around like checkers on a checkerboard.

H Once, San Martin obtained permission from the proud Indians who lived south of Mendoza to cross the Andes through their territory. He knew the enemy would hear of the agreement. The nervous Spaniards moved part of their forces to that region, thereby spreading themselves thinly over a wide front. San Martin had never intended to cross the mountains that far south.

1. Why did San Martin have special horseshoes designed?

_____

_____

2. Draw a circle around the sentence that tells:
a. that San Martin thought the problem of horseshoes was very important.
b. that it was not only step-by-step planning that made him a great general.

3. San Martin believed his army's food supply needed three qualities.

What were they?_____

_____

4. Why did San Martin have church

bells melted?_____

_____

5. Underline the word in paragraph **H** that describes:
a. the Indians
b. the Spanish commanders

6. To what does the phrase "moved their forces around like checkers on a checkerboard" refer?

_____

_____

_____

7. Write a title that tells the main idea of each of the following paragraphs.

B: _____

_____

C: _____

_____

E: _____

_____

G: _____

Name: _____ Date: _____

SOUTH AMERICA: REGIONS OF COLOMBIA AND VENEZUELA

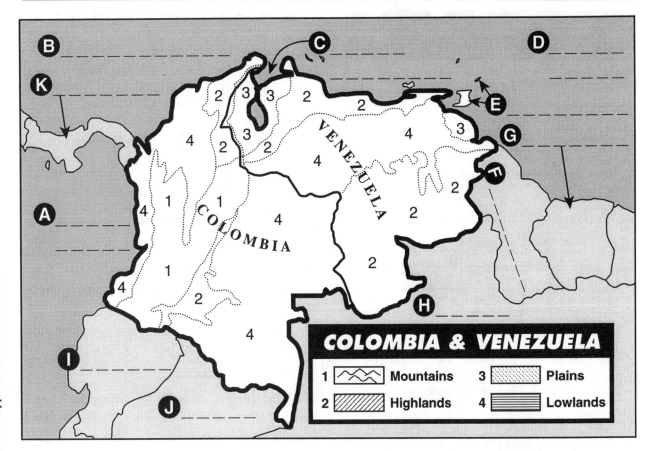

1. Complete the map to show the landform regions of Venezuela and Colombia. The map's key shows the symbols with which you should mark the numbered areas on the map. For example, locate the area that is marked with the numeral 1 on the map. This is where the high Andes Mountains are located. Using the symbol for mountains carefully fill in this area on the map.

Proceed in the same way for the highlands, plains, and lowlands of the two countries.

2. Add the following place names to your map.

A: Pacific Ocean   F: Guyana

B: Caribbean Sea   G: Suriname

C: Lake Maracaibo   H: Brazil

D: Atlantic Ocean   I: Ecuador

E: Trinidad/Tobago J: Peru

                    K: Panama

3.a. Which country is the most mountainous?
_____ Colombia   _____ Venezuela

b. Which country has lowlands along the entire coast?
_____ Colombia   _____ Venezuela

c. Which country has the greatest amount of highlands?
_____ Colombia   _____ Venezuela

4. What kind of land surrounds Lake Maracaibo?_____

5. What kind of land would you meet if you were to go from Brazil to Venezuela?

_____

6. What kind of land would you meet if you were to go from Brazil to Colombia?

_____

SOUTH AMERICA: VENEZUELA—A WORLD LEADER IN OIL PRODUCTION

Country	Barrels of Oil Produced Each Day*
Saudi Arabia	8,224

* In a recent year. 1 barrel = 42 gallons.

1. Use the information from the map to complete the table above. List the countries in the order of their production of oil. Saudi Arabia is the largest producer. It is listed at the top. Find the next largest producer and write in the table the name of that country and the number of barrels it produces each day. Continue in this way until the table is complete.

2. What place does Venezuela have among the world's leading producers? _____

3. What other Latin American nation is included in the list? _____

    What place does this nation hold among the world's top producers? _____

4. What place does the United States hold? _____

    Do Venezuela and Mexico combined produce as much oil per day as the United States? _____ How much more or less? ____

5. **Challenge**: Venezuela produces 2,357 barrels of oil each day. How many barrels does it produce in a 365-day year? _____

© 1996 by The Center for Applied Research in Education

LARGEST OIL-PRODUCING NATIONS OF THE WORLD

Figures in parentheses indicate the average number of barrels of oil produced *each day*.

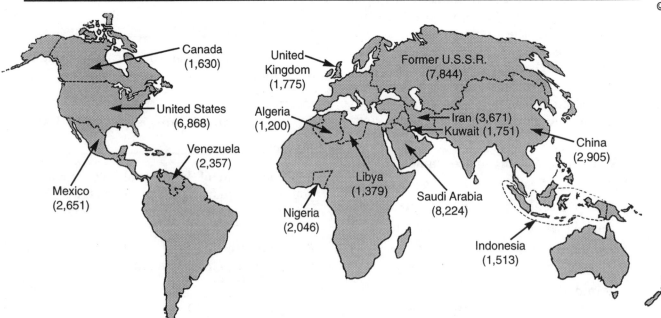

Canada (1,630)

United States (6,868)

Mexico (2,651)

Venezuela (2,357)

United Kingdom (1,775)

Algeria (1,200)

Nigeria (2,046)

Libya (1,379)

Former U.S.S.R. (7,844)

Iran (3,671)

Kuwait (1,751)

Saudi Arabia (8,224)

China (2,905)

Indonesia (1,513)

SOUTH AMERICA:COLOMBIA— A LEADING COFFEE GROWER

The table within the bar graph below shows that both Colombia and Venezuela are coffee growing nations. Colombia, especially, relies on coffee sales as a major source of income. Fifty percent of all of Colombia's exports is coffee. Only 4% of all of Colombia's land is suitable for growing crops, and most of that land is used to grow coffee. Brazil is Latin America's leading coffee grower, but it should be realized that Brazil is more than seven times larger than Colombia.

To Do

Use the information from the table to complete the bar graph. Use color or pencil shading to show the production for each country.

LATIN AMERICAN LEADERS IN COFFEE PRODUCTION

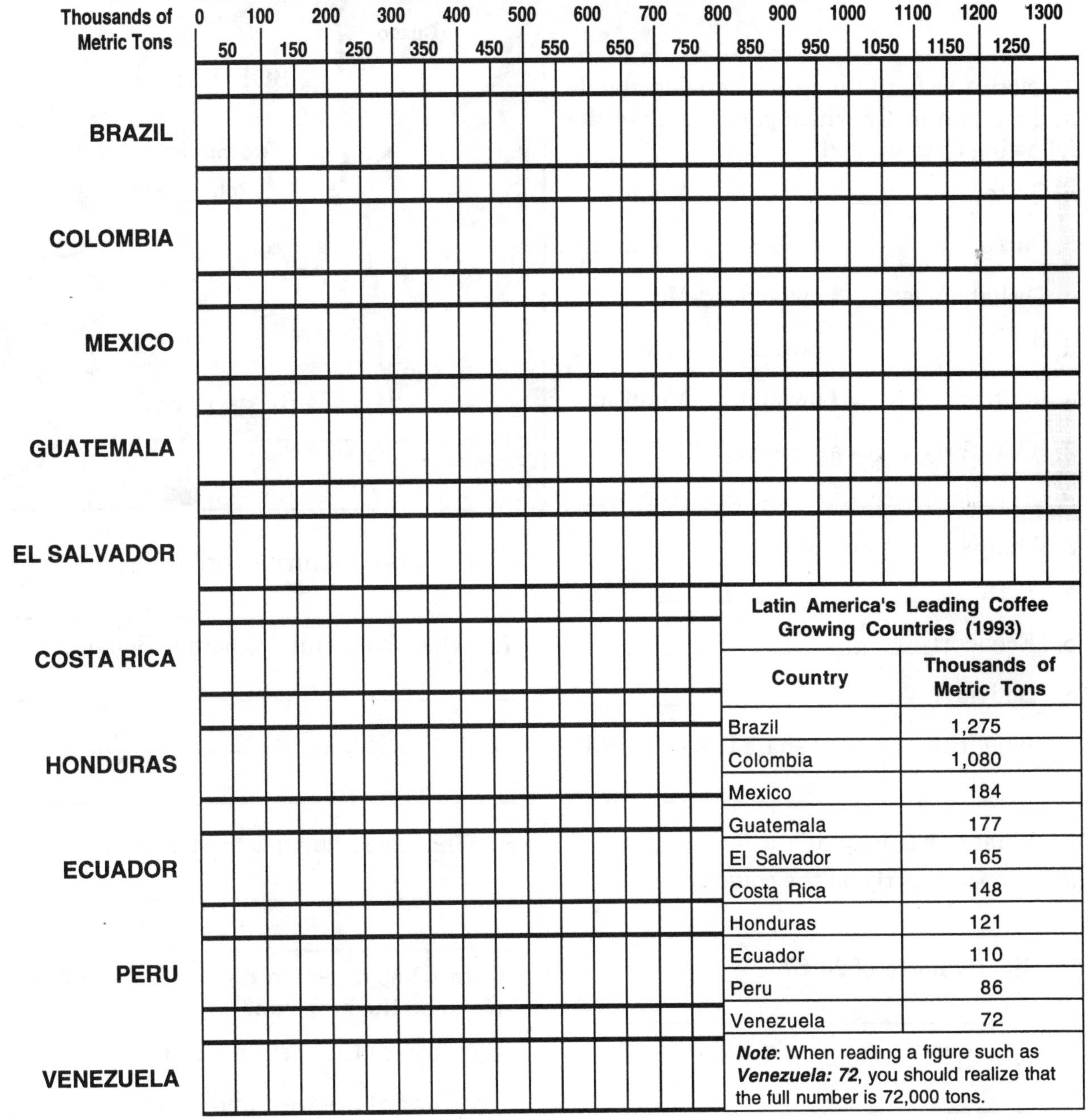

| Thousands of Metric Tons | 0 | 50 | 100 | 150 | 200 | 250 | 300 | 350 | 400 | 450 | 500 | 550 | 600 | 650 | 700 | 750 | 800 | 850 | 900 | 950 | 1000 | 1050 | 1100 | 1150 | 1200 | 1250 | 1300 |

BRAZIL

COLOMBIA

MEXICO

GUATEMALA

EL SALVADOR

COSTA RICA

HONDURAS

ECUADOR

PERU

VENEZUELA

Latin America's Leading Coffee Growing Countries (1993)	
Country	Thousands of Metric Tons
Brazil	1,275
Colombia	1,080
Mexico	184
Guatemala	177
El Salvador	165
Costa Rica	148
Honduras	121
Ecuador	110
Peru	86
Venezuela	72

Note: When reading a figure such as **Venezuela: 72**, you should realize that the full number is 72,000 tons.

　Name: _____ Date: _____

SOUTH AMERICA: ECUADOR, PERU, AND BOLIVIA ON THE MAP

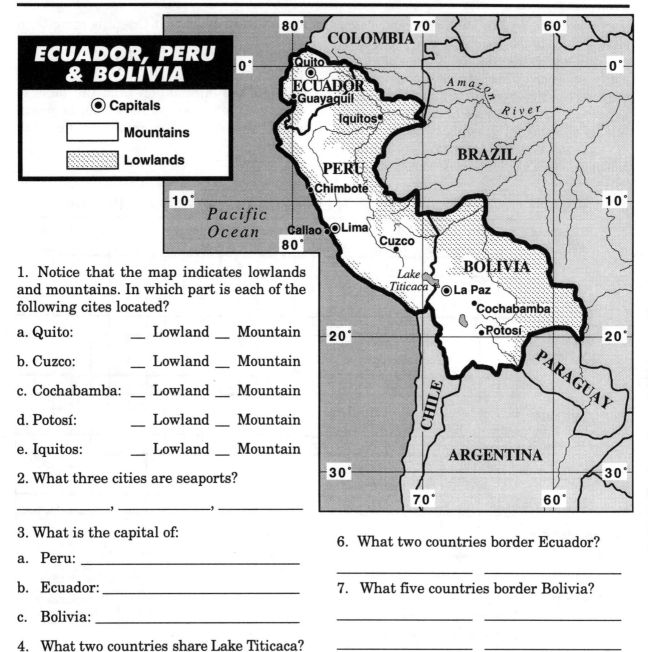

1. Notice that the map indicates lowlands and mountains. In which part is each of the following cites located?

a. Quito: ___ Lowland ___ Mountain

b. Cuzco: ___ Lowland ___ Mountain

c. Cochabamba: ___ Lowland ___ Mountain

d. Potosí: ___ Lowland ___ Mountain

e. Iquitos: ___ Lowland ___ Mountain

2. What three cities are seaports?

_____, _____, _____

3. What is the capital of:

a. Peru: _____

b. Ecuador: _____

c. Bolivia: _____

4. What two countries share Lake Titicaca?

_____ _____

5. What city is located

a. almost directly on the equator?

_____

b. slightly north of 20°S?

_____

c. on 80°W?

_____

6. What two countries border Ecuador?

_____ _____

7. What five countries border Bolivia?

_____ _____

_____ _____

8. What five countries border Peru?

_____ _____ _____

_____ _____

9. In what direction do most of the rivers shown on the map run?

___ Toward the east and north

___ Toward the west and north

SOUTH AMERICA: THE PERU CURRENT

The Peru Current would be a suitable topic for a presentation lesson. Information about the current and suggestions for teaching and student activity follow.

1. Make a transparency of the map to be used during the presentation.
2. Have your students take notes as you proceed through the lesson. Notes should be brief and can be taken under four main headings.
A. Where is the Peru Current?
B. How does the current affect the land?
C. What are some negative effects of the current?
D. What are some positive effects of the current?
3. After the lesson has been presented, some students should be asked to tell what they know about the current. They should be encouraged to use their notes for reminders.

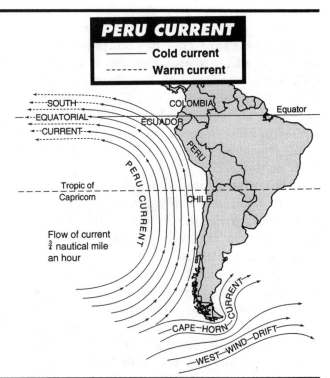

The Peru Current—Some Advantages and Disadvantages

Why are the coasts of Peru and northern Chile barren deserts? The cold Peru Current, sometimes called the Humboldt Current, provides part of the answer to the question.

The prevailing westerly winds of the coast areas cool as they blow over the chilly Pacific waters. As the winds cool, moisture they carry falls as rain on the ocean. By the time the winds reach the coast, they have lost much of their moisture.

Then the coastal land warms the cooled winds. The warmer the winds become, the more moisture they can hold. So, the warm winds take up more moisture from the already dry land. As if this were not enough, the high Andes Mountains block any rain-bearing winds from the east.

About every ten years, especially along the Peruvian coast, there is a complete change. Warm water from the north replaces the cold water of the Humboldt flow. The results are disastrous. Torrential rainstorms beat the coast. Floods occur. Mud homes crumble, irrigated crops are washed out, and raging rivers cut deep paths through the desert.

What good results from the Peru Current? The current does cool the coastal lands, providing a pleasantly warm climate. The winds blowing over the cold water make the current a kind of giant air-conditioning unit.

The current is crammed with very tiny water plants. These plants are eaten by small organisms called **zooplankton**. The zooplankton are eaten by millions of little fish. Big fish eat the smaller fish. The presence of fish in large quantities attracts thousand of fishermen. The fish they catch—bonito, tuna, swordfish, and others—provide needed protein for the diet of Latin Americans. Peru is a world leader in the fishing industry.

The current brings still another benefit. Millions of birds also feed on the fish. These birds nest on the coastal islands. The bird droppings, called **guano**, makes an excellent fertilizer. Some deposits of guano on the islands off the coast are as much as 75 feet deep. Guano was once exported all over the world and was an important source of wealth to Peru. Now its exportation is strictly controlled by the government so that it can be used on Peru's fields.

Name: _____ Date: _____

SOUTH AMERICA: ANIMALS OF THE ANDES MOUNTAINS

Have you noticed how much camels and llamas look alike? They are related. Camels roamed North America thousands of years ago. Some wandered to Asia over the land bridge that once connected North America and Asia. Others grazed their way to South America. Four branches of the family developed: the alpaca, the vicuña, the guanaco, and the llama.

The alpaca are known for their excellent wool. Hundreds of years before Europeans came to South America, the native Indians were skillfully weaving the long strands, some up to 15 inches long, into cloth. Alpaca wool kept not only the alpaca warm in the high, cold Andes Mountains, but also the people who lived there. Wild alpaca were once extensively hunted, but now they are protected by strict laws. Most alpaca are tame and are herded in the same way sheep are herded. Some alpaca wool is exported to be made into very expensive coats and jackets.

The vicuña also have excellent wool, but only a few are tame; most of them are wild and live in the high Andes. And, they need warm wool for they live as high as 18,000 feet—that's more than three miles—above sea level. They are the smallest of the South American descendants of the camel. At the shoulder they average about 2½ feet high, but their long necks make them seem taller. At one time they were in danger of becoming extinct, but strict laws now protect them.

The guanaco look much like the vicuña, but they are larger, about 3½ feet high at the shoulder. They can be found in the mountains of Ecuador, Peru, and Bolivia in the summer. In winter they prefer the shelter of valleys and plains where there is grass to eat. Guanaco are mostly found in the wild. They were once widely hunted by the people of the Andes for their meat, bones, and skins. Now, however, they are protected, but many of them are killed illegally.

To the people of the Andes Mountains the llama is the most important animal. This is especially true for the Indians in the high altitudes. The nimble, sure-footed, wooly animals are their main beasts of burden. They also supply warm wool for clothing and hide for sandals. They are the Indians main source of meat.

The ancient Incas used the strong backs of llamas to help them build roads, bridges, and irrigation systems. The Spaniards used them to carry gold and silver from mountain mines to the coast. Llamas were especially useful in mountains because they could stand the cold and they could pick their way along treacherous mountain trails.

Llamas are good workers, but they also can be very stubborn. If their loads are too heavy they will sit down and refuse to move until the loads are lightened. If tired they will lie down to rest. If they become angry they will spit and kick. Make a llama really angry and it will vomit. Mules are said to be stubborn, but llamas could give them lessons in that trait.

Treated considerately, llamas will carry 100 pound loads twenty miles in a day. They can survive for days without water; they are able to use the moisture in the food they eat. Llamas can find food where other animals would starve.

To Do

Assume that you are a teacher. You assigned your students to read the story on this page. Now, you want to administer a True (T) - False (F) test to determine how much they remember.

Write ten statements, some true and some false. Then, with your instructor's permission have a classmate take the test; likewise, you will take your classmate's test.

Here is a sample statement: Animals such as the alpaca, vicuña, guanaco, and llama came to North American and South America before camels. T or F

Note: Write your statements on the reverse side of this page.

SOUTH AMERICA: BOLIVIA LOSES ITS SEACOAST, LAND, AND NITRATE

That geography is a significant factor in world affairs is beyond dispute. Never was the importance of a country's geography more apparent than in the story of Bolivia, a country that struggled for and lost its most valuable geographic assets—land, minerals, and access to the sea.

Procedure

Read the story to your students, but before reading it refer to the map that shows Bolivia, Peru, Chile, and Paraguay. Point out that at one time Bolivia had a seacoast roughly located in northern Chile and southern Peru, i.e., the Atacama Desert. Also point out the Paraguay River and its route of flow to the Atlantic Ocean.

When Spain was pushed out of Latin America, the boundaries of many of the newly formed nations were indefinite. The boundary between Chile and Bolivia was especially uncertain. Neither country worried about this very much because the land between the countries was considered a wasteland—the Atacama Desert.

The indifference to boundary lines changed when the world began to use more and more nitrate. At that time, the Atacama Desert was the only place in the world where the valuable fertilizer and gunpowder component could be mined in great quantities. The country that controlled the nitrate could become very rich.

It was not long before Bolivia and Chile were quarreling over the region. Peru also had an interest in the dispute. Over a period of years there were many attempts to settle the disagreements peacefully, but none of them were successful.

Eventually, war broke out. Peru joined Bolivia against Chile. The war was called the War of the Pacific. In Chile, it was called the "Nitrate War."

The war began in 1879 and ended in 1883 with victory for Chile. In the treaty following the war, Chile's northern border was moved northward about 150 miles. This meant that Chile took the strip of land that had connected Bolivia with the Pacific. It also meant that Peru lost some land to Chile.

The loss of its coastline meant that Bolivia was a landlocked country. Its people and products no longer had access to the oceans of the world except through some other country.

The loss of its seacoast was an economic disaster for Bolivia. But, there was another possible route to the sea: follow the Paraguay River through Paraguay to the Parana River, which empties into the Atlantic Ocean. But, as the map shows, the Paraguay River flows through the very center of Paraguay. Bolivia tried to negotiate an agreement with Paraguay to use the river. Unfortunately, the negotiations broke down. Even worse, war broke out between Paraguay and Bolivia. Again, Bolivia lost an important war and more land—this time part of the Chaco region, where oil had been discovered.

Bolivia is, of course, still a landlocked country. However, because of the development of railroads, Bolivia is allowed to use them to transport products and people to the ports of Chile, Peru, Brazil, and Argentina. Another helpful development came with the development of air transportation. However, even an airplane flying into or out of Bolivia must fly over another country's land.

SOUTH AMERICA: TROPICAL RAIN FORESTS

The lesson outlined below can help your students arrive at a clear yet simple understanding of the term "tropical rain forest." Also, the lesson will provide opportunities for your students to develop skills in taking notes, labeling a diagram, and locating place names on maps.

Development

Photocopy and distribute the student study guide on the opposite page. As you present the information that follows, have your students write brief notes on the study guide. You may also want to make a transparency of the study guide to complete as you move through the lesson.

Questions and Answers

1. **What is a tropical rain forest?** A tropical rain forest is a thickly wooded area located near the equator that experiences heavy rainfall, high temperatures, and a long growing season—all of which are conducive to the growth and sustenance of a vast amount of plant and animal life.

2. **What is it like to be in a tropical rain forest?** Walking would be fairly easy, although there is very little bright light. The "roof of trees" cuts off sunlight. The absence of bright sunlight inhibits undergrowth so there would be very little brush to trip over. The sounds of birds and other animals would surround us. In spite of the shade, it would be hot and humid.

3. **How is a tropical rain forest structured?** Think of the forest as being "layered." At ground level there would be small, leafy plants. Vines would be climbing toward the sunlight. *Note*: Have your students write "Forest Floor" on the blank line at the bottom of the diagram. Encourage them to draw small plants on the ground and some vines hanging from the trees.

The "Understory" makes up the middle layer of the forest. Vines encircle the straight tree trunks. Young trees with vertical branches meet the lower levels of the uppermost layer. *Note*: Have your students write "Understory" on the appropriate line. Draw leaves on the vertical branches, and continue the vines.

The crowns of the trees compose the roof, or "Canopy." The branches grow horizontally and are densely leaved. *Note*: Have your students write "Canopy" on the appropriate blank line. Your students may draw a profusion of leaves on the branches, giving the impression of denseness.

4. **How many and what kinds of animals inhabit tropical rain forests?** Estimates of the amount of animal life in the forests vary, but it is probable that up to 50% of the world's wildlife make their homes in them. This figure is all the more remarkable because rain forests occupy less than 5% of the earth's surface. Each layer of the forests provides shelter and sustenance for different animals: at the lower level—snakes, insects, crocodiles, lizards; at the middle level—birds, ocelots, tapirs, and animals of the upper and lower level that make forays into it; at the upper level—numerous birds such as toucans and parrots, sloths, monkeys, snakes. *Note*: Encourage your students to draw representative animals in the three layers.

5. **Where are the tropical rain forests?** In general, tropical rain forests are found in regions in which rain falls regularly and totals 80". Most of the forests lie between the Tropic of Cancer (23½°N) and the Tropic of Capricorn (23½°S). Leaves are on the trees all year around because there is very little climatic change from season to season. Latin America's greatest tropical forests are in Brazil's Amazon Basin, Guyana, Suriname, French Guiana, Venezuela, Colombia, eastern Peru, and Ecuador. *Note*: On a large wall map, point out places where tropical rain forests are found. As you name the places, your students may write the names in the spaces provided on their study guides.

6. **Why are tropical rain forests important?** (a) The forests provide habitats for animals and plants that could not survive elsewhere. (b) Trees take carbon dioxide from the air. Carbon dioxide prevents heat from escaping into the atmosphere. If too many trees are eliminated, the earth's temperatures will rise, and this, in turn, will create new deserts and cause disastrous flooding from melted Arctic and Antarctic ice. (c) Important medicines are obtained from tropical trees. (d) Rain forests provide the oxygen needed to keep the mixture of gases in the air in proper balance.

Name: _____ Date: _____

SOUTH AMERICA: TROPICAL RAIN FORESTS

Take careful notes. Keep your notes brief. Complete sentences are not necessary—words and phrases are adequate.

1. What is a tropical rain forest?

_____

_____

_____

_____

_____

2. What is it like to be in a tropical rain forest?

_____

_____

_____

_____

3. How is a tropical rain forest structured?

_____

_____

_____

_____

_____

4. What kinds of animals inhabit tropical rain forests?

_____

_____

_____

_____

5. Where are the tropical rain forests?

_____

_____

_____

Tropical rain forests' locations:

_____

_____ _____ _____

_____ _____ _____

_____ _____ _____

6. Why are tropical rain forests important?

_____

_____

_____

_____

SOUTH AMERICA: MAP-WORD SEARCH

The Word Search puzzle contains 19 of the place names shown on the map. Place names are printed across or down in the puzzle. Names with more than one word have a space between the words. When you find a place name, carefully draw a circle around the entire name.

An effective way to proceed is to find a name on the map, then search the puzzle for it.

F	R	E	N	C	H	■	G	U	I	A	N	A
P	A	R	A	N	A	■	R	I	V	E	R	B
M	O	N	T	E	V	I	D	E	O	V	I	A
X	V	S	A	O	■	P	A	U	L	O	O	P
W	U	R	U	G	U	A	Y	L	K	D	■	O
R	K	M	B	E	L	E	M	K	H	S	D	R
G	E	O	R	G	E	T	O	W	N	U	E	T
U	M	V	A	Y	Z	J	R	M	R	R	■	O
Y	A	N	S	A	N	T	O	S	E	I	J	■
A	N	O	I	Q	W	H	C	N	C	N	A	A
N	A	M	L	P	H	J	H	L	I	A	N	L
A	U	P	I	F	J	K	A	R	F	M	E	E
D	S	C	A	Y	E	N	N	E	E	E	I	G
A	M	A	Z	O	N	■	R	I	V	E	R	R
C	A	P	A	R	A	M	A	R	I	B	O	E

SOUTH AMERICA: BRAZIL AND BANANA PRODUCTION

Bananas are a fruit that we take for granted; the average American enjoys eating them, but doesn't know very much about them. This page will help your students better understand and appreciate the many aspects of growing and distributing the delicious tropical fruit.

Procedure

1. Write the list of banana headings across a chalkboard.

2. Choose a banana fact at random. Then as you tell students the fact, ask them to categorize it under one of the headings. Some facts might fit under more than one category.

3. After the list of facts has been categorized and discussed, project the table that tells the banana production of Latin America's leading banana producing countries. You might ask your students to make a bar or picture graph based on the statistics given in the table.

BANANA FACTS

Banana Plantations

❏ Tropical forests had to be cut to obtain land for thousands of plants.

❏ Roads had to be built and rail lines established to deliver supplies to the plantations and to transport the bananas.

❏ Plantations have homes for the workers, warehouses, shops, and stores.

❏ Banana plants are planted in rows.

Banana Plants

❏ Bananas do not grow on trees. (They are plants with large stems.) They do not have trunks or branches.

❏ Bananas grow in bunches; they grow upward, not downward.

❏ Banana plants are from 10' to 20' tall.

❏ Each banana plant produces one bunch every season. Each bunch has several clusters of bananas called **hands**. Individual bananas are called **fingers**.

❏ Bananas are sprayed with chemicals to prevent them from contracting diseases.

❏ Banana leaves are as much as 10' long and 2' wide.

Harvesting Bananas

❏ It takes about 15 months for a banana plant to produce fruit.

❏ Bananas are not ripe when harvested; they ripen before they reach markets.

❏ Knives attached to long poles cut the bunches from the plants.

❏ After being cut, the bunches are placed in plastic bags.

Miscellaneous Banana Facts

❏ Banana plants are not native to the Americas; they originated in Asia.

❏ Bananas are also grown in great quantities in other tropical countries. Uganda (Africa) rivals Brazil in banana production.

❏ Banana leaves are used for many purposes, including roofing for houses, mats, and baskets.

Banana Distribution

❏ At the plantations bananas are loaded on trucks or trains and hauled to seaports.

❏ At seaports bananas are loaded on wooden pallets and hoisted by cranes to ships' holds.

❏ Temperatures of ships' holds are carefully regulated to prevent premature ripening and spoilage.

❏ Five of the leading banana receiving seaports in the United States are Seattle, Los Angeles, New Orleans, Charleston, and New York.

❏ Some bananas grown on the west coasts of Latin America are shipped through the Panama Canal.

❏ Upon being unloaded at receiving ports, bananas are warehoused, then distributed to stores, where they are sold by the pound.

Latin America's Seven Leading Banana Producers			
Country	**Metric Tons**	**Country**	**Metric Tons**
Brazil	5,593,000	Costa Rica	1,827,000
Ecuador	3,990,000	Mexcio	1,650,000
Colombia	1,827,000	Venezuela	1,215,000
		Panama	1,120,000

SOUTH AMERICA: BRAZIL—A LEADING CACAO BEAN GROWER

Procedure

1. Read or tell "The Cacao Story" to your students.

2. Via a transparency, project the picture graph that shows cacao production among the five leading Latin American countries that grow cacao. **Note**: Several African countries, especially Ghana, Ivory Coast, and Nigeria, are also great producers of cacao beans.

3. Have your students read the graph for amounts grown per country, comparisons, and so on. Some sample questions:

☞ How many of the leading producers are in Middle America? South America?

☞ Do all the countries combined produce as much cacao beans as Brazil?

There is a story that in 1519 Hernando Cortes, Spanish explorer and conqueror of the Aztecs, and his men were being entertained by Montezuma, Emperor of the Aztecs. A strange dark brown beverage with a delightful odor was placed before Cortes. He was probably a bit suspicious that it might be poison, as there was no trust between the Spaniards and the Aztecs. Nevertheless, as the story goes, Cortes did drink the rich and flavorful liquid. The drink was chocolate; it was the first time that a European had tasted the drink.

Chocolate is made from *cacao*, seeds of the cacao tree. The Spaniards called the seeds *cacao beans*. Much later when the drink came to the attention of Americans, and possibly through a mistake in spelling that was never corrected, cacao became know as *cocoa*.

The first cacao beans reached Spain via Cortes in 1528. The chocolate made from the beans became a tightly guarded secret of the Spaniards for many years; there were great profits to be made from the sale of chocolate. However, the secret of chocolate could not be kept forever. People from other countries learned how to process the beans by shelling, roasting, and then grinding them into a paste. Later, methods of making candy and other products were developed. Today, the growing, processing, distributing, and selling of products derived from cacao is a multimillion dollar business.

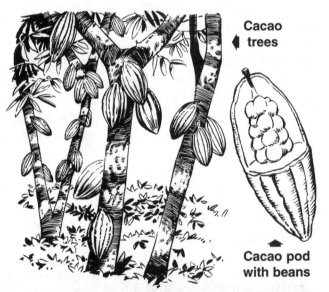

Cacao trees

Cacao pod with beans

Leading Cacao Bean Growers in South America	
BRAZIL	🪙🪙🪙🪙🪙🪙🪙🪙🪙🪙🪙🪙🪙🪙🪙🪙🪙🪙🪙🪙🪙🪙🪙🪙🪙🪙🪙🪙🪙🪙🪙🪙🪙🪙🪙 : 350,000 metric tons
EL SALVADOR	🪙🪙🪙🪙🪙🪙🪙 : 75,000 metric tons
COLOMBIA	🪙🪙🪙🪙🪙🪙 : 55,000 metric tons
ECUADOR	🪙🪙🪙🪙🪙 : 45,000 metric tons
MEXICO	🪙🪙🪙🪙 : 40,000 metric tons

(Figures rounded to nearest 10,000)   🪙 = 10,000 metric tons
(Figures for 1993)

Name: _____ Date: _____

SOUTH AMERICA: PARAGUAY AND URUGUAY ON THE MAP

Using the information from each statement, locate on the map the place name italicized in the sentence. Then add this place name to the map as indicated by the encircled letter at the end of the statement.

1. The *Uruguay* River forms the western border of Uruguay. **A**

2. The *Paraguay River* flows through the middle of Paraguay. **B**

3. The *Gran Chaco* is west of the Paraguay River. It is a region of plains covered by scrub forests and grasses. **C**

4. *Bolivia* is north and west of Paraguay. **D**

5. *Brazil* is east of Paraguay and northeast of Uruguay. **E**

6. The river that flows from Bolivia and forms part of Paraguay's southern border is called the *Pilcomayo River*. **F**

7. *Asunción* is located where the Paraguay River and the Pilcomayo join. **G**

8. The Uruguay River flows into the *Rio de la Plata*, just north of Buenos Aires. **H**

9. *Montevideo* is on Uruguay's southern coast, east of Buenos Aires. **I**

10. Paraguay is located on the *Tropic of Capricorn*. **J**

11. *Concepción* is the city located near the point where the Tropic of Capricorn crosses the Paraguay River. **K**

12. The river that forms Paraguay's southern border and joins with the Paraguay River is the *Paraná River*. **L**'s

13. *Posadas* is an important Argentine town located on the Paraná River and near the Paraguay border. **M**

14. About 200 miles south of Asunción is *Corrientes*. **N**

15. South of Uruguay and east of Argentina is the *Atlantic Ocean*. **O**

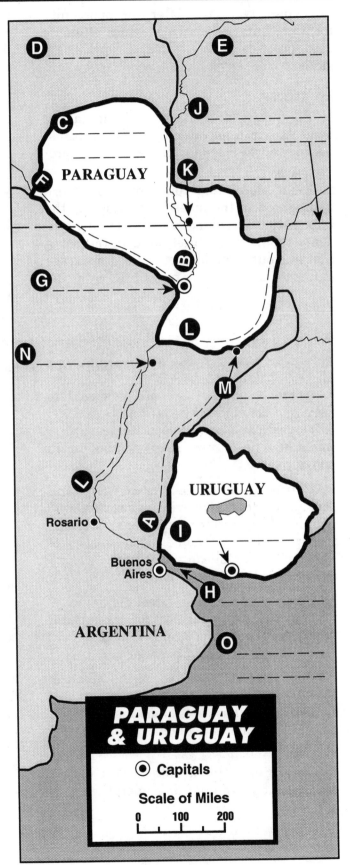

SOUTH AMERICA: CHILE—FROM DRY NORTH TO RAINY SOUTH

These two pages offer an opportunity for a presentation lesson in which students may practice taking notes, a work-study skill.

Procedure

1. Photocopy and distribute the facing page. Also, you may decide to make a transparency of the page to accompany your presentation.

2. Eight places and points of interest are highlighted in the notes that follow. As the information in the notes is presented, students should make brief notes in the boxes that surround the map of Chile. Encourage students to keep their notes brief by using phrases and abbreviations such as "5%" rather than "five percent," "w/o" rather than "without," and so on. They may be able to invent their own note-taking shortcuts, known only to them.

3. After the note-taking lesson is completed students may draw a succession of small symbols for mountains (from the north to the south) on both the east and west sides of Chile's eastern border. This will help them to visualize how constricted Chile is in its position between the Andes Mountains and the Pacific Ocean:

© 1996 by The Center for Applied Research in Education

Points of Interest in Chile

1. **Arica**: seaport . . . once belonged to Peru . . . surrounded by Atacama Desert . . . rich nitrate and copper deposits nearby . . . sometimes no or very scant rainfall in an entire year

2. **Valparaiso**: Chile's main port and second largest city with some 300,000 people . . . modern buildings, schools, transportation . . . name means "valley of paradise" . . . Chilean naval base . . . precipitation 20" to 40" per year

3. **Concepción**: Chile's "steel making city" . . . important shipping port for agricultural products . . . earthquake-proof buildings . . . precipitation 40" to 60" per year

4. **Punta Arenas**: located on the Strait of Magellan . . . Chile's southernmost city . . . Chilean naval base . . . name means "sand points" . . . constant winds . . . wool capital of Chile

5. **Chuquicamata**: world's largest copper mine; an open-pit mining operation . . . copper shipped by rail to the port of Antofagasta

6. **Antofagasta**: northern Chile's most important center of commerce . . . highway and rail center . . . connected by rail and road to Santiago, a distance of about 700 air miles

7. **Santiago**: Chile's capital and principal city . . . headquarters for Chile's mining, industrial, agricultural, and commercial activities . . . a city of modern buildings and palm trees . . . climate much like southern California . . . at the head of Chile's fertile central valley, and where most of Chile's people live

8. **South Chile**: few inhabitants, small farms, heavily forested, very mountainous, extremely irregular coast line . . . a "pioneer land" settled after the defeat of the native Indians (not unlike the United States' settlement of the west) . . . volcanoes, earthquakes, severe Pacific storms

Name: _____ Date: _____

SOUTH AMERICA: CHILE—FROM DRY NORTH TO RAINY SOUTH

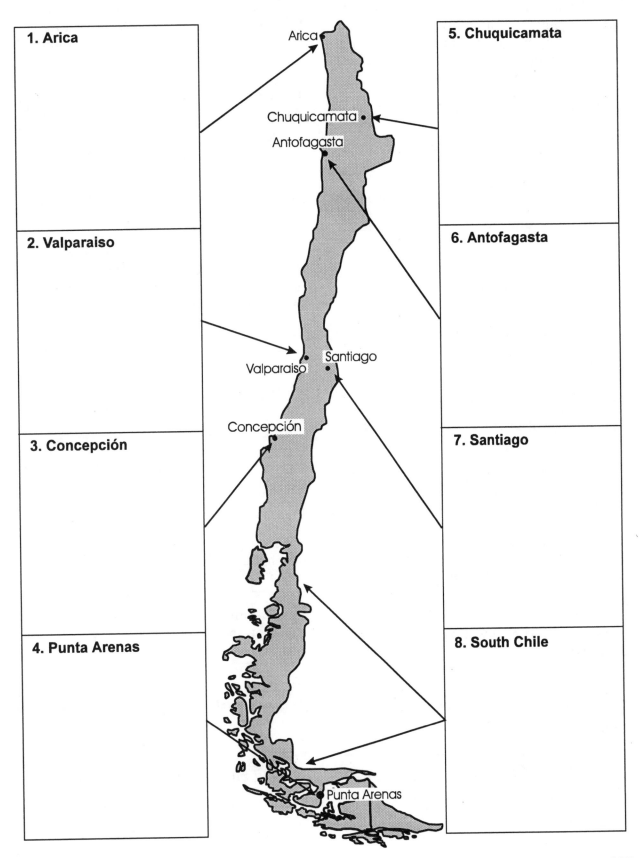

1. Arica

2. Valparaiso

3. Concepción

4. Punta Arenas

5. Chuquicamata

6. Antofagasta

7. Santiago

8. South Chile

SOUTH AMERICA: A TOURIST MAP OF ARGENTINA

The map and information boxes on the opposite page contain information about cities, regions, and places of interest in and near Argentina. That information will help you answer the following questions.

1. What is a person who lives in Buenos Aires called? _____

_____

2. Why would vacationers want to go to Comodoro Rivadavia? _____

_____

_____

3. Why was a statue of Jesus Christ placed at Uspallata Pass? _____

_____

_____

4. The elevation of Mount McKinley in Alaska is 20,320 feet. How much higher is Mount Aconcagua? _____

5. The large grape-production area of Argentina is near what city?

_____

6. What is the world's southernmost town?

_____

What is the southernmost town in Argentina?

_____

7. Where in Argentina could an oil-field worker most likely find work?

_____

8. What Argentine city is the world's leading corn-exporting port?

_____

9. If someone was graduated from the University of Córdoba 380 years after its founding, in what year was the graduation?

_____

10. What is there in Buenos Aires that serves as a reminder of Argentina's independence day? _____

_____

11. What river marks the northern limits of Patagonia? _____

12. Argentina's Northeast is sometimes called Mesopotamia, which means "the land between the rivers." Between what two rivers does the Northeast lie?

_____

_____

13. What two things help make Tucumán suitable for growing sugar cane?

_____

_____

14. In what region of Argentina are the Iguassú Falls? _____

If the Iguassú Falls are 237 feet high, how high are the Niagara Falls?

_____

15. Why might it be expected that English would be spoken in the Falkland Islands?

_____

16. What is the name of the region of Argentina that lies between the Gran Chaco and Patagonia?

_____

17. Why might a tourist from Italy feel "at home" in Mendoza? _____

_____

Name: _____ Date: _____

SOUTH AMERICA: A TOURIST MAP OF ARGENTINA

Frost-free climate... abundant water for irrigation... sugar-cane fields... sugar refineries... Peru trade route

Iguassú means "great waters"... river falls 237 feet, 70 feet more than Niagara... has great possibilities for hydroelectric power... national park

Started in 1573... tourist center for Andes vacation spots... site of one of South America's oldest universities, founded in 1613

Andes highest peak... elevation 22,834 feet

Centuries-old route over Andes... used by San Martín's troops when they marched to liberate Chile... pass is 12,464 feet... highway and railroad cross it

Statue of "Christ of the Andes"... memorial to pact of Argentina and Chile in which each nation promised never to wage a war against the other

Last big city on route to Uspallata Pass... grape-growing, wine-producing region... irrigation farming... home of many Italian immigrants

Capital... Latin America's third largest city... residents called Porteños, or "people of the port"... Avenida 9 de Julio crosses city; named in honor of Argentine independence... beautiful parks, polo fields, a race track, zoo, and other attractions... city is hub of nation

Heart of Argentine corn-growing region... world's leading corn-exporting city... ocean liners load at docks and sail directly to other parts of the world

A million or more vacationists visit here during swimming season, December to April... heart of Argentine oil-producing region

Southernmost town in Argentina... was once world's most southern town before Chile built Puerto Williams, which is 25 miles farther south... Argentine naval base... difficult to reach except by boat or plane

Two large islands surrounded by about 100 smaller ones... British colony of about 2,000 people, mostly British descent... large sheep farms... wool is chief export... whaling station

Tucumán
GRAN CHACO
Córdoba
Aconcagua
Uspallata Pass
Mendoza
Rosario
PAMPA
Buenos Aires
Mar del Plata
Bahía Blanca
Colorado River
ANDES
PATAGONIA
Comodoro Rivadavia
FALKLAND ISLANDS
Ushuaia
Paraguay R.
Parana R.
Iguassu Falls
Uruguay River
Parana River
NORTHEAST

ARGENTINA

⊙ Capital

+ Mountain peak

Name: _____ Date: _____

SOUTH AMERICA: LOCATING PLACES AND THINGS PUZZLES

1. The shapes of the 12 countries and one colony of South America are shown below. Write the name of each on the blank line close to the shape.

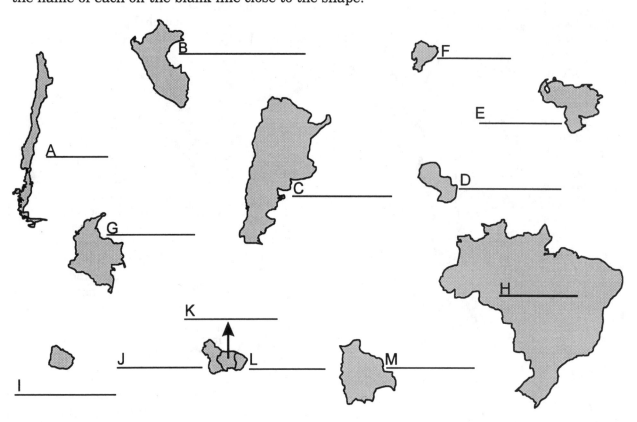

2. Each of the question marks in the two maps below points to a natural feature of Latin America. Write the name of each on the line above the map.

_____ _____   _____ _____

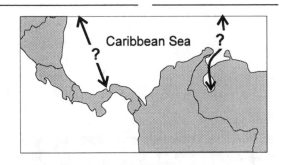

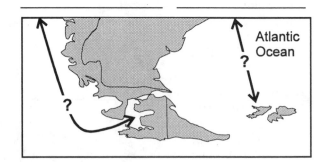

3. Use the clues listed below to identify some South American places and things.

a. A statue . . . located on a 12,000' high mountain pass . . . a memorial to peace between Chile and Argentina:

_____

b. A lake . . . shared by two countries . . . world's largest high-elevation body of water: _____

c. Islands . . . off the coast of Ecuador . . . habitat of unusual animals such as iguanas: _____

Name: _____ Date: _____

SOUTH AMERICA: A PLACE NAME CROSSWORD PUZZLE

If necessary, refer to a political map of South America for help in solving this crossword puzzle.

Across

1. A country with no coast line
3. ___ Guiana
8. South America's second-largest country
9. Brazilian city: ___ de Janeiro
10. Venezuela's capital
11. One of Bolivia's capitals: La ____
13. Its capital is Montevideo.
15. Direction Bogotá is from Caracas (abbr.)
16. ___ del Fuego
17. Brazilian city: São ___
20. Rio de la ___
21. Eastern lowland city of Peru
23. South America's greatest river
24. Dutch Guiana is now called ___.
26. Water passage: Strait of ___
27. Great mountain range

Down

1. The "giant" of South America
2. The mouth of the Orinoco River is in this country.
4. The capital of this country is almost on the equator.
5. The southern tip of South America: Cape ___
6. Lima is its capital.
7. A capital city high in the Andes
11. An inland country
12. Seaport city on the west coast
14. Large lake in the Andes
15. Seaport in Brazil
18. City in Colombia
19. City on the island of Trinidad: Port of ___
22. Bolivia's second capital
25. City in Argentina: Santa ___ (means "faith" in Spanish)

Name: _____   Date: _____

SOUTH AMERICA: REVIEWING THE MAP OF LATIN AMERICA

On this page is an activity that will provide an opportunity for you to test your memory of Latin America geography. Try to complete the entire activity on your own. Then, if necessary, refer to maps to make corrections or fill in the gaps in your memory.

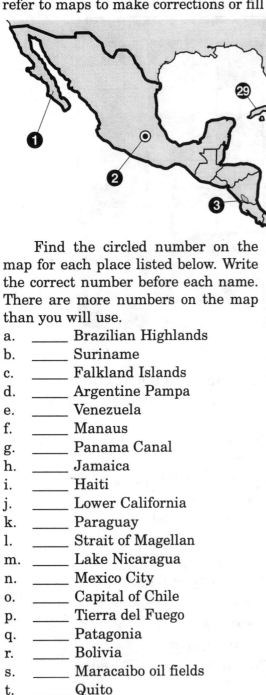
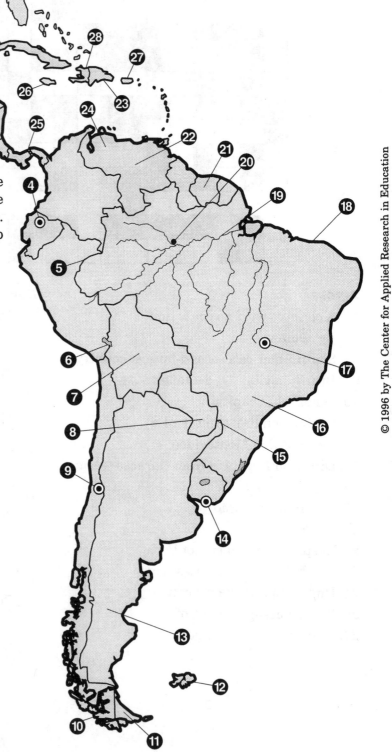

Find the circled number on the map for each place listed below. Write the correct number before each name. There are more numbers on the map than you will use.

a. _____ Brazilian Highlands
b. _____ Suriname
c. _____ Falkland Islands
d. _____ Argentine Pampa
e. _____ Venezuela
f. _____ Manaus
g. _____ Panama Canal
h. _____ Jamaica
i. _____ Haiti
j. _____ Lower California
k. _____ Paraguay
l. _____ Strait of Magellan
m. _____ Lake Nicaragua
n. _____ Mexico City
o. _____ Capital of Chile
p. _____ Tierra del Fuego
q. _____ Patagonia
r. _____ Bolivia
s. _____ Maracaibo oil fields
t. _____ Quito
u. _____ Brasilia
v. _____ Montevideo
w. _____ Lake Titicaca
x. _____ Dominican Republic
y. _____ Puerto Rico
z. _____ Cuba

Activities

ACTIVITIES: GIANT UNITED STATES AND CANADA CROSSWORD PUZZLE

On the facing page is a crossword puzzle about the United States and Canada that will not only challenge you, but also help you review, research, and retain information. Your best help in solving the puzzle will probably come from a map of the United States and Canada.

The list of abbreviations for the various states and Canadian provinces and territories will also be of help.

Across

1. Province on Canada's west coast (abbr.)
4. Capital of South Dakota
6. State bordered on the east by Indiana (abbr.)
7. Chain of mountains: __ Mountains
9. Capital of Washington
11. State bordered on the north by Montana (abbr.)
13. Large bay on the east coast
17. State bordered by Florida on the south (abbr.)
18. State with a small Gulf of Mexico coast (abbr.)
21. Alaskan city on the Bering Sea
22. Province on Canada's east coast
27. State with the Great Salt Lake
31. State on the Gulf of Mexico (abbr.)
33. Canadian province
34. Scenic wonder on the Colorado River
35. Eastern state rich in coal (abbr.)
36. Great city on Lake Michigan
38. State bordered on the southwest by Georgia (abbr.)
39. North central state
40. State with Denver as its capital (abbr.)
41. State capital on the Delaware River
42. State that borders both Lake Michigan and Lake Superior (abbr.)
44. The largest state
46. The largest city in the Florida Keys
49. River on Mexico/Texas border
52. Great Plains state (abbr.)
53. Canadian city on Lake Ontario

Down

2. Capital of New Hampshire
3. State: Ohio River on its entire northern border (abbr.)
4. State on the west side of the Delaware river (abbr.)

5. Smallest state (abbr.)
6. Cities in this state: Dubuque, Cedar Rapids
8. Territory in Canada's northwest (abbr.)
10. River: empties into Chesapeake Bay
12. State with a short Lake Michigan coast (abbr.)
14. Part of the United States, but not a state (abbr.)
15. State: borders Mexico
16. State with the largest population
18. State along the Mississippi River (abbr.)
19. State with the same name as a great river (abbr.)
20. State in which Cape Cod is located (abbr.)
22. Territory in northern Canada (abbr.)
23. River flowing out of Lake Ontario to the Atlantic Ocean
24. Canadian province: Hudson Bay on its north, Lake Superior on its south (abbr.)
25. State: source of the Mississippi River
26. One of the Great Lakes
28. State in which the Willamette River flows
29. State: made up of a chain of islands
30. The smallest Canadian province (abbr.)
32. Great Plains state (abbr.)
37. Capital of Canada
40. The "Nutmeg State" (abbr.)
42. Cities in this state: Bangor, Portland
43. State: great potato producer
45. Canadian province (abbr.)
47. The "Empire State": New ____
48. A city in Pennsylvania and a Great Lake: same name
50. State north of Texas (abbr.)
51. An eastern bay and state: same name (abbr.)
54. State: largest after Alaska (abbr.)

Name: _____ Date: _____

ACTIVITIES: GIANT UNITED STATES AND CANADA CROSSWORD PUZZLE

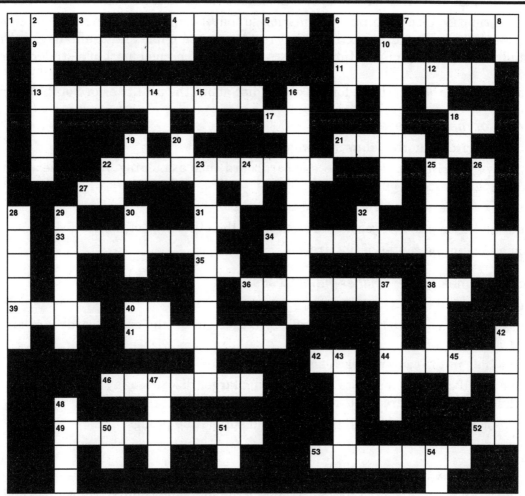

United States Postal Service State Abbreviations

Alabama .... AL	Indiana .... IN	Nebraska .... NE	South Carolina .... SC
Alaska .... AK	Iowa .... IA	Nevada .... NV	South Dakota ...... SD
Arizona .... AZ	Kansas .... KS	New Hampshire . NH	Tennessee .... TN
Arkansas .... AR	Kentucky .... KY	New Jersey .... NJ	Texas .... TX
California .... CA	Louisiana .... LA	New Mexico .... NM	Utah .... UT
Colorado ....CO	Maine .... ME	New York .... NY	Vermont .... VT
Connecticut .... CT	Maryland .... MD	North Carolina ... NC	Virginia .... VA
Delaware .... DE	Massachusetts ... MA	North Dakota ..... ND	Washington .... WA
Florida .... FL	Michigan .... MI	Ohio .... OH	West Virginia ..... WV
Georgia .... GA	Minnesota .... MN	Oklahoma .... OK	Wisconsin .... WI
Hawaii .... HI	Mississippi .... MS	Oregon .... OR	Wyoming .... WY
Idaho .... ID	Missouri .... MO	Pennsylvania ...... PA	
Illinois IL	Montana .... MT	Rhode Island .... RI	Puerto Rico .... PR

Canadian Provinces and Territories

Alberta .... AL	Nova Scotia .... NS	Quebec .... PQ
British Columbia .... BC	Northwest Territories ...... NT	Saskatchewan .... SK
Manitoba .... MB	Ontario .... ON	Yukon Territory .... YT
New Brunswick .... NB	Prince Edward Island .... PEI	

ACTIVITIES: MAKING AN INFORMATION DISC

An information disc organizes information so that it can be easily retrieved when needed. Making the discs is a hands-on activity that results in a tangible and useful device. Through usage and repetition the information the discs contain can become part of a student's memory bank.

Following are the directions for making a disc about the countries of South America.

Directions for making the large disc:

1. Cut out the circles on the following two pages.
2. Glue one of the circles to a stiff piece of cardboard such as oak tag. *Note*: Use a non-puckering glue such as gum cement.
3. Cut the excess cardboard from around the circle.
4. Cut out and then glue the second large circle to the other side of the cardboard.
5. Punch a hole in the center of the circle.

Directions for making the smaller (inner) discs:

1. Cut out the small circles.
2. Glue each small circle to a piece of cardboard; then cut off the excess cardboard around the circles.
3. Punch a hole in the center of each small circle.
4. Lay one small circle on top of its corresponding larger disc; then lay the second circle on the other side. Make sure the three holes line up.
5. Insert a brass fastener through the holes, and spread the prongs.

To use:

1. Turn the inner circle until one of the numerals matches a numeral on the larger circle. The information on the outer circle pertains to the map and country shown on the inner circle.
2. One way to use the device is for the instructor to suggest a numeral found on the disc. After students have made the match, the information may be orally read by one of the students.
3. The same approach and directions may be used for other major topics, for example, the Plains States. However, in this case it can be the students' tasks to find and organize information to be put on the discs. The information for each state could include things such as state motto, state bird, state flower, state tree, and state nickname.

ACTIVITIES: MAKING AN INFORMATION DISC

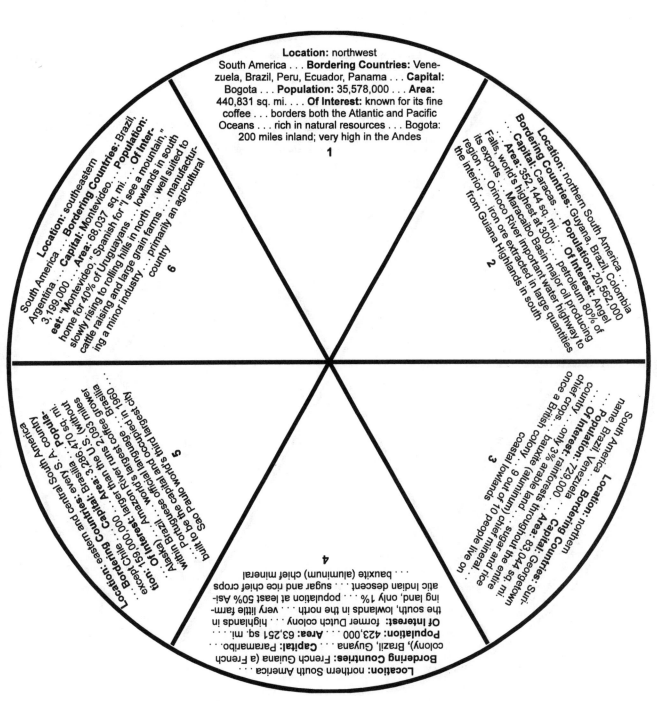

1

Location: northwest South America . . . **Bordering Countries:** Venezuela, Brazil, Peru, Ecuador, Panama . . . **Capital:** Bogota . . . **Population:** 35,578,000 . . . **Area:** 440,831 sq. mi. . . . **Of Interest:** known for its fine coffee . . . borders both the Atlantic and Pacific Oceans . . . rich in natural resources . . . Bogota: 200 miles inland; very high in the Andes

2

Location: northern South America . . . **Bordering Countries:** Guyana, Brazil, Colombia . . . **Capital:** Caracas . . . **Population:** 20,562,000 . . . **Area:** 352,144 sq. mi. . . . **Of Interest:** 80% of petroleum . . . Angel Falls, world's highest at 300 . . . Maracaibo Basin major oil producing region . . . Orinoco River important water highway to its exports . . . iron ore extracted in large quantities from Guiana Highlands in south

3

Location: northern South America . . . **Bordering Countries:** Brazil, Venezuela . . . **Capital:** Georgetown . . . **Population:** 729,000 . . . **Area:** 83,044 sq. mi. . . . **Of Interest:** rainforests through the entire country . . . once a British colony . . . sugar and rice chief crops . . . only 3% arable land . . . bauxite (aluminum) 9 out of 10 people live on coastal lowlands

4

Location: northern South America . . . **Bordering Countries:** French Guiana (a French colony), Brazil, Guyana . . . **Capital:** Paramaribo . . . **Population:** 423,000 . . . **Area:** 63,251 sq. mi. . . . **Of Interest:** former Dutch colony . . . highlands in the south, lowlands in the north . . . very little farming land, only 1% . . . population at least 50% Asiatic Indian descent . . . sugar and rice chief crops . . . bauxite (aluminum) chief mineral

5

Location: eastern and central South America . . . **Bordering Countries:** Brazil borders every S. A. country except Chile and Ecuador . . . **Population:** 159,000,000 . . . **Capital:** Brasilia (without suburbs) . . . **Area:** 3,286,470 sq. mi. . . . **Of Interest:** Amazon River runs through . . . Portuguese official language . . . Sao Paulo the world's third largest city . . . U.S. grower of coffee . . . Brasilia the capital and built to be occupied in 1960

6

Location: southeastern South America . . . **Bordering Countries:** Brazil, Argentina . . . **Capital:** Montevideo . . . **Population:** 3,199,000 . . . **Area:** 68,037 sq. mi. . . . **Of Interest:** est. "Montevideo" Spanish for "I see a mountain," home for 40% of Uruguayans . . . lowlands in south slowly rising to rolling hills in north . . . well suited to cattle raising and large grain farms . . . primarily an agricultural country . . . manufacturing a minor industry

ACTIVITIES: MAKING AN INFORMATION DISC

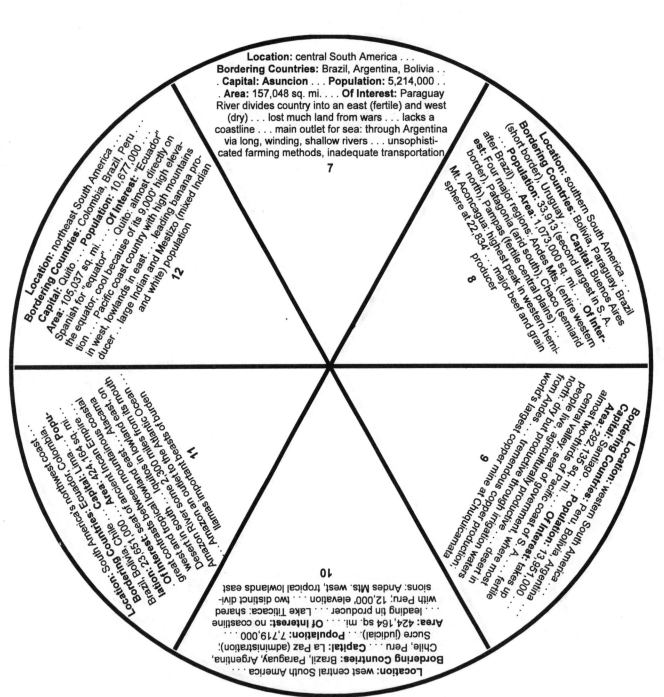

Segment 7

Location: central South America . . . Bordering Countries: Brazil, Argentina, Bolivia . . . Capital: Asuncion . . . Population: 5,214,000 . . . Area: 157,048 sq. mi. . . . Of Interest: Paraguay River divides country into an east (fertile) and west (dry) . . . lost much land from wars . . . lacks a coastline . . . main outlet for sea: through Argentina via long, winding, shallow rivers . . . unsophisticated farming methods, inadequate transportation

7

Segment 8

Location: southern South America . . . Bordering Countries: Bolivia, Paraguay, Brazil (short border), Uruguay . . . Capital: Buenos Aires . . . Population: 33,913,000 (second largest in S.A. after Brazil) . . . Area: 1,073,000 sq. mi. . . . Of Interest: Four major regions: Andes Mts. (entire western border), Pampas (fertile central plains), Chaco (semiarid north), Patagonia (arid south) . . . Mt. Aconcagua: highest peak in western hemisphere at 22,834' . . . major beef and grain producer

8

Segment 9

Location: western South America . . . Bordering Countries: Peru, Bolivia, Argentina . . . Capital: Santiago . . . Population: 13,951,000 . . . Area: 292,135 sq. mi. . . . Of Interest: a fertile central valley, seat of government, where almost two-thirds of people live . . . north: dry desert . . . agriculturally productive through irrigation . . . tremendous copper production . . . world's largest copper mine at Chuquicamata . . . most productive copper mines; from Andes

9

Segment 10

Location: west central South America . . . Bordering Countries: Brazil, Paraguay, Argentina, Chile, Peru . . . Capital: La Paz (administration); Sucre (judicial) . . . Population: 7,719,000 . . . Area: 424,164 sq. mi. . . . Of Interest: no coastline . . . leading tin producer . . . Lake Titicaca: shared with Peru; 12,000' elevation . . . two distinct divisions: Andes Mts. west, tropical lowlands east

10

Segment 11

Location: South America's northwest coast . . . Bordering Countries: Ecuador; Colombia; Brazil; Bolivia; Chile . . . Capital: Lima . . . Population: 23,651,000 . . . Area: 424,164 sq. mi. . . . Of Interest: ancient Incan Empire . . . Atacama Desert . . . late great . . . between mountain east, tropical lowland west and south . . . Iquitos in lowland east, on the Amazon River, some 2,300 miles from its mouth at the Atlantic Ocean . . . Amazon an outlet . . . llamas important beasts of burden

11

Segment 12

Location: northeast South America . . . Bordering Countries: Colombia, Brazil, Peru . . . Capital: Quito . . . Population: 10,677,000 . . . Area: 105,037 sq. mi. . . . Of Interest: "Ecuador" Spanish for "equator" . . . Quito: almost directly on the equator: cool because of its 9,000' high elevation . . . Pacific coast country with high mountains in west, lowlands in east . . . leading banana producer . . . large Indian and Mestizo (mixed Indian and white) population

12

ACTIVITIES: MAKING AN INFORMATION DISC

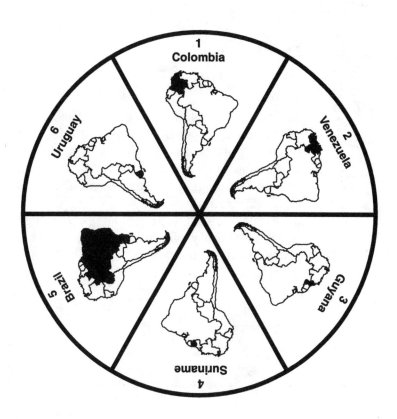

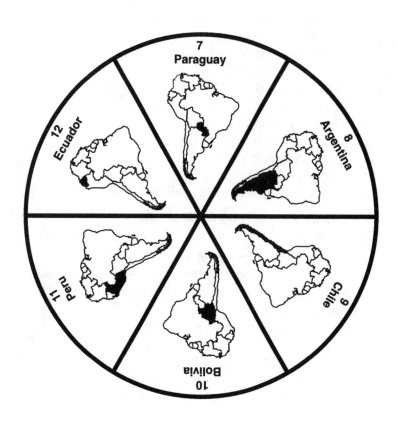

ACTIVITIES: GEOGRAPHY DIORAMAS

Many of the activities and situations told about in *American Continents* may be depicted in dioramas. The materials used in dioramas are inexpensive and easy to obtain. Most materials are readily available in school supply rooms. Making a diorama is a hands-on activity that lends itself well to cooperative learning.

Following are some possible diorama topics that are closely related to the subject matter covered in the *American Continents* and geography textbooks.

- ❑ Gathering Maple Syrup
- ❑ New York State Barge Canal
- ❑ Working in a Shaft Coal Mine
- ❑ The Interior of a Cave
- ❑ Fishing on Chesapeake Bay
- ❑ Key West: Bridges and Roads
- ❑ Fields of Cotton
- ❑ Sod Homes in the Midwest
- ❑ Canal Locks
- ❑ Southwestern Deserts (Death Valley)
- ❑ Tornadoes
- ❑ Cattle Ranching
- ❑ Hydroelectric Dams and Reservoirs
- ❑ Polynesians Approaching Hawaii
- ❑ Volcanic Eruptions in Central America
- ❑ "Primitive" Eskimo villages
- ❑ Eskimos Hunting Whales
- ❑ Crossing the Bering Strait Land Bridge
- ❑ Banana (or Coffee) Plantation
- ❑ Tropical Forests
- ❑ Lake Maracaibo and Oil Deposits
- ❑ On the Amazon River
- ❑ The High Andes
- ❑ Sailing the Straits of Magellan

Suggested Procedures for Making Dioramas

Note: For purposes of illustration, assume we are making a diorama of the lumbering industry in Northwest United States or Canada.

a. Obtain a box (shoebox, small carton).

b. On a piece of paper the same size as the back of the box, draw and color a background: mountains, trees on mountainsides, sun, clouds, indigenous wildlife, etc. (Fig. 1)

238

Figure 1

c. Insert a piece of styrofoam in the bottom of the box. (Styrofoam: obtainable from home supply stores, lumber yards; a package of four pieces each 3/4" × 14" × 48" is relatively inexpensive and good for 16-20 shoebox dioramas)

d. Plant "trees" (spruce twigs are very good) in the styrofoam. Plant the trees in groves with a firelane between the groves. (Fig. 2)

Figure 2

e. Provide for a pile of "cut logs." (wooden dowels from a hardware store, cut to size, or painted plastic straws)

f. Make a "fire tower" from dowels, popsicle sticks, toothpicks.

g. Provide for a small truck or two, preferably flatbeds, but almost any working truck will do. Place some logs on the truck.

h. Make some cardboard workers, glue toothpicks on the backs of the cardboard, and insert in the styrofoam.

i. Add anything else that will make the diorama more authentic, for example, acorns, leaves. (Fig 3)

Figure 3

ACTIVITIES: UNITED STATES GEOGRAPHY TRAVEL GAME

The game on the next five pages will help your students recall geography details and fix them in their memories. All that is needed:

- ❑ the game
- ❑ a spinner or a die
- ❑ question cards
- ❑ a small token for each player (coin, paper clip, eraser)
- ❑ two to four players

How to Get Started

1. Photocopy the game board printed on pages 242 and 243, and trim the pages. Paste the pages to pieces of oak tag. Gum cement is the best for pasting—no "puckering."

2. A set of 56 questions that can be used in playing the game is presented on pages 240 and 241.

3. Photocopy the question pages. Paste the pages to pieces of cardboard, preferably oak tag. Cut the questions out of the cardboard. Print the answers—found in the back of this book—on the backs of the answer cards.

4. Read the rules of the game to your students, and let them start playing.

Suggestions

1. Additional question sets can be developed by students. This could be a beneficial experience for them because they have to do research to find facts suitable for the game. Also, there would be a meaningful language experience in composing the questions and answers.

a. Students choose or are assigned topics: e.g., Canada, Middle America, South America.

b. Students research for facts in references such as textbooks, encyclopedias, world almanacs, and atlases.

c. Students formulate questions and answers and neatly print them on cards. Index cards, whole or cut into halves, are well suited for this purpose.

2. It is helpful to laminate the game boards. Lamination helps keep the game from becoming soiled or "dog-eared." It is not necessary to paste the game on oak tag when laminating. Simply place the two game pages between laminating sheets and pass them through the laminating machine.

3. Several copies can be made from one master copy. Making multiple game boards allows the class to be divided into groups.

4. Making or playing the game also lends itself to a productive and enjoyable learning center activity.

Rules of the Game

1. A player takes the top card and gives it to the person on his/her right.

2. The person on the right reads the question to the player. Player's answer is checked against the answer on the reverse of the card. Person reads the answer regardless of whether or not player's answer was correct.

3. If the player's answer was incorrect, it becomes the turn of the person on his/her right.

4. If the player's answer is correct; the player throws the die (or spins the spinner). The player advances the number of spaces indicated.

5. If the player lands on a special place, he/she must follow the directions printed in the space.

6. If the player lands on a FREE TURN space, he/she takes another card from the top of the pack and follows the procedure outlined in steps 2-5 above.

7. The player who reaches FINISH first is the winner of the game. However, the other players continue until all have reached FINISH.

ACTIVITIES: UNITED STATES GEOGRAPHY TRAVEL GAME

For which one of the following is Washington state noted? a. Lumber b. Copper c. Iron d. Coal	In which state would you be if you lived by the Willamette River? a. Washington b. Oregon c. Idaho d. Wyoming	On which island is Honolulu, Hawaii's capital, located? a. Maui b. Oahu c. Molokai d. Lanai	In what state would you find the Great Salt Lake? a. Utah b. Nevada c. Colorado d. Wyoming
Which of these states does not have the Rio Grande as a border or flowing within it? a. Utah b. Colorado c. Texas d. New Mexico	What state is shown by the map outline?	What direction is Hawaii from San Francisco? a. East b. West c. Southwest d. Southeast	What is Pennsylvania's nickname? a. Mountain State b. Keystone State c. Garden State d. Empire State
Which state produces the greatest amount of cotton? a. Mississippi b. North Carolina c. California d. Texas	In which direction does the Hudson River flow? a. North b. South c. East d. West	What is the name of the state shown on the map?	Which of the following hang from the ceiling of caves? a. Stalagmites b. Stalactites
Which state does not border any of the Great Lakes? a. Michigan b. Ohio c. Indiana d. Iowa	In which of these national parks would you see the Old Faithful geyser? a. Grand Teton b. Yellowstone c. Grand Canyon d. Hot Springs	What state is the only state that borders Maine? a. New York b. Vermont c. Massachusetts d. New Hampshire	Which state is the leader in tobacco production? a. Virginia b. Kentucky c. North Carolina d. Georgia
In which one of these states would sod houses have been common between 1850-1900? a. Nebraska b. Utah c. Louisiana d. Mississippi	Which one of these states grows the most wheat? a. Kansas b. North Dakota c. Montana d. Washington	Which state has the smallest population? a. Vermont b. Delaware c. New Hampshire d. Rhode Island	What river forms the entire northern border of Kentucky? a. Kentucky River b. Ohio River c. Potomac River d. Tennessee River
The Columbia River enters Washington from which direction: a. Northeast b. Southeast c. Northwest d. Southwest	Which two of these four states produce more oil? a. Alaska b. Oklahoma c. Texas d. New Mexico	Which state is the largest of the Northeastern states? a. Maine b. New York c. Pennsylvania d. Maryland	Which one of the following is the only *east-*flowing river? a. Tennessee River b. Savannah River c. Alabama River d. Cumberland River
In which state is the United States' greatest copper mine? a. Colorado b. Montana c. Arkansas d. North Dakota	Which state borders Oklahoma on the north? a. Texas b. Nebraska c. Colorado d. Kansas	Complete this sentence: The Carlsbad Caverns are in the state of __?__. a. Virginia b. Pennsylvania c. New Mexico d. Arizona	In which state is the great Okefenokee Swamp located? a. Florida b. Georgia c. Alabama d. Mississippi

ACTIVITIES: UNITED STATES GEOGRAPHY TRAVEL GAME

Which of these states is the smallest? a. Rhode Island b. Delaware c. Hawaii d. Connecticut	What bay is shown in the map?	Which state was not part of the Louisiana Purchase? a. Kansas b. Wisconsin c. Iowa d. South Dakota	What is the name of the passage of water between Alaska and Asia? a. Straits of Mackinac b. Bering Strait c. Davis Strait d. Hudson Strait
In which section of the country is Key West located? a. Southeast b. Southwest c. Northeast d. Northwest	Which state has the greatest population? a. New York b. Texas c. California d. Florida	Only one of the Great Lakes is wholly within the United States. Which lake is it? a. Superior b. Michigan c. Erie d. Ontario	The Great Lakes are all at the same elevation above sea level. True or False?
Which one of the following states does not border on the Atlantic Ocean? a. New Jersey b. Vermont c. Delaware	Which state does not have part of the Appalachian Mountains within it? a. New Jersey b. Pennsylvania c. Ohio d. Georgia	Which of these cities is not a capital? a. Atlanta b. Cheyenne c. Dallas d. Little Rock	The Brooks Range of mountains is in which state? a. Idaho b. Wyoming c. Alaska d. Washington
Into what body of water does the Mississippi River empty? a. Caribbean Sea b. Atlantic Ocean c. Gulf of Mexico d. Gulf of California	What two states are separated by the Connecticut River?	Which one of the longitudes listed does not touch the United States? a. 60°W b. 75°W c. 90°W	Which one of the following states was once an independent country? a. New Mexico b. Arizona c. Texas d. Nevada
Which degree of latitude is part of the United States' northern boundary with Canada? a. 30°N b. 37°N c. 49°N d. 53°N	Which capital city listed is not located on the Missouri river? a. Bismarck, ND b. Pierre, SD c. Des Moines, IA d. Jefferson City, MO	Which state is the third largest state? a. Texas b. California c. New York d. Alaska	Which state is known as the "Cornhusker State"? a. Nebraska b. Idaho c. South Dakota d. Kansas
Which is the greatest cotton producing state? a. Mississippi b. Texas c. North Carolina d. California	On what river is Hoover Dam located? a. Rio Grande b. Missouri River c. Snake River d. Colorado River	What city is shown on the map?	Which of the two locations has the greatest yearly rainfall? a. Los Angeles, CA b. Portland, OR
What four mainland states border on the Pacific Ocean?	For which agricultural product is Idaho best known? a. Peaches b. Potatoes c. Apples d. Sugar beets	What is the elevation of Mt. McKinley, the USA's highest mountain? a. 13,750' b. 11,900' c. 20,320' d. 14,494'	Which state listed does not border on Mexico? a. California b. Texas c. Arizona d. Nevada

ACTIVITIES: UNITED STATES GEOGRAPHY TRAVEL GAME

ACTIVITIES: UNITED STATES GEOGRAPHY TRAVEL GAME

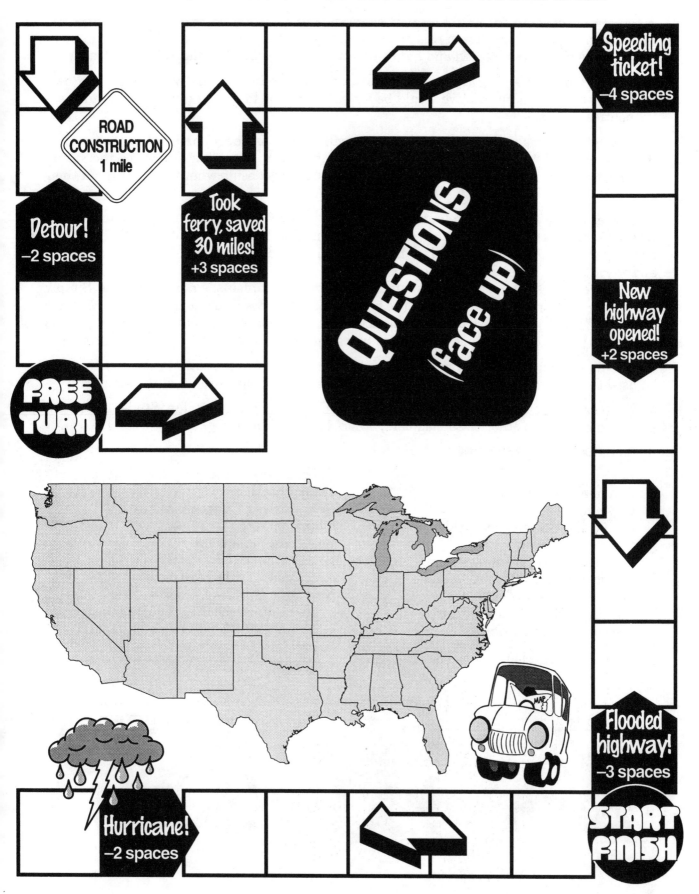

Speeding ticket! –4 spaces

ROAD CONSTRUCTION 1 mile

Detour! –2 spaces

Took ferry, saved 30 miles! +3 spaces

QUESTIONS (face up)

New highway opened! +2 spaces

FREE TURN

Flooded highway! –3 spaces

START FINISH

Hurricane! –2 spaces

ACTIVITIES: DESIGNING POSTAGE STAMPS

Designing a postage stamp that in some way highlights and/or symbolizes a country or state can be a worthy research and hands-on activity. Following is a suggested approach.

1. Choose a particular country or state for which everyone in the class will design their own stamp. Of course, an alternative would be for each student to design a stamp for a particular political entity.

2. Each student makes a decision as to what will appear on the stamp that is chosen. Two or three elements may be selected for and portrayed on a particular stamp, or the stamp may portray only one element. Research will help students decide what to highlight on their stamps.

3. Students should make a preliminary sketch of their proposed stamps. The sketch should include details usually found on a stamp, including the value of the stamp. If the stamp shows, for example, a country's flag, the portrayal should be accurate. Most encyclopedias and world almanacs have sections on flags.

    "Correos de ___" appears on most stamps concerning Spanish-speaking countries. Simply substitute the name of the country in the blank. Thus, *Correos de Chile* translates to *Postage of Chile, Correo Aero* translates to *Air Mail.* **Note**: The example of South American stamps shown at the bottom of the page will prove helpful, especially if shown via a transparency.

4. The final version of the stamp may be drawn on a 5" × 8" index card. Pinking shears can be used to perforate the edges. Of course, color enhances the appearance of the stamps.

5. The complete stamps can make an impressive bulletin board display. Students can explain their stamp to other class members, other classes, or invited guests.

6. Some sample topics for stamps:

Florida: orange trees	Cuba, or any country or state: flag
Panama: Panama Canal	Texas: the Alamo
Guyana: rain forests	New Mexico or Arizona: cactus
California: Golden Gate Bridge	Maine: pine tree
Vermont: maple trees	Barbados: palm trees
Kansas: waving grain	Brazil: a hand of bananas
Massachusetts: Pilgrims' landing	Argentina: gauchos (cowboys)
Mexico: Pyramid of the Sun	New York: Statue of Liberty
Colombia: Bolivar as liberator	United States: constitution, Washington
Nebraska: covered wagon	Monument, Great Seal, a national
	holiday

© 1996 by The Center for Applied Research in Education

ACTIVITIES: GIANT LATIN AMERICA WORD SEARCH

This word search contains the names of 27 countries and 14 capitals, all named in the list that follows.

Here is an effective procedure for solving the puzzle: Take a name from the list, find and circle it in the word search, then cross the name off the list.

Another way to solve the puzzle is to start at the top horizontal line, scan the line for familiar names and circle them, then do the same with the vertical lines. As you find a name cross it off the list.

Notes: a. There are 41 names in the word search
b. If a place has more than one word in its name, a blank space is left between the words.

Countries in the Word Search

Bahamas	Suriname	Barbados	Argentina	
Chile	Brazil	Uruguay	Guatemala	
Cuba	Ecuador	Jamaica	Costa Rica	
Belize	Mexico	Peru	Guyana	
El Salvador	Bolivia	Haiti	Colombia	
Honduras	Dominican	Panama	Paraguay	
Nicaragua	Republic	Trinidad-		
	Venezuela	Tobago		

Capitals in the Word Search

Bogota	Buenos Aires
Georgetown	Havana
Paramaribo	Rio de Janeiro
Lima	Asuncion
Montevideo	Santiago
Quito	San Jose
Caracas	Managua

R	E	U	J	L	P	I	H	O	C	D	L	A	I	S	A	N	T	I	A	G	O	N	O	T
T	S	B	A	H	A	M	A	S	M	B	V	R	D	S	G	P	B	O	G	O	T	A	A	B
R	A	A	M	A	R	T	V	D	O	S	E	V	T	K	U	E	N	Y	R	A	O	G	T	U
I	N	R	A	I	E	A	A	N	I	N	C	U	B	A	O	E	U	D	M	A	X	I	E
N		B	I	T	M	E	N	S	T	L	E	I	A	E	T	A	C	H	I	L	E	I	Q	N
I	J	A	C	I	A	O	A	T	E	H	Z	N	N	R	E	R	O	J	G	O	U	P	C	O
D	O	D	A	L	R	H	W	I	V	E	U	I	E	E	M	C	S	N	W	E	I	V	O	S
A	S	O	Z	S	I	B	E	L	I	Z	E	Y	O	M	A	G	T	B	E	T	A	P	L	
D	E	S	F	R	B	A	E	I	D	E	L		S	A	L	V	A	D	O	R	O	A	O	A
	A	U	N	M	O	U	P	M	E	I	A	G	T	N	A	D		O	P	G	O	R	M	I
T	S	R	I	O	Q	O	A	A	O	E	W	E	I	A	X	I	R	T	I	O	L	A	B	R
O	B	U	P	A	H	O	N	D	U	R	A	S	C	G	V	N	I	E	E	I	I	G	I	E
B	U	G	E	R	E	A	A	G	N	A	R	E	E	U	K	A	C	E	T	B	G	U	A	S
A	S	U	R	I	N	A	M	E	D	D	G	V	Q	A	B	R	A	Z	I	L	U	A	C	S
G	M	A	U	A	I	L	A	R	L	N	E	C	U	A	D	O	R	H	U	L	Y	Y	A	R
O	S	Y	R	A	S	U	N	C	I	O	N	N	I	C	A	R	A	G	U	A	A	S	R	E
G	E	O	R	G	E	T	O	W	N	E	T	R	T	D	A	J	A	O	P	A	N	I	A	O
N	T	Y	U	E	M	U	Z	M	E	X	I	C	O	O	B	O	L	I	V	I	A	D	C	A
R	S	R	I	O		D	E		J	A	N	E	I	R	O	T	H	F	N	T	W	Y	A	E
E	Y	I	W	D	O	M	I	N	I	C	A	N		R	E	P	U	B	L	I	C	Q	S	J

ACTIVITIES: MAKING A MURAL—TRANSPORTATION IN THE UNITED STATES

Mural-making provides opportunities for students to work cooperatively on a common endeavor that results in a tangible product, and it leads to significant subject matter and skill development outcomes. Moreover, students derive a feeling of satisfaction when they see the murals on display. If other classes are invited to see the murals and to listen to explanations of them, a worthy element of whole language (oral presentation) is included.

Following is a lesson plan that demonstrates only one way to develop a class mural. The topic is transportation, a universal geographic concern. The lesson, including the instructor's presentation and the completion of the mural, will take about two periods of 45 minutes each.

The methodology utilized in the lesson can be adapted to almost any topic, for example, quarrying, farming, logging, living in desert lands, and maple sugaring.

The subject matter, skills, and values of the lesson are listed below:

☞ To develop the understanding that adequate transportation has been, and continues to be, a universal need that is either helped or hindered by geography. (Details supporting this conclusion are in the lesson's development section.)

☞ To develop the ability to work with others for a common purpose. Subskills are sharing, compromising, contributing, listening, and behaving appropriately in such matters as talking quietly, taking turns, moving about, and conserving materials.

☞ To develop skill in classifying information.

An appropriate introduction to the lesson would include **Review**, **Motivation**, and **Purpose(s)** of the lesson.

The **Development** section of the lesson follows.

1. Point out that over the years mankind has had to develop ways and means of transporting people and goods. Geographical features have sometimes helped and sometimes hindered transportation. Sometimes a geographical feature can be both a help and a hindrance, depending on the needs of people.

    a. Ask: What physical features have probably been most helpful? **Note**: Students should be given time to jot down some suggestions. Two students may work together if they desire.

    b. List suggestions on the board: (Supplement and explain terms when necessary.)

▪ Rivers*	▪ Straits	▪ Harbors	▪ Oceans
▪ Lakes*	▪ Channels	▪ Flat land (as on a plain)	▪ Fiords

    c. Ask: What physical features have probably been obstacles? **Note**: Students should jot down ideas before orally responding to the question.

    d. List suggestions on the board:

▪ Hills	▪ Swamps	▪ Waterfalls	▪ Rapids
▪ Mountains	▪ Cliffs	▪ Canyons	▪ Deserts

2. Explain that humans have developed various transportation devices to help them better use the helpful geographical features and overcome the nonhelpful features (e.g., rafts and boats to be used on rivers, bridges to cross rivers).

3. Suggest that the class make a transportation mural that will show some of the things that man has invented to help transport people and goods.

---

*   Rivers and lakes may also be considered obstacles.

© 1996 by The Center for Applied Research in Education

ACTIVITIES: MAKING A MURAL—TRANSPORTATION IN THE UNITED STATES

4. Solicit suggestions for a list of transportation devices and aids from the class. Arrange transportation devices under the following headings.

AIR

Mechanical
- ❑ Airplanes
  - ▪ Military
  - ▪ Passenger
  - ▪ Cargo

Nonmechanical
- ❑ Balloons
- ❑ Gliders
- ❑ Parachutes

LAND

Mechanical
- ❑ Trucks
  - ▪ Tractor-Trailers
  - ▪ Vans
  - ▪ Pickups
- ❑ Automobiles
- ❑ Motorcycles
- ❑ Buses
- ❑ Bicycles
- ❑ Trains

Nonmechanical
- ❑ Horse and Wagon
- ❑ Snow skis
- ❑ Sleds
- ❑ Skates

WATER

Mechanical
- ❑ Ocean Ships
- ❑ Motorboats (pleasure)
- ❑ Submarines
- ❑ Trawlers

Nonmechanical
- ❑ Canoes
- ❑ Sailboats
- ❑ Rafts
- ❑ Inflatables

Note: Help students understand the classifications and subclassifications

5. Show partially completed mural. Tell the learners that they are to imagine that they are in an airplane looking at the land from an angle. Help them to see that the scene is a kind of cross-section. (See Page 248 for the stages of the mural and a version of what the mural could look like when completed.)

6. Explain what needs to be done to complete the mural.
   - ❑ Complete bridge with stone- or brickwork
   - ❑ Complete sky (Ask for suggestions as to what should be placed in the sky that is natural: sun, clouds, rainbow, birds, rain, etc.)
   - ❑ Complete water (suggestions: seaweed, fish, etc.)
   - ❑ Complete land (suggestions: houses, grass, trees, fences, flowers, animals, etc.)
   - ❑ Various transportation devices attached at appropriate places

7. Divide the work.
   - ❑ Four volunteers to complete backgrounds
   - ❑ All other students are to make one land, one sea, and one air transportation device
     - ▪ Reasonable size (no more than one-half sheet of paper)
     - ▪ Can be traced or drawn freehand; should be colorful.
     - ▪ As each object is completed, it should be immediately attached to the mural

8. Explain distribution of materials and instructional aids.
   - ❑ All necessary materials and aids on central table (pictures of various transportation devices, paper, scissors, glue, et al.)
   - ❑ "Buffet" style (students take materials as needed)

9. Discuss and set standards of behavior with the children.

10. Children go to work. Teacher supervises, encourages, prods, praises, corrects.

Summary

1. Bring class together. Discuss completed mural and its parts and how they deported themselves in relation to the behavior standards: sharing, talking, working.

2. Remind them of the classifications that took place early in the lesson. In the mural we classified the items, but in a different symbolic way.

ACTIVITIES: MAKING A MURAL—TRANSPORTATION IN THE UNITED STATES

Directions for Making the Mural

1. Three pieces of oak tag, each piece 2' × 3', taped together make a smooth and sturdy 6' × 3' surface on which to draw and/or paste objects. Attach the oak tag to a chalkboard (with taped seams not showing) or thumb-tack it to a bulletin board.

2. A preliminary sketch of the mural should be drawn on a regular piece of paper, and then its basic elements should be transferred to the mural surface. The design should be simple so that students can focus on the aspects of transportation rather than a complex background. The transportation mural described on the previous pages delineates four basic "areas." Figure 1 is an example of a basic sketch.

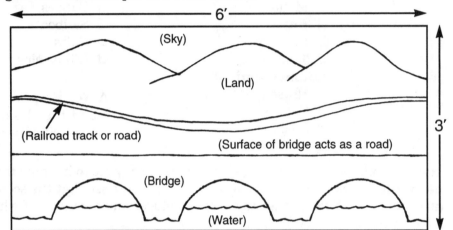

Figure 1

3. Choose a team of four students to work on the nonvehicle aspects of the mural.
   - ❑ Assign one student the **land**: trees, animals, houses, etc.
   - ❑ Assign one student the **bridge**. The main task in this case is to complete the bridge by drawing either stone or brick blocks of either regular or irregular shapes.
   - ❑ Assign one student the **water**: fish, seaweed, sunken boat, et al.

4. Students at their seats draw transportation devices, color them, cut them out, and then attach them to the mural. Students who complete three devices (air, land, water) can make any other device to place on the mural.

5. Figure 2 is an example of how the mural might appear when completed.

Figure 2

ACTIVITIES: GEO BINGO

Learnings that are not rehearsed/repeated will become dim, if not be entirely lost, in learners' minds. Among those things most easily forgotten are facts; and, facts are important. Facts are the building blocks of thinking. Without facts for support, conclusions cannot be validated. As Sir Joshua Reynolds once wrote:

Thinking Point

Invention, strictly speaking,
is little more
than a new combination
of those images
which have been previously gathered
and deposited in the memory.
Nothing can be made of nothing;
they who have laid up no materials
can produce no combinations.

So, there is a place in today's classrooms for drill and rehearsal. Repetition does not necessarily equate with "boredom" If this isn't so, why do we repeat the same songs over and over again? Why do young children want their favorite stories told time after time without any changes—not a single word!

Games such as the "United States Geography Travel Game" (pp. 239-243) can provide interesting and challenging ways of conducting "drill." Thus, the "Geo Bingo" game described below can do much to increase the amount of information relative to the American continents retained in the learners' minds.

Following are suggested sequences for playing "Geo Bingo."

1. Photocopy the gameboard (next page) and distribute.

2. Direct student attention to the word list below the grid. In the squares of the grid they are to carefully write words from the list. Encourage them to choose words randomly so that no two grids will be exactly alike. *Note*: In a class of 20, the possibility of any two grids being exactly alike, using a list of fifty words, is about 1,000,000 to 1.

3. As you read an item from your list (pp. 251-252) players are to determine the correct answer. If the answer they think is correct is on their grid, they cover it with a token. *Caution*: Proceed slowly so as to provide enough time for reaction.

4. When all the squares in any row—horizontal, vertical, or diagonal—are covered on a student's card, he/she should raise a hand and call out "Geo Bingo!"

5. Check to determine if the card has been completed correctly.

Notes:

1. It would increase the effectiveness and progress of the game if all the descriptions and answers were reviewed before the start of the game.

2. The game may be played by omitting the definitions. As the words are called, the players cover the appropriate squares with tokens.

Sample Card

Maple Syrup	Bering Strait	Alaska	Land of Fire
Key West	San Martin	Chile	Coffee
Pittsburgh	El Salvador	Citrus Fruit	Lake Superior
Belize	Llamas	Yucatan	Haiti

Name: _____ Date: _____

GEO BINGO: GAME 2

GEO BINGO: GAME 1

W 1. New Jersey
O 2. Paraguay
R 3. Bananas
D 4. Maine
L 5. Coffee
I 6. Brazil
S 7. Oil
T 8. Yucatan
9. Potomac River
10. Virginia

11. Bering Strait
12. Chicago
13. Wheat
14. Sierra Occidental
15. Pittsburgh
16. Bolivia
17. Missouri River
18. Tallahassee
19. Pampa
20. Potatoes

21. Str. of Magellan
22. Gulf of Mexico
23. Maple Syrup
24. Panama Canal
25. Hudson River
26. Bolivar
27. Columbia River
28. Tierra del Fuego
29. San Martin
30. French Guiana

31. Patagonia
32. Mexico
33. California
34. Stalactite
35. Citrus Fruit
36. Key West
37. Andes Mountains
38. Atacama Desert
39. Chile
40. Amazon River

41. Hudson Bay
42. British Columbia
43. Gran Chaco
44. Caribbean Sea
45. Cuba
46. Jamaica
47. Hawaii
48. Chesapeake Bay
49. Alaska
50. Puerto Rico

51. Lake Superior
52. Bahamas
53. West Indies
54. Llamas
55. Ecuador
56. Pennsylvania
57. Cotton
58. Louisiana
59. Cape Cod
60. Guatemala

ACTIVITIES: GEO BINGO

Note: The items that follow are numbered for easy referral; however, they may be utilized in any order.

1. A state bounded by the Delaware River on the west, New York on the north, and the Atlantic Ocean on the east (New Jersey)

2. A South American country without a coastline and with Argentina as its southern neighbor (Paraguay)

3. A fruit that Brazil grows in great quantities—more than any other South American country (Bananas)

4. The northernmost of the Northeastern States (Maine)

5. An agricultural product of Colombia that is well-known for its quality (Coffee)

6. South America's largest country (Brazil)

7. A product of Venezuela's Lake Maracaibo (Oil)

8. A large peninsula on Mexico's eastern coast (Yucatan)

9. The river on which Washington, D.C., is located and that empties into Chesapeake Bay (Potomac River)

10. A state that is part of the Delmarva peninsula and has Richmond as it capital (Virginia)

11. A narrow water passage that separates North America and Asia (Bering Strait)

12. A city in the state of Illinois that is on the south shore of Lake Michigan (Chicago)

13. A grain that grows in great quantities in Kansas—more than any other state (Wheat)

14. A mountain range in western Mexico (Sierra Occidental)

15. A city at the junction of the Allegheny River and the Monongahela River in Pennsylvania (Pittsburgh)

16. A South American country with no coast, high mountains in the west, and tropical lowlands in the east (Bolivia)

17. The second largest river in the United States; flows from the Rocky Mountains southeast into the Mississippi river (Missouri River)

18. A state capital with two l's two s's, two e's, and three a's in its name (Tallahassee)

19. A major region of Argentina where one can find cattle, gauchos, wheat, and corn (Pampa)

20. An agricultural product that is especially plentiful in Idaho and Maine (Potatoes)

21. A water passage at the southern end of South America (Strait of Magellan)

22. A gulf named after Mexico, but the United States shares it too (Gulf of Mexico)

23. Sweet stuff from Vermont (Maple Syrup)

24. A human-made water passage that connects the Atlantic Ocean and the Pacific Ocean (Panama Canal)

25. A river that flows past Albany and New York City (Hudson River)

26. The liberator of northern South America (Bolivar)

27. A river that separates the states of Washington and Oregon (Columbia River)

28. Spanish for "Land of Fire"; a group of islands off the southern tip of South America (Tierra del Fuego)

29. The liberator of Argentina and Chile (San Martin)

ACTIVITIES: GEO BINGO

30. The only part of South America that is a possession of a European country (French Guiana)

31. A large region of southern Argentina—well-suited for raising sheep (Patagonia)

32. A country that includes Baja (Lower) California, the Yucatan Peninsula, the city of Monterey, and the Sierra Oriental (Mexico)

33. The state containing Death Valley, the Central Valley, and the largest population (California)

34. A formation that hangs from the roof of caves (Stalactite)

35. A kind of fruit that comes in the form of oranges, grapefruit, and lemons (Citrus Fruit)

36. A city in a chain of islands off the coast of Florida (Key West)

37. The mountain range that includes Aconcagua, the highest mountain in the American continents (Andes Mountains)

38. A desert in northern Chile and southern Peru (Atacama Desert)

39. A country in South America well over 1,000 miles from north to south, but no more than 250 miles from east to west (Chile)

40. The greatest river in South America; flows for almost its entire length through Brazil (Amazon River)

41. A large bay in northern Canada (Hudson Bay)

42. Canada's westernmost province (British Columbia)

43. A large region, quite dry, in northern Argentina and southern Paraguay (Gran Chaco)

44. A sea that is bounded on the east and north by many islands, on the west by Central America, and on the south by South America (Caribbean Sea)

45. The largest country and island in the West Indies (Cuba)

46. An island country south of Cuba (Jamaica)

47. A state far out in the Pacific that is made up of numerous islands (Hawaii)

48. A bay that divides Maryland into two parts (Chesapeake Bay)

49. The most northern and largest of all the states (Alaska)

50. A large island east of the Dominican Republic; a part of the United States (Puerto Rico)

51. The largest of the Great Lakes (Lake Superior)

52. A country that is made up of a group of islands and is north of Cuba and southeast of Florida (Bahamas)

53. A group of islands that is made up of numerous small countries and divided into two parts: the Greater Antilles and the Lesser Antilles (West Indies)

54. Animals of the high Andes that are used as beasts of burden (Llamas)

55. A South American pie-shaped country that is crossed by the equator (Ecuador)

56. The state in which the Ohio River begins, whose largest city is Philadelphia, and that borders Lake Erie (Pennsylvania)

57. A plant grown throughout the south, but Texas grows more of it than any other state (Cotton)

58. The state on the Gulf of Mexico where the Mississippi River ends its journey (Louisiana)

59. A Massachusetts peninsula, the first landing place of the Pilgrims (Cape Cod)

60. A Latin American country surrounded by these countries: Belize, El Salvador, Honduras, Mexico (Guatemala)

© 1996 by The Center for Applied Research in Education

Outline Maps

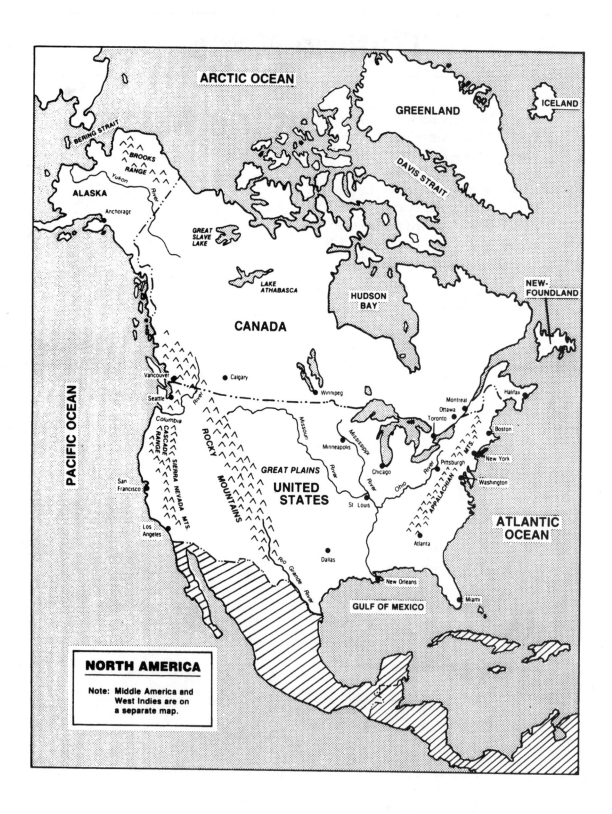

NORTH AMERICA

Note: Middle America and West Indies are on a separate map.

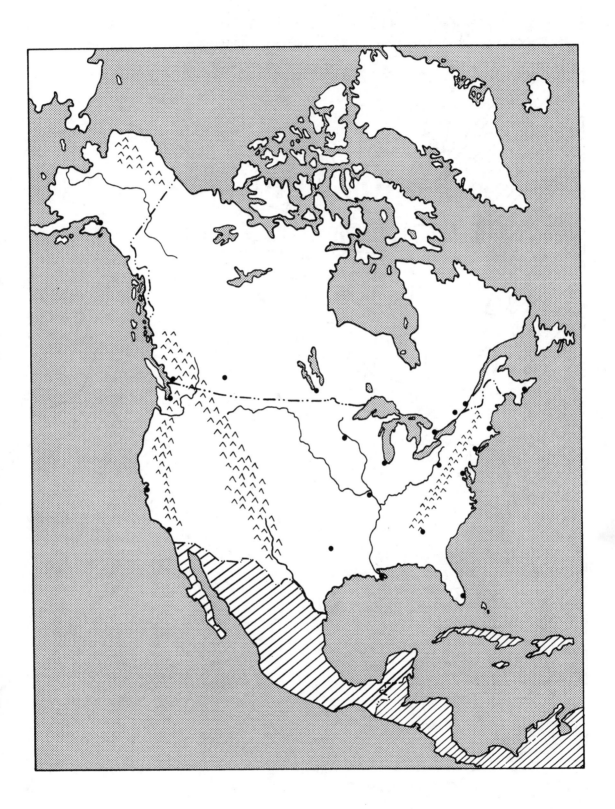

THE UNITED STATES

CANADA

PACIFIC OCEAN

ATLANTIC OCEAN

GULF OF MEXICO

WA Olympia
Columbia River

OR Salem

ID Boise

MT Helena

NV Carson City

CA Sacramento

UT Salt Lake City

WY Cheyenne

CO Denver
Colorado River

AZ Phoenix

NM Santa Fe

ND Bismarck
Missouri River

SD Pierre

NE Lincoln

KS Topeka

OK Oklahoma City

TX Austin
Rio Grande River

MN St. Paul

IA Des Moines
Mississippi River

MO Jefferson City
Missouri River

AR Little Rock

LA Baton Rouge

WI Madison
L. SUPERIOR
L. MICHIGAN

MI Lansing
L. HURON

IL Springfield

IN Indianapolis

OH Columbus
Ohio River

KY Frankfort

TN Nashville

MS Jackson
Mississippi River

AL Montgomery

GA Atlanta

FL Tallahassee

ME Augusta

NH Concord

VT Montpelier
L. ONTARIO

NY Albany
L. ERIE

PA Harrisburg

WV Charleston

VA Richmond

NC Raleigh

SC Columbia

MA Boston

RI Providence

CT Hartford

NJ Trenton

DE Dover

MD Annapolis

ALASKA Juneau

HAWAII Honolulu

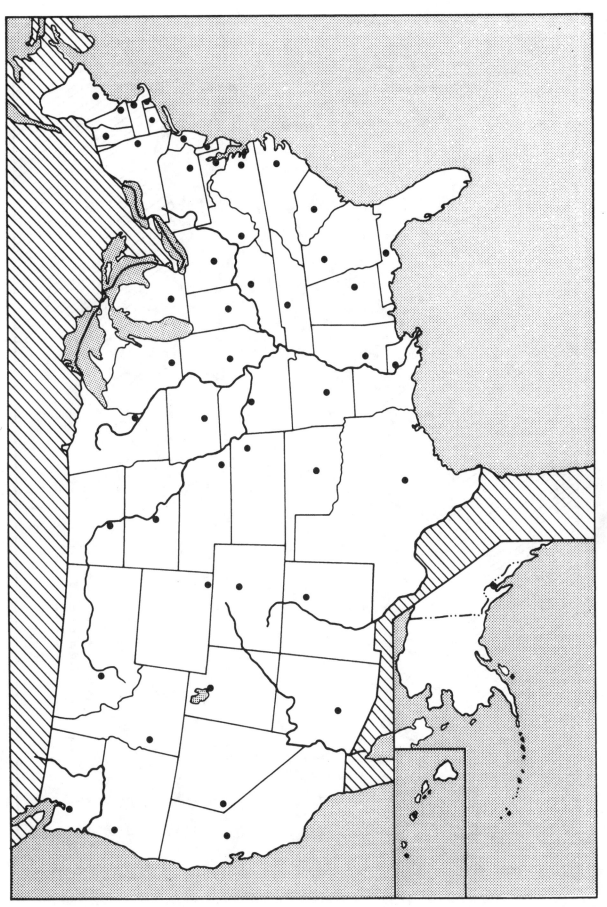

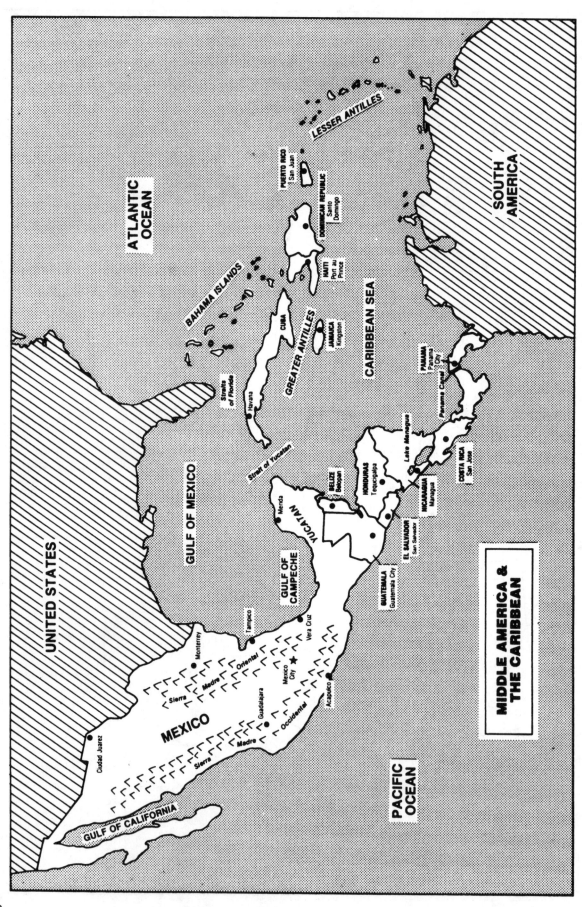

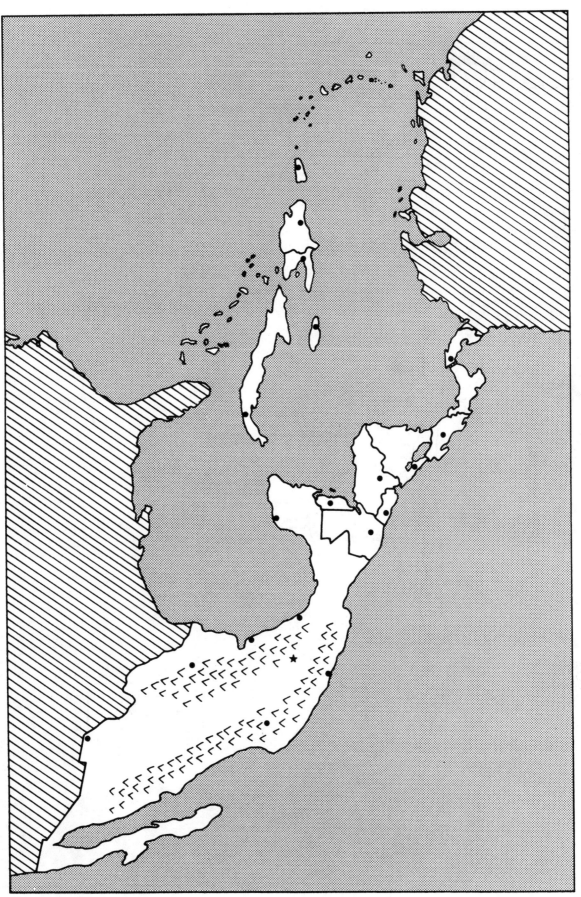

ANSWER KEY

Page 3 **Using Latitude to Locate Places in the Western Hemisphere**

1. - Point Barrow: 71°N   - San Francisco: 38°N   - Quito: 0°
   - Churchill: 59°N   - New Orleans: 30°N   - Brasilia: 16°S
   - Ottawa: 45°N   - Mexico City: 19°N   - Buenos Aires: 36°S
   - Portland: 46°N   - Bogota: 4°N   - Punta Arenas: 53°S
   - Washington, D.C.: 39°N

2. - New Orleans and Quito: 30°
   - Portland and Buenos Aires: 82°
   - Point Barrow and Punta Arenas: 124°

3. a. New Orleans
   b. Buenos Aires
   c. Point Barrow

Page 5 **Using Longitude to Locate Places in the Western Hemisphere**

1. - Nome: 165°N   - Salt Lake City: 112°W   - Belem: 48°W
   - Dawson: 136°W   - Philadelphia: 75°W   - Lima: 77°W
   - Reykjavik: 21°W   - Miami: 80°W   - Rio de Janeiro: 43°W
   - Regina: 104°W   - Guadalajara: 103°W   - Santiago: 71°W

2. - Port Radium; St. Johns

3. - Belem and Lima: 29°; Miami and Nome: 85°

Page 6 **Determining Direction with Latitude and Longitude**

1. a. A   b. C   c. C   d. I
2. a. O   b. H   c. D   d. M
3. a. N   b. E
4. P
5. A, C, G, J, I, L
6. A, B, C, D, E, F, G, H, J, K

Page 7 **Locating Places with Latitude and Longitude**

1. A. 60°N-60°W   D. 30°N-150°E   G. 30°S-45°E
   B. 50°N-45°W   E. 5°S-135°W   H. 40°S-150°E
   C. 40°N-45°E   F. 30°S-75°W

2.

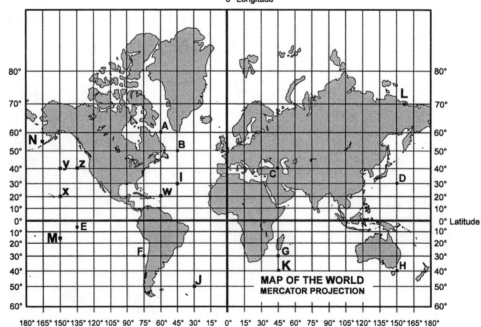

3. a. No   b. Yes

Challenge: z: 40°N-135°W

Page 9   **Using Latitude and Longitude to Compute Distances**

1. a. 2,625 mi.
   b. 1,590 mi.
   c. 1,590 mi.
   d. 4,200 mi.
   e. 6,210 mi.
   f. 6,360 mi.

2. a. 2,800 mi.
   b. 3,500 mi.
   c. 2,100 mi.

   Challenge: 15,325 mi.

Page 12   **Major Physical Features of North America**

Nations: Canada, United States, Mexico
Rivers: Yukon, Columbia, St. Lawrence, Missouri, Mississippi, Ohio, Rio Grande
Straits: Bering, Davis, Florida
Mountain Ranges: Brooks, Cascade, Sierra Nevada, Rocky, Ozark, Sierra Madre Occidental, Sierra Madre Oriental, Appalachian
Islands: Baffin, Greenland, Iceland
Lakes, Great Slave, Athabasca, Winnipeg, Superior, Michigan, Huron, Erie, Ontario
Other Large Bodies of Water: Arctic Ocean, Pacific Ocean, Hudson Bay, Atlantic Ocean, Gulf of Mexico, Gulf of California, Caribbean Sea

Page 15   **The Mississippi Valley**

4. Upstream cities: Wichita, Bismarck, Cincinnati, Fort Worth

5. Tributaries: Yellowstone, Platte, Milk

   Note: The Big Horn River is a tributary to the Yellowstone River

6. Wabash, Cumberland, Tennessee

8. 10 (Minnesota, Wisconsin, Iowa, Illinois, Missouri, Kentucky, Tennessee, Arkansas, Mississippi, Louisiana)

Page 17   **The Panama Canal: Shortcut Through Two Continents**

2. a. 11,061 mi.
   b. 3,873 mi.
   c. 7,188 mi.

3. 8,113 mi.

4. 3,575 mi. (+ or -150 mi.)

Page 19   **The Great Lakes—St. Lawrence Seaway**

1. - Lake Superior: Minnesota, Wisconsin, Michigan
   - Lake Michigan: Wisconsin, Illinois, Indiana, Michigan
   - Lake Huron: Michigan
   - Lake Erie: Michigan, Ohio, Pennsylvania, New York
   - Lake Ontario: New York

2. a. - Lake Superior: 602'
      - Lake Michigan: 581'
      - Lake Huron: 581'
      - Lake Erie: 572'
      - Lake Ontario: 246'

   b. 326'
   c. 246'

   d. - Detroit or Montreal: Detroit
      - Chicago or Duluth: Duluth
      - Montreal or Erie: Erie
      - Hamilton or Detroit: Detroit

Page 20   **Air Distances in the United States**

1. From Chicago to
   - Boston: 875 mi.
   - Washington, D.C.: 600 mi.
   - Miami: 1,200 mi.
   - St. Louis: 270 mi.
   - New Orleans: 860 mi.
   - El Paso: 1,200 mi.
   - Los Angeles: 1,700 mi.
   - San Francisco: 1,750 mi.
   - Salt Lake City: 1,230 mi.
   - Seattle: 1,700 mi.

2. 1½ hours, 4¼ hours, 5¾ hours

Page 21   The United States of America: How It Grew

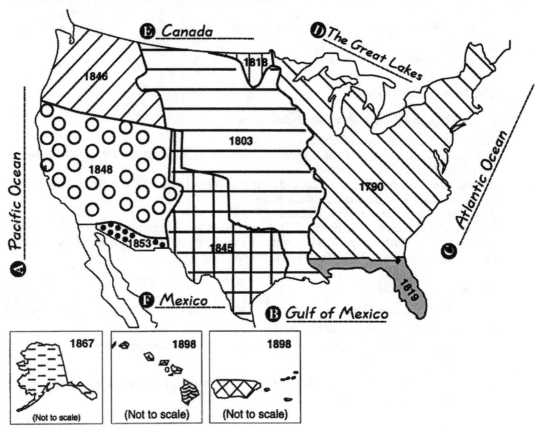

Page 23   United States Place Names Show Our Diversity

A	K	G	L	I	N	C	O	L	N	F
L	P	R	A	T	H	E	N	S	H	K
H	Y	Z	L	I	S	B	O	N	D	L
A	S	U	B	I	T	H	A	C	A	M
M	R	R	L	N	Q	S	P	H	M	T
B	O	I	C	A	I	R	O	E	A	N
R	M	C	U	B	A	W	N	R	S	O
A	E	H	E	G	Y	P	T	O	C	R
P	U	L	A	S	K	I	I	K	U	W
B	E	T	H	A	N	Y	A	E	S	A
L	E	B	A	N	O	N	C	E	R	Y

Page 28 Northeastern States: A Table of Facts

1. New York
2. Rhode Island
3. Vermont and New Hampshire
4. New Hampshire
5. Maine
6. Rhode Island: 50
   Delaware: 49
   Connecticut: 48
7. New York: Empire State
   New Jersey: Garden State
   West Virginia: Mountain State
8. 26
9. Quarrying or Mining

10. 1st: New York
    2nd: Pennsylvania
    3rd: New Jersey
    4th: Massachusetts
    5th: Maryland
    6th: Connecticut
    7th: West Virginia
    8th: Maine
    9th: New Hampshire
    10th: Rhode Island
    11th: Delaware
    12th: Vermont

Challenge: 437 1/3 or 437.33

Page 29 Northeastern States: Capitals and Rivers

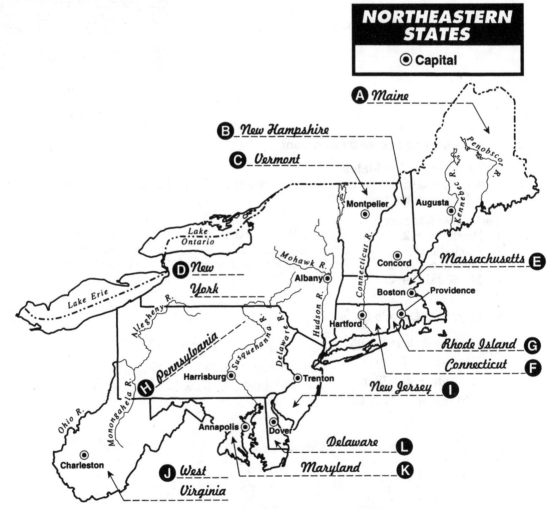

3. a. Monongahela River and Allegheny River
   b. Delaware River
   c. Connecticut River
   d. Hudson River
   e. Susquehanna River
   f. Penobscot River

Page 31   Northeastern States: Acres of Harvested Land

"Square Area" Graphs
1. 54%
2. 46%
3. 8%

"Circle Area" Graphs
4.
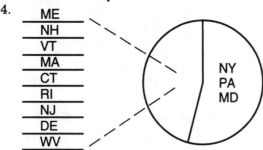

Activity
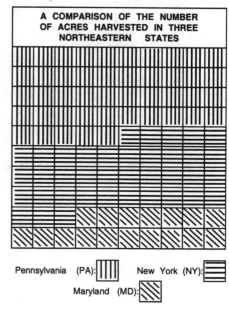

Page 33   Maine: Locating Places by Quadrant

Maine in the United States
1. a. Maine is in the far northeastern part of the United States.
   b. New Hampshire

Maine Map Locations
1. Portland: F-2
2. Augusta: E-3
3. Moosehead: C-2
4. Mt. Katahdin: C-3
5. Allagash Falls: A-3
6. Bangor: D-4
7. Old Orchard Beach: F-2
8. Van Buren: A-5
9. Lewiston: E-2
10. Houlton: B-5
11. Rockland: E-3

Page 35   Vermont: Ski Lover's State

1. - Jay Peak: 2,151', 105
   - Stowe: 2,255', 100
   - Suicide: 650', US-4
   - Killington: 3,175', US-4
   - Sugarbush: 2,600', 100
   - Stratton: 2,003', US-30
   - Middlebury Snow Bowl: 1,020', 125

2. a. 1st: US-7
   2nd: US-4
   3rd: 100
   4th: 105

   Alternate route:
   1st: US-7
   2nd: 105
   3rd: 100
   4th: 105

3. US-7, 17, 100
4. a. 2,525'
   b. 345'
   c. 150'

Page 37 New Hampshire: Locating Places by Quadrant

1.

2c. - Keene: E-2   - Laconia: D-3   - Mt. Washington: C-4
     - Colebrook: B-3   - Conway: C-4   - Portsmouth: E-4
     - Concord: E-3   - Hanover: D-2   - Nashua: F-3
     - Great Stone Face: C-3

Page 39 New York: A Border with Canada and Five Other States

1. Vermont, Massachusetts, Connecticut, New Jersey, Pennsylvania

2. Lake Erie, Lake Ontario

3. St. Lawrence River

4. a. L. Canandaigua
   b. L. Keuka
   c. L. Seneca
   d. L. Cayuga
   e. L. Skaneateles

5. L. Champlain

7. - Albany: Hudson River
   - Schenectady: Mohawk River
   - Buffalo: Lake Erie
   - Utica: Mohawk River

8. 310 mi. (+ or - 15)

9. 355 mi. (+ or - 15)

10. Niagara Falls, Buffalo

Page 41   Massachusetts: Map/Crossword

1. Massachusetts is in the northeastern United States. It has the Atlantic Ocean on its eastern border.
2. Vermont, New Hampshire, Rhode Island, Connecticut, New York

Page 43   Connecticut: Rivers and Cities

1. Middletown, Haddam, Chester, Essex
2. Derby
3. Willimantic, Natchaug; Shetucket
4. New London
5. Two
6. Long Island Sound
7. 90 mi. (+ or - 10)
8. West; 2,380'

9.

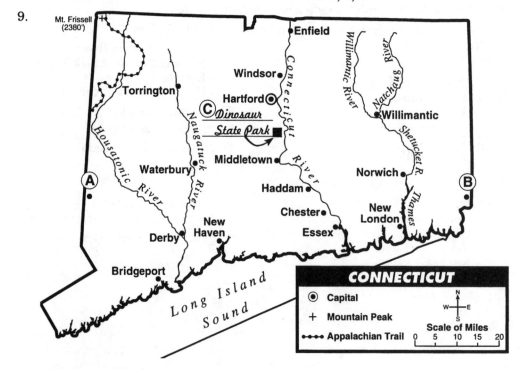

Page 45   Rhode Island: Map-Word Puzzle

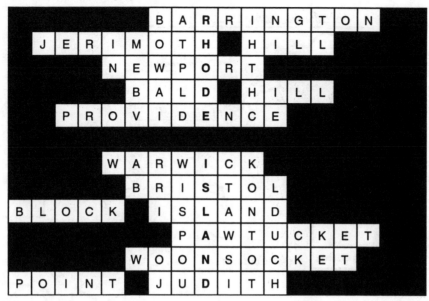

Page 47   Pennsylvania: Computing Distances Between Cities

1. a. 113 mi.
   b. 154 mi.
   c. 75 mi.
   d. 180 mi.
   e. 175 mi.
   f. 120 mi.
   g. 195 mi.
   h. 125 mi.

3. 3,213'

Page 49   New Jersey: Gaining Information from Maps

New Jersey in the United States

1. a. New Jersey is in the northeastern part of the United States. The Atlantic Ocean is on its eastern border.
   b. New York, Delaware, Pennsylvania

New Jersey on the Map

1. New York; Pennsylvania
2. Delaware River; Delaware Bay
3. Atlantic Ocean
4. Hudson River
5. Trenton
6. 150 mi. (+ or - 15), 35 mi. (+ or - 10)
7. Toms River, Mullica River, Great Egg Harbor River
8. Musconetcong River
9. Maurice River
10. Raritan River; Passaic River
11. Southeast
12. Northeast
13. Delaware and New York
14. Delaware Bay, Delaware

Page 51   Delaware: Transportation Crossroad

Delaware in the United States

1. a. Delaware is located in the southern part of the Northeastern States. It has a short coastline along the Atlantic Ocean.
   b. New Jersey, Maryland, Pennsylvania

Cape May-Lewes Ferry

1. b. 15 mi.
   c. US-9

Intracoastal Waterway
Chesapeake and Delaware Canal

United States Highway 13

1. b. 95 mi. (+ or - 5)
   c. 34 mi. (+ or - 5)

Maryland: Points of Interest

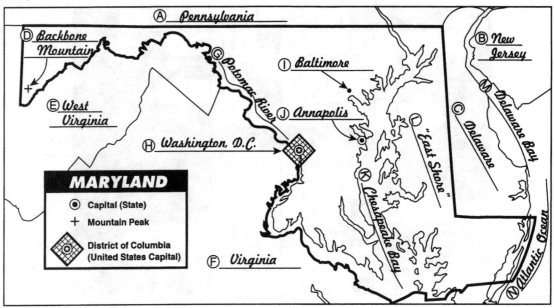

Page 55 West Virginia: Mountain Peaks and Rivers

1. Spruce Knob: 4,861'
   Whitman Knob: 3,900'
   Bickett Knob: 3,330'
   Pine Swamp Knob: 3,104'
   Cottle Knob: 3,048'
   High Knob: 2,814'

2. a. Fishing Creek
   b. Mid Island Creek
   c. Muskingum Creek
   d. Little Kanawha River
   e. Kanawha River
   f. Raccoon Creek
   g. Guyandot River
   h. Scioto River

3. South Branch Potomac River and Shenandoah River

4. Elk River, New River

5. Eastern

Page 59 Southeastern States: A Table of Facts

Populations of the Southern States Compared															
States															
Florida	☺	☺	☺	☺	☺	☺	☺	☺	☺	☺	☺	☺	☺	◡	13½
Mississippi	☺	☺	☺	☺	☺	☺	☺	☺	☺	◡					9½
North Carolina	☺	☺	☺	☺	☺	☺	☺								7
Georgia	☺	☺	☺	☺	☺	☺	☺								7
Virginia	☺	☺	☺	☺	☺	☺	◡								6½
Tennessee	☺	☺	☺	☺	☺										5
Louisiana	☺	☺	☺	☺	◡										4½
Alabama	☺	☺	☺	☺											4
Kentucky	☺	☺	☺	☺											4
South Carolina	☺	☺	☺	◡											3½
Arkansas	☺	☺	◡												2½
Key: ☺ = 1,000,000 people ◡ = 500,000 people															

2., 3.

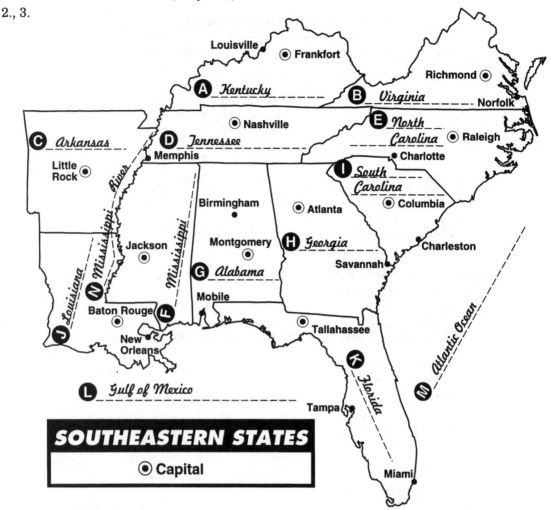

4. - New Orleans: Louisiana
    - Mobile: Alabama
    - Miami: Florida
    - Savannah: Georgia
    - Tampa: Florida
    - Charleston: South Carolina

    - Birmingham: Alabama
    - Charlotte: North Carolina
    - Louisville: Kentucky
    - Memphis: Tennessee
    - Norfolk: Virginia

Page 61   The Southeastern States and the Appalachian Mountains

1. Arkansas, Mississippi, Louisiana, Florida

2. horses, carts, oxen. rake, shovel, hoe, axe. guns, protection, game. rivers, mountains, valleys. trees. cliff.

3. candle mold for making candles

4. 40 days

5. Perhaps the river runs too swiftly and has falls and rapids; perhaps the river is flowing in a direction opposite to where the pioneers want to go.

Page 63   Cotton Production in the Southeastern and Other States

MAJOR COTTON PRODUCING STATES

STATE	AMOUNT	RANK	STATE	AMOUNT	RANK
Alabama	460,000	9	Missouri	345,000	11
Arizona	895,000	6	New Mexico	107,000	14
Arkansas	1,120,000	4	North Carolina	415,000	10
California	3,155,000	2	Oklahoma	265,000	12
Florida	85,000	15	South Carolina	210,000	13
Georgia	720,000	7	Tennessee	550,000	8
Louisiana	1,110,000	5	Texas	5,148,000	1
Mississippi	1,560,000	3			

* Number of bales of cotton produced in a recent year. One bale = 500 lbs.

Page 65   Virginia: A Geography History Tour

Virginia in the United States

1. a. Virginia is the most northern of the Southeastern States. The Atlantic Ocean and Chesapeake Bay border Virginia on the east.
    b. West Virginia, Maryland, North Carolina, Kentucky, Tennessee

Population Growth of Virginia

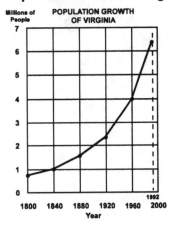

Page 67   Kentucky: Map/Crossword

274

Page 69   **Tennessee: An Aerial Survey**

1.
1. Memphis
2. Arkansas
3. Missouri
4. Tennessee R.
5. Nashville
6. Kentucky
7. Knoxville
8. Virginia
9. Great Smoky Mtns.
10. North Carolina
11. Georgia
12. Chattanooga
13. Alabama
14. I-65
15. Mississippi

2. From the north and clockwise: Missouri, Kentucky, Virginia, North Carolina, Georgia, Alabama, Mississippi, Arkansas

3. *Suggested*: Tennessee is in the southeastern part of the United States. It does not border on the Atlantic Ocean. There are eight states that border on Tennessee.

Page 71   **North Carolina: Airline Distances**

1. 400 mi.

2. 335 mi.

3. 450 mi.

4. 180 mi. (+ or - 10)

5.
- Raleigh to Elizabeth City: 140 mi.
- Elizabeth City to Wilmington: 175 mi.
- Wilmington to Fayetteville: 80 mi.
- Fayetteville to Charlotte: 110 mi.
- Charlotte to Asheville: 100 mi.
- Asheville to Winston-Salem: 135 mi.
- Winston-Salem to Raleigh: 90 mi.

6. 830 miles

Page 73   **South Carolina: Locating Places by Quadrant**

- Columbia: C-3
- McCormick: C-2
- Rock Hill: B-3
- Lancaster: B-4
- Myrtle Beach: C-6
- Wahalla: B-1
- Georgetown: C-5
- Sassafras Mtn.: A-2
- Lake Marion: C-4
- Florence: B-5
- Augusta: C-3
- Spartanburg: B-3
- Greenville: B-2
- Orangeburg: C-4
- Hardeeville: D-3

Page 75   **Georgia: Matching Places and Descriptions**

15 - Southern end of the Appalachian Trail
14 - Georgia's highest point—4,784' high
7 - Forms border with Alabama
11 - City on Georgia's South Carolina border
8 - Coastal city
10 - Seaport, and US-280 ends/begins there
4 - City on US-27
17 - Formed by the Ocmulgee River and the Oconee River
12 - Crossed by I-95 as the highway enters Florida
1 - Capital
6 - River that enters the Atlantic Ocean south of Brunswick
16 - World's largest single piece of granite, 683' high
2 - Forms border with South Carolina
13 - Lake southeast of Springer Mountain
5 - Swamp in southwest Georgia
9 - Large city in central Georgia
3 - State on Georgia's northwest border

Page 77   **Florida: Some of Its Tourist Attractions**

1. Pensacola
2. 345
3. Apalachicola
4. Tallahassee
6. Jacksonville
5. Suwannee
7. St. Augustine
8. 1565
9. Daytona Beach
10. Cape Kennedy
11. Orlando
13. Miami
12. Lake Okeechobee
15. Tampa
14. Everglades
16. Gulf of Mexico
17. Panama

Page 79   **Alabama: Cities, Rivers, and Mountains**

1. a. T
   b. T
   c. F
   d. F
   e. F
   f. T
   g. T
   h. T
   i. F
   j. T
   k. T
   l.. T
   m. T
   n. T

2. Student options

Page 81   **Mississippi: Rivers, Reservoirs, Cities**

1. Biloxi, Clarksdale, Columbus, Greenville, Gulfport, Hattiesburg, Jackson, Meridian, Vicksburg
2. Yazoo River, Big Black River, Homochitto River
3. Pascagoula River, Biloxi River, Wolf River, Pearl River
4.. Pearl River Res., Grenada Res., Enid Res., Sardid Res., Arkabutla Res.
5. The highest point in Mississippi is in the far northeastern part of the state.
6. A star should be drawn next to Jackson in the listing above.

Page 83   **Louisiana: Place Names on a Map and in a Puzzle**

P	E	A	R	L	K	T	R	V	W	G	K	L	Z	N	N
F	O	H	J	B	A	T	O	N	R	O	U	G	E	E	E
A	D	N	M	N	P	O	U	X	Z	Y	K	L	W	W	W
T	R	K	C	S	A	B	I	N	E	A	C	B	A	O	I
C	I	D	E	H	F	H	J	K	W	D	R	T	F	R	B
H	S	A	R	K	A	N	S	A	S	F	O	W	A	L	E
A	K	U	V	C	A	R	L	M	P	Q	R	B	Y	E	R
F	I	A	D	K	N	A	T	C	H	E	Z	Y	E	A	I
A	L	A	K	E	C	H	A	R	L	E	S	P	T	N	A
L	L	B	O	G	A	L	U	S	A	G	F	H	T	S	D
A	K	T	E	X	A	S	M	P	F	I	A	B	E	R	C
Y	C	Y	D	G	H	J	K	R	M	O	N	R	O	E	O
A	C	A	L	C	A	S	I	E	U	M	P	U	Z	D	K

276

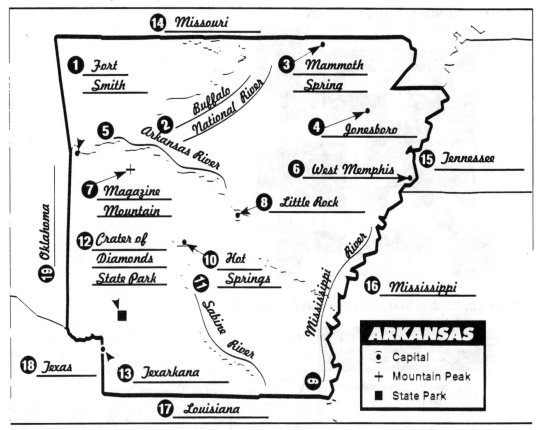

1. Minnesota, Wisconsin, Michigan
2. Wisconsin, Michigan, Indiana, Illinois
3. Michigan
4. Ohio, Michigan
5. Lake Michigan
6. Illinois
7. Iowa, Missouri
8. Minnesota
9. Ohio, Indiana, Illinois
10. Rainy River, Lake of the Woods, Rainy Lake
11. Iowa

First Column
- Kansas City, Missouri River
- Des Moines, Missouri River
- Minneapolis or St. Paul, Mississippi River
- St. Louis, Illinois River
- Toledo, Cleveland

Second Column
- Chicago, Wisconsin
- Duluth, Lake Superior
- Detroit, Cleveland
- Cincinnati, Ohio River
- Indianapolis, Evansville
- Milwaukee, Lake Michigan

CROSS-NUMBER PUZZLE

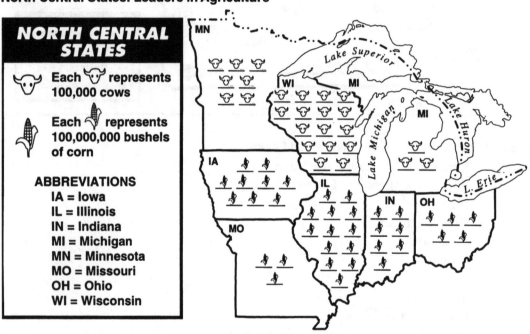

	1 4	5	**2** 1	7	4	1	**3** 6		
4 1				2			5		
5 1	2		**6** 2	3	0	1	4		
0				5			9		**7** 3
9		**8** 3				**9** 5	7	9	1	8
10 1	5	4	9			0			
3				**11** 2	3				
0			**12** 2		7				**13** 1
14 1	1		**15** 1	1	6	9	7	7	3	6
		16 2			2				7
		17 5	2	3	3	8	4	9	0

NORTH CENTRAL STATES

Each 🐂 represents 100,000 cows

Each 🌽 represents 100,000,000 bushels of corn

ABBREVIATIONS
IA = Iowa
IL = Illinois
IN = Indiana
MI = Michigan
MN = Minnesota
MO = Missouri
OH = Ohio
WI = Wisconsin

1. Michigan
2. Ohio River
3. Kansas City
4. Ohio
5. 49°N
6. Milwaukee
7. Lake Superior, Lake Michigan
8. Four
9. Automobiles
10. Iron
11. Detroit
12. Minneapolis, St. Paul
13. Canton, Ohio
14. Iowa (West Branch)
15. Robin
16. Flowering Dogwood
17. Harry Truman
18. Forward
19. 1816
20. Chicago, 1454', Sears Tower
21. Minnesota, -34°F
22. Illinois River
23. Iowa, Missouri
24. Indiana
25. Indiana

Page 95 Minnesota: Finding Places with Latitude and Longitude

1. 45°N
2. 94°W
3. 48°N
4. 44°N
5. 48°N
6. 420 miles
7. 47°N-48°N and 94°W-95°W

Page 97 Wisconsin: Coded Place Names

1. ASHLAND
2. TIMMS HILL
3. EAU CLAIRE
4. WAUSAU
5. GREEN BAY
6. APPLETON
7. OSHKOSH
8. LAKE WINNEBAGO
9. LA CROSSE
10. SHEBOYGAN
11. MADISON
12. MILWAUKEE

Page 99 Michigan: Lakes, Cities, Distances

2. Wisconsin, Indiana, Ohio
3. Straits of Mackinac
4. - Au Sable River into Lake Huron
   - Kalamazoo River into Lake Michigan
   - Muskegon River into Lake Michigan
   - Manistee River into Lake Michigan
5. - Lansing - Saginaw: 60 mi. (+ or - 10)
   - Lansing - Chicago: 180 mi. (+ or - 10)
   - Lansing - Detroit: 85 mi. (+ or - 10)
   - Lansing - Madison: 270 mi. (+ or - 10)
   - Lansing - Ironwood: 410 mi. (+ or - 20)
   - Lansing - Escanaba: 260 mi. (+ or - 15)
6. 3,021'
7. 1,270 mi. (+ or - 150)

Page 101 Iowa: Rivers and Cities

1. Missouri; Minnesota
2. Illinois and Wisconsin
3. Nebraska and South Dakota
3. - Skunk River: 5
   - Turkey River: 2
   - Des Moines River: 6
   - Upper Iowa River: 1
   - Wapsipinicon River: 3
   - Iowa River: 4
4. - Floyd River: 1
   - Boyer River: 3
   - Little Sioux River: 2
   - Nishnabotna River: 4
5. - Des Moines: Des Moines River
   - Dubuque: Mississippi River
   - Fort Dodge: Des Moines River
   - Ottumwa: Des Moines River
   - Davenport: Mississippi River
   - Iowa City: Iowa River
   - Council Bluffs: Missouri River
   - Waterloo: Cedar River
   - Cedar Rapids: Cedar River

Page 103 Illinois: Cities, Rivers, and Lakes

1. SPRINGFIELD
2. CHARLES MOUND
3. DECATUR
4. WAPSIPINICON, ROCK, ILLINOIS, MISSOURI, KASKASKIA, OHIO
5. EVANSTON, WAUKEGAN
6. EAST ST. LOUIS
7. INDIANA, KENTUCKY
8. ILLINOIS
9. ROCKFORD
10. CARLYLE, SHELBYVILLE
11. MISSOURI, IOWA

Page 105 Indiana: Rivers, Highways, and Cities

1st Column Descriptions	2nd Column Descriptions
- 6	- 7
- 1	- 18
- 17	- 16
- 13	- 5
- 12	- 3
- 2	- 11
- 4	- 9
- 8	- 10
- 14	- 15

Page 107 Ohio: Locations on the Map

1st Column	2nd Column
- G	- W
- N	- D, E, F
- C	- U
- T	- O
- X, N, Z	- H
- U	- K
- A	- X
- P	- S, M
	- Y

Page 109 Missouri: Finding Rivers, Cities, and States on a Map

MISSOURI CROSSWORD PUZZLE

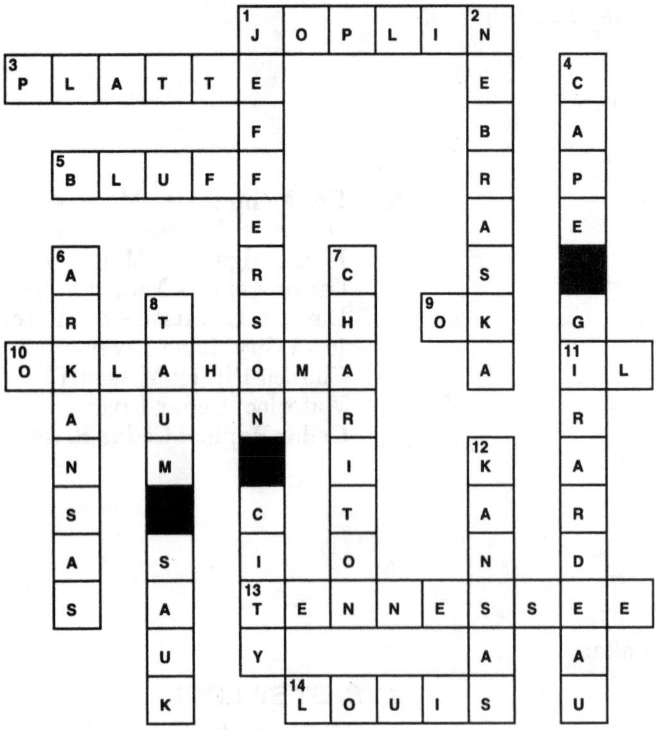

Across/Down answers:
- 1 JOPLIN
- 3 PLATTE
- 5 BLUFF
- 10 OKLAHOMA
- 13 TENNESSEE
- 14 LOUIS

Down words: JEFFERSON(S), NEBRASKAS(A), CAPE GIRARDEAU, ARKANSAS, TAUMSAUK, OHIO, CHARITON, OKA, KANSAS, ILLINOIS

Page 112 Great Plains States: Capitals, Major Cities, and Rivers

2. A North Dakota: Bismarck
   B South Dakota: Pierre
   C Nebraska: Lincoln
   D Kansas: Topeka
   E Oklahoma: Oklahoma City
   F Texas: Austin

4. - Wichita: Kansas
   - San Antonio: Texas
   - Sioux Falls: South Dakota
   - Omaha: Nebraska
   - Houston: Texas
   - Fargo: North Dakota
   - Dallas: Texas

Page 113 Great Plains States: A Table of Facts

1. *Note*: South Dakota and North Dakota are interchangeable in the puzzle

```
M H A R N E Y   P E A K
            S O K L A H O M A
S S O U T H   D A K O T A
        M W H I T E   B U T T E
      N C O R N H U S K E R
  S N E B R A S K A
              N S U N F L O W E R
  N C O Y O T E
        M B L A C K   M E S A
    S N O R T H   D A K O T A
      S T E X A S
    S K A N S A S
```

2. *Numbers Challenge*
   a. 8,450,962
   b. South Dakota: 1,962'
      Nebraska: 146'
      Texas: 3,469'

Page 114 Great Plains States: Measuring Distances with Latitude

3. Houston - Kansas City: 630 mi.
   Austin - Fort Worth: 210 mi.
   Lincoln - Sioux City: 210 mi.
   Wichita - Oklahoma City: 210 mi.

Page 115 Great Plains States: Interesting Facts

GREAT PLAINS FACT CLASSIFICATION TABLE							
History	Geography	Population	Personalities	Agriculture	Mining	Climate	Miscellaneous
15, 19, 20	2, 13, 16	7, 17	12, 14	4, 8,10	3, 18	5, 6 , 21 *	1, 9, 11

* Also appropriate under Agruculture

Page 116 North Dakota: Road Distances

Distances Within North Dakota
- Minot and Fargo: 260 mi.
- Williston and Grand Forks: 338 mi.
- Bismarck and Grand Forks: 276 mi.
- Fargo and Williston: 400 mi.
- Bismarck and Minot: 114 mi.
- Devils Lake and Fargo: 163 mi.

Distances to and from North Dakota
- New York and Bismarck: 1,659 mi.
- Chicago and Bismarck: 837 mi.
- Los Angeles and Bismarck: 1,669 mi.
- Seattle and Bismarck: 1,236 mi.

Table of Distances

ROAD DISTANCES INSIDE AND OUTSIDE NORTH DAKOTA						
	Bismarck	Devils Lake	Fargo	Grand Forks	Minot	Williston
Bismarck		180	191	276	114	243
Chicago	837		646			
Fargo	191	163		78	260	400
Grand Forks	276	89	78		210	338
Los Angeles	1669		1839			
Minot	114	121	260	210		126
New York	1659		1468			
Seattle	1236		1427			
Williston	243	249	400	338	126	

Page 117 North Dakota: Rivers, Lakes, Cities

1. Yes
2. No
3. Yes
4. Yes
5. No
6. Yes
7. Yes
8. Yes
9. No
10. No
11. Yes
12. No
13. No
14. Yes
15. No
16. No

Page 119 South Dakota: Rivers, Bordering States, Mountains

1. a. eastward
   b. eastward, north
   c. eastward
   d. north-to-south
2. Thunder Butte Creek and Rabbit Creek
3. Aberdeen
4. Yes. The boat would float downstream.
5. Oahe Dam
6. Fort Randall Dam
7. 7,242'
8. a. North Dakota
   b. Minnesota
   c. Iowa
   d. Nebraska
   e. Wyoming
   f. Montana

Page 121 Nebraska: Road Mileage and Air Distance

1. - 138 mi.
   - 66 mi.
   - 49 mi.
   - 124 mi.
   - 377 mi.

2. - 58 mi.
   - 166 mi.
   - 60 mi.
   - 119 mi.
   - 403 mi.

3.e. North Platte
4. 210 mi. (+ or - 10)
5. 460 mi. (+ or - 10)
6. South Sioux City, Omaha

Page 123 Kansas: Communities and Quadrants

INDEX OF KANSAS COMMUNITIES AND THEIR QUADRANTS			
Quadrant	Community	Quadrant	Community
D6	Arkansas City	D8	Independence
B6	Belleville	B9	Kansas City
D8	Chanute	D3	Liberal
D7	El Dorado	C6	Newton
C7	Emporia	D9	Pittsburg
D9	Fort Scott	D5	Pratt
D3	Garden City	C6	Salina
B2	Goodland	B8	Topeka
C5	Great Bend	D2	Ulysses
C4	Hays	D6	Wichita

Page 125 Oklahoma: Latitude and Longitude, Rivers and Cities

Latitude and Longitude Quadrants

1. - McAlester
   - Enid
   - Muskogee
   - Oklahoma City, Norman
   - Guymon
   - Elk City

Rivers and Cities

2. - North Canadian River
   - Cimarron River
   - Cimarron River
   - Washita River
   - Red River

3. Arkansas River, Canadian River, North Canadian River

Page 127 Texas: Coded Place Names

1. Dallas
2. Austin
3. Lubbock
4. Brazos River
5. Brownsville
6. Waco
7. Laredo
8. Houston
9. Guadalupe Peak
10. Amarillo
11. Odessa
12. Rio Grande
13. El Paso

Page 131 Western States: Captials, Rivers, and Boundaries

2.
   1. Columbia
   2. Snake
   3. Missouri
   4. Yellowstone
   5. Colorado
   6. Green
   7. Sacramento
   8. San Joaquin
   9. Gila
   10. Rio Grande

3.
   a. Olympia
   b. Boise
   c. Helena
   d. Salem
   e. Cheyenne
   f. Sacramento
   g. Carson City
   h. Salt Lake City
   i. Denver
   j. Phoenix
   k. Santa Fe

5. Utah, Colorado, New Mexico, Arizona

6. Oregon, Washington, California

7. Washington, Idaho, Montana

8. California, Arizona, New Mexico

Page 132 Western States: Water in the West

1.

		Average Monthly Precipitation (in inches)											
	J	F	M	A	M	J	J	A	S	O	N	D	TOTAL
Los Angeles	2½	3¼	2½	1¼	¼	T	T	T	¼	½	1	3	14½
Portland	5½	5	4	2½	2	1½	½	½	1½	3½	6	7	39½
Albuquerque	¼	¼	½	½	¾	¾	1½	1½	1	½	½	½	8½

2. 16½ inches
3. winter
4. summer
5. June, July, August

Page 133 Western States: A Table of Facts and a Number Puzzle

Page 135 Washington: Mountains, Rivers, Cities, and Coastline

1. Tacoma
2. Spokane
3. Columbia River
4. Snake River
5. Mt. Rainier
6. Olympia
7. Vancouver
8. Cascade Range
9. Bonneville Dam
10. Yakima
11. Seattle
12. Grand Coulee Dam
13. Walla Walla
14. Longview
15. Okangon River
16. Bellingham

Page 137 Idaho: Map Puzzle

T	W	I	N	F	A	L	L	S	E	A	I	N	B	S	M
W	Y	E	F	S	C	A	N	A	D	A	D	E	O	A	F
A	O	S	L	E	W	I	S	T	O	N	A	V	R	N	P
S	M	N	A	S	M	I	L	V	J	R	H	A	A	D	O
H	I	A	T	M	O	R	E	G	O	N	O	D	H	P	C
I	N	K	H	A	N	R	Y	S	A	L	F	A	P	O	A
N	G	E	E	T	B	O	I	S	E	A	R	E	I	T	
G	M	R	A	S	A	L	M	O	N	N	L	O	A	N	E
T	O	I	D	E	N	A	M	P	A	D	L	I	K	T	L
O	S	V	L	W	A	L	L	A	C	E	S	T	H	U	L
N	C	E	A	L	B	U	R	L	E	Y	O	R	N	T	O
A	O	R	K	B	O	Z	E	M	A	N	J	E	A	A	N
M	W	I	E	C	W	E	I	S	E	R	H	E	A	H	L

Page 139 Montana: A Mountain and Plains State

True or False

1. F		5. F
2. T		6. T
3. T		7. T
4. T		8. F

Complete the Sentences
1. Powder
2. Jefferson, Madison, Gallatin
3. west
4. 130 mi. (+ or - 10)
5. British Columbia, Alberta, Saskatchewan

Page 141 Oregon: Mountains and Rivers

1. *Table*
   - Mt. Hood
   - Mt. Jefferson
   - South Three Sisters
   - Sacajawea Peak
   - Strawberry Mountain
   - Eagle Gap
   - Mt. McLoughlin
   - Mt. Thielson
   - Steens Mountain
   - Rock Creek Butte

2. Willamette River, Deschutes River, John Day River, Umatilla River, Snake River
3. Washington
4. Owyhee River, Malheur River, Grande Ronde River

Page 143 Wyoming: Mountain Peaks and Distances

1. a. Montana
   b. South Dakota
   c. Nebraska
   d. Colorado
   e. Utah
   f. Idaho

2. a. 45 mi.
   b. 355 mi.
   c. 330 mi.
   d. 270 mi.

3. Gannett Peak: 13,804'
   Grand Teton: 13,770'
   Fremont Peak: 13,745'
   Downs Mountain: 13,349'
   Cloud Peak: 13,167'
   Francs Peak: 13,153'
   Lizard Head Peak: 12,842'
   Washakie Needles: 12,518'

Page 145 California: Places on the Map

2. a. 14,495'
   b. Mexico and California

3. Santa Rosa
   San Francisco
   San Jose
   Santa Barbara
   San Diego
   San Joaquin River

Page 147 Nevada: Places and Things of Interest

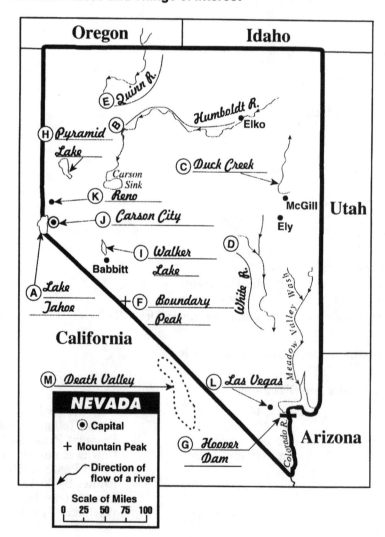

Page 149 Utah: Dry Lands, High Mountains, and Rivers

1. a. Great Salt Lake Desert, Sevier Desert, Escalante Desert
2. a. Dirty Devil River, Green River, San Juan River
   b. Muddy River, Fremont River
   c. north, southwest, Sevier Lake
   d. Bear River
   e. Jordan River
   f. Idaho and Utah
3. 270 mi. (+ or - 25), 350 mi. (+ or - 25)
4. 409'

Page 151 Colorado: Cities, Rivers, Distances

1. Yes
2. Yes
3. No
4. Yes
5. No
6. Yes
7. No
8. No
9. Yes
10. No
11. Yes
12. Yes

Page 153 Arizona: Map-Word Puzzle

```
C O L O R A D O K
A M E X I C O V W
L A S █ V E G A S
I F P H O E N I X
F L A G S T A F F
O C N I P U Y N P
R O E L R C U E K
N O V A E S C W L
I L A █ S O C █ N
A I D R C N A M O
Z D A I O U G E G
M G R V T T Y X A
E E M E T A U I L
S H V R K H M C E
A R I Z O N A O S
```

Page 155 New Mexico: A Trip Around the State

1. Texas
2. 65-75 mi.
3. US-285
4. Portales
5. I-40
6. I-40
7. Tularosa
8. US-70
9. Arizona

Page 156 **Alaska: Area and Population**

How Big is Alaska?

1. 18%
2. 7%
3. 18%, 6%
4. 5%

Alaska's Population

Title: (Students' titles will vary.)

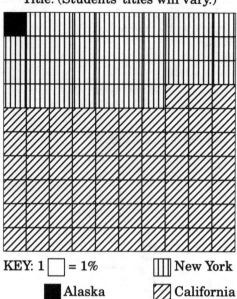

KEY: 1 ☐ = 1% |||| New York

■ Alaska   ⧄ California

Page 157 **Alaska: The USA's Largest and Most Northern State**

1.

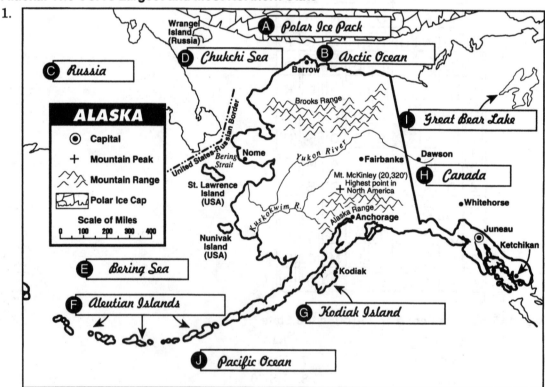

2. 20,320'
3. Juneau
4. United States
5. 675 mi.
6. The danger of ice packs and floating ice would make it difficult.

Page 159 Hawaii: The Island State

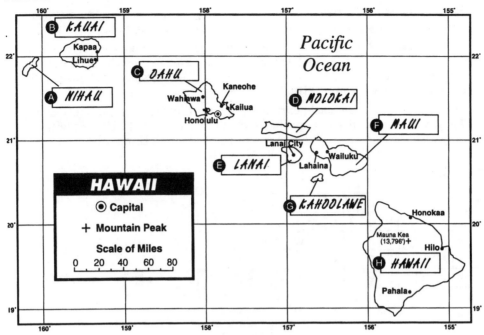

2. a. 158°W
    b. 21°N and 22°N
    c. Kahoolawe

3. a. Hawaii
    b. 13,796'

4. Kauai and Ohau; 80 mi.

Page 163 Canada: Reading and Completing a Map and Table

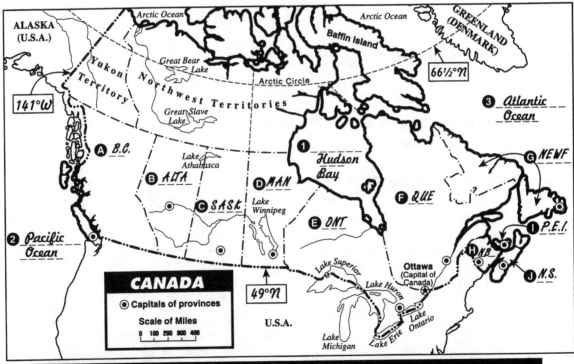

AREAS OF CANADA'S PROVINCES			
Province	Area in Square Miles	Province	Area in Square Miles
Quebec	594,860	Manitoba	250,947
Ontario	412,581	Newfoundland	156,949
British Columbia	365,947	New Brunswick	28,355
Alberta	255,287	Nova Scotia	21,425
Saskatchewan	251,866	Prince Edward Island	2,185

Page 166 Activity #1: Eskimos and Their Environment

1. *Sampling of facts:* two dogs, a woman, three children, man, boat (kayak), caribou, house, rack for storage, fish, warm clothing, high boots, fish

2. *Sample story:* Father has returned from a fishing expedition. While he is beaching the boat his family is admiring the big fish he caught. All the children are laughing and smiling, even the baby on the mother's back. The dogs are excited, too; they are probably hoping to eat some of the fish.

   The animals in the back, caribou, are browsing for food, probably clumps of grass. They will supply milk and, perhaps, cheese for the family. During winter months they may also provide meat. Their furs will be used for clothing and bedding.

Page 167 Canada: Map Puzzle

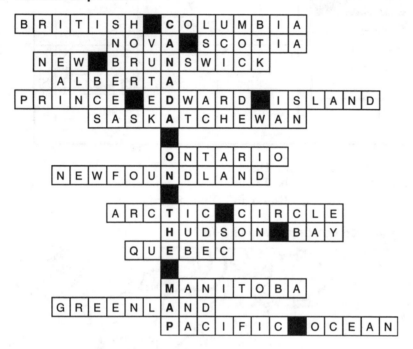

Page 168 Canada: Lumbering and Wood Products

Sentence Sequence: 1, 2, 6, 8, 9, 7, 3, 5, 4

Page 169 Canada: Lumbering and Wood Products

1. FOOD
   Nuts
   Fruit

2. FOLIAGE
   Oils
   Extracts
   Decorations

3. GUMS
   Varnishes
   Soaps
   Medicines
   Waxes
   Turpentine
   Crayons
   Insecticides
   Perfumes
   Chewing Gum
   Latex (rubber)

4. SAP
   Sugar
   Syrup

5. BARK
   Tannin
   Oils
   Dye

6. STUMPS
   Charcoal
   Rosin
   Pine Oil

7. ROOTS
   Smoking Pipes
   Tea
   Oil

8. CORDWOOD
   Paper
   Fuel
   Charcoal
   Plastics
   Rayon
   Alcohol
   Insulation

9. LOGS
   Poles
   Piles
   Posts

10. LUMBER
    Flooring
    Furniture
    Shingles
    Construction
       Lumber
    Baskets
    Plywood
    Sawdust
    Woodchips

Page 171 Canada: Fishing and the Grand Banks

1. southwest, about the same size as
2. Quebec, New Brunswick, Prince Edward Island
3. Cod, haddock
4.

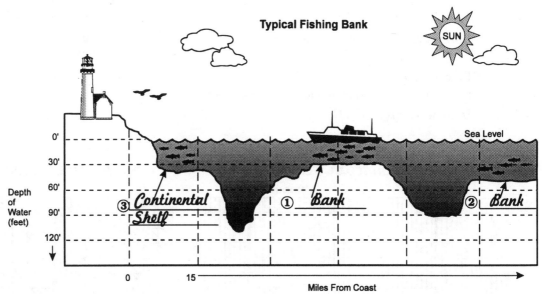

Typical Fishing Bank

5. 30'

Page 175 Latin America on the Map

Latin American List of Countries*

Middle America
1. Mexico
2. Belize
3. Guatemala
4. Honduras
5. El Salvador
6. Nicaragua
7. Costa Rica
8. Panama

West Indies
9. Cuba
10. Jamaica
11. Haiti
12. Dominican Republic

13. Puerto Rico (USA)
14. The Bahamas
15. St. Kitts & Nevis
16. Antigua & Barbuda
17. Dominica
18. St. Lucia
19. Barbados
20. St. Vincent & the Grenadines
21. Grenada
22. Trinidad & Tobago

South America
23. Colombia
24. Venezuela

25. Guyana
26. Suriname
27. French Guiana (France)
28. Ecuador
29. Peru
30. Brazil
31. Bolivia
32. Paraguay
33. Chile
34. Uruguay
35. Argentina

* Exceptions: Puerto Rico and French Guiana

Page 177 Mexico: A Map of Its Highways

1. 3, 5, 1, 2, 6, 4

2. a. Monterrey
   b. San Felipe
   c. Hermosillo
   d. Chihuahua
   e. Monterrey

3. a. 57
   b. 40
   c. 180
   d. 15

4. a. 1,544 mi.
   b. 719 mi.
   c. 2,263 mi.

5. a. Sierra Madre Occidental
   b. Sierre Madre Oriental
   c. Sierra Madre del Sur

6. a. 600 mi. (+ or - 25)
   b. 550 mi. (+ or - 25)
   c. 180 mi. (+ or - 10)

291

1. T	5. T	9. T
2. F	6. T	10. T
3. F	7. F	11. F
4. F	8. F	12. F

Complete the following sentences.

A. experience

B. cotton, cattle

C. . . . they were alarmed at the number settling there.

D. Nueces River, Rio Grande

Page 180 Mexico: Size and Population

COMPARING THE UNITED STATES AND MEXICO

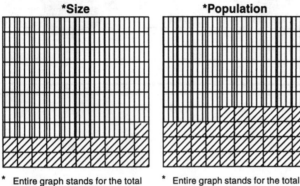

*Size	*Population

* Entire graph stands for the total area of the United States and Mexico.

	USA	79 squares
	Mexico	21 squares

* Entire graph stands for the total population of the United States and Mexico.

	USA	64 squares
	Mexico	36 squares

COMPARING MEXICO AND CENTRAL AMERICA

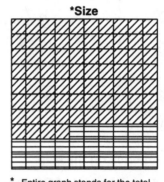

*Size	*Population

* Entire graph stands for the total area of Mexico and Central America.

	Mexico	74 squares
	Central America	26 squares

* Entire graph stands for the total population of Mexico and Central America.

	Mexico	66 squares
	Central America	34 squares

COMPARING SOUTH AMERICA AND MEXICO

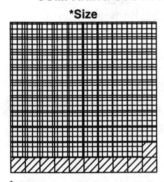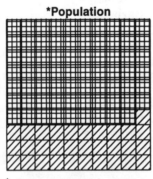

*Size	*Population

* Entire graph stands for the total area of South America and Mexico.

	South America	89 squares
	Mexico	11 squares

* Entire graph stands for the total population of South America and Mexico.

	South America	69 squares
	Mexico	31 squares

Page 181 Mexico: Spanish and English Words

1. agua: water   cabra: goat   muchacho: boy
   casa: house   huerta: garden   montaña: mountain
   maiz: corn   hombre: man   sombrero: hat
   mujer: woman   puerta: door   cacto: cactus

2. a. The hat acts as a shield from the sun.
   b. Northern Mexico has a slight rainfall; so, it is not necessary to have a slanted roof to shed lots of water.
   c. There is not enough rain to support extensive tree growth.
   d. Goats yield meat and milk, from which cheese can be made; chickens yield meat and eggs; the garden yields vegetables; and the corn patch yields corn that can be cooked and eaten or ground for cornbread.
   e. Goats can more easily withstand hot temperatures; also, goats will eat almost any vegetation, whereas cows are mainly grass eaters.
   f. The water is coming from the hills. Another use of the water is for irrigating the garden and corn.

Page 182 Central America: Countries and Capitals

C	A	R	I	B	B	E	A	N		S	E	A	P
L	B	G	E	R	E	C	M	P	E	C	T	M	A
S	E	L		S	A	L	V	A	D	O	R	E	C
A	L	E	K	N	L	A	R	N	O	S	A	X	I
N	I	C	A	R	A	G	U	A	E	T	X	I	F
	Z	F	E	I	V	P	N	M	I	A	W	C	I
S	E	M	M	E	R	I	D	A	Y		I	O	C
A	L	A	U	D	H	O	N	D	U	R	A	S	
L	A	N	B	C	O	L	O	M	B	I	A	D	O
V	S	A	N		J	O	S	E	A	C	L	R	C
A	N	G	U	A	T	E	M	A	L	A	I	B	E
D	Q	U	T	E	G	U	C	I	G	A	L	P	A
O	H	A	W	S	A	J	B	E	L	O	P	A	N
R	X	Y	U	C	A	T	A	N	I	D	F	N	Y

Page 183 Central America: Land of Volcanoes

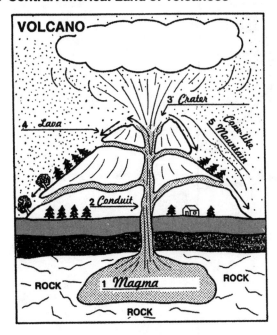

VOLCANO

3 Crater

4 Lava

5 Cone-like Mountain

2 Conduit

1 Magma

ROCK   ROCK

ROCK

1. C: Facts and figures about the lake
    D: A means of transportation for local traffic
    A: Ocean fish in lake water
     : Water for irrigation (Blank)
    E: A possible canal route
     : Water sports on Lake Nicaragua (Blank)
    B: A lake that was once a bay

2. sharks, sawfish, tarpon

3. "Several ideas, or theories, have been suggested."

4. "Even today the possibilities of a canal through Nicaragua are mentioned in newspapers and magazine articles."

5. Tipitapa River

6. 105'

7. 15'

8. 270 (+ or - 20)

9. 280 mi. (+ or - 20)

10. San Juan River and Lake Nicaragua

11. 170 mi.

12. a. 200 lbs.
    b. Ometepe
    c. Steamboats and dugout canoes
    d. 1,000 or more

13. _____

Page 187 The West Indies: Geographical and Historical Facts

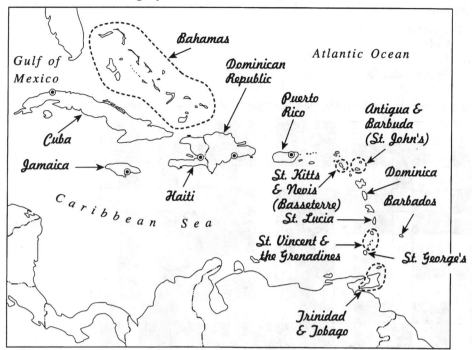

Page 189 The West Indies: Puerto Rico

MAP INDEX			
Quad-rant	Place	Quad-rant	Place
B1	Aguadilla (C)	B3	La Plata (R)
B2	Arecibo (C)	B1	Mayaguez (C)
B3	Bayamon (C)	B2	Ponce (C)
B3	Caguas (C)	B1	Pt. Jiguero
B3	Cayey (C)	B4	Pt. Puerca
B2	Cerro de Punta (Mtn)	C4	Pt. Tuna
B5	Culebra (Is)	B4	Pt. Vaca
B3	Coamo (C)	B1-B2	Rosario (R)
B4	El Toro (Mtn)	B3	San Juan (C)
B4	Fajardo (C)	B4-B5	Vieques (Is)
C3	Guayama (C)		
C: City R: River Mtn: Mountain			
Is: Island Pt: Point or Cape			

2. a. Ponce: 18°03'N
    b. Fajardo: 18°20'N
    c. Caguas: 66°04'W

Page 190 The West Indies: Trinidad's Asphalt Lake

1. "grayish-black, tar-like material"
2. 1st paragraph, 2nd sentence: road pavements, roof shingles
3. It is cheaper to make asphalt from petroleum.
4. "ichthyologist"
5. The fish may have been washed in by floods.
6. Digging, carrying, loading
7. The tracks sink into the asphalt and disappear.

Page 191 The West Indies: An American Outpost on Cuba

2. 800 mi.

3. a. 1,150 mi.
    b. Cuba
    c. 1,500 mi.
    d. Mexico and Cuba

Page 192 Middle America and West Indies: Crossword Puzzle Review

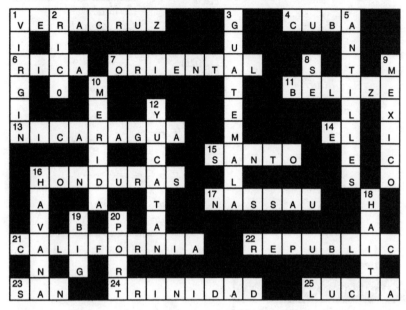

Page 193 Middle America and West Indies: Identifying Countries by Shape

1st row, left-to-right: Belize, Jamaica, Puerto Rico, Trinidad and Tobago
2nd row, left-to-right: Panama, Dominican Republic, Honduras
3rd row, left-to-right: Nicaragua, Guatemala, Haiti
4th row, left-to-right: Cuba, El Salvador, Costa Rica

Page 198 South America: Twelve Countries and One Colony

1. CO: Colombia
    CA: Bogota
    A: 440,831 sq. mi.
    P: 35,578,000

2. CO: Venezuela
    CA: Caracas
    A: 352,144 sq. mi.
    P: 20,562,000

3. CO: Guyana
    CA: Georgetown
    A: 83,044 sq. mi.
    P: 729,000

4. CO: Suriname
    CA: Paramaribo
    A: 63,251 sq. mi.
    P: 423,000

5. CO: French Guiana *
    CA: Cayenne
    A: 43,740 sq. mi.
    P: 101,000

6. CO: Brazil
    CA: Brasilia
    A: 3,286,470 sq. mi.
    P: 159,000,000

7. CO: Paraguay
    CA: Asuncion
    A: 157,048 sq. mi.
    P: 5,214,000

8. CO: Uruguay
    CA: Montevideo
    A: 68,037 sq. mi.
    P: 3,199,000

9. CO: Argentina
    CA: Buenos Aires
    A: 1,073,000 sq. mi.
    P: 33,913,000

10. CO: Chile
    CA: Santiago
    A: 292,135 sq. mi.
    P: 13,951,000

11. CO: Bolivia
    CA: La Paz, Sucre
    A: 424,164 sq. mi.
    P: 7,719,000

12. CO: Peru
    CA: Lima
    A: 496,225 sq. mi.
    P: 23,651,000

13. CO: Ecuador
    CA: Quito
    A: 105,037 sq. mi.
    P: 10,677,000

* French Guiana is not an independent country.

Page 199 South America: Latitude and Longitude

1. a. 20°S - 70°W: Iquique
    b. 3°S - 60°W: Manaus
    c. 38°S - 57°W: Mar del Plata
    d. 11°N - 75°W: Barranquilla
    e. 10°N - 66°W: Caracas
2. a. Salvador: 13°S - 38°W
    b. Georgetown: 6°N - 58°W
    c. Punta Arenas: 53°S - 71°W
    d. Brasilia: 16°S - 48°W
3. - Rosario to Manaus: 2,050 mi. (+ or - 100)
    - Punta Arenas to Iquique: 2,310 mi. (+ or - 100)

Page 200 South America: Seasons South of the Equator

To Do

1. fall
2. summer
3. If the earth were not tilted there would be no seasons because a specific location would always be the same distance from the sun.
4. December and January is the southern hemisphere's growing season.
5.

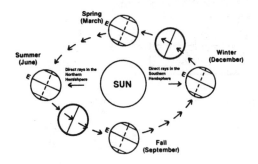

Page 201 South America: Seasons South of the Equator

2. 39°N
3. 39°S
4. 8°S
5. They are equidistant from the Equator; they are both coastal cities.
6. Washington, D.C.: December, January, February
7. Bahia Blanca: June, July, August
8. When Washington, D.C., is having spring during the months of March, April, and May, Bahia Blanca is having fall.
9. 41°
10. 27°
11. At or near the Equator there are no seasons with respect to significant changes in temperature.
12. - Bahia Blanca: 73° average high in January; 46° average low in July
    - Washington, D.C.: 78° average high in July; 37° average low in January and February
    - Recife: 81° average high in January, February, March; 75° average low in July and August

Note: All temperatures are Fahrenheit.

Page 202 South America: A Physical Map

Mountains:
a. Andes Mts.
b. Guiana Highlands
c. Brazilian Highlands

Rivers:
a. Magdalena R.
b. Orinoco R.
c. Amazon R.
d. Parana R.

Land Regions:
a. Amazon Basin
b. Chaco
c. Pampa
d. Atacama Desert
e. Patagonia
f. Hills, valleys, lowlands, coastal plains

Oceans and Seas:
a. Atlantic Ocean
b. Caribbean Sea
c. Pacific Ocean

Ocean Current:
Humboldt Current

Water Passage:
Strait of Magellan

Islands:
a. Falkland Islands
b. Tierra del Fuego

Page 203 South America: Interpreting Elevations

1.

Place	Elevation	Place	Elevation
A	500'	D	2,000'
B	1,000'	E	2,500'
C	1,500'	L	500'

2. I. -1,000'
   H: -500'
   J: -400'

3. J; M, G, B

4. 3,500'

5. height, altitude

6.

A CROSS SECTION SHOWING ELEVATION

KEY — ELEVATION IN FEET

more than 2500 · 1500 to 2000 · 500 to 1000 · 0 to -500
2000 to 2500 · 1000 to 1500 · 0 to 500 · -500 to -1000

2.

DISTANCES BETWEEN SOUTH AMERICAN CAPITALS	
Air Flight	**Distance in Miles**
Caracas, Venezuela to Georgetown, Guyana	600
Georgetown, Guyana to Parimaribo, Suriname	200
Parimaribo, Suriname to Cayenne, French Guiana	200
Cayenne, French Guiana to Brasilia, Brazil	1,450
Brasilia, Brazil to Asuncion, Paraguay	750
Asuncion, Paraguay to Montevideo, Uruguay	625
Montevideo, Uruguay to Buenos Aires, Argentina	150
Buenos Aires, Argentina to Santiago, Chile	700
Santiago, Chile to La Paz, Bolivia	1,050
La Paz, Bolivia to Lima, Peru	750
Lima, Peru to Quito, Ecuador	650
Quito, Ecuador to Bogota, Colombia	450
Bogota, Colombia to Caracas, Venezuela	675
Total Miles Traveled	8,250

3. Total Distance: 8,250 miles

4. North-to-South: 4,400 (+ or - 50 mi.)
   East-to-West: 3,250 (+ or - 50 mi.)

Page 208 South America: Simon Bolivar, "The Liberator"

1. 4, 1, 7, 6, 2, 8, 5, 3

2. 8, 7, 4

3. Suggested: "Spain is so far away. Why should they rule us?"

4. a. strong, determined. He is obviously a leader.
   b. determined, motivated, hurrying

5. Country #1: Venezuela
   Country #2: Colombia
   Country #3: Ecuador
   Country #4: Peru
   Unidentified Country: Bolivia

Page 210 South America: San Martin Prepares to Free Chile

1. The horses hooves had to be protected from the sharp rocks in the Andes Mountains

2. a. The last sentence of paragraph B
   b. The second sentence of paragraph A

3. The food had to be nourishing, light for transportation, and not easily spoiled.

4. Church bells were melted to make guns and bullets.

5. a. 1st sentence: proud
   b. 3rd sentence: nervous

6. The efforts of the Spaniards to move their forces to places they thought San Martin's forces would attack.

7. B: Providing Horseshoes for Horses
   C: Providing Food for a Long Campaign
   E: Providing Containers for Water and Metal for Bullets
   G: Strategies to Confuse the Enemy

Page 211 South America: Regions of Colombia and Venezuela

1 & 2.

3. a. Colombia
   b. Colombia
   c. Venezuela

4. Plains
5. Highlands
6. Lowlands

Page 212 South America: Venezuela—a World Leader in Oil Production

1.

Country	Barrels of Oil Produced Each Day*
Saudi Arabia	8,224
Former USSR	7,844
United States	6,868
Iran	3,671
China	2,905
Mexico	2,651
Venezuela	2,357
Nigeria	2,046
United Kingdom	1,775
Kuwait	1,751
Canada	1,630
Indonesia	1,513
Libya	1,379
Algeria	1,200
* In a recent year. 1 barrel = 42 gallons.	

2. 7th place
3. Mexico; 6th place
4. 3rd place; No; 1860 fewer barrels
5. *Challenge:* 860,305 barrels per year

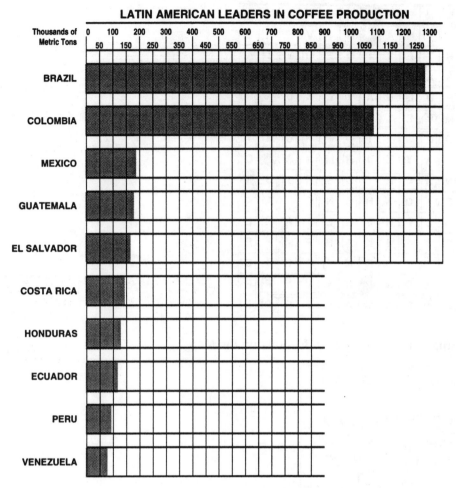

LATIN AMERICAN LEADERS IN COFFEE PRODUCTION

Page 214 South America: Ecuador, Peru, and Bolivia on the Map

1. a. Quito: Mountain
   b. Cuzco: Mountain
   c. Cochabamba: Mountain
   d. Potosí: Mountain
   e. Iquitos: Lowland
2. Guayquil, Chimbote, Callao
3. a. Peru: Lima
   b. Ecuador: Quito
   c. Bolivia: La Paz
4. Bolivia and Peru
5. a. Quito
   b. Potosí
   c. Guayaquil
6. Colombia, Peru
7. Brazil, Argentina, Chile, Peru, Paraguay
8. Ecuador, Brazil, Bolivia, Chile, Colombia
9. Toward the east and north

Page 216 South America: Animals of the Andes Mountains

Questions will vary from student to student.

Page 219 South America: Tropical Rain Forests

Notes will vary from student to student.

F	R	E	N	C	H	■	G	U	I	A	N	A
P	A	R	A	N	A	■	R	I	V	E	R	B
M	O	N	T	E	V	I	D	E	O	V	I	A
X	V	S	A	O	■	P	A	U	L	O	O	P
W	U	R	U	G	U	A	Y	L	K	D	■	O
R	K	M	B	E	L	E	M	K	H	S	D	R
G	E	O	R	G	E	T	O	W	N	U	E	T
U	M	V	A	Y	Z	J	R	M	R	R	■	O
Y	A	N	S	A	N	T	O	S	E	I	J	■
A	N	O	I	Q	W	H	C	N	C	N	A	A
N	A	M	L	P	H	J	H	L	I	A	N	L
A	U	P	I	F	J	K	A	R	F	M	E	E
D	S	C	A	Y	E	N	N	E	E	E	I	G
A	M	A	Z	O	N	■	R	I	V	E	R	R
C	A	P	A	R	A	M	A	R	I	B	O	E

Page 223 South America: Paraguay and Uruguay on the Map

D Bolivia   E Brazil

C Gran Chaco

J Tropic of Capricorn

F PARAGUAY

K Concepción

Pilcomayo River   Paraguay River   B

G Asunción

L   Paraná River

N Corrientes

M Posadas

Paraná River   Uruguay River

L

URUGUAY

Rosario

A

I Montevideo

Buenos Aires

H Rio de la Plata

ARGENTINA

O Atlantic Ocean

PARAGUAY & URUGUAY

◉ Capitals

Scale of Miles

0   100   200

Page 225 South America: Chile—From Dry North to Rainy South

Notes will vary from student to student.

Page 226 South America: A Tourist Map of Argentina

1. Porteños (People of the Port)
2. Seashore resort
3. In memory of an Argentine-Chile peace pact
4. 2514'
5. Mendoza
6. Puerto Williams; Ushuaia
7. Comodoro Rivadavia
8. Rosario
9. 1993
10. Avenida 9 de Julio (July 9)
11. The Colorado River
12. Uruguay River and Paraná River
13. Frost-free climate, water for irrigation
14. Northeast
15. 167'
16. Pampa
17. Home to many Italian immigrants and their descendants

Page 228 South America: Locating Places and Things Puzzle

1. A: Chile
   B: Peru
   C: Argentina
   D: Paraguay
   E: Ecuador
   F: Venezuela
   G: Colombia
   H: Brazil
   I: Uruguay
   J: Guyana
   K: Suriname
   L: French Guiana
   M: Bolivia

2. 1st map: Isthmus of Panama, Lake Maracaibo
   2nd map: Strait of Magellan, Falkland Islands

3. a. Christ of the Andes
   b. Lake Titicaca
   c. Galapagos Islands

Page 229 South America: A Place Name Crossword Puzzle

Page 230 South America: Reviewing the Map of Latin America

a: 16	j: 1	s: 24
b: 21	k: 8	t: 4
c: 12	l: 10	u: 17
d: 15	m: 3	v: 14
e: 22	n: 2	w: 6
f: 20	o: 9	x: 23
g: 25	p: 11	y: 27
h: 26	q: 13	z: 29
i: 28	r: 7	

Page 233 Activities: Giant United States and Canada Crossword Puzzle

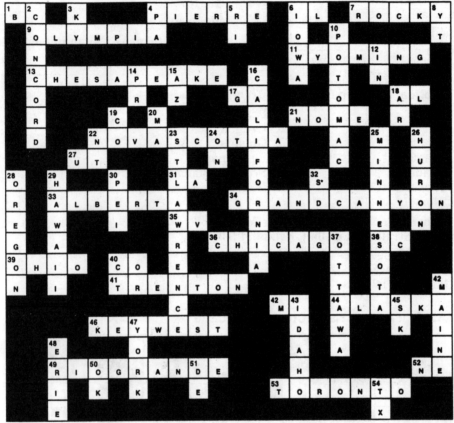

* ND is also acceptable.

Page 240 Activities: United States Geography Travel Game

1st line: Lumber, Oregon, Oahu, Utah
2nd line: Utah, Oklahoma, Southwest, Keystone State
3rd line: Texas, South, Massachusetts, Stalactites
4th line: Iowa, Yellowstone, New Hampshire, North Carolina
5th line: Nebraska, Kansas, Vermont, Ohio River
6th line: Northeast, Alaska and Texas, New York, Savannah River
7th line: Colorado, Kansas, New Mexico, Georgia

Page 241 Activities: United States Geography Travel Game

1st line: Rhode Island, Delaware Bay, Wisconsin, Bering Strait
2nd line: Southeast, California, Lake Michigan, False
3rd line: Vermont, Ohio, Dallas, Alaska
4th line: Gulf of Mexico, New Hampshire and Vermont, 60°W, Texas
5th line: 49°N, Des Moines, California, Nebraska
6th line: Texas, Colorado River, Pittsburgh, PA; Portland, OR
7th line: Washington, Oregon, California, and Alaska; Potatoes; 20,320'; Nevada

R	E	U	J	L	P	I	H	O	C	D	L	A	I	S	A	N	T	I	A	G	O	N	O	T
T	S	B	A	H	A	M	A	S	M	B	V	R	D	S	G	P	B	O	G	O	T	A	A	B
R	A	A	M	A	R	T	V	D	O	S	E	V	T	K	U	E	N	Y	R	A	O	G	T	U
I	N	R	A	I	A	E	A	A	N	I	N	C	U	B	A	O	E	U	D	M	A	X	I	E
N	■	B	I	T	M	E	N	S	T	L	E	I	A	E	T	A	C	H	I	L	E	I	Q	N
I	J	A	C	I	A	O	A	T	E	H	Z	N	N	R	E	R	O	J	G	O	U	P	C	O
D	O	D	A	L	R	H	W	I	V	E	U	I	E	E	M	C	S	N	W	E	I	V	O	S
A	S	O	Z	S	I	B	E	L	I	Z	E	Y	O	M	A	G	T	B	E	T	A	P	L	■
D	E	S	F	R	B	A	E	I	D	E	L	■	S	A	L	V	A	D	O	R	O	A	O	A
■	A	U	N	M	O	U	P	M	E	I	A	G	T	N	A	D	■	O	P	G	O	R	M	I
T	S	R	I	O	Q	O	A	A	O	E	W	E	I	A	X	I	R	T	I	O	L	A	B	R
O	B	U	P	A	H	O	N	D	U	R	A	S	C	G	V	N	I	E	E	I	I	G	I	E
B	U	G	E	R	E	A	A	G	N	A	R	E	E	U	K	A	C	E	T	B	G	U	A	S
A	S	U	R	I	N	A	M	E	D	D	G	V	Q	A	B	R	A	Z	I	L	U	A	C	S
G	M	A	U	A	I	L	A	R	L	N	E	C	U	A	D	O	R	H	U	L	Y	Y	A	R
O	S	Y	R	A	S	U	N	C	I	O	N	N	I	C	A	R	A	G	U	A	A	S	R	E
G	E	O	R	G	E	T	O	W	N	E	T	R	T	D	A	J	A	O	P	A	N	I	A	O
N	T	Y	U	E	M	U	Z	M	E	X	I	C	O	O	B	O	L	I	V	I	A	D	C	A
R	S	R	I	O	■	D	E	■	J	A	N	E	I	R	O	T	H	F	N	T	W	Y	A	E
E	Y	I	W	D	O	M	I	N	I	C	A	N	■	R	E	P	U	B	L	I	C	Q	S	J

Special Acknowledgment

As mentioned on page iv, Acknowledgments, special thanks and appreciation are given to Silver Burdett Ginn—past publisher of author Silver's books. The *American Continent* pages listed below are those which include maps and illustrations, originals and adaptations, from Silver Burdett Ginn's *American Continents*, *Changing New World*, and *Learning About Latin America*.

Pages: 3, 4, 6, 15, 17, 18, 19, 20, 21, 29, 60, 61, 70, 88, 89, 92, 122, 132, 134, 142, 144, 146, 148, 163, 166, 168, 177, 181, 182, 193, 198, 200, 201, 205, 206, 209, 211, 212, 215, 217, 223, 225, 228